MW00614497

Bernie Saggau & the Iowa Boys

The Centennial History of the

Iowa High School Athletic Association

To Kent –

Bernie Saggau & the Iowa Boys

The Centennial History of the
Iowa High School Athletic Association

Chuck Offenburger

11-18-05

Iowa High School Athletic Association
Boone, Iowa

Also by Chuck Offenburger:

Iowa Boy: Ten Years of Columns by Chuck Offenburger. 1987. Iowa State University Press

Babe: An Iowa Legend. 1989. Iowa State University Press

Ah, You Iowans! At Home, At Work, At Play, At War! 1992. Iowa State University Press

Don't Look Back...we aren't going that way! The Bill Krause Story. 2001. Internet Book at www.Offenburger.com

E. Wayne Cooley and the Iowa Girl: A celebration of the nation's best high school girls sports program. 2002. Iowa Girls High School Athletic Union

Need more information regarding this book? Contact N&K Publishing, Madison, WI. Neelum Chaudhry, who edited, designed and is now marketing this book, grew up in Pakistan and Kuwait and came to the U.S. to attend the University of Iowa. She stayed to become a high school journalism teacher in the towns of Washington and Ames, then at Iowa State University. She began her publishing career in 1987, working in marketing for the Iowa State University Press and later the University of Minnesota Press. She resides in Madison, Wisconsin where she owns and operates N&K Publishing. This is her sixth book in collaboration with Chuck Offenburger. Members of the media and booksellers may contact her at neelumc@hotmail.com, or 608-274-7418/608-345-1789.

Cover photos by Bruce Wagman Photography, West Des Moines

Printed in the United States of America by Sigler Printing, Ames, Iowa

ISBN - Cloth edition: 0-9764875-0-0
ISBN - Paperback edition: 0-9764875-1-9

First printing, 2005

CONTENTS

PREFACE

Boone, Iowa

By Chuck Offenburger

Happenstance brought me through the central Iowa town of Boone on December 28, 2004, an historic day in Iowa high school sports.

It was exactly 100 years ago – December 28, 1904 – that the Iowa High School Athletic Association was founded.

For 27 years, the IHSAA sanctioned both boys' and girls' sports in the state. Then, in what now seems an incredible fuss over whether the game of girls' basketball would continue to be offered, the Iowa Girls High School Athletic Union split off to administer girls' athletics. The two organizations, now often working together, have built what is arguably the best high school sports program in the U.S.

But on this Tuesday in 2004 that was centennial day, all seemed quiet around the beautiful IHSAA headquarters building on the south end of the town of 12,800.

In Iowa, there is no longer regularly scheduled high school athletic competition during the Christmas and New Year's holidays. So the association shuts down its offices for about a week, allowing the staff to recover some of the hundreds of hours they spend working weekends and nights the rest of the year.

However, seeing one sports utility vehicle parked in the employee lot in the early afternoon, I decided to see who might be in the building, and whether they'd allow me to take a walk-through in my own sort of corny observance of the 100th anniversary.

Of course, I was probably more aware and interested in the history of that moment than anybody in the state. I'd already spent 18 months on what would become a two-year project – reporting and writing this book "Bernie Saggau & the Iowa Boys: The Centennial History of the Iowa High School Athletic Association."

So I tried the side door, and finding it unlocked, I walked into the darkness. Florescent light streamed from a front office, though, so I headed that way. I walked in on a scene I'll never forget.

Here was Bernie Saggau, 76, who would officially retire four days later, after 37 years as executive director of the IHSAA, 41 years as a staff member. I'd known him for 30 years, but I'd never before seen him dressed any way but coat-and-tie, or business casual, or sports casual at a track meet or baseball game. On this day, though, he was wearing blue jeans, a golf sweatshirt, a U.S. Open golf cap. He sat at his desk, glasses low on his nose, rummaging through papers he was pulling from the drawers.

The walls were bare. The cabinets were empty. A few legal tablets were on the floor.

I knocked lightly on the door, walked in and shook hands with this man who is the most widely known and respected high school athletic administrator in the nation.

"I've been here since 7 o'clock this morning emptying it all out," Saggau said with a smile. "I've got my SUV out there loaded as tight as I can get it, and I'm now down to my two personal drawers in the bottom of my desk. I've kept a few letters and other things in here that mean a lot to me."

The fact that it was the 100th anniversary day of the IHSAA had slipped Saggau's mind. As we started reminiscing about it, around the corner came Rick Wulkow. He'd already been named the successor to Saggau, and he was taking over as executive director January 1.

Wulkow, who had been Saggau's top assistant for 24 years, became only the fourth executive director in the IHSAA's 100 years.

"You know what's special about today?" Saggau said to Wulkow. "It's the 100th anniversary of the athletic association. And you want to know why I know that? Because Chuck just reminded me."

It's been quite a run, we all agreed.

For the first 23 years of the organization, school superintendents and principals ran it. When the flow of business and activities warranted it, George A. Brown was hired as part-time executive director in 1923, then he went full-time in 1927. He was succeeded by Lyle T. Quinn, who served from 1941 until his death in 1967. Then Saggau took over.

Wulkow is normally as sharp a dresser as his mentor Saggau is. But let the record show that on centennial day, he, too, was wearing blue jeans and a sweatshirt. Of course, he was cleaning out his own office, getting ready to move into the quarters the boss was vacating.

They were the only two people in the building.

We spent a nice few minutes, calling to mind some memorable IHSAA moments. Then I said I wanted to snap a photo of the two of them together in the office on centennial day.

As I did that, the phone rang – Saggau said he'd been answering it all morning.

"Athletic association," he said this time.

"No, I'm sorry," he told the caller. "The office is closed this week. There's nobody here but us two custodians."

Custodians, indeed – of one of Iowa's most important institutions.

The IHSAA and its programs, over the past 100 years, have given us some great athletes and teams. More importantly, they've produced legions of young people whose lives have been forever enriched by the competitive experience. And they've also given us a whole lot of mostly wonderful entertainment.

All of us in Iowa probably owe a debt of gratitude to the Iowa High School Athletic Association, for the way its programs have impacted us, our families, friends, schools and communities.

And we can also thank those like Saggau and Wulkow who for 100 years have made it all run right.

Even when they're supposed to be on vacation, like on December 28, 2004.

I OWE MORE GRATITUDE THAN MOST. Wulkow and the members of the IHSAA's Board of Control commissioned me in mid-2003 to do this centennial history and to include in it Saggau's biography. They could not have been more understanding, patient and supportive.

I had estimated I would interview about 150 people and write about 125,000 words, which would fill about 300 pages. But the stories just would not stop coming. I wound up extending the project almost a year while I was interviewing more than 400 people. I wrote more than 193,000 words, which will fill about 500 pages.

All that for a book about boys' high school sports?

If you are kind enough to read it all, I hope you will realize that this book has almost as much Iowa history in it as it has Iowa sports. It is also loaded with biography, not just of Saggau but also of many of our state's most fascinating people, who believe that some brush they had with high school athletics was important in their own personal development. You will come to know and understand them in new and different ways after reading their stories here.

A SUBJECT EVERYONE SEEMS HAPPY TO TALK ABOUT. It is amazing how quickly phone calls are returned, if you leave word that you want to talk to somebody about their high school sports experience.

My favorite story about that involves Robert James Waller, the internationally-known author of "Bridges of Madison County" and other books. Many will remember that Waller was a professor of business at the University of Northern Iowa when "Bridges" was published in 1992 and quickly became one of the biggest successes in book publishing history. Despite the proven popularity of the book, many in the media – including some colleagues of mine at the Des Moines Register – made fun of the story and of Waller. It was unseemly, they wrote, that a business professor, a good thinker and a serious writer would win such fame and financial reward for what they characterized as a shallow love story. He was the target of some real cheap shots, even in the Register, the newspaper that had launched him as a writer in the 1980s when it began publishing his essays on a wide variety of topics. Waller thereafter began refusing interview requests from Register reporters and columnists, a policy he has basically followed ever since.

Several times over the years, I attempted to reach him, usually through our mutual friend J. R. Ackley of Marble Rock, Iowa. I would point out that I had known Waller 15 years before he ever became famous, and that I'd never written anything critical about him – before or after "Bridges." In fact, I wrote favorably about his UNI career, about his visionary thinking about Iowa's future and even about how he conceived the idea for "Bridges" and put the story together.

But he'd never talk to me, although he generally would later send word that it was "nothing personal against you." He'd just been so personally wounded by the Register's scorn that he did not want to talk to anybody who was writing for the paper – or had written for it, as became clear after I left it in 1998. I still occasionally sought interviews with him, unsuccessfully.

There were two things about Waller that made me want to try once again to talk to him, for this book. First, I remembered being told years ago about what an outstanding basketball player he was at little Rockford High School in north central Iowa, where he graduated in 1957. He had one of the finest jump shots ever, people said, and he went on to use it both for the University of Iowa Hawkeyes and ultimately for the Panthers of what today is the University of Northern Iowa. Second, I had pulled out my copy of his essay "Jump Shots," which was originally published in the Register. It is one of the finest sports stories I've ever read anywhere. Actually, it's a story about the pursuit of excellence. Waller tells it through the metaphor of how he developed his jump shot back home in Rockford, where it took him and why he eventually decided to walk away from it. I wanted to ask if he'd help arrange permission from the book publisher that now owns the essay, for it to be re-published in this book.

So on Sunday evening, May 23, 2004, I got back in touch with J.R. Ackley and told him I'd really appreciate him contacting Waller in Texas about a possible interview. "Tell him about this book and that I want to talk to him about his basketball experience in high school at Rockford," I told him, "and ask how I can get permission to use 'Jump Shots' in this book." Ackley was polite as ever. "Oh, Chuck, I'll get in touch with him, but you know how he is on this stuff," he said. "He's never said 'yes' yet, so I doubt he will now. But I *will* ask him."

Just before 8 a.m. the next morning, May 24, 2004, I was out front of our house, putting up our American flag to start another today. Suddenly my wife Carla opened the front door and, with a special urgency, yelled, "You better get in here right now!" What was the matter? "Nothing's wrong! Robert James Waller is on the phone for you! Get in here!"

He could not have been more congenial as he talked at length about basketball and other sports in his Rockford boyhood, about his college sports experiences and about his evolving view of sports since then. It told me a lot about Waller that he not only knew where his old Rockford High basketball coach Paul Filter is today, but said that he talks to him frequently. In fact, he gave me the coach's phone number, encouraging me to call him. And in several follow-up conversations and messages, Waller indeed helped arrange permission for "Jump Shots" to appear here.

A BIOGRAPHER'S DREAM. Bernie Saggau and his wife Lois have been wonderful to work with, in the way they opened their memories, memorabilia and files for me. I dipped farther into their hearts and minds than any interviewer ever has before, even exploring some old heartaches. And we're still friends afterward.

I loved the way Bernie was still making bold, sometimes controversial decisions, even in his final weeks as IHSAA executive director. And then he went right on to helping get the long-awaited Iowa Hall of Pride open in Des Moines. When you're writing a book about someone, it's a plus when they stay so prominently in the news.

One other thing I must say about Saggau. Everyone in Iowa knows what a dynamic and prolific public speaker he has been. He's been telling stories all around Iowa for 40 years. You know what? The stories are all true.

I've checked them out, as a reporter and biographer should.

His credibility is as good as his stories are, and that's made him all the more interesting and admirable to me.

A REQUIEM FOR FIVE WHOSE SPIRITS LIVE ON IN THIS BOOK. I was at work on this book so long that five people who helped me greatly with stories and insights have died.

They were Charley Schram, the super fan and statistician from Manilla; Duane Schroeder, who had recently retired as sports information director at Wartburg College in Waverly; Bill Reichardt, the Des Moines clothier and raconteur whose memories about earlier athletes were especially helpful; my brother Dan Offenburger, a former high school coach and teacher in Iowa, later athletic director at Creighton University in Omaha and later in his career the Chamber of Commerce and economic development director in our hometown of Shenandoah, and Mike Henderson, the sports information director of the Iowa Girls High School Athletic Union, the most knowledgeable person ever in the state about prep sports – boys' sports as well as girls'.

I interviewed Schram in mid-June, 2003, when he was 83 years old and knew he was dying of cancer. As lousy as he felt, he said he was more than willing to talk at length about his love for high school athletics. "My mouth still works," he said, "even if not much else does." I volunteered to leave two or three times, fearing I was wearing him out, but he kept telling me story after riveting story until more than two hours had passed. When I left, I was apologizing for the interview going on so long. "No problem, I'll rest an hour, and then I'll be ready to go," he said. Huh? Go where? He was heading to Charley Schram Field in the western Iowa town to once again do the public address duties for an IKM Hawks baseball game, just as he'd done on that field since 1946!

A few days later, I got a letter from Schram, listing several athletes he thought should be considered for the list of Iowa's 25 all-time greatest that now appears in this book. And he had one crusty piece of advice for me about the final list: "Prioritize – the people that are still living, they might buy the book."

Oh, we'll miss Charley Schram, and those others also mentioned in this requiem.

SEVERAL OTHERS PROBABLY WERE THINKING THEY

MIGHT DIE, TOO, BEFORE I FINISHED. That list would include those I've leaned on the most.

Bud Legg, the information specialist for the IHSAA, has chased down every name, fact and statistic that I've pestered him for, and somehow he's always done it cheerfully. He has picked up the yoke that was long shouldered by Henderson as chief advocate for the high school athlete with Iowa's media. In Chapter 6, when you read the story about how Legg has researched and created the first authoritative list of boys' sports records in the state, you will realize the depth of his commitment.

This is the sixth book I have done since 1987 with Neelum Chaudhry as my editor, book designer and marketing consultant. Her patience and skills have helped a half-dozen different people become authors over the past decade. Luckily for her, they don't stretch deadlines as much as I do. Chaudhry is unfailing in her support of the journalistic code of ethics that I bring to book projects – that the fair and honest reporting and presentation of our stories will not be compromised. I hope we will work together on books for years to come. She may faint when she reads that last sentence.

Chaudhry worked with Sigler Printing in Ames, Iowa, for the actual publication of this book. We had worked before with the imaginative and reliable crew there – and in their "Innova" division for creative ideas and services – on our 2002 book "E. Wayne Cooley and the Iowa Girl." Sigler Printing is a real asset for Iowa's authors and readers, playing an increasingly prominent role in book publishing in the state with each passing year.

Finally, my wife Carla continues to be my chief inspiration and motivator, while carrying more than her share of the load in our partnership in life. While I worked overtime on this book, she essentially moved us by herself from Storm Lake to our Simple Serenity Farm near Cooper in southern Greene County. She single-handedly supervised the renovation of our 105-year-old farmhouse, handled all our finances, scheduled and re-scheduled trips and other projects around my need to be away on interviews, on the phone or in front of the computer.

I close with one final word of thanks – to the teammates, coaches, athletic administrators and fans I came to know as a below-average athlete at Shenandoah High School a long time ago. Thanks to all of those old Mustangs for helping introduce me to the love of the game that I have tried to convey in every page of this book.

FOREWORD

Boone, Iowa

By Bud Legg
IHSAA Information Specialist

Bernie Saggau has dedicated over 40 years to the students and schools as an administrator of the Iowa High School Athletic Association. Under his watch, Iowa has enjoyed unprecedented growth in expanding athletic opportunities and on a proportionate basis of student participation to state population, Iowa has consistently led the nation. It is therefore only fitting that the history of the organization be entwined with his biography.

Historically, the Board of Control's hirings, including Bernie, have strengthened the IHSAA's philosophy of employing educators to administer programs for Iowa's youth. Often it is hard to separate the organization from the personality of its leader. Just as a team often takes on the persona of its coach, Bernie's personality and integrity are pervasive in the organization and permeate the decisions that are made. He has never shied from the difficult decisions. Anyone can make the easy ones. And while it is common nature to question outcomes, no one can argue with the rationale and thinking, as well as the caring that is readily apparent in them. He has the uncanny knack of being able to explain a decision or a rule without being self-serving – a characteristic of his tenure.

I once heard him tell an interviewer during the State Basketball Tournament that he preferred to be a "back row" spectator, soaking up the atmosphere and the effervescence of the tournament, rather than being courtside and visibly directing the event. The game, indeed the tournament, or any of the 10 sports administered by the IHSAA, is for the kids. That has been a constant mindset of the IHSAA under Bernie, along with promoting sportsmanship and citizenship. Those are strong and deep roots to have and why his leadership has been steadfast. As much as anyone who has gone before him, he understands the history of the IHSAA, where high school athletics have gone and where they can go in the future. When school administrators have a concern or question, the IHSAA and Bernie are at the top of their assistance list.

Philosophically, and in practice, each sport is important to him because it showcases our state's youth and the regular season and tournaments are testimonials to the high caliber of sportsmanship, citizenship and the purism of amateur athletics. He is a champion of classification, but in a larger and real sense, he really champions opportunities for kids. Iowa proudly boasts one of the largest awards programs in the nation. In addition to trophies at the state tournament, students receive a medal, certificate and picture plaque of their team. In championship games, special autograph balls are presented, courtesy of the support of the Iowa Farm Bureau, to the players of each team. An adult cannot watch an IHSAA activity or tournament without feeling proud and reflecting on the positives of their own experiences as a student-athlete.

Although tournaments are one of the most visible functions of the IHSAA, he has expanded the office to a full-service organization. The Association carries a catastrophic insurance policy on each student who participates in its sanctioned sports and a supplemental accident insurance policy on participants in IHSAA tournaments. In addition, the Association furnishes schools with calendars, sportsmanship posters which feature prominent Iowans, regulation manuals, monthly bulletins, summary booklets, sponsors sportsmanship-leadership conferences, and provides resources for substance-alcohol programs, and redressing academically deficient students.

Bernie never misses an opportunity to speak up for schools, education, activities and kids. Throughout a career in public service, he has tirelessly articulated the values of activities, Iowans, the ideals of patriotism and what each means to students. No one believes more passionately than Bernie in the value of American youth and the benefits they can derive from athletic participation. He is an unabashed proponent of rules and regulations that govern the welfare of student-athletes in Iowa, never compromising his integrity or responsibility to school administrators. And while some may take exception to his positions, no one loses their respect for him and therein is the essence of his leadership.

He is regarded as one of the most influential figures in prep sports in the U.S. The IHSAA and his persona have become synonymous. He is on a first name basis with virtually every school administrator, coach, official, media representative, and fan. Moreover, that familiarity is nationwide, where executive directors of other state athletic associations and the leadership of the National Federation of State High School Athletic Associations seek and value his opinion. His officiating experience in football and basketball on a collegiate level for 18 years and his leadership as President of the National Federation of High School Athletic Associations and service as a member of the United States' Olympic House of Delegates Committee have embellished his image as a national leader. He has also served the NFHS for many years of service on their basketball and football rules committees.

Among other numerous honors he has received are the recipient of the National High School Coaches Distinguished Service Award and an Award of Merit from the National High School Athletic Directors Association, which is the highest honor given by that organization. In 1996 he was selected by *Referee* magazine as one of the top 20 individuals in last 20 years to have done the most to improve officiating. He was inducted into the National Federation of State High School Association's Hall of Fame in 1993. The Board of Control, in 1989, established an award for students in his name. The award honors an outstanding citizen athlete (boy or girl) in every one of the 400 high schools in the state for modeling the values of patriotism, integrity, citizenship and sportsmanship.

My initial contact with Bernie came earlier in my career. As a young coach in 1967 I heard him speak when our athletic director invited him to talk to our staff. I came away from the speech a bit in awe but believing that I could make a difference and armed with some general principles as to how to do just that. Later as an official, an administrator and now as an employee, the message remains constant. The passion and excitement are still prevalent.

As a motivational speaker, Bernie is virtually without an equal and has remained in high demand over the years. His public speaking has made him a favorite at keynoting high school and collegiate conferences, school awards assemblies, teacher workshops, civic clubs and graduations. His personal charm, ability to relate to an audience, and his genuine, honest approach effectively enhances his message, which is full of humor, real-life drama, and common sense. You can be laughing and crying during the same talk, but always he leaves you reflecting and challenged as to how you can move forward. His words are woven with the red, white and blue fabric of citizenship and integrity, each a value and a cornerstone of the IHSAA.

There are many firsts that can be attributed to his management style of high school sports in Iowa. Perhaps, none is greater than his leadership to include special education students in the varsity athletic program. Not separate teams, but on the school's team. It has been a decision that has paid huge personal dividends to the lives of all kids. He is not afraid to think outside the box, implementing the three-point field goal in basketball two years before other states and the NCAA adopted it. He took the state wrestling tournament out of Waterloo, the mat capital of Iowa, to Des Moines where it has become the toughest ticket to obtain in Iowa prep sports. He also helped energize a struggling football program by creating a play-off format and later district football so schools could have full schedules. When behavior at athletic events nationwide became suspect, Iowa became a national leader in developing sportsmanship programs and ideas many states imitated. His tenure has also created a concern for the total student and the student body in our schools. The state tournament sportsmanship award and captains of the all-tournament teams now carry cash awards to the student government program of the winning school. He does not mull problems rather he searches for ways to solve them and build consensus. And he has the vision to be proactive so that potential problems that plague others are not experienced in Iowa.

Another innovation in recognizing students is the Governor's Scholar Program created in 2003. It has touched the state's 400 high schools, as outstanding students were honored in a special ceremony with the governor.

So proud is he of the accomplishments of Iowans that he passionately promoted a dream – the Iowa Hall of Pride, an interactive, technology based attraction that pays tribute to the quality of citizens our schools produce in all areas. For that reason all school activities for boys and girls are included. Vocal and instrumental music, speech, and drama stand just as tall as girls and boys athletics. The achievements of adult Iowans in politics, science, service, education, entertainment and other life endeavors are also highlighted. He has spearheaded the public and private fund raising to ensure the fruition of the dream.

In an effort to hold escalating costs at a minimum, particularly with the premiums of catastrophic insurance the Association carries on each participant, he successfully sought an exclusive corporate partner for the IHSAA – the Iowa Farm Bureau. The recurring theme of his life and administration is family and family values. They are readily in evidence whenever you attend an IHSAA tournament or visit the offices in Boone.

It is important that his story be woven into the fabric of the history of the IHSAA. His is a story that needs to be told. It is one that can inspire and educate. His life has had great success but has also experienced the tragic loss of a son. He has been able to move forward with family and friends because of a deep faith in the Almighty and a value system as straight and tall as Iowa corn in August. His passion is equaled only by his compassion and he is a thinker and leader from whom there is much to learn.

We know that the "Iowa Boy," Chuck Offenburger, will capture in words, the essence of the "Iowa Boy" from Denison.

Bernie Saggau & the Iowa Boys

Part I

Chapter One

It's not the winning that's important

One evening in the long ago autumn of 1939, the boys on the sixth grade football team in the western Iowa town of Denison were beyond excited. They were about ready to experience what had become a thrilling local tradition – playing one of their games each fall "under the lights" on the same field the high school varsity used.

Coach Clarence Luvaas Jr., then a 29-year-old elementary school teacher, knew the boys were playing mind games that were bigger than the actual game that was about to happen. Any doubt he had about just how big they were making it surely was erased when one of the boys said, "We ought to have a prayer" – just like the high school team did before its games. So the young coach thought quickly, asked the little football players to huddle and bow their heads, and this is what he said:

"Lord, let these boys learn something tonight that will make them better men tomorrow."

That moment – that simple little vignette 65 years ago – is really the foundation upon which one of the nation's finest high school athletic programs is built.

On December 28, 2004, the Iowa High School Athletic Association observed its one hundreth anniversary. Since September 9, 1967, the executive in charge of it had been Bernie Saggau, and he had been groomed for the leadership the previous four years.

Back on that fall night in 1939, "under the lights" on the Denison football field, Bernie was one of those sixth grade boys.

He still says today that Coach Luvaas and his prayer "made a difference in my life – and in the lives of about three million kids who've heard me tell that story."

Helping boys become better men. Helping athletes become better citizens. Helping average Iowa teenagers become more successful and productive adults.

That's not the official mission statement of the Iowa High School Athletic Association, but it could be.

Especially in the Saggau era, which was over with his retirement on January 1, 2005. Succeeding him as executive director is Rick Wulkow, his loyal assistant for 24 years.

All around Saggau are signs and testimonials that his mission was accomplished. In 2004, he was the longest-serving executive of all the state high school activities associations in the nation.

"We will not see his likes again, I'm sure," said Robert F. Kanaby, the veteran executive director of the National Federation of State High School Associations, based in Indianapolis.

Saggau's satisfaction with what he accomplished runs deep, as deep as the appreciation he holds for the job he held.

He talked about that when he was giving yet another high school commencement speech – he has given hundreds – on May 18, 2003, which happened to be his seventy-fifth birthday.

"Seniors!" he almost yelled, to the graduating class at Fredericksburg High School in northeast Iowa. "If there's a hell on this Earth, it is getting up and going to a job you hate. And 60 percent of adults in America do that every Monday morning. But during the 40 years I've been at the athletic association, I can honestly say I've worked 20 days. The rest has been fun!"

In his job, "I get paid to make tough decisions," he often says. And his 20 days that have not been fun "are when I had to go to court" to defend, explain, or be ordered to change some of those tough decisions.

And yet, the very nature of Saggau's job – running high school sports in Iowa – should indeed make it fun. Just as fun as he said it's been.

About 83,000 boys are now competing each year in the 10 sports that the Iowa High School Athletic Association sanctions – football, cross country, swimming, wrestling, basketball, golf, tennis, track & field, soccer and baseball. Three other sports are recognized but not yet sanctioned – bowling, competitive cheering and rodeo.

In addition, about 60,000 girls now compete in the nine sports that the Iowa Girls High School Athletic Union sanctions – cross country, volleyball, swimming, basketball, tennis, golf, track & field, soccer and softball. The girls' organization also recognizes drill teams, bowling, competitive cheering and rodeo.

Those participation figures, if compared to other states on a per-capita population basis, are very high.

And several of the state tournaments are generally recognized as the best in the nation – wrestling and baseball for the boys, with basketball and football also highly regarded; basketball and softball for the girls.

"Iowa is unique," said Nelson Hartman, now retired after 30 years as an executive with the Kansas High School Activities Association. "It's a state with a good-sized population but being small enough geographically to make it easy for teams and fans to get to Des Moines for the state tournaments. Kansas is three times as large geographically and has less population. It's difficult to get the attendance Iowa has at the state tournaments. Because of the difficulty and expense of traveling, we have our state tournaments at about six sites around the state. If you add up all the crowds, we probably do as well as Iowa, but with the sites split like that, we can't match the magic Iowa has at its state tourneys."

For boys sports in Iowa, the IHSAA sets the rules for team play, operates the tournaments, offers several innovative educational programs related to exercise and health, and conducts an ambitious awards program, both for athletics and general scholarship, that is unrivaled in the nation. It also houses and helps fund the Iowa High School Music Association. The IHSAA's annual operating budget for the 2004-05 year was a "net income"-based figure of $2,334,700, which represented the income from all events, less expenses. The 399 member schools paid the same absurdly low annual membership fee of $2 each – that's right, two dollars per school – as the schools have paid from the organization's beginning. Schools pay no entrance fee for tournament competition. Hence, most of the IHSAA's operating revenue comes from gate receipts during the tournaments.

For the girls, the IGHSAU operates similarly, except that instead of assisting with the music program, it houses and helps fund the Iowa High School Speech Association. The IGHSAU's 2004-05 operating budget was $2.66 million. That is a "total revenues"-based figure, including the anticipated receipts from all its sports events ($2.4 million) plus income from television broadcasts, registration of officials and sales of merchandise.

Both organizations are "owned" and operated by the member schools. As Saggau has often said, "The rest of the staff and I are just the hired help."

If you add the operating budgets of both organizations, the total means that in Iowa, more is spent on high school athletic programs, on a per capita basis, than is the case in all the neighboring states.

In addition, Iowa is the only state in the nation with separate organizations sanctioning boys and girls sports, as well as separate ones sanctioning music and speech activities. In all other states, all those functions generally rest with one activities association.

What does all of the above indicate?

Some might say – and have argued in the past – that it represents inefficiency.

However, the member schools watch that closely. They have considered mergers of the organizations several times over the years and have ultimately decided they want to maintain the four separate ones, even if it does cost a little more.

Why?

The short answer is that in Iowa, high school extracurricular activities – especially sports – hold a higher place in the local culture than those activities do in other states.

Indeed, many alumni of the Iowa programs who go on to athletic success at higher levels, where they meet athletes who have grown up in other states, realize what they've had in Iowa. In terms of a) community support, b) the supervision and conduct of games, c) the coverage of the local and state media, and d) the enthusiasm of the fans, there may be no better place in the United States to be a high school athlete than Iowa.

Dave Stead, the executive director of Minnesota's high school activities association, said, "The support that the people of Iowa have supplied for high school activities in general, and directly to the high school athletic association, is phenomenal." He lived it in the late 1950s and early '60s, when he was an outstanding athlete and musician at Monticello High School in eastern Iowa, and he observes it now from his position in Minnesota.

And why is the public support in Iowa so strong?

First, while there are excellent athletic programs at the universities and colleges in Iowa, there are no major league professional sports competing for the attention and support of the fans and media. Additionally, in the two-thirds of Iowa that is made up of rural areas and small towns, those high school activities are the communities' main forms of entertainment.

It's partly because of that additional public interest, and partly because of a historical rift long since ended, that high school boys' and girls' athletics are overseen by the separate organizations. In Iowa, both the IHSAA and the IGHSAU are regarded as very prominent players in public life, with influence far beyond what the high school activities organizations have elsewhere. The long tenure of the administrators who in the past have headed the Iowa organizations adds stability, credibility and respect. E. Wayne Cooley headed the Girls Union for nearly 49 years before retiring in the fall of 2002.

Another reason Saggau has had so much fun on the job, as he told those Fredericksburg graduates in 2003, is undoubtedly because he and the IHSAA have been such innovators.

In the early 1960s, his predecessor Lyle T. Quinn asked Iowa's football coaches to begin addressing concerns about player safety in their sport. Iowa soon became the first state in the nation to require mouthpieces. Then in 1969, with Saggau heading the IHSAA, Iowa was first to eliminate use of the helmet to "spear" opponents in tackling and blocking, and two years later became the first to ban below-the-waist blocking.

In the 1963-64 school year, the IHSAA Board of Control became a national leader again, by ruling that special education students who are making satisfactory progress in school are eligible to compete in sports.

Later in the 1960s, the IHSAA started "classification" in all sports, so the competition was conducted among athletes from similarly-sized schools. As that idea was expanded during the 1970s and '80s, it meant there were more champions, more awards and more interest among more players.

In 1970, Saggau oversaw the move of the state wrestling tournament from Waterloo, where it had been drawing about 10,000 fans per year, to Des Moines. It's now grown into the nation's largest high school wrestling tourney, with nearly 90,000 paid admissions, and a total crowd of nearly 100,000 when competitors, coaches, cheerleaders and media are counted.

In 1972, the IHSAA added football playoffs with state championships, reversing several years of declining interest and participation in the sport of players and fans alike.

In the basketball season of 1982-83, the IHSAA became the first high school athletic organization in the nation to add the three-point shot in basketball.

In 1986, high school baseball became exclusively a summer sport, and, although Iowa is the only state playing its high school season then, the state tournament has become one of the nation's best in number of schools competing, paid attendance and media coverage.

In 1989, the IHSAA put in place the nation's first alcohol and substance abuse awareness program for high school athletes, with its own director. A little later, the first wellness program was developed, also with its own director, to address issues of nutrition, hydration, curiosity about performance-enhancing stimulants and concern about blood-transmitted diseases like HIV and AIDS. The IHSAA's AIDS-awareness video is believed to have been the first ever made anywhere, and the U.S. Department of Defense wound up distributing copies of it to its armed forces across the nation and around the world.

In 1990, competition in track was expanded to include wheelchair bound athletes. In 1994, soccer was added as a sport, with state tournament competition.

In 2000, the IHSAA brought back eight-player football, after the smallest schools began having trouble fielding 11-player teams, and it became wildly popular – among all fans, not just those in the smaller communities.

In 2003, after the schools' and the IHSAA's budgets became strained in the first years of this century, the association negotiated a first-ever "corporate sponsorship" with the Iowa Farm Bureau Federation, but "we picked them, they didn't pick us," Saggau said. "We picked them because they have the same philosophies toward kids that we do." That helped pay for a major enhancement of the trophies, mementos and certificates the athletes receive for participation and success in state competitions, and that awards program was already one of the best in the nation.

The sponsorship also made it possible for the IHSAA to start a unique "scholar recognition event" in 2003, bringing together the top student in each of Iowa's high schools, along with his or her parents, for a reception with, and recognition by, Iowa's governor. Each of those students could designate a favorite teacher to receive a certificate.

And, perhaps most innovative of all, just after the IHSAA observed its one hundreth anniversary in December, 2004, it opened a very high-tech, very interactive, $12 million "Iowa Hall of Pride" in Des Moines in February, 2005. With music, art, sculpture, accessible archives, professionally-produced video, eye-popping graphics and other special effects, the 26,000-square-foot facility showcases the high achievement that has been happening for decades in the state's high schools, not only in sports but in all activities.

Saggau has unusual perspective on all this – particularly about the relative importance of sports – and it may surprise those who don't know him.

"Over my 41 years (on the job), no one's ever heard me say that athletics are more important than any other activities," Saggau said in press conference in June, 2004, in Sioux City, where a group of officials and referees from northwest Iowa were honoring him. "Band, chorus, speech, debate, drama – all the activities are just as important as sports are. The key is getting our kids involved in something, and we've done a pretty good job of that in Iowa, because 80 percent of our high school students are involved in at least one extracurricular activity. You know, we have too much 'I' and not enough 'we' in our society today, and it's in our school activities where we really teach the 'we's' – the teamwork that our society needs."

And even though Saggau has personally been about as competitive as a person can get, it has been his constant refrain over the decades that, in the high school sports programs, winning just isn't that big a deal.

Check what he said in a speech he delivered in 1959 to the athletic banquet of the Booster Club in little Breda in west central Iowa, where he was billed as "the well-known Iowa high school basketball referee," then from the northwest Iowa town of Cherokee. "My pet peeve is the statement that somebody has to win and somebody has to lose," he told the Breda crowd. "That doesn't prepare us for the game of life, because in that game, there are no losers."

And here's what he said 45 years later, when he spoke at the 2004 banquet of the Iowa chapter of the Fellowship of Christian Athletes, held in West Des Moines: "In athletics, I don't know why losing is so terrible. I sometimes think it'd be better if we'd all go 50-50 all the time."

He may have said it best in August of 2003 when he was the keynote speaker at a first-ever "Sportsmanship Summit" that the South Dakota High School Activities Association organized in Pierre, with each high school sending at least one athlete, coach and administrator. "It's not the winning that's important," Saggau told them. "It's the wanting to win that's important."

But even deeper, he always has stressed that the bedrock –what the Iowa High School Athletic Association is really all about – is education.

"Bernie's message, time and time again, is that this is all part of education," said Kanaby, the National Federation executive. "He's not only made it that way in Iowa, he's created that same mindset which has been adopted and followed by the high school associations all over the country."

In an interview in the fall of 2003, Saggau said one reason high school athletics "has to be an integral part of the schools' program, a vital part of education," is that otherwise, "it will all go to 'club sports' and it'll be out the door and out of control." If the coaches of young athletes are not certified educators, he argued, there is less of a chance that the real values of athletic competition will be taught.

Saggau has been talking about just what those values are for more than 30 years.

In a 1970 speech to a national convention of athletic directors, he asked, "Does education stop when we have academic achievement alone? I don't think so. I think we agree that a nation of academic great achievers is important. If our country fails, if our secondary schools fail, they will fail because we do not educate good citizens as well as intelligent people.

"We must train citizens to become individuals and leaders who believe in dedication, desire, determination, and respect, and who develop pride and learn responsibility, and above all, who learn to be a competitor and learn to accept defeat with honor. There is no subject taught in the American secondary schools today that teaches more of the American way of life and more democracy than is taught on the athletic fields of our secondary schools. Interscholastic athletics is nothing more than a laboratory to teach these values.

"What is closer to the American way of life than to teach a boy that he can be what he wants to be, if he wants it bad enough? America is the one country left in the world where you can be what you want to be, if you have the courage and the desire and the determination to try.

"You can take a boy and you can put him out on a basketball court, and he can shoot at the backboard, and maybe at first only two or three out of 15 go through the basket. But all of a sudden, through hard work and practice, he develops a skill where maybe it is five or six out of 15 that go through the basket.

"Oh, perhaps he will never be a first-teamer, maybe never an All-Stater or All-American. But the most important thing is that he is learning, that he tries, that he is not frightened of competition or of losing, that he can prove that he as an individual can make himself better, and that he as an individual develops dignity within himself."

In winding up that speech, Saggau said something that he's repeated hundreds of times since: "I could care less about all the All-Americans we produce. I am concerned about all the good Americans, not the All-Americans."

The truth is, the Iowa program has turned out a whole lot of those good Americans, and actually, a pretty impressive number of All-Americans, too, especially considering the relatively small population of the state. Some former Iowa preps have even transcended All-American status.

Five became members of professional baseball's Hall of Fame: Adrian Constantine "Cap" Anson of Marshalltown in the late nineteenth century; player-manager Fred Clarke of Winterset in the 1890s and early 1900s; Clarence Arthur "Dazzy" Vance of Orient in the 1920s and '30s; Urban Charles "Red" Faber of Cascade in the early 1900s, and Bob Feller of Van Meter from the late 1930s into the '50s.

Two Iowa boys went on to win college football's Heisman Trophy: Jay Berwanger of Dubuque Senior High School, who won the first of what became the Heisman while playing for the University of Chicago Maroons in 1935, and Nile Kinnick, of Adel High School, who won his Heisman for his play with the University of Iowa Hawkeyes in 1939.

Nine won Olympic gold medals. Five of those were wrestlers: Allie Morrison, of Marshalltown, in 1928; Glen Brand, of Clarion, in 1948; Bill Smith, of Council Bluffs Thomas Jefferson, in 1952; Dan Gable, of Waterloo West, in 1972, and Tom Brands, of Sheldon, in 1996. Three of the gold medalists were in track: Morgan Taylor, of Sioux City High School, in 1924; Sabin Carr, of Dubuque, in 1928, and George Saling, of Corydon, in 1932. Craig Oppel, of Valley of West Des Moines, won a gold in swimming in 1988.

There was Davenport High School alumnus Jack Fleck, who in 1955 shocked the golf world by upsetting heavily favored Ben Hogan and winning the U.S. Open Golf Championship.

And in 2002, Marshalltown's Jeff Clement became high school baseball's national home run king when he finished his prep career with 75 round-trippers.

Iowans have had great fun celebrating the successes of all those star athletes, and many others, too.

But Saggau is right when he says it's what all those other "good Americans" have done, after they've grown up in the Iowa programs, that's most important.

It is inspiring, sometimes even amazing, to hear many of them talk about what they learned from participating in high school sports and other activities, and how that has helped them later.

"It gave me confidence," said Norman Borlaug, a 1932 Cresco High

School graduate who went on to win the Nobel Peace Prize in 1970. His research in and advocacy for increasing grain production in the poorest areas of the world has – and this is no overstatement – saved the lives of millions of people. In more recent years, he became the founder of the World Food Prize, which is based in Des Moines and each year gives international recognition to one or more people working to relieve world hunger.

I almost felt foolish in the summer of 2004, telephoning the 90-year-old Borlaug at his office in Mexico to ask about his high school sports career. But with his enthusiastic response and vivid memories, I was quickly at ease – and completely impressed.

He became a wrestler in his sophomore year, he told me, when a group of boys from his rural neighborhood 14 miles south of Cresco, which is located in northeast Iowa, reached an age at which they could take turns driving the group in for school and home after practice. He practiced but didn't get to compete that sophomore year because of "a tremendous case of boils that kept me inactive most of the year. That was a common curse in that era of old cotton mat covers that were seldom ever laundered. There was a lot of impetigo and a lot of boils among wrestlers."

Borlaug played football his junior and senior years, too, and he played on a baseball team in the farm neighborhood, but he was mostly known for his wrestling. The high point of his high school high career was when he finished fourth in the state at 145 pounds in 1932.

"I got to the semifinals at the state wrestling tournament that senior year, but then I got licked," he recalled. "And I had to wrestle right away again, maybe an hour later, and I got licked again."

He went on to become a varsity wrestler at the University of Minnesota. But how does he look back now on his high school involvement in athletics?

"Well, first of all, I enjoyed it, but it was the confidence it gave me that was most important," Borlaug said. "Many times all down through life, I have used that. In tough debates, with bankers and agricultural and policy experts from many nations, I drew on an inner strength. And I think a lot of that came from what I learned in athletics.

"Many times, I've found myself in situations around the world in which I was really all alone, trying to implement new research or new procedures, and it was very difficult. Often, it reminded me of being alone in a wrestling match, that I had to remember what I had been taught, and then put it into action. Of course, it was different because the lives of millions of people might be on the line. But it was still a matter of having confidence that I could do something about the situation."

Most of Iowa's athletes, later in their lives, never have to think or act on that level. Instead, most take the values and skills they've learned while participating in high school sports and other activities, and use them more anonymously in their careers, their communities and their families.

And, oh, the memories!

Whether it's a bad case of boils from a nasty wrestling mat in the long ago, or the thrill of a state basketball championship for a small school in our modern day, the memories last a lifetime. Maybe longer.

In the 2004 state basketball tournament, little Dunkerton from northeast Iowa capped a magical season by winning the Class 1A championship at Veterans Memorial Auditorium in Des Moines. The Raiders had been good all year, bringing a 24-1 record to "Vets," as it's always been known. Their success made everybody recall another magical Dunkerton season, 1933, when the team knocked off mighty Burlington and Des Moines Roosevelt and won the one-class state tournament played back then.

It was like the 2004 Raiders somehow took their game several levels higher once they reached Des Moines.

"It seemed like we were a different team here," senior Brian Brungard, the team's leading scorer, told Jim Sullivan, sportswriter for the Waterloo Courier, after the title game. "We hit our peak here."

Was Brungard relieved it was over? Was he contemplating how he would remember it all? The questions seem to bewilder him.

"I wish we had about 20 more games," he said. "I love playing with these guys, and playing for our community, too. I don't know if I'm ready to leave yet, to tell the truth."

At that moment in his young life, there was no way he could understand how that season which was just completed is never really going to end – that, in fact, it will get even better as the years and decades pass.

14

Chapter Two

How it all began for Bernie Saggau

It was one of those moments when somebody you think you know fairly well, and have pretty well figured out, says something that makes you look at him or her in a whole new way.

One of those happened for me with Bernie Saggau in August of 2003, when we were driving on Interstate Highway 90 in South Dakota. We were on the way to the state capital of Pierre, where he was to be the keynote speaker at a "Sportsmanship Summit" meeting of high school administrators, coaches and athletes in that state.

I had known Saggau for more than 25 years as the executive director of the Iowa High School Athletic Association. I knew him as an excellent speaker, one who often peppers his talks with stories and lessons from his years as an athlete at Denison High School and Buena Vista College in western Iowa. I guess I'd never really thought of him as being more than a former athlete and strong administrator of Iowa's excellent high school sports program for boys.

"You know, I was always very interested in music," I suddenly heard him saying, in the middle of a tale about his boyhood in Denison. "In high school, I was in the glee club, the mixed chorus and I even had the lead in a couple of operettas. I especially remember being 'Ralph' in 'HMS Pinafore.' "

The next thing I knew, here was the 75-year-old Saggau, at the wheel of his Lincoln Town Car, going into a lilting tenor voice and singing a line from one of his songs in that production: "Is there not one maiden here?"

Bernie Saggau? "Ralph" in an operetta? Singing about maidens?

And that was only like a prelude to a rush of old tales that suddenly flowed, amazing me.

In the next hour, before we saw the black dome of the South Dakota Capitol looming over a barren hillside on the horizon, I also learned:

When he was in grade school, his parents, two sisters and Bernie attended the Lutheran Church, but his cousins were attending St. Rose of Lima Catholic Church and its school. St. Rose had a grade school basketball team, and Bernie's cousins recruited him to play with them on it. He recalls the Rev. Edmund J. Casey, who was pastor of St. Rose for 30 years, ruling that "he has two cousins on my team, and that's good enough for me."

In junior high school, "I was so small they wouldn't let me play football," Saggau recalled, "so I became one of the cheerleaders. I've still got my cheerleader's letter sweater to prove it, too. It's got a couple of moth holes in it, but I'm still proud of it."

In high school, besides being in sports and music, his 75 classmates elected him president of the junior class, he was a reporter for the Monarch News student newspaper and he was a workin' fool. He held down very demanding jobs at a local shoe store and in the summers on a Northwestern Railroad section work gang. He thought the shoe store job held such promise that, after graduating from Denison High in 1946, he nearly opted to skip going to college and move into management of the store – until a sage old railroad worker gave him a good piece of advice.

Story after story spilled out of Saggau about his childhood, youth and early career. I was scribbling notes as fast as I could, trying to keep up with him. One thing was immediately clear to me.

"Bernie," I said to him, "we're going to have to spend some time together in Denison."

One chilly day in November, 2003, we met there.

The town, which has consistently had a population of about 7,500 from the 1930s to today, sits on and among the rolling hills of west central Iowa, about 125 miles from Des Moines, and 75 miles from Sioux City and Omaha.

Saggau had told me that when he was growing up in Denison, that after a big victory in high school football or on other "real special" occasions, he'd go to Cronk's Café and have a chicken-fried steak.

16

So the two of us started and finished our tour in that landmark café, which opened in 1929 at the junctions of U.S. Highways 30 and 59, and thrives today.

You can learn a lot about people by going back to their roots with them. That happened for me with Saggau in Denison, even though I'd probably already spent 25 hours or more interviewing him, another couple of hours with his wife Lois and had already talked with his old high school football coach Marion Wilson and several teammates.

But the hometown tour gave me a completely different perspective.

Walking and driving around Denison today, Saggau says things don't seem nearly as big as he once thought they were.

That sidewalk that circled the Crawford County Courthouse and which served as the "track" for the neighborhood kids' races? It seemed like it must be a half-mile around there in the 1930s. Now it's a one-minute stroll.

The old high school a couple blocks southeast of the business district? It's still in good shape, now as the Denison Middle School. But its attached gymnasium, which was one of the best in western Iowa in the 1940s, now seems a humble crackerbox.

The "vast" lawn around the old hospital that administrator Lydia Krall had young Bernie mow, a couple blocks west of the courthouse? Looks like it might be a 20-minute job with one of today's power mowers.

But Saggau and I agree that there's one thing in Denison that's just as good now – maybe even better – as it was when he was a kid.

That chicken-fried steak at Cronk's Café is by-God special!

The town is now known for its meatpacking and for being the hometown of Academy Award winning actress, the late Donna Reed, but it grew up in the late 1800s and early 1900s as a service center for the railroad and agriculture.

The Saggaus, of German-Belgium stock, first came to Crawford County in the second half of the 19th century. Brothers Martin and John Saggau, who were born in Germany, probably rode a train to Clinton, Iowa, and then came on west to the Denison area by covered wagon.

They farmed for a few years before both decided to move to town, where each of them opened a tavern in the same block of the business district, across the street south from the courthouse. The names of those places? "I believe they were 'John Saggau's Saloon' and 'Martin Saggau's Saloon,' " Bernie Saggau said. "They didn't get very fancy with the names."

An old photo shows the sign on the front of Bernie's grandfather's place as being more direct. "M. Saggau – Saloon," it said. But he must have had a good sense of humor because under that name on the sign, there was a business motto painted in the German language that so many people were still often speaking then: *"Heute fur Geld. Morgen umsonst."* That translates as: "Today for money. Tomorrow for free."

Older Denison citizens today remember two things about those taverns, Bernie said: "John Saggau's Saloon had a 'cigar store Indian' out front and Martin Saggau's Saloon had a parrot named Polly that was in there. That parrot probably lived about 30 years, because even after my grandparents got out of the tavern and retired, they had Polly up at their house, and he'd perch on a little stand out in their yard. What I remember most about Polly was could he ever swear!"

That cigar store Indian, an advertisement for the Otto Cigar shop that operated in John Saggau's place, is now in the McHenry House museum operated by the Crawford County Historical Society.

Each of the tavern-owning brothers also married a Jepsen sister, meaning there are succeeding generations of "double cousins," making the family tree a little tricky to trace. That first generation continued to speak German to each other, but not to their children or grandchildren as they came along.

Bernie's father Bernhard E. Saggau was born in 1902 to Martin and Caroline Saggau. He never was heavier than 150 pounds, but the stories are that he was incredibly strong and became an All-State high school football player in 1923. He worked for a time at a local gas station and automotive garage, then bought a bulk gas and oil service, delivering to farmers all over the area. And he was a dedicated member of the volunteer fire department.

Bernie's mother Angie R. Satterlee Saggau was born in 1906 in Ida Grove. She met her husband at a high school football game.

She was a homemaker during the years she was raising their three children – Bernie, his older sister Norma Jean, now retired in Arkansas, and his younger sister Lydia, now retired in California. Later, she opened the very popular Angie's Café, also just across the street from the courthouse. She ran it for 16 years, offering good meals – hot beef sandwiches were a specialty along with her famous pies and cakes – and doing catering, too.

"They were great people, really hard working people," Bernie said of his parents. "Everybody loved my mother, just loved her. Now, my dad, if anybody crossed wires with him, he was a fire-eater! And he'd let them know in no uncertain terms!"

Father and son spent a lot of time hunting together.

"The phone operators in Denison were used to calling all the volunteer firemen when there was a fire in town," Bernie said. "So when we'd be going hunting, Dad would call the operator the night before and say, 'We're going to go out tomorrow morning, so would you give us a call at 5 a.m.?' The next morning, she'd call right at 5 and say, 'Bernie, wake up little Bernie, it's time to get up and go hunting.' That's the kind of environment I grew up in. Everybody looked out for everybody else."

So even though his childhood came during the tough economic times of the 1930s and then the World War II years, "it couldn't have been any happier," Saggau said.

"We were busy all the time – work and play, play and work, and it was hard to tell the difference a lot of times. My memory from my young boyhood is of getting on our bicycles and going swimming in the afternoons. It seems like we'd always carry a football, baseball gloves, bats, basketballs and boxing gloves right along with us, and there'd be some kind of game break out every day."

On Saturday mornings, there was always a race among the kids in town to see who could be the first to get to the high school and make the first basket during the "open gym" time.

Bernie's cousins Jack, Bobby and Tommy Saggau were among the good young athletes, and all three eventually played football at Notre Dame. In fact, Bob was an All-American for the Fighting Irish in the late 1930s. Jack, the oldest of the three, ran a :09.7 100-yard dash when he was in high school. After starting his college career at Notre Dame, he transferred to Creighton University in Omaha. Later he became a well-known sports broadcaster for WHO radio in Des Moines, and ultimately he became one of the top sales executives with the insurance company Mutual of Omaha.

But in Denison in the 1930s, Bobby and Tommy Saggau were the cousins on the Catholic side of the family who recruited Bernie to play for the St. Rose of Lima grade school basketball team. The Catholics had a significant rivalry with the Lutheran church in which Bernie was then being raised, and not just in grade school basketball.

"There was the Lutheran church on one block in our old neighborhood, and the Catholic church on this other block," Saggau recalled in a speech to a Iowa Fellowship of Athletes banquet in the spring of 2004. "They hated each other, and all the other churches in town hated both of them. But I never bought into any of that."

Sunday nights usually meant supper at his grandparents' home.

"The whole extended family would be there," he said. "Sometimes there'd be as many as 25 of us. My sisters and I had two choices about those suppers – it was either go to Grandpa and Grandma's house, or death, because not to go was an insult to them."

As Bernie and I began our tour of the town, we drove north off U.S. Highway 30, up the hill on South Twelfth Street, looking directly at the courthouse. The first home he remembers is right below the courthouse, at 23 South Twelfth. He told me how when people would gather for livestock auctions across the street at the downtown stockyards, he and his pals would launch snowballs "and see if we could scatter the crowd."

When he was about 11, the family moved just west around the corner to the home at 1119 Broadway, also across the street from the courthouse and just to the west. That's where he lived until he left home for college. Saggau was pleased to see that the family in that home now flies an American flag out front.

"You want to know why I've always been so patriotic?" he said, looking back across the street. "There on that corner of the courthouse lawn, see that old Civil War cannon and monument over there? Where they've still got all those flags flying? I can't tell you how many hours I spent right there, climbing on that cannon and looking at that monument."

We walked over and read the inscription on the monument: "In memory of the men of this vicinity who gave their lives in the defense of their country, 1861-1865."

In addition, his uncle Hugo Saggau "was big in the American Legion – even headed it in Iowa for a while – and I remember that a day didn't go by that he didn't put up the American flag and take it down," Bernie said. "I think it rubbed off on me."

And, of course, he was in high school while World War II was raging.

He remembers exactly where he was when he heard that Pearl Harbor had been bombed, prompting America's entry into the war. On that December 7, 1941, in his eighth grade year, Bernie was on a duck hunting trip with his father and local dentist "Doc" Vosgerau on Blackhawk Lake at Lake View. It took them a few minutes to believe what they were hearing.

"Then Doc started walking up and down a row, singing 'We're in the Army now!' " Saggau recalled. "I remember Dad saying to him, 'By God, Doc, it might be sooner than you think.' And six months later, Doc was in the Army!"

Bernie also remembers a day or two after the attack, sitting in an all-school assembly, "listening to President Roosevelt talk to the nation – they had his radio speech on the PA system – and everybody was quiet, real quiet."

Soon they were all involved in a county-wide campaign by public and parochial school students to sell U.S. Savings Bonds and stamps to help raise money for the war effort. In fact, the school children of Crawford County raised $235,446 – more than their counterparts in any other Iowa county – and that was enough to purchase a B-25 medium-range bomber, according to stories in the archives of the Denison Bulletin newspaper. The Crawford County kids got to name the plane, and they dubbed it "The Wild Rose of Iowa." It flew into service in the Pacific Theater in 1944.

Saggau said that as he and the rest of the students went on through high school, "war wasn't something you necessarily feared fighting. We all thought about our friends in the war, and we all took it for granted we'd go to the service, too, right out of school. But still, I don't think we really understood what it might be like."

The military stopped drafting new soldiers on May 15, 1946. Saggau's eighteenth birthday, which would have made him eligible for the draft, came three days later.

As he went through school, Saggau said he was never more than "an average student," except in one area: "citizenship."

He recalls that "when I was a boy, when we got our report cards to take home from school, they'd have the academic grades on the left side and the 'citizenship' grades on the right side. When I'd give that report card to my parents, my dad would cover up the academic grades and first look at those citizenship grades. I've never forgotten what he'd always say: 'If somebody is a good citizen, he'll always do his best.' And that's what became most important to me. That's how I've based my own philosophies."

When he tells that story in speeches, as he has done hundreds of times, he often says he's "going to write a book some day called 'When Education Changed.' It's going to be about what's happened since they took those citizenship grades off the report cards."

As an athlete, Saggau had a good four years with the Denison High "Monarchs." (The nickname was taken from the kingly lions, and not the pretty butterflies, as opponents often contend.) He was especially good for his size. He was about 5 ft., 6.5 in. tall and, by his recollection, weighed 117 pounds as a junior, maybe 125 as a senior. He played football, basketball, track and baseball.

Nearly every time he made the newspapers, his size was mentioned.

The Denison Bulletin, in a baseball story, noted, "Bernie Saggau, undersized Denison rightfielder, was the biggest gun of the Monarch attack, getting three hits, one of them a three-bagger, out of four trips to the plate."

The student newspaper Monarch News led a story about a basketball victory over Jefferson this way: "Led by little Bernie Saggau with 19 points, the rejuvenated Monarchs came out of the fog here last Friday night to score a smashing 46-17…"

In another game story, that student paper called him "the diminutive dynamo."

And here is student reporter Shirley Slechta's brief "senior profile" story about Saggau late in his senior year:

"If you hear anyone asking about a little man with a little beard, you can take it for granted that they are paging Bernie Saggau.

"Bernie's a senior this year, and we are hoping that he will graduate, because he says that he will not shave until he does.

"You can find this little man at the bottom of every pile at the football or basketball game. Confidentially, he is the streak of white you see racing down the floor to make a super duper basket. He participates in track meets and comes out with an award every time. In football, as you all know, he is quite a flash. Yep, that's our Bernie.

"Bernie isn't only outstanding in athletics, he sings, too – a regular Bing Crosby. He has played the lead in several operettas and has done some wonderful acting in the class plays.

"Someday when Bernie is a great big boy, he is going to become a doctor. So girls, when you sprain your wrists beating your men, call on Dr. Bernard Saggau!"

But pound for pound, he was probably about as tough as they come.

The sports editor of the town paper wrote in his column that Bernie and his teammates Tommy Saggau and Jimmy Saggau "are all cousins and tougher than whang leather."

Bernie saw his first varsity football action as a sophomore, as a back-up quarterback. He started as a junior, but only played one complete game. In the second game, at Ida Grove, he suffered a broken collarbone and broken ribs and was out for the rest of the season. He saw lots of action as the starting quarterback in his senior year, helping the team to a 4-5 record. He also "drop-kicked" most of the points after touchdown. That season ended with a hard-fought 12-7 loss to Harlan in the Armistice Day game, with what appeared to be a winning Denison touchdown waved off because time had run out.

"I liked to play football in high school, but I can't say I ever really loved it," Saggau said. "The contact was too much. I wasn't a coward, but at 117 pounds, I didn't bull anybody over, that's for sure. When I got to BV and was playing college football, I really enjoyed it more because I'd gotten stronger and more mature. I knew how to handle it a little better by then."

Terry Knott, a classmate who went on to play with Saggau at Buena Vista, too, was a 6 ft., 2 in., 190-pound lineman in high school who tried to keep the opponents' maulers away from the Monarchs' little quarterback.

"Bernie was guttier than hell," said Knott, who spent most of his career as a teacher and coach in western Iowa and retired in Denison. "He was speedy and he was brainy, and that helped."

Saggau had more success in high school in basketball, starting for three years, "even though in that sophomore year, I probably wasn't any more than about 5 ft., 3 in.," he said.

During that sophomore season, he also learned what it felt like to be the goat.

"We got beat in the county tournament on a Saturday night," Saggau said, "and I had the dubious honor of missing two free throws after the gun, to lose the game. There wasn't any hiding from it. I think everybody in town was at that game, and I felt terrible about it, the way any kid would.

"On that Sunday afternoon, it was so cold we couldn't even go hunting. But all of a sudden there was a knock on our door at home. Dad told me to go to the door, and when I opened it, there was my Latin teacher Mrs. (Hilda) Catron. She said, 'Bernie, I was at last night's game,' and I said, 'You, too, Brutus,' from a story she'd taught us. Then she said, 'I just wanted to come by and tell you something: If you always try as hard as you can, you will never fail, and you have my word of honor.'

"We sat and visited some more, and then after a while, I walked her home. It really hit me how she'd taken time, on a day when it was way below zero, to walk to our house, knock on our door and give me that little consolation. I've told that story to hundreds of thousands of kids in the years since. I tell them how we all ought to be 'door-knockers,' and that 'if you try as hard as you can, you'll never fail, and I give you my word of honor.' Then I tell them that that's not me talking – it's my old Latin teacher – and that the real lesson is that you never know who is going to carry your message on through the years. I've carried Mrs. Catron's message every since that cold Sunday afternoon when I was a sophomore in high school."

By his junior year of basketball, he'd grown a little and improved a lot, nearly always scoring in double figures. In one game, he made 28 points, and that stood as Denison High's one-game scoring record for some time.

In baseball, Saggau generally was in the outfield, but in those war years Denison did not field a team every year. He also played on various local fast-pitch softball teams.

Denison was a track powerhouse in those years, and Saggau became one of its best sprinters, once running the 100-yard dash in :10.3 seconds, and usually running the leadoff legs on the 440- and 880-yard relays.

On those relays, he teamed with Don Chandler, Dick Boeck and Tommy Saggau. Their heyday came in the Valley Relays in West Des Moines in 1946 when they set meet records in both those events. And Denison's two-mile relay team also set a new meet record that day. The Des Moines Register reported that "an unheralded Denison High cinder crew came charging out of western Iowa to steal Knoxville's thunder in Friday's opening-day session of the Valley Relay," and ran a photo of the sprint relay team.

Marion Wilson, the young Denison coach at that time, carried that photo in his wallet for the next 55 years before recently telling Saggau he wanted him to have it.

In 2004, Wilson was 83 years old and retired in California. His attachment to his athletes in Denison was so strong that five decades later, he was still coming back to Iowa most summers, gathering a bunch of his old Monarch athletes and spending a day playing golf and remembering old stories. Saggau usually joins them.

"Bernie, for his size, was probably the best athlete I ever coached," Wilson said. "But when I got to Denison, they were on a 20-year run of great success in sports. It was an athletic town, for sure. I couldn't believe the speed. I'd coached at Villisca earlier, and I didn't have one kid who could break 60 seconds in a quarter-mile. At Denison, I had 20 that could."

Wilson had attended high school in little Patterson, southwest of Des Moines, and then went on to William Penn College in Oskaloosa. His first teaching and coaching position was at Prairie City, located just east of Des Moines; then Villisca in southwest Iowa, and he arrived in Denison in the fall of 1945 when he was 24 years old.

Denison was a member of the Midwest Conference with Ida Grove, Sac City, Jefferson and its biggest rivals Carroll and Harlan. They would also play non-conference games with schools from Omaha and Council Bluffs, as well as with other western Iowa teams.

"Remember, it was war time," Wilson said. "I might not have been able to get that Denison job except that there just weren't many men available to teach and coach right then."

His assignment in Denison was to teach high school physical education, an eighth grade orientation class and to be the high school coach – that's right, the only one, in whatever sports Denison was offering. His recollection is that he received no pay for his coaching, just for his teaching.

He only had Saggau and his classmates for their senior year.

"Bernie's group had had four different coaches in four years," Wilson said. And, as Saggau tells it, they had more than their fill of new coaches coming in year after year, meaning they'd barely learn one coach's system before he'd be gone and another one would arrive.

"At the end of our junior year, our old coach left because he wanted to go to a larger school," he recalled in his speech at the Sportsmanship Summit in South Dakota. "Then the next fall, this young dude appears in baggy sweatpants and sweatshirt. We football players took one look at him, and we voted 58-0 that we weren't going to like him. Then somebody said, 'But what's his name?' We didn't know, but we weren't going to give him a chance. And we decided we wouldn't call him 'Coach' because that was the magic word that we respected somebody."

So the newly-arrived Wilson started football drills, with more strain on his squad than he may have realized.

The turnaround, Saggau said, came after one of the first practices when the boys were all in the showers, whooping it up as usual.

"Suddenly it got real quiet," he said. "I turned around and there was the coach, naked as a jay bird, getting ready to come into the shower with us. And that's when we realized for the first time that he only had one leg – the other one was cut off at about the knee. He was standing there in front of this vat of athlete's foot treatment chemicals that was right in front of the shower room. As we were all standing there, he hopped on the one foot into that vat, then into the shower and started taking his shower right with us.

"That changed everything," Saggau continued. "After that shower, some of us went up to him and said, 'Coach, you tell us what to do and we'll get it done.'

"What Coach Wilson taught us was that we should never judge another human being until you get to know him."

Over time, they not only got to know and respect Wilson, they came to love him.

Eventually, Wilson shared the story of how, when he was two years old, his father was using a mowing machine on their farm near Weldon in southeast Iowa, didn't realize his toddler Marion had wandered into his path and hit him. The left leg was severed, and his right foot was badly mangled but saved.

"I look back on that and it's a wonder I didn't bleed to death," Wilson said. "It was 1923, and medical care wasn't nearly what it is now, of course. But they were able to take care of me okay, get me patched up and then eventually get me an artificial leg. I got over it. In fact, I've never really looked on it has a handicap, but instead, more of a motivator."

He went on to be a letterman in both basketball and baseball in high school and in tennis in college.

But his father, he said, "never got over what happened, I don't think. He died four years after the accident, when he was only 34 or 35 years old. I think it was his heart, and his worrying that I'd never have any kind of life after losing my leg like that. If he'd have just lived long enough, he'd have seen, man, I've had the best life in the world. I spent my whole career in schools, around young people, and now look at me – over 80 years old and friends all around me. I've had a great life."

In that 1945-46 school year, he coached the Monarchs to a 4-5 football season, after the disappointing loss to Harlan in the final game; then a .500 basketball season, and then the great track season in which the Denison boys set records running everywhere they went in western Iowa. A year later, he coached Denison High to its first state championship in any sport – indoor track. Then he was off to California, where he served 31 years as a principal, and then superintendent, in an elementary school district in the community of Lemoore. When he retired, they named the school's library after him. And then for the next 21 years, he served on the board of education for the local high school district.

Wilson said he has "never forgotten how good Denison was to me as a young guy. There were three former coaches on the school board, and I remember worrying that they'd think they were experts and might want to be doing the coaching, but they were real supportive. Other people helped, too. The Presbyterian minister came down and helped me coach the sprinters and hurdlers in track, because I really didn't know much about that."

Saggau said it was a real head-turner among the boys when that minister, Rev. William L. Tillman, first showed up at track practice, which was a year or two before Wilson came to town.

"Rev. Tillman was a little squirt, about my size," he recalls. "He came walking up to this high hurdle and did one of those quick high-steps over it, like good hurdlers do. He got our attention right away!"

He also had an active youth program at his church, and that intrigued Saggau and his pals.

"We all started going to those youth group meetings," he said. "It became a real popular way to spend our Wednesday nights.

"My family had not been overly religious up to then. We went to the Lutheran church on Sunday, but I missed some, too – going hunting. Finally, I remember one time having a catechism lesson that we were supposed to go to church and do before school started in the morning. It was at the same time we had our music practices before school. I asked the minister, who was kind of a stern old Lutheran, if I could miss the catechism lesson, and he said, 'You must think more of music than you do of religion.' That sort of put me off, and by that time, I knew Rev. Tillman, so I started going to the Presbyterian church. I even became an usher and got real active."

That was fine with his parents.

"My dad told me I could go to any church I wanted, but that I was going to church," he said.

Saggau looks back on that time period as being when his faith really started to come alive.

"When I went on to Buena Vista, which has always had the Presbyterian affiliation, I kind of put religion on hold again, like a lot of college kids do," he told the Fellowship of Christian Athletes. "We had to go to chapel, and we all complained, but the truth is, I loved going."

The other hangouts for high school boys back then included the pool halls, the movie theater and the roller skating rink.

"I loved to play pool," Saggau said. "Kids could go into the pool halls, but only from 4 to 5 p.m. – then out! The old German guys had a pinochle kind of game they played, too, and it turned out that there were only two kids they'd let get in those games – Terry Knott and me. But if we made a dumb play, or were careless, then they'd throw us out of the game."

By 5 p.m., the adults would take over the pool halls, where the daily norm "was to have one beer, get the news and then when the fire whistle blew at 6 o'clock, go home," Saggau said. "There were three places people in Denison got their news back then – in the Denison Bulletin newspaper, at church and in the taverns."

He "dated a girl from Manilla," located southeast of Denison, and a date was "usually either a movie or roller skating."

The movie house in Denison then was the Ritz Theatre. The roller rink was the "Stardom." There were also dances at ballrooms in nearby Arcadia as well as at "Columbia Hall" in Denison, later known as the "Moonglow Ballroom."

The Ritz was near demolition when, in 1988, it was saved by a new community foundation formed to honor the memory of Donna Reed. They raised money locally, secured some preservation grants and began a long renovation that in 1995 allowed it to be reopened as the Donna Reed Theater. The 550-seat theater is now the hub for the Donna Reed Festival held every June, which besides being a community festival, brings Hollywood stars in to work with aspiring young actors and actresses.

Reed was born in Denison in 1921 as Donnabelle Mullenger. She went to Hollywood when she was 16 to finish high school and study acting. She died in 1988 after a long and distinguished career, which including winning an "Oscar" for her performance in "From Here to Eternity" and starring with Jimmy Stewart in "It's a Wonderful Life." She also starred in her own weekly television show from 1958 to 1966.

Donna Reed was enough older than Saggau that he never really knew her, although her younger brother Bill Mullenger was a teammate.

Saggau always had a job while growing up. As a young boy, he used his bicycle to deliver prescriptions for a pharmacist. He mowed lawns and scooped walks, especially for Lydia J. Krall, the woman who owned and operated Denison's hospital and who was a close friend of Bernie's parents. Krall became an influential figure in Bernie's life, always encouraging him to consider medicine, even having him sit-in on surgeries and childbirth procedures.

"She was just like a second mother for us, and in fact, one of my sisters is named after her," Saggau said.

Krall had grown up in the small nearby town of Vail.

"Talk about an independent woman, ahead of her time," Saggau said. "Here was a gal who was not married, but she used her medical training, saved some money, bought and then ran the local hospital."

Later she also became the anesthesiologist for surgeries.

The white, wood-frame hospital building at 103 South Ninth Street has long since been converted to apartments.

Saggau recalls that when it was a hospital, it had nine or 10 rooms for patients as well as examination rooms, an operating room and a snack shop in the basement. Krall lived diagonally from the hospital in her own home. Both around her house and behind the hospital, she had substantial yards and gardens, which she paid Bernie to mow and weed.

"Since she was dealing with doctors all the time, she wanted to be on their social level," Saggau said. "Two of our doctors back then were good golfers, so Miss Krall drove her own car to Omaha in the 1930s to take golf lessons. She wanted to be able to show them she could play with them, and she could – I was her caddy."

She traveled a good bit, and would occasionally take Bernie with her – to Chicago, where she would buy him school clothes at the famous Marshall Field Store and treat him to a major league baseball game, or to Minnesota on fishing trips.

"I've always thought she sort of picked me out as having some potential," he said, "and she wanted to give me a few more experiences than I would have had otherwise."

Krall stayed single until her late 30s, when she married Bernie's uncle Hugo Saggau. She died in about 1990.

Saggau had other jobs in high school that kept him even busier.

During the summers, he joined a railroad section gang and did heavy work on the Northwestern Railroad mainline that ran east-west through Denison.

And during the school year, he also became a sales clerk, window washer and janitor at a shoe store, Hallit's Bootery. Owner Bill Hallit had been summoned to military service and left his wife Mary in charge. It was located in what today is the east wing of the Donna Read Theater. Late in Saggau's high school years, the Hallits asked if he wanted to go into a partnership with them, the idea being that he'd eventually own the store.

"That was quite an opportunity for a young guy, especially back then right after World War II," Saggau said. "I mean, that was a good business there, right in the business district."

The summer after he graduated, he was still thinking of going full-time with the shoe store, while he was spending weekdays working the railroad job.

"Our section boss was an Irishman named Jim Burke, who wasn't even five feet tall and was kind of stooped-over besides that," Saggau said. "He didn't have much of an education – I think he had real trouble even reading the train schedules – but, oh, what a worker that guy was.

"One day that summer after my senior year, we were working west of Denison on the tracks right alongside Highway 30. I told Jim that I was debating on whether I really wanted to go to college, where I might go or whether I should just stay home and go to work at the shoe store. He stopped what he was doing and said, 'Bernie, you know, if you don't go to college you'll work your whole life here. That's what I've done, and it's O.K., but I think there's a whole lot more out there for you if you want it.' "

And?

"I put my tools away, walked across the tracks up on to the highway and hitchhiked back into Denison," Saggau said. "I decided I was going to go to college."

A few days later, Saggau was mowing the grass in front of his grandparents' home when a car pulled up and stopped. Approaching him came "two men wearing white shirts and neckties," he said, and they introduced themselves as President Henry Olson of Buena Vista College in

Storm Lake and a member of the BV Board of Trustees Z.Z. White, a Storm Lake attorney.

They told him they wanted him to come to BV, play some football and run track, and they had a small scholarship and a part-time job for him.

"I hadn't been that great of a high school football player to warrant them recruiting me for that," Saggau said. "But my uncle Eddie Saggau had been a star at BV years before, and they knew about my cousins Bob and Tommy. I think they were probably recruiting the Saggau name, more than anything."

That name had certainly been a big one in Denison.

"There were lots of Saggaus in Denison, and they all lived there a long time," said Bernie, "but then they began their migration to California."

Now there are no Saggaus left in the community.

But one of them remains forever loyal.

"I always tell everybody it's the best hometown in America," Bernie said, a warm twinkle in his eye. "And I always watch for the Denison-Harlan score in the sports pages."

Bernie Saggau's heritage and life before the IHSAA

Bernie Saggau's boyhood in the town of Denison in west central Iowa "couldn't have been any happier," he says. The lower photo shows him now, standing in front of the house where he lived in his high school years, just across the street south from the Crawford County Courthouse.

Personal Collection

Personal Collection

Personal Collection

Chuck Offenburger

Clockwise from right top: Bernie Saggau's grandparents Martin and Caroline Saggau, his parents Bernie and Angie Saggau, his sisters (left) Lydia Ann and Norma Jean with Bernie, and the front of Martin Saggau's Saloon, with the German motto underneath the business' name translating, "Today for money. Tomorrow for free."

Bernie Saggau was a four-sport athlete for the Denison High School Monarchs. In the football team photo, he's second from the left in the front row. On the record-setting track relay team, shown in an old Des Moines Register clipping, Bernie is second from the left, next to Coach Marion Wilson. Bernie's cousin Tommy Saggau is on the right. In the picture of the track squad from the school yearbook, Bernie is first person on the left in the front row. In the inset photo Coach Wilson is shown in a 2003 photo, in a golf cart during a visit back to Iowa. In the basketball team photo from his junior year, Saggau is No. 22 in the front row.

Personal Collection

Track

Sitting—Bernie Saggau, Tom Gaines, Jerry Lehr, Eris Willadsen.
Second Row—Pete Jepsen, Little Young, Bob Eshbaugh, Wayne Roepke, John Gunnett, Kevin Guenther.
Third Row—Allen Hanafan, Mark Van Voorhis, Wubho Johnson, Coach Bob Otte, Bob Allen, Norman Neilsen, Don Castle.

DASH MEN	FIELD EVENTS	DISTANCE MEN
Saggau	Guenther	Eshbaugh
Willadsen	Roepke	Van Voorhis
Gaines	Hanafan	
Lehr	Castle	
Warner	Jepson	
Castle	Young	
Johnson		

— 124 —

Personal Collection

They Couldn't Be Stopped

Personal Collection

Chuck Offenburger

Personal Collection

Bernie Saggau at his 1946 graduation from
Denison High School and with his favorite
dog "Pal."

Bernie Saggau in his Buena Vista College years in Storm Lake, where he graduated in three years.

Above: In a recent photo Saggau points to his old BV football helmet, which has quite a dent from a long-ago collision on the gridiron.

When Bernie Saggau was a senior at Buena Vista College, he met first-year student Lois Kretzinger, from Coon Rapids, Iowa, and fell in love. Lois is shown here in a formal portrait and walking in front of BV's Old Main building with her friend DeeAnn Carlson, from Paton, Iowa.

Right: Bernie and Lois were married in Coon Rapids in 1952, when he was teaching and coaching in Cherokee and she had been teaching in Lytton.

The young Saggau family spent three summers in Missoula, Montana, while Bernie earned his master's degree at the University of Montana. Here Bernie, Lois and infant son Jeff are shown beginning their long drive to Missoula in 1953.

Below: Bernie Saggau worked four years for the Jostens Company from 1957 to 1961, and became one of the company's top producers in soliciting schools' yearbook production accounts and other services. He is pictured, second from right in the front row, among the top Jostens salesmen. Company owner Dan Gaine is first on the left in the back row.

Personal Collection

Chuck Offenburger

Above: Saggau in a recent visit to his parents' graves in Denison. *Right:* One of Saggau's keepsakes is a carved wooden statue of a Buena Vista "Beaver" given to him by IHSAA board members.

Chuck Offenburger

Chapter Three

Bernie Saggau's route to the IHSAA

In 1946, when Bernie Saggau and 450 other students enrolled at Buena Vista College in the northwest Iowa town of Storm Lake, it was a time when everybody was in a hurry – to get their lives started again.

World War II had ended, and veterans were streaming back to campus to use their military benefits to pay for their college education. They were marrying, having babies and were anxious to begin their careers. Hence, it was a rather odd time to go to college as an 18-year-old. Freshman Saggau's teammates on the BV Beavers football team were as much as 10 years older than he was. Their sense of urgency was contagious, and Saggau wound up graduating in just three years.

It seems like he's been on the fast track ever since.

In the fall of 1949, he became a science teacher, football and basketball coach at the junior high school in Cherokee, 25 miles west of Storm Lake. In 1952, he married his BV sweetheart Lois Kretzinger, of Coon Rapids, Iowa, and in 1953 he was promoted to junior high principal in Cherokee, a position he held for four years. In that time period, the Saggau family began to grow, with the births of son Jeff in 1953 and daughter Becky in 1955.

In 1957, Bernie left education to go into sales for Jostens, a Minnesota company that sold high school class rings, produced yearbooks and offered graduation robes and invitations. And in 1958, Jostens moved the Saggaus to Storm Lake, where they also bought, lived in and operated an apartment house with five adjacent cabins on the lakeshore. In 1959, son David was born. In 1961, Bernie was recruited back to Cherokee to go into insurance and real estate.

By that time, he had also become one of the best football and basketball referees in the Midwest, working major college as well as high school games. Through officiating, he had come to the attention of Lyle T. Quinn, the executive secretary of the Iowa High School Athletic Association. Quinn assigned Saggau and his partners to many of the biggest and sometimes most contentious games in the state, and to the basketball state tournaments. In fact, Saggau officiated eight consecutive boys' state championship games from 1954-61. As Quinn's health began to fail, he frequently asked Saggau to take his place conducting "rules meetings" around the state for other game officials and coaches.

By the fall of 1963, Saggau had realized his heart was not in the insurance and real estate business, and he had an opportunity to buy The Oaks golf course near Ames. He made an offer, which was accepted, but before the transaction was complete, Quinn summoned him to Boone and offered him a position as assistant executive secretary at the IHSAA, with the understanding he would eventually be Quinn's successor.

On October 14, 1963, Bernie Saggau's long tenure with the IHSAA began.

If it sounds like it was a dizzy dozen years getting there, you really don't know the half of it, Lois Saggau says. "When we were leaving Cherokee to buy the golf course in Ames but then wound up going to Boone, between selling our house, moving into an apartment, moving to a rental house in Boone and then finally buying another house in Boone, we moved three times in three months."

There's another aspect of their lives back then that tells you a lot about the times, and a lot about Bernie Saggau, too.

When he took the two jobs he loved most – the teaching-coaching position in Cherokee and the IHSAA job – each time he took a cut in pay.

Quinn gave him an annual salary of $8,400 at the athletic association in 1963. Saggau had been making "one and a half times that" in insurance and real estate, and the income from the golf course he was planning to buy would have been even higher.

34

But even more amazing, the $3,050 annual salary he was paid for that first teaching and coaching position in 1949 was less than he'd made the previous year as a college student, when he worked nearly full-time as a waiter at Storm Lake's Cobblestone Ballroom. He started out there in his freshman year making $5 per night and all the tips he took-in, and as a popular BV athlete, he quickly became a favorite waiter of the Cobblestone crowds. He became one of owner Junior Lawrence's key employees, working five or six nights a week and even longer hours during the summers.

He did so well financially then, in fact, that Z.Z. White, the Storm Lake attorney who had helped BV President Henry Olson recruit young Saggau, told him during his last year on campus, "Bernie, you're the first student I ever helped do his income tax!"

Remember, when he came out of Denison, Saggau was no stranger to work.

His football and track scholarship at Buena Vista paid $95 per semester. In addition, White paid him $3.75 per week to keep the floors swept and waxed in his law office. And the college's athletic department paid him 65 cents per hour to be a custodian in the gymnasium and "to wash the T-shirts, shorts, jocks and socks," Saggau recalls. And since there were no dormitories at Buena Vista then, the athletic department had also helped him find a room with a Storm Lake family, for which he paid $6 per week.

He was so young and so small when football practice started his first fall on campus, that he went through a little hazing from the older players on the team.

"But in the second game of the season, we played the University of Dubuque, which was a real powerhouse back then," Saggau said. "Our tailback was a real speedster, and a key player for us, but he had a rough first half, so the coach brought me into the game in the second half. I did pretty well. That next week, John Rutan, one of the older guys on the team, and his roommate Sam Reed, who was another older athlete, invited me to come over to the little cabin they shared and have dinner with them."

Rutan told him "he'd be happy to block for me any time I wanted to carry the ball," Saggau said. "And then they asked if I liked my janitor's job. I told them I'd like to find something else, and Sam Reed said he'd get me on

35

at the Cobblestone Ballroom."

"The Cob" was a lively place, to say the least, back then in the mid and late 1940s. Besides being a fine supper club and dance hall, it had three or four bars in it, the most notorious of which was a balcony-level "Circus Lounge," with a tent-like canvas ceiling and paintings of animals and trapeze artists on the walls. It is well documented that there were slot machines available at different times in the Cobblestone's history, and the liquor laws were often given only cursory attention. But there is no question that the owner was good to the college students working for him.

"Junior Lawrence did have some bad habits," Saggau said, "but he was responsible for putting a lot of guys through college, too."

Buena Vista was regenerating its football program after the war, and Saggau recalls "the equipment wasn't as good as what we'd had in high school." The Beavers played in two conferences at the same time – the Iowa Conference and the Dakota-Iowa Conference. In one season, they finished last in the Iowa while winning the championship in the Dakota-Iowa.

As the tailback in a single-wing offense, Saggau was both throwing and running the ball, and he was fast and shifty enough that he began causing opponents lots of problems.

In his sophomore year, they traveled to the University of Dubuque and quickly fell behind "by two or three touchdowns," he recalled. "We kept trying to run the ball on them, and we were getting nowhere. So we said the heck with the single-wing, we're putting the ball in the air! We started coming back, and we wound up getting beat by one point."

Saggau threw, ran and caught the ball while running all over the Dubuque secondary late in that game. Afterward, when the team was in the showers, he received a highly unusual salute for his effort.

"All of a sudden, somebody snapped me on the butt with a towel," he said. "I wheeled around and there stood 'Moco' Mercer, the UD coach, in his street clothes, right in our shower room! He said, 'Are you Saggau?' I said, 'Yes, sir.' He said, 'I just wanted to see if you are as small as they say, because you're the toughest little son-of-a-bitch I've ever seen!' And then he walked out."

In his third year, BV limped into the football season with some key players injured, new coach Bob Otto told the Storm Lake Pilot-Tribune. "But Bernie Saggau has pulled through scrimmage clutches, as has Gordon McKinstry," the newspaper noted. "Saggau, with his fog horn voice and bowl-full of energy, and McKinstry, whose booming punts and dead-eye passes have clicked, promise to give York College punishment" in the opener.

By then, there was enough public interest in the team that the squad had grown to "45 to 50 players," Saggau said, "and you know, it seems to me like every afternoon when we'd practice, there might be 100 people from around town who'd come out and watch."

When BV began a football Hall of Fame, Saggau was one of the original three inductees. "I think the reason they put me in there was as a token," he said, "as a representative of all the athletes who were average in talent but who gave 110 percent. Honestly, I was an average football player, maybe a little better than some expected just because of my size, but very average."

Saggau also played a half-season of basketball when BV's squad was short of players, but his main focus after football was track.

He was a sprinter, running on the BV sprint relay teams as well as the open 100- and 220-yard dashes. He lowered his 100 time to :09.9. He captained the track team in his third season and was named its MVP.

But the biggest moment of his college career – of his whole life, he'll tell you – was meeting freshman Lois Kretzinger, a head-turning farm girl from Coon Rapids, in the fall of 1948.

"He looked young, kind of like his senior picture from high school," Lois recalled. "I guess I'd say he looked like a halfback, but he was a friendly guy.

"He evidently had a bet with one of the boys that he could get a date with me," she continued. "So, my friend DeeAnn Carlson, from Paton, Iowa, and I were walking out of Old Main, and here were Bernie and several other big football boys on campus, all stretched out on the grass and making funny noises at us. Dee Ann and I were rather cool – we didn't want them to think we were that kind of girls – so Bernie called us stuck up. But I thought he was really cute. Of course, Bernie won his bet, and we have had a great love affair ever since."

She had followed her brother Ronnie Kretzinger to BV, where he'd been an athlete in the early 1940s. Ronnie had a rather notable high school classmate in Coon Rapids who also wound up at BV – E. Wayne Cooley, who later headed the Iowa Girls High School Athletic Union for 49 years.

Lois Kretzinger had opted for music over sports in high school, and when she came to BV, she played clarinet in the college's marching band, orchestra and stage band, and also sang in the choir. She was enrolled in the two-year teacher-training program that BV and most other colleges offered back then.

She loved playing pinochle in an ongoing game in the basement of Old Main, and she was just as avid about fishing, as she still is today. She recalls going night crawler hunting on the BV football field one night before she, Bernie and his teammate Bob Willadsen were going fishing early the next morning.

They dated often, but their time together was limited because Bernie was working nearly every night. They'd go to movies, bowling and take walks along the lake.

"He'd take me to dinner at the bowling alley, and then he'd go work at the Cobblestone," Lois said. "Sometimes I'd go out there, too, with a big bunch of girlfriends. We'd all get out and dance. Bernie never liked to dance, but I loved it. When the big bands would come in – Harry James, Glenn Miller, Tommy Dorsey, Jimmy Dorsey, Gene Krupa – the Cobblestone would be packed to the hilt. I'd never seen anything like it before, and probably will never again. It was great!"

Bernie Saggau concurs that it was a happy time at Buena Vista.

"There was a wide age difference among all the students there then," he said. "And we were all poor, but we didn't know it. We were all going up hill together, and it seemed fun."

Many friendships that he and Lois formed there are still important in their lives – Bob Willadsen and his wife Marge, still living in Storm Lake; John Gannon, longtime superintendent of the Emmetsburg, Iowa, schools and also a member of the Board of Control of the IHSAA; Vernon "Dutch" Huseman, who went on to become athletic director for years at Fort Dodge High School; Dick Utter, still of Storm Lake, and his wife Jan, and many others, some now deceased.

It was also while he was at BV that Bernie Saggau began doing the officiating and the public speaking that, within just a few years, made him known all over Iowa – and beyond.

"I always think my refereeing career started back when I was in sixth grade in Denison," he said. "From sixth through the eighth grade, I 'refereed' the varsity basketball practices every afternoon. I always liked to go to those practices, and the coach Al Dallagher would have me be the referee for the scrimmages."

When he started college, "I started officiating right away, although you know when I look back on it, I'm not so sure I really had passed the test and gotten certified," Saggau said. "But I must've done that before long.

"The fall of my freshman year, I probably did some junior high or high school junior varsity football games. But then in basketball, I went right into high school varsity games. I think I was getting $12.50 a night if I was working with somebody else, or $15 if I worked alone, and there were a lot of those small schools that wanted you to work alone just to save a little money. I'd work at places like Truesdale, Rembrandt, Sulphur Springs, Schaller, Ute, Charter Oak, Schleswig, Kiron, Highview, Larrabee, Calumet, Meriden. None of them even have their own schools any more."

In subsequent football seasons, "generally I'd officiate a high school game on Friday night, and then play in a college game on Saturday," he said. He formed a football crew with Utter and Jim Reese, another Storm Laker, and the three of them "would sometimes do one game on a Friday afternoon at one of the little schools that didn't have lights, then we'd go on and do another game that night at a larger school," Reese recalled.

Saggau said, "Right from the start, I decided that when I was refereeing, I'd work those games hard. I'd be hustling all the time. I'll tell you what, when it came to basketball, I worked just as hard in the girls' games as I did in the boys'. I'd take good control of the game, but I also made it fun, and I think the coaches and athletes – even the fans – picked up on that."

What that led to, he said, "was I started getting invitations to come out and speak at sports banquets around the area. I was somewhat of a freak because I'm so small and, back then, I looked so young. I think the coaches and administrators at the high schools thought a lot of their kids would identify with me. So I'd go speak and try to give them a pretty good message, something that might help them in school or in sports. I think BV probably was glad to have me out there speaking, too. It kind of connected high school kids around the area to the college."

His way with students caught somebody else's eye, too.

In the spring of his third year at BV, with his graduation assured, Saggau was walking across campus when he was stopped by a man carrying a clipboard with several sheets of paper on it.

"Are you Bernie Saggau?" the man said.

"Yes, sir," he answered.

"Good," the man said, thrusting the clipboard at him, "sign here!"

The man was Rankin Creel, then superintendent of schools in Cherokee. What he wanted Saggau to sign was a contract that he'd come teach at the Cherokee junior high school, and coach junior high football and basketball. It must have been the oddest way a job was ever offered to a prospective teacher.

"I'd never met him before," Saggau said. "It turned out that he had watched me play a couple of football games, and I guess he had checked me out with some of my BV coaches and professors."

The superintendent's thinking, Saggau said, "was that their football coach Otto Huebner, was going to coach three more years and leave, and then they'd offer me the head football job at the high school."

In Huebner's eight years as head coach, which ended after the 1952 season, Huebner's teams had four undefeated/untied seasons.

Saggau gave the opportunity some thought, eventually signed a contract and started his teaching career in the fall of 1949. He taught general science at the junior high, in addition to his coaching there. He got a room in the home of a Cherokee family.

Meanwhile, Lois Kretzinger finished her sophomore year at Buena Vista, got her two-year teaching degree, then landed an elmentary school teaching job in Lytton, southeast of Storm Lake. They continued dating, their relationship bloomed, they decided Lois would leave teaching, and they were married February 10, 1952 in her hometown of Coon Rapids.

Chapter 3

So, how was Bernie Saggau as a classroom teacher?

"I've always told people I must've been an outstanding teacher that first year, because they had three school board meetings just for me," he said.

He was called in, he said, to explain "why I'd gotten a little rough with some of the students. That was after one of our athletes questioned the heredity of one of our coaches, right to his face. Another time, a kid spit in the face of one of our teachers. After one of those incidents, I grabbed one of those kids and threw him down one flight of stairs and up two others, getting him straightened out. The school board wanted to ask me about that. I can remember telling the board president, 'I didn't want this job when I got it, and I won't tolerate people acting like some of these people are acting.' I thought if they fired me, well, at least I wouldn't have backed down.

"What they did, after three years, was make me principal of the building."

It was quite a step for a 24-year-old, and, in fact, it was quite a year. Saggau was also invited for the first time by the Iowa High School Athletic Association to officiate in the boys' state basketball tournament in Iowa City.

Paul Fuhrman was a student who had Saggau as a teacher, football coach and principal back in those early years of the 1950s.

"He had a passion for teaching, that's for sure," said Fuhrman, who retired in 2001 after a long career as an English teacher, athletic director and eventually high school principal in Cherokee. "I can remember Bernie coming into the science classroom. He was very fiery, just like he is now. You could tell he was excited about being there, and he got all of us students excited about it, too. He made us want to go to class, I'll tell you that."

As a coach? "He was tough," Fuhrman said. "He expected you to do what he said, but he was fair, and he made it a lot of fun. I can still remember him talking to us at the junior high sports banquet. He told us that 'some day you're going to get knocked down, maybe hurt and it might be just as easy for you not to get up. But the tough guys do get up, and right then is when you become successful.' That was a great lesson for junior high students getting ready to go into high school."

Fuhrman also had a brush with Saggau in his role as principal, and it was an incident that "was a turning point" in my life, Fuhrman said.

"When I was an eighth grader, I started kind of running with the wrong crowd," he said. "Bernie pulled me out of the hallway one day, took me into an empty classroom, sat me down and talked to me for about a half-hour. He looked me right in the eye and told me I was headed down the wrong road, that I needed to think about where it might take me. He was right, of course, and I've always thought that when he took time to tell me that, it really straightened me out."

Lynn Schwier was a junior high industrial arts teacher who served under Saggau for two years, then succeeded him as principal at the school in 1957.

"When Bernie was running that school, he was so young looking and small, but at the same time he was such a fired-up individual, a real leader," Schwier said. "He could handle kids better than anybody I've ever seen."

When Saggau was getting ready to leave education and go into business, "he called me in and told me he thought I ought to become the principal," Schwier said. "I was just a shop teacher at that point, and he changed my career." Schwier wound up serving 33 years as a principal in the Cherokee schools before he retired in 1991. And, when Saggau came back to Cherokee as a real estate and insurance salesman in 1961, Schwier "was the first person to buy a house from him, I think."

Cherokee High's head football coaching position, which had been tentatively promised to Saggau when he was recruited out of Buena Vista, opened up in 1953. But with his family and career responsibilities and his love of officiating all growing, he decided against pursuing the job.

That left the position open for Bruce Pickford, a Chicago native who had attended Morningside College in Sioux City and then coached two years at Sanborn, Iowa.

Pickford not only continued Cherokee's strong football tradition – his Braves teams won six consecutive Lakes Conference championships – he also teamed with Saggau for officiating in basketball. They became two of the best in the Midwest, working not only high school games but also contests on the college and university levels in the Iowa, North Central, Missouri Valley and Big Eight Conferences.

Pickford went on to coach football at Sioux City Central for three years, including one season there when his team was unbeaten, and then he coached 15 years at Fountain Valley High School in southern California, where his football teams were consistently top-rated among the largest high schools in that part of the state.

"I think the most fun I ever had coaching was in Cherokee," said Pickford, who in 2004 was 75 years old and retired in Huntington Beach, California. "And I doubt very many officials ever had more fun working together than Bernie and I did when we were both there. We really worked a lot – I can remember one basketball season when we were out 84 nights – and I think we developed a great rapport with the coaches."

Indeed.

"It was a big deal when Saggau and Pickford came to town to work one of your basketball games," my late brother Dan Offenburger told me, before his death in early 2004. He coached in the early 1960s in northwest Iowa at Fonda Our Lady of Good Counsel High School and at Rolfe High School. "The players, coaches and fans – everybody – loved it when they walked into the gym. It was kind of an event, in fact. No one knew the rules as well as they did, and no other officials could keep a game moving like they could. They made it fun for everybody."

Well, almost everybody.

There was a rather unhappy fan right there in Fonda, in fact, a few years before my brother started coaching there.

"We did get called on quite a bit to work in highly-competitive games, ones where there might be some extra antagonism," Pickford said. "One night, one of those tough games was in a tournament at Sac City, involving the Fonda public high school. We got the game started, and everything seemed fine except with this one kind of small, little guy sitting about four rows up in the bleachers. He had a very large woman sitting right next to him. So anyway, this guy started in on us. He was yelling about every call we made. He'd yell at us all the way up and down the floor, and he was even shaking his fist at us. The woman sitting next to him – must have been his wife – wasn't saying anything.

"One of the coaches called a time out, so the game stopped and it got pretty quiet – all except for the one little guy still yelling at us. I looked over at Bernie. He was standing across the floor holding the ball – and he was glaring at that fan. Bernie must have heard a word he wasn't going to put up with because, all of a sudden, he blew his whistle real loud, and then everything stopped! You could have heard a pin drop!

"Bernie started walking across the floor, right toward the guy, and as he did, the crowd around the man and woman started scooting away from them. Bernie got right down in front of the man and he said, 'One more word out of you, and you are out of here!' That was all the woman needed. She stood up, yanked the man up on his feet and she said to Bernie, 'Don't you worry, sir, he's out of here right now!' She pulled him out of the gym and pushed him out the door. Everybody else in the crowd loved it!"

Saggau and Pickford lived right next door to each other, near Cherokee High School. Their wives, both named Lois, became "Big Lois" (Saggau) and "Little Lois" (Pickford). Their kids played with each other.

"Bernie and I both liked to hunt, and we'd keep the freezers pretty well full in the fall," Bruce Pickford said. "When we were headed out to referee, if we could get out of town just a little early, we'd throw our shotguns in the car and road-hunt a little bit on the way. We'd get a rooster pheasant here and there, then go on to the game.

"One late afternoon we were on our way to do a basketball game over west of us somewhere, in the Missouri River flyway. We were both wearing our street clothes, and we thought we saw a flock of Canadian geese, just over the hill. Bernie always thought he was the best hunter since Daniel Boone, so he said we had to get out of the car, sneak up over that hill and get those geese. We did that, and by the time we got to the top of the hill we were so muddy and cold, you wouldn't believe it."

And?

"It turned out those Canadians were actually 18 goose decoys sitting there in the field. We didn't let each other forget about that for a long time."

Pickford said by working closely with Saggau, "I learned that he's always got a quick line. He's also got a long, long needle, and a lot of times he'd be sticking it into me."

Saggau confessed "there was the time when we were going to be officiating a basketball game between South Dakota and South Dakota State.

44

Bruce stepped out of the dressing room for a minute before we were going out on the floor, so I stole the pea out of his whistle. Then when he came back in, I bet him I'd make a call before he did in the game. You should have seen the look on his face the first time he tried to below his whistle."

Life was good in Cherokee. In his first summers there, before he was married, Bernie was director of the town's recreation program for kids. By the mid 1950s, he and Lois would take their toddler Jeff and their infant Becky and make a long drive to Missoula, Montana, where he studied three summers at the University of Montana for his master's degree in educational administration.

Between his school salary and the money he brought in from officiating, Bernie was able to save money, invest wisely and provide his young family with a comfortable lifestyle.

"My parents had never had much when I was growing up, but one thing they taught us was the importance of saving money," he said. "I've always done that, and I was able to become fairly independent financially with some good investments I made while I was teaching."

Lois was a devoted stay-at-home mother. "I wasn't working and none of my friends were, either," she said. "We women would all get together for coffee, bring the kids and it'd be wild."

Both of the Saggaus were active in community affairs, took part in Chamber of Commerce activities, and Lois sang and performed in such musicals as "Show Boat" with the Cherokee Community Chorus.

The family had a close call with tragedy in late November, 1957, when Becky, then two years old, sat down in a pail of very hot water Bernie had just used to scald pheasants he was cleaning. She suffered second-degree burns requiring hospitalization for several days, first in Cherokee and then in Sioux City.

"For the first time in my life, I'd run into something I couldn't buy, whip or change," Bernie said, recalling the incident in a speech to the Iowa banquet of the Fellowship of Christian Athletes in 2004. "I was being tested, and I started trying to make deals with God – 'you can take me, God, if you leave her here.' Well, we were lucky that time, and Becky came out of it fine."

But it was a jolting reminder to the family, he said, of just how precious life is. They would be reminded again in later years, with a more sorrowful outcome.

It was in that year of 1957 that Saggau left his principal's job with the Cherokee schools and joined the Jostens Company, which has long recruited coaches and athletes to become its sales force making calls on high schools. He covered a wide territory in northwest Iowa, and quickly became a top producer for the company, attracting several yearbook production accounts that had been held by competing companies.

"Jostens gave me a real opportunity," Saggau said. "It could have been very rewarding financially. I really enjoyed it for four years. The first one, they let us stay in Cherokee, then they asked us to move to Storm Lake. We knew so many people there, that we knew we'd like living there, too. But in 1960, Jostens started asking me to accept a job as an assistant sales manager, which would have been a good promotion, but it was going to mean moving to Owatona, Minnesota. We might not have minded that, but they were also going to have me go to Jacksonville, Illinois, for a year for training."

The Saggaus' third child, David, had been born by then. And with Bernie traveling frequently for sales, for refereeing and for speaking, he and Lois decided the promotion and moves were just too much, and he declined.

About the same time, two partners in insurance and real estate in Cherokee – Lee Miller and A.I. "Mac" McClintock – offered Bernie a chance to join their business.

McClintock had earlier in his career been a teacher and coach in Cherokee, and Miller had recruited him into the business, too.

"They were putting a silver spoon in my mouth," Bernie said. "Neither McClintock or Miller had a son, and I think that is why they wanted me. The opportunity was a perfect fit for my family, too. We were really happy to go back to Cherokee."

And Cherokee was happy to have the Saggaus back when they moved in 1961.

"I was thrilled," said Joan Ballantyne, who was working as a secretary at the agency then but is one of the partners today in the firm still called Miller-Mac, The House of Insurance & Real Estate.

"I thought Bernie would be a great asset to our business. He was so well known around Cherokee. He was the kind of person you were glad to see come in the office every day – fun to be around, always full of energy, enthusiastic, always presented himself so well to the public."

Alas, within a year, Saggau could tell, "it just wasn't for me. I could sell real estate or insurance just fine, but I couldn't stand to collect the money for it. I remember selling some kind of fire policy to an older woman for about $30, and when I told her how much the payment was going to be, I could tell she didn't have it. I couldn't stand to turn her down, so I just paid it myself. I knew then that I wasn't going to make it in that business. The hardest thing about it was feeling like if I left, I'd be disappointing the people at Miller-Mac, because they'd been so good to me."

But they could see it coming.

"He'd worked for us for about a year, and then he realized that insurance wasn't going to be his long suit," said Ballantyne. "You can always tell when the match is good, or not, and I knew sports was his first love. With all his talent, we all kind of felt that there was probably more for him out there."

He had come into the business with the plan of buying in and becoming a partner. As he was leaving, he encouraged Ballantyne to do that herself. "He said, 'Well, Joan, you should be the new partner here'," she said. "I said, 'Do you think they'd take a woman in here?' That was unusual back then. He really encouraged me to try it, and that probably helped my confidence to do it."

She not only became a partner, she became very active in the state associations, serving as president of the Iowa Association of Realtors in 1981 and national president of the Women's Council of Realtors in 1988.

After Saggau left in 1963, the agency in Cherokee continued to write his family's personal insurance for more than 30 years, and Ballantyne and her husband Keith have visited back and forth with Bernie and Lois often through the years.

"I'll tell you, his heart's got to be just about as big as a drum," Ballantyne said of Bernie, "because he's done so much good in his life for so many people."

Saggau had become an increasingly avid golfer early in his career, and about the same time he realized he wanted to leave insurance and real estate, "I read where a golf course 'The Oaks' was for sale near Ames, straight north of town. I looked it over, and I thought it could be gold mine. They had a nice clubhouse, and a little place where we could live, and it was in a great location with the way Ames was growing. I think the price was about $175,000. I made the offer, and we were negotiating it, but a 30-day clause in the purchase agreement ran out before we got the deal made."

And it was right then that Lyle Quinn, the ailing executive secretary of the Iowa High School Athletic Association, asked Saggau to come work for him at the headquarters in Boone.

Quinn's admiration and respect for Saggau had grown as he watched the young man develop as a referee. By 1963, Saggau was regularly working major college football and basketball games. He appreciated Saggau having been willing to take over conducting some "rules meetings" for high school coaches and officials, and he knew the reports back on Saggau's performance at those were glowing. He thought Saggau's master's degree, his administrative experience in the Cherokee schools and his success with Jostens had prepared him well for executive-level work at the IHSAA.

And after an incident Quinn had witnessed a couple of years earlier, he knew Saggau was a guy who could make a controversial decision and stand by it.

"Mr. Quinn – and in those years that's what I called him – would often send me out to work some game he anticipated might be trouble, and he always would remind me to keep it under control," Saggau said.

"So one year he sent me to Spencer to do a sub-state final basketball game between Spencer and Sioux City Heelan. It got started a little off-kilter – a lot of talk, some shoving. The next thing I knew there were two big guys inside, one from each team, and they were throwing elbows at each other as they were moving around. I stopped the game and warned them. A couple of minutes later, they did it again. I blew my whistle, stopped the game again and threw them both out. We went ahead and finished the rest of the game with no problems.

"So afterward, I was in the officials' dressing room, and the door swung open. It was Mr. Quinn. I hadn't even known he was there! All he said was, 'Well, Mr. Saggau, I was glad to see you take hold of this game tonight. Good work.' He shook my hand, turned around and left."

That was probably a very significant moment in the history of the Iowa High School Athletic Association.

Chapter Four

Bernie Saggau in his IHSAA years

The late Gordon Gammack, a columnist for the Des Moines Register & Tribune, was an astute observer of the Iowa scene. And in a 1970 column about Bernie Saggau, Gammack pegged him perfectly.

"Bernie Saggau," Gammack wrote, "is the evangelistic executive secretary of the Iowa High School Athletic Association."

It was not only a good description of the young Saggau at that point in his life and career. It also turned out to be an accurate prediction of what he was like in his 37 years at the helm.

Saggau had been evangelistic, all right – about kids, education, the importance of all school activities, sports in particular, and about good sportsmanship.

He was also an unapologetic, flag-waving American patriot, always reminding everybody of the choices and opportunities so readily available in this country, not so in many other places, and how we should be thankful for them every day.

Faith, family and citizenship.

All of that is Bernie Saggau, now at 76 years old and retired.

But he is more than that, too.

He is a workhorse, one who through much of his career was away from home as many as 200 evenings per year.

Current and former employees describe him, generally, as a tenderhearted boss.

He is a wizard at finances and investments.

He is a multi-tasker.

He is a masterful negotiator.

And he is the finest orator from Iowa since Harold Hughes, the former All-State football player from Ida Grove who went on to become governor, a U.S. senator and a candidate for the U.S. presidency.

Or maybe he's the finest orator since another Harold from Iowa. I'm thinking of Professor Harold Hill, the fictitious "Music Man" in Iowan Meredith Willson's 1950s musical that was a smash hit on Broadway and as a movie. When Saggau is on the stump, he is, as Mayor Shinn said of Professor Hill, "a by-God spellbinder."

There is no doubt in my mind Saggau could indeed sell the concept of a mythical boys' band to any community in Iowa, just like in "The Music Man." After all, over the years he has sold the whole state on such ideas as the 3-point goal in basketball, having playoffs in football, using a "safety base" at first in baseball, building the new $12 million "Iowa Hall of Pride" and a lot of other innovations – things that nobody else around here had heard of or thought about before he peddled them.

More than 1,200 audiences in 45 states have heard Saggau speak. And he is nearly always invited back.

Saggau is about as animated a speaker as you've ever seen. He waves his arms. He rolls his eyes and grabs his forehead as if he is going to faint. His voice soars and dives, sometimes in a whisper and other times in almost a scream. He even growls. He gets an emotional catch in his voice at just the right moments. And his timing with his pauses, facial expressions and punch lines is something to behold.

Fred Moore, president of Saggau's alma mater Buena Vista University in Storm Lake, Iowa, tells how "several years ago for Homecoming weekend, we had Bernie speak to our football team the night before the game, and I went along.

"He put on one of his classic stem-winders, and you could hear a pin drop in there," Moore said. "He had a profound impact on our football players. And on me, too. I was ready to go out and hit somebody myself!"

But Saggau also has an uncanny ability to leave his listeners feeling calm, focused and forward thinking.

He often winds up his presentations by having the entire audience holding hands, while he softly recites his own twist on a favorite line from the 19th century poet Robert Browning:

Come,
Go forth with me,
Because the best of life
Is yet to be.

And nine times out of 10, he leaves to a standing ovation.

He is just as effective with the media – and he has been a biographer's dream, the way he seems to stay in the news. Most reporters he deals with think of him as a great interview, since he is readily accessible, generally candid and almost always quotable.

He delivers his message another way, too. Unlike most men, especially younger men, Saggau is a prolific letter writer.

That's a practice, or discipline, he learned from his father, who used to send postcards of encouragement to customers and others around their hometown of Denison, after he'd seen or heard something good about them. Like his dad, Bernie Saggau sends out many notes of praise and encouragement.

Some he makes very personal.

He and his wife Lois Saggau know the agony of losing a child. You'll read later in this chapter that their son Jeff Saggau died after a car wreck in 1976 when he was only 23 years old. "After that happened, I've probably written 500 letters to people who've lost a child," Bernie Saggau told me. "I know how they feel. I feel their pain. I tell them that once you quit asking 'Why?' then you can smile more and cry less. Or you can smile while you cry. And then there'll be more good memories than bad."

There have been letters when he's been free with his advice, even when unsolicited.

Friends chuckle at one example of that. Several years ago, Saggau was attending a luncheon event at which Tom Osborne, then the head football coach at the University of Nebraska, was the featured speaker. Osborne raced into the room as most of the guests were eating desserts, gulped down his whole meal, gave a strong speech, then raced back out of the room on the way to his next appointment. Saggau wrote the coach a stern letter about

how he had to slow himself down, that his career was too important to his
athletes and the people of Nebraska, and that he should not be risking his
own health.

And there also have been some letters in which Saggau figured
somebody needed a good scolding. In such instances, he can be
breathtakingly blunt, even excessively so.

One of those became the talk of Iowa in the summer of 2003. That
was a dust-up between Saggau and Bob Feller. When Saggau felt Feller was
out-of-line in his harsh treatment of an IHSAA staff member, he wrote a
sharp letter that was eventually quoted in newspapers across the state.

"You, Mr. Feller, may have been a great baseball player," Saggau
wrote, "but your ill-mannered, inconsiderate actions reveal what kind of a
person you really are." Later in it, he added: "If you had worked for me, you
would have been fired this morning at 8 a.m. No one on my staff would ever
treat anyone in such an ill-mannered and disrespectful way. The second thing,
if we were in a clubhouse I could describe your actions much better, but I
guess it is safe to use the words, 'You acted like a big jerk!' "

Whew!

When both men calmed down, apologies were extended in both
directions, and they've had cordial personal contact since then.

To his credit, Saggau knows he "can be pretty spirited," as he says.

And the few times he has said or written something he later
determined he was wrong on, or that he'd gone over-the-top in his reaction
to, he has indeed stepped up publicly with apologies. "Anybody who can't
swallow their pride to do what you know is right, will never get very far or
get much respect," he told me.

There have also been many times when he's been on the other end of
some misinformed criticism, perhaps delivered in anger. How does he handle
that when, if right were right, he'd be receiving an apology?

"I do my best to remember that I get paid to make difficult and
sometimes unpopular decisions," he said. "And I get paid to take it when
people get mad at me and say bad things. I get paid for that."

That's how it often goes for evangelists, you know. They're real
lightning rods.

Saggau has headed the IHSAA for so long, most of his constituency has no memory of his predecessor Lyle T. Quinn or what the association was like back then.

But those who do remember will tell you that when Bernie Saggau came on board in 1963, it was like a fresh breeze came blowing across the prep sports scene in Iowa.

That was even more so, after 1967, when Saggau became the executive secretary, following Quinn's death.

The contrast between the two men could not have been more apparent.

Quinn, who was 61 when he died, was 5 ft., 11 in. tall and weighed more than 300 pounds in his late years. He wore his hair slicked back, his eyeglasses had heavy dark frames, he generally wore conservative business suits to work. You seldom see photos of him smiling. Saggau, who was 35 when he joined the IHSAA, was about 5 ft., 7 in. and weighed maybe 140. He was wearing a flat-top haircut then – a few years later he went with longer hair and sideburns – and was a much sportier dresser. With his charisma and story-telling ability, he would light-up any room of people he entered.

How could Quinn be described, in a word or two?

"Rigid," said Morris "Mo" Kelley, who covered Quinn and the IHSAA as the sports editor of the Boone News-Republican. Kelley was hired by Saggau to become the association's publications director for 30 years. "I liked Lyle a lot," said Kelley. "He was a good guy, but he was very set in his ways. There was one way – his."

Saggau also had great respect for Quinn – "he was a great man, and an intellect" – but he challenged him, too.

"Mr. Quinn had been an English major," Saggau said, "and he'd learned at an early age that 'No' was a complete sentence. Especially in his later years, when I was around, he hated change. He hated it with a passion."

Maybe that's because Quinn dealt with so much change in the first few years after he joined the association in 1940.

As Saggau, Kelley and others who know the deep history are quick to tell you, and as you will read in Chapter Six, Quinn should be remembered as a great hero in IHSAA history. In his early years in the job as executive secretary, he saved the association from financial collapse. And he calmed member schools which had been ready to secede and form a new organization, so upset were they at the heavy-handed reign of his predecessor George A. Brown.

Quinn is also the reason the IHSAA headquarters is in Boone, which was his hometown and where he spent his early career as a teacher and coach at Boone High School. He never moved from Boone after he joined the IHSAA, and instead commuted to work at the offices the association then had in the capital city of Des Moines. But by January, 1944, he had persuaded the Board of Control to move the office to Boone, a town of 12,803 located 45 miles north and just west of Des Moines.

By the early 1960s, Quinn began having health problems with hypertension, diabetes and glaucoma. He had by then become well aware of Saggau as an excellent referee, school administrator and public speaker, so he asked Saggau if he would begin conducting some of the IHSAA rules meetings. Up till then, either Quinn or his assistant executive secretary Harold Schmickley had conducted those, teaching the coaches and officials about the rules of the games, especially any rules changes.

Saggau got rave reviews from his audiences at those meetings.

"Mr. Quinn had a photographic memory," Saggau said. "He had the rule books for the sports completely memorized – right down to the numbers and letters – and when he did the rules meetings, he'd stand up there and recite those rules in pretty much of a monotone voice. I think most people thought the rules meetings were kind of boring when he did them. I just tried to put a little more life and enthusiasm into them."

In 1963, Quinn knew that with his health worsening, he better begin grooming his successor. Schmickley was about the same age as Quinn, and although he was brilliant as a rules interpreter, especially in baseball, he was not a particularly strong personality. Quinn apparently favored bringing on someone younger, especially someone with the knowledge, energy and respect he sensed that Saggau had.

He offered Saggau the job as an assistant executive.

"I turned down the position twice," Saggau recalled. "He offered me $8,400 a year, which was quite a bit less than I was making then, and I had a wife and three kids to think about. The second time I turned it down, he seemed a little hurt and said, 'What's the reason?' I said, 'Well, Mr. Quinn, I make one and a half times what you're making!' And he said, 'Is money that important to you?' I had to admit that it really wasn't.

"Then he said, 'What's the real reason?' I said, 'Mr. Quinn, with all due respect, you're too stubborn. I'm pretty strong-minded myself, and I'm not sure we could get along' "

Quinn must have been surprised at young Saggau's candor. But he also did not want to lose him.

"I remember him pausing, then saying, 'How often do you have to be right?' " Saggau said. "I said 50 percent of the time. He said, 'That's not a problem for me – you've got the job.' Then I said, 'Mr. Quinn, I'd never work for somebody who isn't the boss – you can be right 51 percent of the time, but I have to be able to call my 49 percent at any time.' We shook hands on that, and he hired me."

After the IHSAA Board of Control made the hiring official, Saggau reported for work at the headquarters, which were then located in a former bank building in downtown Boone.

Ruth Ingalls, who retired in 2003 after 51 years at the IHSAA, most of it as chief bookkeeper, recalled that when Saggau came to work, "his office was at one end of the same area where we girls worked, but he spent a lot of his time working directly with Mr. Quinn in his office. Mr. Quinn spent a lot of time teaching him."

It did not take long for the two strong-minded men to have their first argument.

"I drank coffee," Saggau said, "and so I'd go across the street to a café at 10 in the morning and have a cup of coffee. After a couple days of that, Lyle came by my desk and said, 'Do you like coffee?' I said, 'I sure do!' And he said, 'No one else here in the building leaves the building for coffee.' I was surprised, but I said, 'Well, if you don't want me leaving the building for coffee, that's fine.'

"The next day, I brought my thermos, a big 16-ounce thermos. He came by my desk that morning and asked why I had that, and I said, 'Mr. Quinn, I'm going to have my coffee here at my desk.' He said, 'The girls don't have coffee at their desks,' and I said, 'Mr. Quinn, let's go talk in your office.' "

Their private conversation started, Saggau said, with him saying, "Mr. Quinn, I'm not one of the girls."

Quinn then told him that a few years earlier, office coordinator Cheryl Kane had come to him and had asked for coffee breaks of 10 minutes in the morning and 10 minutes in the afternoon for "the girls." Quinn told Saggau he had agreed to the coffee breaks, but then had asked Kane "whether the girls wanted to come to work 20 minutes early, or stay until 20 minutes after closing time at 5 p.m., to make up for that coffee break time," Saggau recalled. "So the women dropped it."

Saggau didn't. He told Quinn right then that he'd continue to drink coffee at his desk, even if he had to bring it in a thermos, and that he thought it only right that the rest of the staff could, too.

Quinn was undoubtedly exasperated.

"He didn't have anybody ever argue with him," Saggau said.

But the boss surprisingly relented at this upstart's coffee challenge. He told Saggau to call a plumber, have a new water line installed in the office's basement and buy a coffeemaker.

"After that, you could go down, get your coffee, put 10 cents in a jar and bring your coffee back to your desk," Saggau said.

"The girls were happy as could be. But you know who enjoyed the new coffee thing most? Lyle Quinn! I'd get him a cup of coffee and bring it to him. He wasn't walking well by then, and he really got to where he liked having that cup of coffee at his desk."

Saggau said he learned volumes at Quinn's desk. "I picked his brain on everything I could think of" about the association's operations, he said.

Quinn gave him two blunt lessons about the fiscal responsibility of the executive in charge.

"When Mr. Quinn was showing me the ropes, he introduced me to Ruth Ingalls," Saggau recalled. "He said, 'You've got a lot of talent, Bernie, but I don't think you know much about bookkeeping. So the best thing for you to do is to stay the heck out of there and let Ruth take care of it.' I found out that was right, so I pretty well stayed out of that bookkeeping department. When it came to money, I knew how to make it, Ruth knew where to put it."

Ingalls laughs when she hears that story.

"I've heard he says that," she said after her retirement. "Bernie's quite a guy. But I can assure you he's no slouch when it comes to figures. He'd come in about finances, or I'd go down to his office, and he'd be down the road twice as far as I was on what we should be doing, and it'd take me a while to catch up.

Quinn's other financial lesson for Saggau was especially unusual. "The very first month I got paid, Mr. Quinn brought the check out to my desk and said, 'Let's go to the bank and you can cash this,' " Saggau said. "I told him I was really busy right then and that there was no hurry for me with the check. He said, 'No, I want you to go to the bank with me and cash this.'

"So we walked over there, went to the teller and cashed the check. Then Mr. Quinn said, 'Do you see that check is good?' I told him yes, but that I was already sure it would be. And then he said, 'Bernie, the first three checks I got when I came to work here, I couldn't cash because the association had no money in the bank. I had to take warrants for payment later. It is your job to make sure that never happens again.' "

It hasn't.

Besides making the IHSAA financially solid, Saggau has impacted the organization in countless other ways. You read about many of the innovations in Chapter 1. You will see much more evidence of his management and guidance as you read on through this history.

One thing he's done is find strong assistant executives and other staff members – there are 20 full-time and one part-time at the IHSAA – and then let them work.

"One of the secrets of my service of 41 years," he said in the summer of 2004 as he accepted a major award for career service from the National Federation of State High School Associations, "is that I have been fortunate to hire good people. And after they have been with me two years, they don't work for me – we are partners."

Dave Harty, who made Iowa's wrestling and baseball tournaments two of the best high school sports events in the U.S., was assistant executive director for 32 years before retiring to part-time status in 2002 and fully retiring in early 2005. Rick Wulkow, 59, one of the best in the nation at administering football and basketball, has been on the executive staff for 24 years and took over as executive director at Saggau's retirement. There are three or four other top-level staff members at the IHSAA who have credentials and experience that match or exceed what the executive directors of many of the other states' athletic associations have.

"Bernie is the kind of leader who isn't afraid of delegating authority," Harty said. "And, of course, he expects accountability, too."

When he was hired in 1970, "I was going to be Bernie's successor," Harty said. "That was the plan, but Bernie elected to stay longer than either of us had expected, because of his success, his good health and because he loves to work. Gradually, I got older, and time wasn't right for me to succeed him. But I have no regrets. I had opportunities elsewhere through the years, but I chose to work here because I have a love for the state of Iowa, and a great working relationship with Bernie and the board. Bernie's philosophy and mine on interscholastic athletics is the same. Then Rick came along and his philosophy is the same as Bernie's and mine. We've complemented each other. It's been great how well we all get along together."

It's that philosophy – and his articulating it, implementing it, enforcing it – that may be Saggau's most significant contribution in his long IHSAA career.

He took an early, firm and enduring stand that high school sports in Iowa be conducted as part of the education system, not outside it. Almost as important has been his insistence that real values be taught and coached, right along with athletic skills.

As a result, said Ron Sadler, chairperson of the Board of Control when the IHSAA turned 100 years old, "Bernie Saggau has had a bigger influence on schools in Iowa than any other individual in the history of the state."

That, of course, is a big statement, perhaps an arguable one, but certainly an interesting one. Why does Sadler, the veteran superintendent at Crestwood of Cresco in northeast Iowa, believe it?

"The vision of Mr. Saggau that the program be a model for

discipline, credibility, being truthful, adhering to the rules, teaching character – all of that has gone way beyond athletics," Sadler said. "The reason it has is because our school people in general began emphasizing all those values after Bernie began stressing them." He noted that through the decades, many, if not most, of Iowa's school superintendents and principals have been coaches early in their careers. "The schools in this state are a reflection of Bernie," said Sadler, a former coach himself. "We can all thank him for that."

Saggau's importance to education in general in Iowa was echoed in June, 2004, at the banquet held in his honor by the high school referees and officials in the Sioux City area. Among the speakers that evening was Ted Stilwill, then nearing his own retirement as director of the Iowa Department of Education. The DOE gives the IHSAA and the Iowa Girls High School Athletic Union the authority to administer the school sports programs in the state, and also places a representative on the boards of the organizations – that board member currently is Carol Greta, of Des Moines. The DOE could, in fact, order the athletic organizations to do this, or do that. But that has rarely happened through the years. In fact, Stilwill told the crowd, the DOE has often summoned Saggau for help on matters that transcend sports.

"Throughout the whole time I've worked for the Department of Education," Stilwill said, "when things needed to be worked on, when we needed an enforcer, Bernie was usually that person."

Because Saggau has had that kind of role, and because he has been such a consistent and eloquent spokesman about athletics being built on a foundation of education, he has had very little difficulty with, or even interaction with, the Iowa legislature. That's in an era when in many other states, fusses between the athletic associations and legislators have become annual bouts.

Other than the lobbying he did in recent years for state government help with the Iowa Hall of Pride project, Saggau hasn't had a serious dispute with legislators since the resolution in 1972 of the "Bunger case," which will be discussed more fully in Chapter Six. But explained briefly, Saggau had some legislators howling at him – others were praising him, too – when in the late 1960s and early '70s, he was zealous in enforcing a "Good Conduct Rule" that the IHSAA had adopted. Athletes who were caught drinking

– generally it was beer – or were at a party or in a car where beer was found, even if they were not drinking themselves, were ruled ineligible for competition for six weeks.

Saggau presided over the declaration of more than 3,500 being ineligible in one year's time, according to a story in the Des Moines Tribune in January, 1970. It did seem to dramatically decrease the number of alcohol-related incidents – there were only 350 two years after that one big year, the Tribune reported. One reason for the decline, Saggau told the newspaper, was that "high school students no longer think that drinking beer is the 'in' thing to do."

But the policy produced the lawsuit by attorneys for Bill Bunger, a Waverly-Shell Rock athlete who had been ruled ineligible. The Good Conduct Rule was upheld by the Iowa District Court but then overturned by the Iowa Supreme Court. Thereafter, the individual school districts have had to adopt and enforce their own conduct rules for athletes, if they decide to, and there has been no consistency statewide.

It was the biggest legal fight of Saggau's career, and an exhausting one. But he learned a lot.

"One of the things I've told other executives of the associations around the country is, 'Don't get out of our field,' " Saggau told me. "I remind them that we're not lawyers, so don't be thinking about going to court to fight this, or defend that. That's what you pay lawyers to do."

That hints at another of the major accomplishments of his IHSAA career. Saggau has helped give the IHSAA a national reputation as a model – perhaps *the* model – high school sports program.

That's partially because of his long tenure, of course, and his willingness to counsel other states' associations. But it has even more to do with his innovative management, his popularity as a motivational speaker and his involvement with the National Federation, for which he served as president in 1990.

"Bernie is truly the leader among the executive directors across the nation, and he has been for years," said Nelson Hartman, who led the Kansas High School Activities Association until his retirement in 1993.

"In those executive director positions, you have to make hard decisions in emotional situations," Hartman continued. "And then you have to enforce them in an even but firm way, so that you don't wind up making martyrs of people who break rules and need to be corrected. It's tough."

Hartman said he thinks Saggau learned one of his most effective management skills when he was a basketball floor official.

"I think that's when I first came to know of Bernie, as a basketball official," Hartman said. "I was asked by the old Big Eight Conference to go out and assess the officials they had working.

"Bernie was phenomenal. In fact, I don't know if I ever saw a better official, particularly the way he kept those coaches in the palm of his hand. He did it by being stern, using great discipline and also by having a smile on his face. He could 'sell' his calls to the coaches better than anybody I ever saw. He was the outstanding official in the Big Eight Conference back then, for sure.

"But my real point here is that Bernie's ability to communicate under duress – to 'sell' his decisions to coaches or any other audience – has been a real attribute in his association work."

That ability has certainly been critical to the fundraising success for the Iowa Hall of Pride, and for underwriting the costs of several of the IHSAA's most innovative recognition programs. On those projects, Saggau's salesmanship turned around a particularly skeptical audience – the board of directors of the Iowa Farm Bureau Federation – and he turned them around in a big way.

"I had known of Bernie Saggau ever since I played high school sports back in the late '60s," said Craig Lang, now the Iowa Farm Bureau president, a dairy farmer from near the east central Iowa town of Brooklyn. "But I never really met him until the first time he came to meet with our board, and I think that was at our summer retreat meeting back in 1997. We knew ahead of time that he was coming in to ask us to be the lead sponsor for this Iowa Hall of Pride he wanted to build.

"Now, see if you can imagine this scene. We have 12 pretty well seasoned, pretty conservative farmers, and in comes Bernie with Jack Lashier, who was working on the Hall of Pride project with him, to give us the presentation. I think it's fair to say that we had already pretty well decided ahead of time that taking a half million dollars of our members' money to build a Hall of Pride was not a very good way to use it.

"But Bernie started talking, and about 45 minutes later, we had decided it was not only a good way to use the members' money, but that maybe it was the best way we could use it!"

Saggau had described how each school, each community, in the state would be featured in the Hall of Pride, and how each school's leading students, athletes, singers, instrumentalists, actors – they'd all be mentioned.

"I'm pretty sure that, at that point, Bernie had all of us board members imagining in our minds how the displays on our communities might be right inside the front door of this Hall of Pride," said Lang, with a laugh. "And we were probably thinking, hey, you know what? Some of our names might be mentioned there, and if they are, maybe they'd have some little explanation in parentheses about what we'd done in high school!

"That's the kind of salesman Bernie is," Lang continued. "We could imagine just how neat it was going to be. He fully convinced us of the value of having an Iowa Hall of Pride, and how it directly tied to the core values of the Iowa Farm Bureau."

They agreed to a $500,000 donation.

Three years later, Saggau came back.

"This time he had an idea for a new program to recognize the outstanding scholars of each graduating class in Iowa's schools," Lang said. "He wanted to bring the top students, their parents and maybe a favorite teacher all together for a recognition ceremony with the governor every spring. We loved the idea that in these programs, every student in every school has an equal opportunity to participate, that it doesn't matter whether you're a student in West Des Moines or Rockwell City, you've got just as much chance at being one of those recognized scholars."

In addition, Saggau told the Farm Bureau board, he wanted to do a better job with the awards the IHSAA gives to the individual athletes participating in the state tournaments in all the sports.

"He said he needed to find a corporate partner to help the IHSAA do this," Lang said, "and he thought the Iowa Farm Bureau would be the perfect one. The ideas he was describing fit a lot of what we want to encourage –

scholarship, leadership and the value of our school systems all over the state. It took him only a half-hour to convince us on this one."

And thus, the Iowa Farm Bureau became the IHSAA's first-ever corporate sponsor, contributing $200,000 per year, over a five-year period, a total of $1 million.

It was also the first time the Farm Bureau had agreed to become a corporate sponsor of any on-going entity outside its own organization. Part of the commitment, Lang explained, is coming from Farm Bureau's insurance/financial arm, FBL Financial, a reflection of the deep interest and involvement the organization's insurance agents have in the communities and schools they serve across the state.

Undoubtedly a key to the strong new relationship between the Farm Bureau and the IHSAA has been the dual role of Dennis Presnall, of Ankeny. He serves on the school board at Ankeny, and is the designated representative of the Iowa Association of School Boards on the IHSAA's Board of Control. Presnall works full-time as the organization director of the Iowa Farm Bureau Federation.

In the spring of 2004, Saggau came back again to the Farm Bureau board, seeking more financial support to help complete the fundraising for the Iowa Hall of Pride.

"I suggested to our board ahead of time that we should consider contributing more to this project," Lang said. "Their reaction was really interesting this time. They said, 'Don't even send Bernie in here – we don't have a chance if he starts talking to us – it's already a done deal as soon as he walks in the door – we know we're going to endorse anything he's selling!' "

And so they did – again.

This time they agreed to a $1.5 million gift to the Hall of Pride, which is in addition to the $500,000 they gave five years ago, with the new contribution to be spread over a 10-year period.

"With that, our members and their families all get free admission to the Hall of Pride for 10 years," Lang said. "We think that will be a tremendous benefit. But we'd also eventually like to see admission be free for everybody who walks in there. The reason we feel that way is we think the Hall of Pride is going to showcase the best of Iowa life – our schools,

Bernie Saggau's 41 years with the IHSAA

Bernie Saggau joined the IHSAA in 1963. *Top left:* Bernie on a trip with then-Executive Secretary Lyle Quinn and his wife, Kathryn. *Top Right:* Saggau in 1967 with wife Lois, children David, Jeff and Becky and dog Sam. *Bottom:* Saggau near the end of his career, at the 2004 state basketball tournament, chatting with friends, retired broadcaster Bob Wilson, of Sioux City, and Chuck Van Hecke, athletic director at Muscatine High School.

Personal Collection   Personal Collection

Chuck Offenburger

Bernie Saggau became one of the best basketball officials in the nation, in demand for major college games, as well as for clinics and rules meetings. In his 30-year officiating career, he worked both high school and college games, but stopped doing prep games when he joined the IHSAA. Once when his refereeing partner was injured, the Kansas and Kansas State coaches told Saggau he'd been doing such a good job he should work the second half all by himself – and he did! Acclaimed cartoonist Brian Duffy of the Des Moines Register saluted Saggau with a caricature of him officiating for a gift from the School Administrators of Iowa.

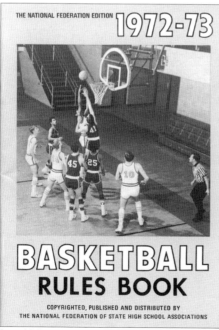

THE NATIONAL FEDERATION EDITION 1972-73

BASKETBALL
RULES BOOK

COPYRIGHTED, PUBLISHED AND DISTRIBUTED BY
THE NATIONAL FEDERATION OF STATE HIGH SCHOOL ASSOCIATIONS

Personal Collection   Personal Collection

Top: Bernie Saggau is not only one of the best speakers ever from Iowa, he's also one of the most animated. He has spoken from coast to coast *Above:* Six pals who have done a lot together in Iowa high school sports. Seated in the front row are sporting goods dealer Dwight Hauff, retired broadcaster Bob Wilson, both of Sioux City, and the late coach Russ Kraai, of Holstein. In the rear are Saggau and fellow IHSAA administrators Dave Harty and David Anderson. *Left:* In 1990 Saggau was president of the board of the National Federation of High School Associations. During their convention in Minneapolis, he threw out the ceremonial first pitch at a Minnesota Twins game. *Bottom Left:* With Craig Lang, president of the Iowa Farm Bureau Federation, at the 2004 state basketball tournament. Saggau negotiated the deal which made Iowa Farm Bureau the corporate partner of the IHSAA, a "first" for both organizations.

Chuck Offenburger

Top: The Saggau family, Christmas 2002. Back Row: Lois, Bernie, their son Dr. David Saggau, son-in-law Leonard Russo, daughter Becky Saggau Russo. Front Row: David's wife Kris Saggau and their children Anna, Bernie, Lydia and Helen. *Above:* The Saggau home in West Des Moines and a younger Bernie with David after they'd won a father & son golf tournament in Boone in 1969. *Right:* Four generations of Saggaus, in 1989: Bernie Sr. holding his great-granddaughter Helen, her father David at the left, grandfather Bernie Jr. behind them.

Personal Collection

Personal Collection

Chuck Offenberger

Personal Collection

Bernie and his grandchildren, hitting the pool at the Saggau home. Left to right are Helen, Anna, Lydia, Bernie and "Little Bernie."

The Saggaus' oldest son Jeff died in 1976 after a car wreck, when he was only 23 years old. He had been a scholarship wrestler at the University of Wisconsin, spent a summer panning for gold in Idaho (shown after that adventure with his brother David) and went on to become a favorite teacher and coach at Fort Dodge High School.

Right: The Saggaus have been in the audience for presentations by many noted Americans at their alma mater, Buena Vista University in Storm Lake, Iowa. Here they are pictured with the former Secretary of State, Colin Powell.

BUENA VISTA UNIVERSITY
2000 WILLIAM W. SIEBENS

Above: Saggaus at BVU with opera great and Iowa native Simon Estes. *Right:* Bernie and Lois Saggau have remained loyal to and very involved at BVU, where he serves on the Board of Trustees. In 2002, he gave the commencement address and received an honorary doctorate. *Bottom Right:* Saggaus at BVU with retired CBS-TV News Anchor Walter Cronkite.

Below: Bernie Saggau was given the highest honor of the National Federation of High School Associations, the "American Tradition" award, at the 2004 convention in San Diego. With him as he accepted the award were members of the Board of Control of the IHSAA. Left to right: Robert Busch of Riverside of Oakland, Dan Delaney of Mason City High School, Bob Tesar of Cedar Rapids Jefferson, Saggau, Ron Sadler of Crestwood of Cresco, Mike Billings of Roland-Story, Dwayne Cross of Rockwell City-Lytton, Dennis Presnall of Ankeny and Carol Greta of Des Moines.

Personal Collection

Personal Collection

Above: Saggau was proud to lead the Grand March at the IHSAA state wrestling tournament, one of the biggest high school sports events in the U.S. *Left:* Saggau and longtime friend Brice Durbin, retired executive director of the National Federation of State High School Associations, were inducted into the National High School Sports Hall of Fame in 1993.

Above: Bernie Saggau (right) visits with Rick Wulkow, his successor as executive director of the IHSAA, during the 2004 state basketball tournament. *Right:* Iowa Governor Terry Branstad, in 1998, signing an appropriation by the State of Iowa for $100,000 to assist in planning for the Iowa Hall of Pride. Left to right are IHSAA special projects director Jack Lashier, Saggau, Branstad and Jim Boyt, an East Des Moines business leader. *Bottom Right:* Saggau being interviewed by broadcaster Tim Seaman during the last state basketball tournament he directed in 2004.

communities and the achievements of our young people. It goes way beyond just sports. In fact, part of our Farm Bureau gift is going to sponsor the displays that are being done on the choral music and band programs."

Lang said he was especially proud of the music display sponsorship because in addition to being an All-State honorable mention football tackle when he was at BGM High School, he was also a Division I-rated singer in the state music contest. He later performed with the Iowa State Singers, when he was studying dairy science at Iowa State University, and he's sung in a gospel quartet as an adult.

Lang said with all the interaction with the IHSAA, he and several other Farm Bureau board members have come to treasure their close relationship with Saggau himself.

In fact, when Lang spoke at the June, 2004, banquet in Sioux City honoring Saggau's career, he told the crowd, "There are few men I admire as much as my father, but Bernie is one."

Earlier that same night, Saggau told the Sioux City media that arranging the corporate partnership with the Iowa Farm Bureau is "one of the things I'm most proud of" in his IHSAA career.

"With budget concerns being what they are now for schools and organizations like ours, we were at a point where we were going to start having trouble doing all the things we'd like to do for the young people of Iowa," Saggau said at the press conference. "So we changed our philosophy a little – we'd always stayed away from sponsorships – and then the first place we went was Farm Bureau. We picked them, they didn't pick us, and we picked them because they have the same philosophy toward kids that we do."

So salesmanship was one thing that Saggau learned from more than 25 years of officiating basketball and football games.

But it wasn't the only thing.

His refereeing experiences undoubtedly strengthened his resolve that good sportsmanship must be encouraged and enforced at IHSAA events.

On the college level, he was never quite sure what he and his officiating partners might be seeing or hearing.

"I can remember working basketball games at South Dakota State University up in Brookings, and the fans would bring in fenders from cars and trucks, then beat them with sledgehammers," he said. "That was in a metal building back then, and it sounded like cannons going off.

"Then one time at Vermillion, Wayne Lichty from Waterloo and I were working a basketball game with South Dakota State playing there at the University of South Dakota. It was snowing hard and they'd delayed the start of the game by two hours, and when Wayne and I walked out from the dressing room, we looked in under the bleachers and we couldn't believe how many empty bottles there were. We didn't know what to expect. We got the game started and things were going well enough, then there was a time out. All of a sudden, someone threw a freshly-killed, bloody jackrabbit – that's the South Dakota State mascot – out on the floor and it slid across with a big streak of blood after it. Then another fan ran out there, picked it up and threw it back up into the stands. It was quite a night."

At a game between South Dakota State and the University of Sioux Falls in a new arena in Sioux Falls, Saggau was working with Floyd Magnusson of Fort Dodge. "Floyd had played basketball at the University of Iowa, and he was getting to be a good official," Saggau said. "As we were going up there, I told him something screwy always seems to happen up there. It started when the fans threw about 20 dirty, scroungy chickens out on the floor. And before the night was over, they'd also thrown hundreds of M&Ms out on the floor. Other than that, they played pretty good basketball up there that night."

Saggau saw live chickens turned loose on a basketball floor another time, too. That was during a game at Kansas State in Manhattan, and they were painted up to resemble the University of Kansas Jayhawk mascot.

But there were a lot of fun, positive experiences, too.

One of the best happened at a televised Kansas vs. Kansas State basketball game in Manhattan in March of 1966.

"I think I may have worked more of those games between KU and K-State than any other human being," Saggau said. "That particular game, I was working with Tom Glennon, and we got through the first half just fine. But right after Tom threw up the ball to start the second half, he pulled a muscle or ligament in one leg and he couldn't go on.

"So when we had the game stopped there, I called both coaches together and I said, 'Those fellows who officiated the freshman game did a good job, so why don't you see if one of them is still here and will work with me.' The two coaches walked away, then they came back to me and one of them said, 'We've made a decision.' Then they told me they wanted me to work the game alone, that I'd do just fine. I couldn't believe it."

Saggau told the coaches he'd give it his best effort, but that "I hope you'll be kind when you evaluate me after the game." Then he called together the players from both teams and told them, "I won't see everything out here, so here's what we'll do. If I don't see something that should have been a call, I'll say so and then we can figure it out."

They started the second half with Saggau racing back and forth on the floor, doing the best he could as the solo referee.

"All of a sudden, I see this big ol' boy on one of the teams start pushing and shoving inside," Saggau said. "I yelled at him to stop it, but the next time down the floor, he did the same thing, pushing and shoving. So I blew the whistle and stopped the game. I went over and grabbed him by the elbow, walked him over to his bench and said, 'Coach, we've made a decision – he'd like to rest for a while. If he gets to feeling better, then maybe he can come back into the game.' "

A few minutes later, when the action was stopped again, Saggau ran by the bench and asked the player, "Are you ready to come back in and play a little now? He said, 'You better believe I am!' I said, 'Well, come on in.'

"I'll never forget what happened after that," Saggau continued. "When he checked back in at the scorer's table, that big ol' boy walked out on the floor in front of 12,000 people, reached down and put his arm around me and apologized. I said, 'Oh, that's okay, we're both competitors. Let's get it on and have some fun.' "

The game moved into its final minutes and, typical of that rivalry between KU and K-State, it could have gone either way at the end.

"With about 20 seconds left, the ball went out of bounds, and there were enough players between me and where it happened, I couldn't see it," Saggau said. "So I went running over yelling, 'I didn't see it! I didn't see it!'

"That big ol' boy I'd put on the bench earlier looked right at me and said, 'I knocked it out of bounds – it's their ball.' "

Everybody in the arena seemed moved by such an unusual display of good sportsmanship, the Wichita Eagle & Beacon reported, not only on that late play but also throughout the second half of the contest.

Bob Prewitt, an assistant coach at Southern Methodist University who was in Manhattan scouting the KU team, wrote a letter to the Big Eight's supervisor of officials to praise Saggau and the players on both teams, according to the newspaper. "I thought Saggau did an excellent job and the players were tremendous the way they cooperated with him," Prewitt wrote. "In a game like that where there was so much rivalry and so much at stake, there could have been a lot of problems."

Saggau pulled a great stunt on a renowned heckler in a 1972 game at Oklahoma University.

Grace Mills, a rabid Sooner fan, was a terror to all of the Big Eight officials who worked games in Norman. A former high school foreign language teacher, she would sit right behind the scorer's bench, and her husband, OU professor R. C. Mills, would sit right behind her.

"Grace appears sedate and ladylike until the opening tip-off," wrote Bob Hurt, sports columnist for the Daily Oklahoman. "Then she starts to instruct the officials – even as she instructed her foreign language students. But the tone of voice is different. It carries, and it cuts."

Saggau said one weekend as he was driving to Oklahoma to referee a game there, "I decided to take care of Grace," he said. "I picked up three roses before I went to the fieldhouse, and then I had one of the guys on the scorer's bench take them out, turn around and give the roses to Grace. I wrote on a little note, 'From a secret admirer,' but I didn't sign it.

"So the game started and pretty soon I called a foul on one of the OU players. Grace was sitting there holding the roses, but she started screaming at me, like usual. 'Bernie, that was a bad call!' I was right there at the scorer's bench, giving them the player's number, so I leaned over the table and said to her, 'One more word from you and I'm taking my roses back.' From then on, I never heard another word from her all the trips I made back to Oklahoma."

Saggau said all his officiating indeed "helped me as executive director," just as former Kansas association director Nelson Hartman suggested earlier here. "It helps people have confidence in you, your knowledge of the rules and regulations," Saggau said.

When he joined the IHSAA in 1963, he of course had to give up refereeing high school games in the state. He remained very active doing college games for another dozen years.

But by the end of 1976, the year Jeff Saggau died in a car wreck, Bernie was a changed man, holding together a changed family. As far as officiating, and a lot of other things that were not directly connected to his IHSAA work, "I was burned out," he said. "I wanted to stay home."

Jeffery J. Saggau was the oldest of the three Saggau children, a good high school wrestler and golfer for Boone High School before his graduation in 1971, a full-scholarship wrestler at the University of Wisconsin, a good piano player and more.

"Jeff was a banty rooster," Bernie Saggau said. "You know, I didn't have to go to school but once for anything our three kids got in trouble for. That one time I got called in because of something Jeff did. A kid in one of his classes had called a teacher 'an old whore,' and Jeff went over a row of chairs and decked the kid. So, I went to school and I told them that fighting is certainly wrong, and Jeff would be disciplined at home, but that I couldn't promise if that kid called that teacher a whore again, my son wouldn't deck him again."

Jeff grew up to become an adventurer. For example, he and his college roommate Steve Evans, another Wisconsin wrestler, would get out of bed before dawn and go bow hunting for deer.

But most adventurous of all, the two of them spent the summer of 1974 pursuing a wild idea Evans came up with – prospecting for gold in the most remote areas of the mountains of Idaho using the traditional picks, shovels and pans.

The Ames Daily Tribune, in a follow-up story about the expedition, reported that when they left for the West, "packed into Steve's four-wheel drive jeep were two motorcycles, sleeping bags, a tent, clothes, camping equipment, two rifles and two pistols."

Bernie and Lois Saggau and their young son David, then 15, later drove to Idaho to visit the gold prospectors, and left David there with them for a week's stay.

"We drove way up there in the mountains where they were, and it was rough," Bernie recalled. "They were living in this little cabin that no one had lived in for seven or eight years. But Jeff was real proud of the way they had fixed it up, especially for our visit. He'd walked all the way into town and bought a new sheet so his mother would have something clean to sleep on. They were telling us about having to shoot rats around there, so when it came time to go to bed, Lois decided she was going to sleep in the car. She was still out there about midnight, and it was pretty cold. So I went out, tapped on her window, reminded her that her son had walked all the way to town to get that sheet for her, and I told her how warm it was in the cabin. She came back in, got between me and David, and that's the last complaint we heard from her."

That summer's experience produced about $1,200 worth of gold for Jeff, which he figured was as good a summer's wage as he would have made at some job back home. But it gave the two young gold miners a whole lot more than that. "I wouldn't give this summer up for anything," Jeff told the Ames newspaper. "It was a real education."

After graduating from Wisconsin in 1975, Jeff landed a teaching job at Fort Dodge High School in northwest Iowa. He taught English and mass communication, was faculty advisor to the student newspaper, coached the debate team and girls' golf, helped coach the wrestling team, got involved with the Fellowship of Christian Athletes and was beginning to work with church youth groups in his new community.

"Jeff was an excellent young teacher," said Bob Bargman, then the Fort Dodge High principal and now retired, with homes at the Iowa Great Lakes and in Arizona. "He really got involved, and the kids loved him."

Then on the last weekend of January 1976, Jeff and his girlfriend Rachel Robinson, who was teaching home economics and coaching synchronized swimming at Fort Dodge High, decided to go to Minnesota for some snow skiing. It was also a trip home for Robinson, who was from the town of Mound, west of the Twin Cities. They stayed at her parents' home on Friday evening, went out dancing – which both of them loved – and were up early Saturday morning, January 31, to go skiing.

Jeff was driving about 35 miles per hour four miles east of St. Paul, where his car hit a small patch of ice, went out of control and flipped end over end. He was not wearing a seat belt, and was severely injured. A priest was the next motorist to come along and called for help. Three hours later, Jeff Saggau died in Ramsey Hospital in St. Paul. Robinson was hospitalized three weeks in St. Paul for treatment of her injuries, which included seven broken bones in her pelvis, a broken ankle and a severe wound from a ski pole penetrating her foot.

Bernie Saggau was in Denver, Colorado, about ready to speak to that state's high school athletic association membership, when he got a phone call from his wife Lois about the accident. He went immediately to the airport and flew to Minneapolis-St. Paul. In Boone, Dave and Kay Harty picked up Lois and raced to St. Paul.

The news hit Boone like a thunderbolt.

Ruth Ingalls, the IHSAA bookkeeper, was spending that Saturday morning sitting with a dying friend in a Boone nursing home. Ingalls recalls the phone call from Lloyd Courter, a Boone attorney who represented the IHSAA and was one of the Saggaus' closest friends, with the sad news. "As soon as I heard his voice, I knew something was wrong," Ingalls said. "I got off the phone and told Estella, and I wasn't sure she even understood. 'Well, Dearie,' she said to me with very labored breathing, 'you must remember, it's not the storm that sinks the ship, it's the water that gets inside.' It was actually one of the last things she said to me. She was telling me to keep perspective on what was happening, and don't let it get inside, that otherwise you can battle the storms."

It was difficult consoling the Saggaus, of course.

"It was very hard for Bernie and Lois," Ingalls said. "They were just devastated. You could read 'loss' all over their faces, their mannerisms, the way they looked. They grieved over it a long time."

Bernie Saggau, speaking at Fellowship of Christian Athletes annual banquet in Des Moines in the spring of 2004, said a key moment in their healing came a day or two after Jeff's death. The Boone funeral director came to their home with the young man's suitcase, recovered from the car.

"I thought, 'Oh, boy, this could be tough,' " Bernie said. "But I walked downstairs with the suitcase, opened it up and there were the typical socks and T-shirts. Right there under them was the Bible. It just stopped me. A 23-year-old boy going skiing for a weekend, and he takes his Bible with him?"

He spent some time reading favorite verses, including one saying, "Those who learn to love one another are my disciples." Bernie said when he read that, "I thought, that's it – that's what this is all about – it's a call to us to make people a little better if we can. Ever since, Jeff has been very much a part of a lot of the good things I try to do."

The funeral at Boone's First United Methodist Church was packed. Fort Dodge High School sent four busloads of students, including its whole concert choir, which performed during the service.

The Saggaus' pastor Rev. William Miller presided, with a family friend Monsignor J.E. Tolan delivering the sermon. Tolan, a Catholic priest who served several parishes in northwest Iowa, was especially close to Bernie Saggau and many other sports figures in Iowa.

Rachel Robinson, after recovering from her injuries and the shock of what she had been through, was able to return to her Fort Dodge High classroom after Easter that spring. She eventually married a Fort Dodge man, they moved to Texas and she went on with her life. After 17 years of marriage, they divorced. Rachel, 52 in 2005 and the mother of four grown children, later married Navy pilot Steve Rose, who now flies for United Airlines. In early 2005 they moved to Pensacola, Florida from Yorba Linda, California. Rachel has continued teaching home economics-related courses the rest of her career, most recently in adult education programs.

It took a long time for her to heal emotionally.

"I was pretty crazy about Jeff," Rachel (Robinson) Rose said in 2004. "We'd gone together about five months then, and he was such a wonderful young guy. We had such a good time together. We did several of those weekends where we'd go to the Twin Cities, go dancing on Friday night, skiing all day Saturday and then church on Sunday. We were both very active Christians, and you know, we really encouraged each other in that. His death was such a tragedy, such a loss."

She and the Saggau family stayed close for a time after the accident, "but then I thought it would probably be better for all of us to kind of move on with our lives," Rachel said. They haven't been in contact for many years.

The Saggau family's grief lifted ever so slowly.

"It was a while before I could even read a sports page," Bernie said. "I kept it going at work as best I could, but I had to be careful because I had a torn family. Having the two younger ones still at home really helped us, I know that."

Eventually, said Ingalls, "Bernie began to go out speaking again, and he would talk about Jeff and how they got through it after losing him. Lois was going along on a lot of those trips then, and I think maybe it helped both of them."

By Christmas of 1976, when Bernie sat down to write his traditional holiday newsletter for the family, he gave a powerful description of what they'd been through since January 31 of that year. After giving a humorous update on what level of learning each member of the family happened to be in then in school or life, he wrote:

"Jeff has graduated. He has had the course, and we know he passed. He is finding out first-hand what Christmas is all about, because of where he is spending it. Jeff had his fatal accident when he was on his skiing trip. He had taken along some new luggage that his grandparents had just given him last Christmas. It was our task to unpack Jeff's luggage. Even though he was going to be gone for only two days, Jeff had taken the time to pack his Bible, the one that one of his wrestling buddies had given him. A young man, 23 years old who goes on a skiing trip, who takes along his Bible, pretty much has passed the course. Jeff's tragedy has made us a stronger family. It has proven to us that there are many, many wonderful people who do care and who do love. Even the strangers whom we have never met expressed love, compassion and concern. I assume that all the people who have ever lost loved ones at a young age ask the question, 'Why?' We did. We couldn't find the answer, but I finally figured it out. We are not to know the reason why. All our hearts were broken, but they are on the mend. Things that Jeff said and did have helped us a great deal. In Jeff's room, there is a sign that reads, 'Quitters never win and winners never quit.'

"The easy thing was not to write this Christmas letter to our friends and to

the people we love, but Jeff would never have forgiven us for that because it would have destroyed everything we ever taught him. Jeff loved Christmas more than any other time of the year, therefore we are going to make Christmas a little more meaningful than ever before.

"Every year I try to end with something that I think is important to the people that we love. This year, I would just like to say this: To protect oneself from ever having a broken heart, just don't love, but oh, what a price to pay. Too high a price, to say the least.

"From all of us to all of you, Merry Christmas and a Happy New Year. God bless. The Saggaus."

At home through that year, the family had done its best to stay busy. Becky, who had graduated from Boone High in 1974, was in the middle of her years at Iowa State University in nearby Ames, where she was a scholarship golfer. David was a senior at Boone High, a wrestler and cross country runner.

All three young Saggaus were excellent students, and all really enjoyed music, in which they were encouraged by both parents, but especially by Lois.

In fact, one of Bernie's best stories when he is out speaking, told with the full Saggau flair, tells how Becky became an outstanding violin player.

"Seniors!" he yelled, in the middle of his speech to the graduating class at Fredericksburg High School in northeast Iowa in 2003. Long pause. "I hope none of you ever have a daughter who plays the violin!" He paused again, and the reaction across the packed gymnasium seemed to be, "Huh?"

"Now I love my daughter Becky, but when she was a little girl, she started taking violin lessons," he continued. He paused, and started doing a fiddling motion and uttering screeches and moans, like an instrument being tortured. "It'll about drive you nuts, I tell you. I'd come home from work, and Becky would be going on and on, and I'd say to my wife, 'Lois, for God's sake, how much longer is she going to play that thing?' Lois would say, 'Fifteen more minutes, just 15 more minutes.' And she'd keep playing it."

More fiddling motions. More screeching noises.

"But then you know what happened?" he continued, getting increasingly animated. "She got better, a lot better. And on the night she was graduating from our Boone High School, they introduced Becky Saggau, and she walked out in the middle of our football field in front of 3,000 people, all by herself with that violin. It was a great moment. She looked so beautiful out there in a flowing dress, and she played a wonderful piece of classical music, and everybody in the crowd was nodding toward Lois and me, and we were proudly nodding back to them."

Long pause, and he was beaming.

"So then when the ceremonies were over, we were starting to walk away, and this one woman comes up and says (he goes into a falsetto voice), 'Oh, Mr. Saggau, your Becky is such a natural on the violin, such a natural!' And I just lost it! I started yelling at this poor woman. 'A natural, you say? The hell she is! That girl worked her head off on that violin, one hour a day, five days a week, since third grade, and it about drove me nuts! Do you have any idea, lady? She is not a natural! Who ever heard of a natural violin player?' The woman walked away. I kept yelling, too. Lois had to get me out of there. You can tell I get excited a little."

There was a lesson about tenacity and hard work in that tale, which, 1) had those graduating seniors in Fredericksburg rocking with laughter, and 2) they'll never forget.

The Saggau family – parents, grown children and now grandchildren – are a very close and loving bunch, with their affection for and loyalty to each other enhanced by the great loss most of them lived through in 1976.

Becky Saggau Russo now lives on a golf course in Sacramento, California. She was highly successful in sales of stocks, bonds and securities in her early career. More recently she is operating her own art gallery, which offers African art that she and her husband Leonard Russo travel to Africa to purchase. That gallery is named "J.R. David Gallery Africa," with the initials and name in it representing the three Saggau kids in birth order – Jeffery, Rebecca and David. Leonard Russo, whose career has been in insurance, has four grown children and grandchildren from an earlier marriage.

Becky, incidentally, is still a fine golfer, so much so that it is difficult to get a straight story out of Bernie Saggau on who is winning when they play together.

David Saggau is now one of the top retinal surgeons in the Midwest, working for the acclaimed Wolfe Clinic, which is based in Marshalltown with centers in 30 Iowa communities. He and his wife Kris have daughters Helen, 14, Anna, 12, and Lydia, 8, and 11-year-old little Bernie named after you know whom.

David Saggau is an occasional golfing partner of his father, infrequent fishing buddy and always a key adviser to him. He gave a fun glimpse into their relationship in June of 2004 at the banquet in Sioux City honoring Bernie's career.

"I grew up in a house where we always had contests," David said. "Ping pong, pool, throwing rocks, climbing stairs – if we were going to do it, we usually made a competition out of it. Now, you all know that my dad is always all about sportsmanship and citizenship. But let me tell you, he is also all about competing. That never manifested itself, really, when we kids were younger – Dad would always beat us in our contests back then. But the playing field seemed to change as we all got older and could challenge him, maybe even beat him sometimes. And now, I'm enjoying watching as my son little Bernie and my dad big Bernie are having some real contests."

He went on with a nice reflection about his father's career.

"What Dad has really done over the years hasn't been about sports, or even about extra-curriculars," David said. "It's been about kids. I've always been proud that he 'walks the walk,' as they say. He's been able to do something he loves for a long time now. My sister and I are very proud of all he's done in this long career."

Bernie and Lois Saggau moved from Boone to West Des Moines in the fall of 1998, buying a beautifully renovated former farmhouse that is now in the middle of a very affluent suburban neighborhood. David and Kris Saggau and their kids live only a few minutes away.

"I never expected to be working as long as I have," Bernie explained, "but I promised the Board of Control that I would stay on until we got the Iowa Hall of Pride built and opened. I'd always promised Lois that we could live wherever she wanted after I retired, and of course, she wants to be close to the grandkids. That's why we made the move to West Des Moines. A nice house came available, and it was already beyond when I had planned to retire. So we bought it and I commuted to Boone the last few years."

Their house was originally the home and farm headquarters of the pioneering Potts family. History has it that for years, one evening a month, the Pottses would gather all the neighbors for supper – nothing fancy, just good food with paper plates, cups and napkins, to make more time for conversation. The Saggaus have continued that tradition in the neighborhood.

Another big gathering in their home has been the IHSAA staff Christmas party, a wonderful evening of snacks, punch, coffee and singing carols – all around a piano with Dr. David Saggau playing.

The Saggaus attend the West Des Moines United Methodist Church. They were long active in the Methodist Church in Boone, before they moved. In fact, earlier in his career, when groups wanted to pay Bernie when he was out speaking, he often had them write a check to the Boone church.

Since the mid-1980s, Lois and Bernie have also had a home at the Iowa Great Lakes in the northwest part of the state. In 1991, they built a new home there on Pocahontas Point on the west Okoboji Lake. In retirement they hope to spend more time there.

"I'm going to make sure Lois gets to go fishing more often," Bernie said. "She's always loved to fish. That's one of the main reasons we have the place at Okoboji. She's got her fishing buddies up there, and she loves to get out there, either in the boat or off the dock. They have a great time at it. And I go enjoy the golf courses."

Lois' fishing buddies through the years have been Marie Kellen, 88 at this writing, from Remsen in northwest Iowa, and Warren "Van" Vanden Brink, 80, who lives at the lakes after spending most of his business career in Sheldon, also in northwest Iowa.

They both kid Lois about how fashionable she always looks when they're out fishing. Kellen said she worries "that Lois will get the fish line caught on those gold earrings." And Vanden Brink added that Lois "goes fishing looking like she's come right out of a bandbox, with her hair just so and her nails all painted. But I'll tell you, she's not afraid to get those fingers into a worm can or tackle box."

The Saggaus enjoy excellent health, especially for people in their 70s. Both are very trim, and they walk in place on workout machines at home.

Bernie had a heart attack in November, 1989, but bounced back from that well, and he is moving about much easier at retirement after having a hip joint replacement in September, 2003.

There is little doubt he has given his all for the young people of Iowa. Dan McCool, a grizzled veteran sportswriter at the Des Moines Register, said of Saggau, "I've always been amazed at how that man has kept a fire burning for the high school athlete for so long. How long has he been in his office now? Forty years or more?

"Think about it. He's the man who gets accused of hating this sport, this school, that sport, that school. He gets accused of keeping this team or that team out of the state tournament. He's the reason in a lot of people's minds when some bad thing has happened to their favorite athlete or team.

"They're forgetting that he's the person who has made it possible for 80,000 or more people to see the state high school wrestling tournament. I've always felt that what he really wants to do, in whatever sport, is to make it all memorable for the kids. There's nothing about it for him. It's all for some kid out there in Iowa, so he can grow up and say, 'You know, I participated in the best state wrestling tournament in the country.' Or to be able to say 'I shot a basket at Vets Auditorium,' or 'I scored a touchdown in the UNI-Dome.' That's what Bernie Saggau has done."

PROCLAMATION

WHEREAS, BERNIE SAGGAU HAS DEDICATED HIS LIFE TO EDUCATION AND THE VALUES OF HIGH SCHOOL ATHLETICS AND ACTIVITIES IN THE DEVELOPMENT OF SECONDARY SCHOOL STUDENTS; AND

WHEREAS, MR. SAGGAU HAS WORKED AS A TEACHER AND A PRINCIPAL, AND FOR THE PAST 37 YEARS HAS SERVED AS THE EXECUTIVE DIRECTOR OF THE IHSAA, THE LONGEST TENURE OF ANY OF THE 50 STATE HIGH SCHOOL ATHLETIC ASSOCIATION DIRECTORS; AND

WHEREAS, MR. SAGGAU WAS ONE OF THE HIGHEST RATED BASKETBALL AND FOOTBALL OFFICIALS IN THE STATE, SERVING AS A BIG 8 BASKETBALL OFFICIAL FOR 18 YEARS, AS BIG 8 CONFERENCE SUPERVISOR OF BASKETBALL OFFICIALS FOR SEVEN YEARS, AND A COLLEGE FOOTBALL OFFICIAL FOR OVER 15 YEARS; AND

WHEREAS, MR. SAGGAU HAS CHAIRED A NUMBER OF COMMITTEES FOR THE NATIONAL FEDERATION OF STATE HIGH SCHOOL ASSOCIATIONS, AND SERVED ON THE BOARD OF DIRECTORS OF THE IOWA GAMES AND THE GOVERNOR'S TASK FORCE FOR SUBSTANCE ABUSE; AND

WHEREAS, MR. SAGGAU IS A NATIONALLY RENOWNED PUBLIC SPEAKER, HAVING DELIVERED KEYNOTE ADDRESSES AT A NUMBER OF NATIONAL CONVENTIONS, AND BRINGING AN INSPIRING MESSAGE TO OVER 1,200 STUDENT BODIES ACROSS THE COUNTRY; AND

WHEREAS, WHEN THE IOWA HALL OF PRIDE OPENS, MR. SAGGAU WILL HAVE ACHIEVED A LEGACY THAT WILL STAND AS THE ULTIMATE TRIBUTE TO IOWA HIGH SCHOOL ATHLETICS AND ACTIVITIES AND THE OUTSTANDING PEOPLE THEY CREATE; AND

NOW, THEREFORE, I, THOMAS J. VILSACK, GOVERNOR OF THE STATE OF IOWA, DO HEREBY PROCLAIM BERNIE SAGGAU TO BE AN

OUTSTANDING IOWAN

AND ON BEHALF OF ALL IOWANS, I THANK HIM FOR HIS MANY CONTRIBUTIONS AND WISH HIM ALL THE BEST FOR CONTINUED SUCCESS IN ALL HIS FUTURE ENDEAVORS.

IN TESTIMONY WHEREOF, I HAVE HEREUNTO SUBSCRIBED MY NAME AND CAUSED THE GREAT SEAL OF THE STATE OF IOWA TO BE AFFIXED. DONE AT DES MOINES, IOWA THIS 26TH DAY OF MAY IN THE YEAR OF OUR LORD TWO THOUSAND FOUR.

THOMAS J. VILSACK
GOVERNOR

ATTEST:
SALLY J. PEDERSON
LT. GOVERNOR

A Salute to Bernie Saggau by a member of the Board of Control

Born to Bernhard and Angie Saggau 76 years ago
What kind of future life lay ahead, no one could know
Growing up in Denison, the place of his youth
Developing his strong character of pride, dedication and truth

Work and play such important parts of his younger ways
Establishing patterns, ethics and goals for future days
A janitor, sales clerk and member of the Northwestern Railroad crew
Mowing lawns, washing windows, shoveling snow – hard work nothing new

In the summers riding his bike, swimming and making the rounds
In physical stature, not very big at five feet, seven inches and 125 pounds
Very active in athletics, participating in baseball, basketball and football
But as a sprinter on a record-breaking track relay team is where he did stand tall

Recruited and on to Buena Vista College in nearby Storm Lake
One of his toughest decisions in life – a good choice he did make
Three short years and graduation with a teaching and coaching degree
That first job in education and eventually, administration at Cherokee

High school and college officiating become a big part of his life
Inducted in the National High School Hall of Fame accompanied by Lois, his wife
A charter member of the Iowa High School Officials Hall of Fame
Receiving "The Golden Whistle Award," the highest officiating honor in the game

Joining the Iowa High School Athletic Association in 1963
Spending the next 41 years of his life – this was where he was meant to be
Serving 37 years as Executive Director for the Board of Control
The honor of working with him on the Rep Council or Board, for so many a goal

The "Iowa Hall of Pride," his vision, legacy and lifelong dream
Showcasing every past and present Iowa boy and girl activity and team
The Iowa High School Athletic Association celebration 100 years in 2004
Highlighted by the "Iowa Hall of Pride's" opening of the front door

Sought out as the number one speaker for high school graduation day

Expressing his passion for Iowa's youth and athletics in his own way
As he approaches his retirement, so humble, he will not boast
This is to Mr. Saggau, "Bernie" as he is known to most!

Dwayne Cross

(The author is superintendent at Rockwell City-Lytton and is a member of the Board of Control of the Iowa High School Athletic Association. It was done in calligraphy, framed and presented to Bernie Saggau at a banquet held in June, 2004, in Sioux City, in honor of his impending retirement.)

Chapter Five

100 years of great sports moments

Let the reminiscing begin.

In 100 years of high school boys' sports in Iowa, there are 100,000 great memories, moments and characters. Or maybe a million. We'll never get them all covered, but sharing some of my favorites will undoubtedly prompt your own recollections, and thus your own little celebrations of what the Iowa High School Athletic Association programs have given us.

There was legendary Davenport High School basketball coach Paul Moon wearing spats at games from the late 1920s into the early 1950s. The Roland Rockets essentially became the whole state's basketball team in the 1950s, and the Palmer Panthers did that again in the 1980s. We've all been thrilled with the small-school baseball powers like the Bancroft St. John's "Johnnies," mighty Norway and in more recent years Kee High's Kee Hawks from Lansing and New Albin. We've read about, or remember, the football juggernauts at Cedar Rapids High School in the early years, later at Waterloo East, Dowling Catholic, Emmetsburg and Harlan. We watched Dan Gable start his heroic wrestling career by going undefeated at Waterloo West. We loved it when sprinter Clyde Duncan of Des Moines North electrified track fans nationwide with his performances in the Drake Relays and state championship meets. There was the "home run derby" summer of 2002 in baseball, when Marshalltown's Jeff Clement and Winterset's James Peterson both took aim at the nation's record for home runs in a high school player's career. So many stories.

THE SINGLE BEST SPORTS STORY that has come out of

100 years of high school boys' competition in Iowa may well be that of the Palmer Panthers' run to glory in basketball in the late 1980s.

The hold that this small school and town had on the hearts of Iowans was well-told in a column in 2002 by Marty Gallagher, now 35 and a writer for several Internet sites from his home base in Storm Lake. That's just 30 miles west of Palmer, but when the Panthers went on their streak of 103 consecutive victories and three straight state championships from 1985 to '88, Gallagher was growing up 200 miles away in Strawberry Point in eastern Iowa.

Nevertheless, he so admired the Palmer basketball story, he's talked about it ever since, especially after he moved to northwest Iowa. And on Father's Day in 2002, his wife Heather Gallagher gave him a gift he will never forget – a surprise trip to the old Palmer High School gymnasium in the town of 214.

The story Marty Gallagher subsequently wrote about that gift speaks volumes about the high regard Iowans have for high school sports.

It is the first of several stories we will reprint in this chapter – a couple of them my own, a couple by other Iowa writers – to remind you, or give you the feel for, how special that certain individual athletes, teams, coaches and games were.

A Great Father's Day Gift

By Marty Gallagher

June 23, 2002

PALMER, IOWA – Father's Day is supposed to be a day marked by bad neckties and cheap gadgets, isn't it?

Not for me, I guess.

My wife pulled off a pretty good one for me last Sunday. We were at her parents' house near Pocahontas, and she told me that we were going to go for a drive to look at some neat houses on a lake somewhere. (The U.S. Open coverage had just started, so I can't remember EXACTLY what she was telling me.)

"Uh, O.K.," I said. I'm pretty sure that my enthusiasm didn't overwhelm anyone.

So, my wife, my daughter, my wife's sister and her parents all loaded up into the van of my father-in-law and off we went.

About 20 minutes later, we were driving into the town of Palmer. (Traffic wasn't too bad, in case you're wondering.)

"Let's drive by the school," I suggested to my father-in-law.

"O.K.," he said. I had only seen the old Palmer High School once before. And that was around 15 years ago, back when the Panthers were in the middle of their 103-game winning streak in boys' basketball.

And I had never been in the school.

My father-in-law pulled up in front of the school and asked, "You want to go inside and look around?"

"Sure," I said, without hesitation. When nobody else in the van voiced a concern about what we were doing, I figured something was up.

Here's what I learned: My wife and her parents set it up so that I could get into the old Palmer school, check out the gym, the trophies, the awards, the classrooms, the locker rooms, the scrapbooks and all the memorabilia of the Palmer basketball teams of the 1980s.

And I loved it.

It was like walking into a "real-life" setting of the movie "Hoosiers." Just incredible.

Immediately, I stepped into the gym and shot a few baskets. I felt like a 12-year-old kid. It's hard to explain.

And this part should surprise no one: Two minutes after we entered the building, a few high school-aged boys walked into the gym to shoot hoops. It was 85 degrees outside, a perfect day, and these boys wanted to get some "work" done in the gym.

Perfect.

My mother-in-law, who graduated from Palmer in 1970, gave me the grand tour.

The lockers for grades 9 through 12 ran along one wall outside the gym. There were only a handful of classrooms. And the locker rooms? Unbelievably small. Smaller than what you're thinking right now, I'll guarantee it.

The trophy case was fantastic, of course. Trophies for a state title in 1983, a fourth place finish in 1985, a title in 1986, another title in 1987, a third straight title in 1988 and a third place finish in 1989. Remarkable.

There was a letter from Jim Valvano displayed prominently, commending the Panthers for having a zest for life, written not long before the North Carolina State coach passed away.

There were scrapbooks full of congratulatory letters and best wishes from people across not only the state of Iowa, but the nation. People who had seen the team featured on ABC-TV's "Good Morning America" or some other national news show and felt compelled to wish the Panthers good luck on their road to another state title.

There was a letter from a man in Texas who was impressed with "the class" the Panther boys showed in their interviews. There was a woman in Missouri who wanted a purple Panther sweatshirt, "but not one with frills around the collar." There was a man in California who sent a check to be used "for scholarships, the athletic programs or wherever it might be needed." There was a coach in Minnesota who was desperate for Coach Alden Skinner to send him some shooting drills for his own players to execute. There was a boy in Michigan who just wanted some autographs. And on and on.

Then, there were the composite photos of each class that graduated from Palmer. The Class of 1988 included basketball greats Troy Skinner and Brian Pearson, of course. And that wasn't a very large class. But what really struck me was that the classes of 1987 and 1989 had only SEVEN students apiece. Not boys. STUDENTS.

And they still dominated in basketball!

How could something like this happen? Over such a sustained period of time? The Panthers only lost 25 games, TOTAL, from 1975 to 1989.

The answers, of course, were right in front of me.

● *There were the photographs of Coach Skinner, the man who directed basketball at Palmer during that entire period. The work that he spent building that program in the early '70s is still paying off for that community today. Pomeroy-Palmer won its second straight state title this season, and it can't be questioned that the tradition that Coach Skinner helped construct is a big factor in the continued success in that consolidated school system. "I don't think you have great teams — you have great programs," Coach Skinner told me this spring. And he should know. He was the architect of one of the all-time greatest programs in Iowa's history.*

● *There were the photographs of all of the Palmer boys, who put in countless hours working on ball handling, passing and shooting. Boys like Norm Weimers, Bob Beneke, Brent Aden, Bill Francis, Eric Hanson, Troy Skinner, Brian Pearson and Jamie Peterson. Those recognizable names that will never be forgotten in northwest Iowa. But, there were so many others. Boys who were NOT first-team all-state players. Boys who worked hard at the game to be an important part of Palmer's success. Boys like Jeff Buenting, John Beneke, Kyle Skinner, Scott Martin, Mark Pearson, Marty Flaherty, Dallas Janssen, Chad Melco, Brad Gutz and so many others. And you couldn't look at these photos without seeing that there were so many families who must have sacrificed a lot of time over the years, for the good of the program. Everywhere I turned, I saw names like Aden, Beneke, Wessels, Buenting, Martin, Abrahamson, Francis, Skinner, Pearson, Wilken, Janssen, Hartman, Wiemers and Melco.*

● *And last — but certainly not least — the secret to Palmer's long-term success could be found just a few steps away. In the gym. Two hours after I entered the old school building, those same boys who were shooting hoops and working on ball handling were STILL in the gym. Working on their games. On a beautiful summer day, there they were. Dribbling. Passing. Shooting.*

Today's practice equals tomorrow's success.

I don't know how many high school-aged boys there could be now in Palmer. There can't be very many. But, here's what I do know: Five of them spent two hours on a Sunday afternoon getting better.

And that, my friends, is the secret to their success.

Hard work. Countless hours of dedication to getting better. Making sacrifices for the good of the team.

These are good lessons for our young people today, of course. I'd love to be able to take my kids through the old Palmer school someday and explain how those lessons still apply to everything they set out to achieve.

And as I walked out of that gym last Sunday, I couldn't help but feel like I'd just walked out of a museum. In a way, I think I did.

A building with a rich and proud history of showcasing what a great work ethic and teamwork can accomplish.

And what those people and teams achieved in this small northwest Iowa town during that 15-year stretch remains one of the most incredible sports stories in our state's history.

Will we ever see something like that again? I doubt it.

"Happy Father's Day," said my wife.

"Thanks," I said. And we drove away.

Coach Skinner who turned 59 years old in 2005, and lives in the Des Moines suburb of Pleasant Hill having retired in 2000 after 32 years as a business teacher, school administrator and basketball coach. After 27 years at Palmer and Pomeroy-Palmer, he spent the last five year of his career in education as the assistant superintendent at nearby Southeast Polk High School. Since retirement, he is now doing real estate appraisals for his son Kyle's appraisal business. Son Troy, a lawyer and lobbyist, and daughter

Darcee, are also close by, giving Alden and Donna plenty of opportunity to be doting grandparents.

The old coach said he is amazed that so many people remember his name when he meets them, and immediately associate him with Palmer basketball.

"Yeah, it happens all the time, for some dumb reason," Skinner said. "That's getting to be a long time ago. You'd think people would forget that stuff, wouldn't you?"

Actually, the story is even better than most remember.

Alden Skinner was a three-sport athlete at little Runnells High School, which is now part of the Southeast Polk district, before graduating in 1963. As a football quarterback, he led the state in passing yardage in his senior year. He went on to Drake University, played freshman sports then focused on earning his teaching and coaching credentials. When he graduated in 1968, he learned of a teaching and coaching vacancy in Palmer from Don Goode, an old high school buddy, who was on the faculty there as a math teacher.

"I went up and was interviewed at the grain elevator office by Don Reiter, who was the manager of the elevator and the school board president," Skinner said. "He hired me on the spot."

Alden, Donna and their four-week-old son Kyle moved that August to Palmer, where he was paid $5,200 per year to teach, be head coach of the boys' basketball team – which had not won a game in two years – and assist in several other sports. The Skinners paid $45 per month for a small apartment over the telephone office, right downtown.

"It was fine," Alden said, "but then when you're young, anything's okay."

The senior class in that fall of 1968 had 10 students, nine of them boys.

"It was pretty obvious who was going to be homecoming queen," Skinner said. "There wasn't much excitement about sports. Truth was, I only had one boy in that senior class who even came out for the team. In fact, I think we only had about 12 come out from all four grades."

Slowly, Skinner went about building the program.

"We won five games that first year, and the town kind of got excited with that," he said.

In his third year in Palmer, Skinner started a basketball program for kids from the third grade on up.

"I did most of the coaching myself, but I always involved the high school players with the young ones, too," he said. "It's a great teaching experience for high school kids to do that. Having that opportunity was as important for them as the opportunity to play and learn was for the young kids."

In his fifth year, the 1972-73 season, Skinner's Panthers had their first winning season. "Our older players were struggling the first half of that season," he said, "so about midway, we moved three freshmen into the starting line-up, which already had two sophomores on it, and we went on to win 12 games."

There was never another losing season.

"One of the biggest sales jobs any coach has to make," Skinner said, "is to get the kids to understand what it takes to win consistently, then to get them to buy into that. They have to make a commitment to do what it takes, if you're going to be winners year after year."

When he got the Panthers into the state tournament for the first time in 1977, "the whole community went nuts," he recalled. "When we came home after winning the sub-state tournament at Spencer, a caravan of fire trucks led us into town."

By then, Skinner was also high school principal as well as being basketball coach. In 1983, he became superintendent – and coach.

Meanwhile, he had the team back in the state tournament in 1979 and 1980, then came back in 1983 to win the first of his four championships. The incredible streak of 103 victories ran from the first game of 1985 until the semi-finals of the state tournament in 1989, when Palmer lost to Keota. Then the Panthers came back to win the consolation game for a third place finish.

"Usually those consolation games don't mean as much," said Skinner, "but I pushed the kids for that one, because it was Palmer High School's last basketball game. We wanted to go out with a victory, and we did."

They also went out with a decade of unparalleled success in the '80s. They averaged more than 20 victories per year. They didn't lose a home game "from 1981 until we closed the gym in 1989," Skinner noted.

Capacity in that gym was about 800.

"Our home games became such big events that when we'd get out of school about 2:30 on the day of a game, there would already be people lining up at the gym doors," Skinner said. "The seats and standing room would fill completely up, so we hooked up a closed-circuit TV system and the spillover crowd could watch the gym in the study hall."

People came from all over the Midwest to see the Panthers play at home.

The fun reached its zenith at the end of the 1987- 88 regular season. Reporters from the regional and state newspapers were regulars at Palmer games by then. As tournament time neared, and word was out that the team from the small town in northwest Iowa was going for its third consecutive state championship, the national media founds the way to Palmer, too.

On the afternoon of the last regular season game, the acclaimed ABC-TV broadcaster Dick Schaap arrived in town, and a crew from the ABC network's "Good Morning America" show stayed with the team from the start of the district tournament right on through the state championship game. Schaap's morning reports turned the Palmer Panthers into America's team.

Each day during state tournament week, "Good Morning America" opened with a live picture from outside the Palmer High gym. Schaap's daily stories ran about 10 minutes each, with videotape from the previous game and live interviews with Skinner, his players, townsfolk and other fans in front of the cameras and bright television lights that were set up in the gym.

There were also stories on the evening news and morning shows of the NBC and CBS networks, as well as in newspapers and magazines from coast to coast.

The result?

"We had three notebooks full of letters from people from all over America," said Skinner. "It was just amazing."

How did the Palmer players react to all that?

"Well, it seems almost crazy when I say this now, but I think we managed to keep things in perspective," the coach said. "We talked to the kids about what was happening, and we tried to keep them from getting their heads inflated over it all. We told them that a lot of the media was around just waiting for us to lose, because that would be a big story.

"But, you know what? We also reminded the kids – and the whole community – how much fun it was. One line I remember someone saying was, 'It's not going to last forever, people, so let's enjoy it while it's here. Don't miss out on it now!' "

Broadcaster Schaap seemed to have as much fun as any of them.

"He was very positive here," Skinner said. "He was always congratulating the team and the fans. He said later he really had enjoyed his time with us."

At the end of the season in the spring of 1989, Palmer could look back on a record of 103-1 in its previous four seasons. In a way, it made closing the school and consolidating with nearby Pomeroy a little easier.

"That last graduation in 1989 was sad, but we'd been successful right to the end," Skinner said. "The impact of winning so much in basketball had a positive impact on our whole educational program. It seemed to bring excellence to every area of our school – music, speech, academics, everything.

"By that time, we'd talked for five or six years about what we were going to do with the school. We'd had so many town meetings about it. But we all knew something had to happen. That last year, I think we were down to 42 kids in grades nine through 12. So when we made the decision to consolidate with Pomeroy, it was kind of a relief. There were no more battles to fight. We just had to make the change."

If you know Iowa high school basketball, you know that Pomeroy-Palmer basketball became an instant juggernaut and stayed strong through the 1990s and into the new century. Skinner coached the boys' basketball team one year, just to oversee a smooth transition, then devoted all his time to being superintendent.

Now, 16-plus years after that last state championship at Palmer High School, hardly a day goes by that strangers with out-of-county license plates doesn't drive into town. They loop through the business district, swing up past the gym, which is still used for a few school activities, and smile about what once happened there. And downtown at the Palmer House bar and grill, it's still real easy to strike up a conversation about Palmer Panther basketball.

THE BEST PERFORMANCE BY AN INDIVIDUAL

ATHLETE? In 100 years of high school sports history in Iowa, can you possibly pick one athlete's performance as the most remarkable?

Talk about arguable!

But in my view, nobody's athletic achievement tops that of Jack Mustapha, who in 1965 pitched Boone High School's Toreadors to the state championship in baseball.

More than two decades later, I talked to Mustapha about it for a story in the Des Moines Register, which is reprinted here. Read it, and then we'll come back for a visit with Mustapha today.

Catching up years later with Jack Mustapha, Boone's high school baseball legend
By Chuck Offenburger
June, 1989
Des Moines Register

BOONE, IOWA – When you tell people today what senior right-handed pitcher Jack Mustapha did in the 1965 Iowa high school baseball tournament, they think you're making it up. But you can look it up:

●He pitched six of the Toreadors' nine tourney games on the way to Boone's first state baseball championship. All six were shutouts. Even more amazing, five were no-hitters, including three in a row that brought the final three victories over North Tama and Shenandoah in the substate and against Burlington in the title game.

● If you include Mustapha's two victories immediately before tournament play and another one after – Boone had to play that late game to clinch the conference championship because of an early season rainout – he allowed just two unearned runs and seven hits in about 60 innings. He struck out 118.

● *What made it even more incredible is that Mustapha came down with infectious hepatitis after his first game early that summer and was hospitalized 13 days. He missed nearly a month of the season. When he came back just before the tourney series began, he had lost 35 pounds from his normal weight of 180 and constantly battled exhaustion.*

"I've never heard of any high school athletic accomplishment in any sport to rival what he did in those tourney games, especially when you consider how he was just getting over such a serious illness," said his coach, Bill Sapp, who is now 64 and still teaching at Boone High School, although he has given up coaching.

"When you realize he had the three no-hitters in a row in the substate and championship games, you know those didn't come against any humpty-dumpty ball teams. Those were good clubs. He was the best I was ever associated with as far as high school pitchers go."

Rick Davis, now 40 and the current Boone baseball coach, was Mustapha's catcher in 1965. "Jack was as good as I've ever seen in amateur ball, and I caught two years for Iowa State and played semi-pro and service ball," Davis said. "None of the pitchers I caught anywhere could compare to him."

Staff Sgt. Jack Mustapha, 42, is now a full-time recruiter for the Iowa National Guard. He was in the process of moving from Boone to Cedar Rapids, when he was asked about that season 24 years ago.

"Wow, that's a long time ago, isn't it?" he said. "Yeah, I'm proud of what I did then, but my main memory is of how much fun we all had playing baseball. We really had a great time, but of course, we were always winning, too."

The people of Boone saw it coming. The gang of boys that included Mustapha had won the state championship as Little Leaguers and old clipping show that 1,000 people turned out to welcome the young team home from that title game. A couple of years later, the same boys won state and regional championships to qualify for the Babe Ruth baseball World Series in New Jersey before losing. In their sophomore year of high school, they challenged for the conference title and Mustapha was 10-0 as a pitcher. In their junior year, they were 20-5 and Mustapha was 12-2.

By the senior year, people were already talking about how Lenore Wyckoff, who had taught the great Bob Feller in fourth grade in Van Meter, had taught Mustapha in fourth grade after her move to Boone.

The team was certainly expected to be a great one, and Coach Sapp knew it. He went to the school board and told them that although Boone's football and basketball teams traveled to away games in chartered Greyhound buses, his baseball teams always had to go in school buses. He thought it was time to go first class in baseball, too. The vote was unanimous for Greyhounds.

Boone fans who drove to road games almost always outnumbered the home team's crowd. At home games, attendance was in the range of 900 up to 2,000, said Mo Kelley, now the publications director for the Iowa High School Athletic Association, which is headquartered in Boone. Back then, Kelley was the sports editor of the Boone News Republican and also served as sports director and broadcaster for KWBG radio, which carried all Toreador games, live.

"You look back on it now, and in a way, it doesn't seem real," Kelley said. "it was very exciting around town. It was like all the people were thinking, hey, we've really got something here. We reflected that excitement in the way we covered the team in the paper. We ran complete box scores and printed game-by-game batting averages, which was real unusual in a paper in a community this size."

Mustapha's illness soon after the season started sent shockwaves through the town. "They traced the hepatitis down to a water bottle that this kid was using to bring water to us during the games," Mustapha said. "It was a real scare because it not only meant that I was quarantined in the hospital, but everybody else on the team had to take shots and then wait to see if they got it, too. Luckily, nobody else did."

Coach Sapp remembers just about getting sick himself when he got the news about Mustapha. "I thought, 'Holy smokes, we build up to having this great team with one of the greatest pitchers there's ever been, and he gets sick.' That was a real rugged time for us. All five games we lost during that season were when he was gone."

Professional scouts who became regulars at Boone games because of Mustapha were the talk of the town. The most persistent among them was "Iron Mike" Ryba of the St. Louis Cardinals who had been the catcher for that team's "Gas House Gang."

After high school Mustapha was offered several college baseball scholarships. He visited Parsons College in Fairfield and Western Kentucky, but signed with Iowa State. On the ISU freshman team, which played only four games, he had two victories. He was frustrated that collegiate rules kept freshmen from playing for the varsity. And he had overextended himself academically, taking tough courses for a chemistry major and a physics minor.

He dropped out of school and signed a contract with the Cardinals. But, because military draft pressure was on him as the Vietnam buildup was growing, he and Ryba decided it would be best to put his pro career on hold, enlist in the Army and then go back to baseball as soon as his service hitch was completed.

The pro career never happened. In Vietnam, Mustapha, who was a door gunner in a helicopter, was in two crashes. In the first, he was not hurt. In the second, during the 1968 Tet offensive, he was wounded and broke his back when the chopper went down. Two of the five crew members were killed. The survivors spent four days on the ground in hostile territory before being rescued.

When he came back to the United States and completed his hospital stay, "I could still throw, but it wouldn't be long before my back would stiffen up and I couldn't go on. I knew my baseball career was over. I was a little bitter about that for a while then, but I'm not now. There's no doubt in my mind that I would have made it in pro ball if all that hadn't happened. That's O.K., I had my shot in the limelight, then it was somebody else's turn."

As a boy, he had been groomed for that limelight by his father, the late Jack Mustapha Sr., who was Boone's fire chief. Once little Jack got old enough, they played catch almost every night.

"He taught me control, how to work a strike zone and be able to hit the corners at knee height and at shoulder height," Mustapha said. "He wouldn't let me throw a curveball until I was 14, so we worked on speed and placing the ball. We played every day like that until I was about 15, when Dad couldn't hold me any more."

By then the fastball was a lively one. "There were no radar guns around then, but I think he was probably throwing at 90 miles per hour or so in that senior year," said Davis, his former catcher. "His curve was a great one by then, but he didn't really need it all that much. He didn't need a lot of rest between games because he didn't throw that many extra pitches. He averaged 15 to 16 strikeouts per game. It was 1-2-3 sit down, 1-2-3 sit down."

Despite his 31-2 career pitching record in high school, Mustapha said the Cardinals planned to turn him into an outfielder. "I was always a pretty good hitter — my average was .377 that senior year — and they wanted me as an everyday player," he said.

When the war injuries ended his dreams for pro ball, Mustapha elected to stay in the Army. He stayed until 1975 when he returned home and became an Iowa State Patrol trooper, serving till 1985. He was police chief of Madrid for two years, did private investigations for a year and joined the National Guard in March. He's married and has two children.

"When I'm around town in Boone, a lot of people still mention what happened in the '65 summer, and it's kind of nice to be remembered," he said. "But it's certainly not something I've dwelled on. In fact, I've talked more about my high school baseball with you today than I have in all the years that have gone by since then."

The interview ended with a photograph session, and Mustapha was asked if he had a glove and a ball tucked away somewhere. "Hey," he said with a smile, "I've always got a glove and a ball."

Fiftten years later, in 2005, Jack Mustapha, 57, is glad to be alive, walking on his own and able to go to work every day for Iowa Workforce Development in Des Moines. Shortly after that story was published in 1989, Mustapha suffered a heart attack and then a stroke. Later, he battled the intestinal disorder diverticulitis, which required frequent hospitalization.

His health problems – "most of them related to the old wounds from Vietnam" – not only forced him to retire from the National Guard, they also put him in a wheel chair for about a year. "I wouldn't stay down," he says now. "I refused to stay in that wheelchair."

By 1990, he was up and working as a veterans' representative with Iowa Workforce Development, the state agency that assists in matching people with jobs around the state. In 2004, he was still there, working as a management analyst, specifically monitoring the state's welfare payments for abuses. "Life is good," he says. "Oh, it'd be better if I was rich, but it's just good to be alive and active. I get around great now."

He said a turning point in his recovery was in 1995, when the old Boone High state champion baseball team had a 30-year reunion in Boone. "I actually pitched a few innings," Mustapha said. "Someone in the stands said, 'Oh, my goodness, he looks like an old man out there on the mound!' My wife told them how far I'd come back even to be out there."

The Mustaphas, who have two children, now live in the eastern Des Moines suburb of Pleasant Hill.

When he looks back on his pitching in that summer of 1965, does it seem unreal now? "No, not really," he said. "My dad was the co-founder of the little league program in Boone when I was about eight years old. All of us on that team played together from that time on. We worked hard, played together, we were groomed to win and we expected to win. It carried over from baseball to other sports, too. That year we won the baseball championship, we also won the mythical state football championship. So we had a good bunch of athletes, obviously.

"I do still occasionally look back on it and wonder what would have happened if I hadn't gotten sick at the start of that season. Mike Ryba, the Cardinals scout who had been following me for two or three years, really helped me get through that. He was coming to Boone quite a bit then, and when he heard what happened, he came to see me one day when I was really low. I remember he said, 'Well, you can lay down and die, or you can go ahead, get better and do what you wanted to do.' That's what I did."

OUR MOST INSPIRING ATHLETE? There have, of course, been some very inspiring athletes over the past 100 years in Iowa high school sports. Maybe the most inspirational has been a wrestler who finished no better than sixth place in the state tournament in his senior year.

Doesn't sound so inspiring?

Well, what Nick Ackerman of Colfax-Mingo had accomplished as an athlete prompted more than 11,000 rabid wrestling fans at Veterans Memorial Auditorium in Des Moines to give him a standing ovation after he'd been defeated in his last match back in 1997. Dan Gable, perhaps the greatest wrestler in the history of the sport, walked up and asked the high school boy for his autograph.

At that point, there was much more wrestling glory in Nick Ackerman's future – including his stunning individual national championship for Simpson College in 2001. But before we get to that, let's go back to a story that explains why Ackerman still ranks as one of Iowans' all-time favorite athletes. The story by the Des Moines Register's outstanding wrestling reporter Dan McCool was published as Ackerman started the tournament trail in his senior year at Colfax-Mingo, located 20 miles northeast of Des Moines.

Loss of legs no deterrent
Ackerman compiles 26-3
record with special "ability"
By Dan McCool
February 1997
Des Moines Register

COLFAX, IOWA – Nick Ackerman considers himself just a normal kid. Sure, he can get instant attention by sticking a knife into his leg and faking the pain. "My legs don't get cold," silences anyone who thinks he's daffy to be wearing shorts in mid-winter.

But despite the fact his legs are artificial, he considers himself just like all the other high school wrestlers who are setting out on their quests to reach the state tournament.

Ackerman's legs were amputated just below the kneecaps when he was 1 1/2 years old to stem a fast-moving form of meningitis that threatened his life. He doesn't let that stand in his way.

"I always thought I was normal," said Ackerman, 17. "I used to break the legs off my G.I. Joe guys to make them look like me, a bunch of stupid stuff like that, because I always thought I was the normal one."

Years ago, Nick corrected a school nurse who was explaining his situation to younger students. The nurse had told them Nick had a special disability, but Nick corrected her, saying it was a special ability – "I can take off my legs, and nobody else in this school can," he said.

His mother, Cindy Ackerman, said Nick used to tell his older brother, Nathan, to take off his legs, too, when it was time to go to bed.

Since his friends have grown up with him, any teasing is mostly good-natured, Ackerman said.

"Nobody ever gives me any stuff," he said. "Maybe once in elementary school some kid did, but it was no big deal. I mean, nobody liked him anyway."

Ackerman's wrestling teammates at Colfax-Mingo High School consider the senior just one of the guys.

Principal David Morgan said: "You don't even think about him as somebody without legs. He's just a regular student. You forget the fact he has two artificial legs."

Ackerman has a 2.8 grade-point average. In story-telling, Ackerman might be a straight-A student.

Growing up, whenever he was asked how he lost his legs, he said he told far-fetched tales. One was that his father was a lumberjack in Oregon who accidentally cut off Nick's legs. Another had an airplane running over his

Soap Box Derby car at the end of a race, after Ackerman crashed through a protective hay bale.

Wrestling coach Bryan Poulter said Ackerman's attitude has been consistently upbeat.

He's a pleasant young man with a sense of humor, a 26-3 record that includes 15 pins, a busy social schedule and a desire to wrestle in college.

"Ever since I've known him, his attitude has been positive, mischievous, the whole ball of wax," Poulter said. "I can't think of a day when he's been down, even when he came back from surgery. It was just a matter of getting back at it."

Ackerman said, "I've never gone up to bed and cried because I didn't have legs."

His great-great grandfather, Jake Tharp, lost a leg when he fell into a well. His great grandfather, John Tharp, lost both legs in a train accident.

Nick's artificial legs cost from $8,000 to $22,000 a pair, said his father, Kurt Ackerman. As Nick grew, he got different sets of legs. "You can understand why there are people that maybe don't have a prosthetic arm or leg, because the cost is astronomical," Kurt said.

Ackerman and his Colfax-Mingo teammates will be in a Class 1-A sectional. The top two wrestlers in 13 weight classes advance to districts. The top two from eight districts will make up the 16-wrestler bracket in each weight class of the state tournament, which is at Veterans Memorial Auditorium in Des Moines.

Ackerman will wrestle at 152 pounds. He advanced to the district last season, placing third at 140 pounds.

"I don't think there's much of a higher goal for me than (making state)," Ackerman said. "It's the goal I've been pushing for for four years. I'd be so proud and so thankful for the people who helped me make it there - my coach, my parents and people like that."

Chapter 5

Ackerman's legs were at the center of a life-or-death battle when he was 1 1/2 years old. He had contracted meningococcemia, a bacterial meningitis that gets into the blood stream and can kill in a matter of hours. The first signs of trouble came when he was taking a bath, Ackerman said. His parents noticed bruises on his legs and rushed him to Iowa Methodist Medical Center in Des Moines.

"By the time they got me there, the bruises were bigger," Ackerman said. "It was spreading that fast. It was like my legs were dying. The doctors decided they could cut the legs off and maybe save my life or they could try to leave them on and I'd maybe not make it. They decided to cut them off."

He was near death several times after the surgery, Cindy Ackerman said.

At one point during the two-month hospital stay, Nick was in a coma. His mother was desperate just to hold him. When he was placed in her arms, he awoke and said "Hi, Mom."

Since the amputation, Ackerman said he's had at least 25 surgeries, mostly to control the growth of the leg bones. They sometimes had to cajole him into surgery by giving him a piggy-back ride instead of rolling him on a hospital gurney, his mother said.

Ackerman stands 4 feet 3 inches tall from his head to his kneecaps. The short portions of his legs remaining below the knee provide a base after he removes his prosthetics at matside and walks on his kneecaps to the center of the mat.

"I like to not think about the past, or if I had legs or if I had this I could have been that," Ackerman said. "I always think I'm here as I am, so make the most of it."

When Nick was born, his father said, he envisioned hunting and fishing trips with his son. After the surgery to remove Nick's legs, Kurt cried at the thought his son wouldn't be able to play in Little League. They've always done such outdoor activities, with Kurt even carrying Nick in a backpack.

Artificial legs didn't keep Ackerman from hunting, fishing or Little League — nor from participating in flag football, track, soccer, swimming, snow and water skiing and roller skating. He even played football in junior high.

Ackerman said he might have been playing basketball in high school. His brother, Nathan, stands 6-7 and plays basketball at Simpson College in Indianola.

"I don't know if I would have been a basketball player, but I would have been taller than (Nathan) because the doctors said I would have been 6-10," Ackerman said.

Ackerman said he got into wrestling in third grade by default. "They didn't have a basketball league, only a wrestling league and everybody wrestled," Ackerman said. "Once basketball started, a lot of people switched and played basketball. I could run but I just didn't like it as much. I could wrestle with my legs off and I liked that better."

Colfax-Mingo's Poulter said that in coaching Ackerman he worked to foster a can-do attitude.

"My objective was to never tell him 'no' on anything," he said. "I would never say 'You can't do this' and I never have. He's never said it to himself."

Wrestlers usually need a strong mind, strong body and strong legs. Josh Eastvold, Colfax-Mingo's 130-pounder, said Ackerman handles it well.

"A strong mind is probably the biggest thing" for a wrestler, Eastvold said. "He's got a strong upper body, and a strong mind compensates for the absence of legs."

Ackerman said he still finds an opponent who will take it easy early in the match because of his apparent handicap. The opponent usually changes his mind, especially if Ackerman works his crossface cradle, his favorite way to pin an opponent.

Nevada Coach Jim Pappas, who has watched Ackerman for four years, said Ackerman doesn't need the state tournament to be a winner.

"If he's not a role model, who can be?" Pappas said. "Everyone's got odds they have to overcome. His odds he's overcome. As far as I'm concerned, that kid's a champion right now."

Nick Ackerman, 26 years old in 2005, and living in Davenport, is a graduate-school-trained prosthetist, meaning he makes and fits artificial legs and arms for people who have had amputations. The company he works for, American Prostetics & Orthotics, based in the Des Moines suburb of Clive, is the same one "that's made my own legs for 23 years now," he says. "It's pretty rewarding work to be able to help people get up and going again after they've lost a limb."

His own story offers a lot of hope to his patients, of course, especially if they happen to be young athletes.

Ackerman has been an inspiration to other athletes ever since he was high school, actually. But that reached new levels of importance after his success in NCAA Division III wrestling at Simpson College in Indianola, south of Des Moines. He followed his brother Nathan Ackerman, the basketball player, there. He majored in environmental science and loved campus life.

Wrestling was a real challenge for him in his first two years at Simpson.

"My freshman and sophomore years were really depressing in wrestling," he recalls. "Everybody was a whole lot better at that level. I wasn't just losing, I was really getting beat bad. On the varsity level, I probably didn't win a half-dozen matches those first two years."

By his junior year, he "had matured, was stronger and smarter – mostly smarter – and I was more successful. I wound up third in the Iowa Conference that year."

Then came his amazing senior year, the 2000-01 season, when he ran up a 38-4 season record at 174 pounds by winning the national championship in the tournament held in Waterloo. In the final match, he won a 13-11 victory over Nick Slack, the undefeated defending champion from Augsburg College.

"For him to have the type of tournament he had, against the quality of kids in that bracket, and in the championship match defeat the defending national champion, I don't think it's going to fully set it for any of us for a long time," his Simpson coach Ron Peterson told the reporters afterward. "He had every reason not to go out and put himself in those situations. But his attitude is, 'I don't have a disability, I have ability and I'm going to use it,' and he certainly has."

Ackerman went on to Northwestern University in Evanston, Illinois, for his training in prosthetics. In 2005, he was completing the national examinations for certification in the field.

"I'm very committed to my work as a prosthetist," he said. "This is where I'm supposed to be. The people in this field, and in this company, have been very good to me over the years, and I love being able to help other people now."

He said while he never expects to be too far from wrestling, he doubts he'd ever want to coach full-time.

"Coaching wrestling is very difficult," he says. "You know, the sport is as much mental as it is physical, and as a coach, you have to get 10 guys mentally prepared so they're all ready to go at the same time on the same day. You can't really be doing that and trying to do some other career at the same time."

Ackerman has stayed in excellent shape, though, by working out regularly with several old wrestling friends in the martial arts sports of jujitsu. "I've been in a couple of tournaments, but I'm doing it just for a good workout and fun, nothing serious," he said.

That's how Ackerman was physically ready to respond when he got a phone message in the fall of 2004 from a Lance Wetter, who said he was from Boscobel, Wisconsin.

He'd been a three-sport high school athlete, but he lost a leg in a corn augur accident in September of 2003, Wetter said. He explained he had now started his freshman year at the University of Dubuque and wanted to continue wrestling, a sport in which he'd had a 36-7 high school record and had twice fallen just short of the state tournament. He wondered if Ackerman could give him some tips about wrestling now that he has only one leg.

"I called him back and left a message that I could probably tell him some things over the phone that might help," Ackerman said. "But I told him what we really needed to do was get some mat time together so I could show him some things. I said since my job takes me to Dubuque, maybe we could

104

find a time and get together."

The 20-year-old Wetter was astonished at that response, which came within a day.

He said he'd "had no idea" how to approach Ackerman for advice. When he made his initial phone call to the wrestling legend, "luckily I got his answering machine and I left him a message. I was extremely surprised to find a message back from him on my phone. He sounded very willing to help and real down to earth."

When they finally connected on the phone, "I couldn't believe that he was willing to come to the University of Dubuque and train with me," Wetter said. "At first I was nervous, and I didn't know how to talk to him or anything, but instantly he treated me like one of his friends."

That led to Ackerman not only stopping for a personal workout with Wetter, but eventually signing on as a volunteer assistant to UD head wrestling coach Jon McGovern. His assignment was to work directly with Wetter on Thursday evenings, after Ackerman had spent the day in his company's Dubuque office. And frankly, McGovern leaped at the chance to have Ackerman around, simply because he is now recognized coast-to-coast as an inspiration by all wrestlers.

Wetter began the 2004-05 season with a 3-10 record at 149 pounds, "which isn't bad when you consider this is the first year he's wrestled without his one leg," said Ackerman. "I mean, I lost my legs when I was 18 months old, and started wrestling when I was three years old, so I had a whole lot longer to learn than Lance has had."

As far as help with his wrestling, Wetter said "the main thing that Nick has taught me is to never get discouraged. He keeps reminding me that he only won a few matches his freshman and sophomore year. The main wrestling technique he has taught me is to always have hand control and that hand control is the important concept in wrestling."

Having that kind of help and attention from a national champion like Ackerman, especially one who overcame challenges similar to what Wetter is facing, meant so much to the college freshman.

"Nick Ackerman is a great guy and more inspirational than any other person, besides Jesus," said Wetter, who hopes to enter the ministry eventually. "I'm very grateful for the help I've received from Nick. If it wasn't for him, I might have given up on wrestling."

THE MOST EXCITING FINISH EVER TO AN IOWA HIGH SCHOOL GAME? There have been many thrilling (or heartbreaking, depending on your perspective) last-second victories (or losses) in Iowa prep sports history. But let me share the story of my favorite ending to a game – and of my effort 18 years later to find the hero of that game.

The most incredible finish
to a high school football game
that I've ever heard of
By Chuck Offenburger
October, 1987
Des Moines Register

ESSEX, IOWA – The high school football season is winding down, but the '87 season should not pass without an examination of the play of the year, if not the play of a much longer period of time. Here in Essex, a southwest Iowa town of 1,000, conversation hasn't been the same since. And a videotape of it is in danger of being worn out.

On October 2, the Essex Trojans were facing the Hamburg Wildcats in a rivalry that was Essex' homecoming. It was late in the game when Essex, trailing 14-12, mounted a last assault – a drive that stalled on the 20-yard line. The host Trojans attempted a field goal but it was blocked. Hamburg, now seemingly sure of victory, took the ball with two minutes remaining.

The Hamburg team marched down the field.

"We know now, with hindsight, that we should have killed the clock instead of trying to score," said Hamburg coach Jim Zuck, "but then, we were repeatedly giving the ball to our best back, Clay Boatman, and he's about as safe a player as you could find in taking a handoff."

With six seconds left, Hamburg was on the Essex 7 yard line. Quarterback Clint Crain handed again to Boatman, who started left. As he did, Essex lineman Mike Murray poked his hand beyond a blocker and touched the ball, still in Boatman's grasp.

It was enough of a jostle to make Boatman start bobbling it. The ball went behind his back, but he kept juggling it as he ran across the goal line. Three yards deep in the end zone, the ball – which Boatman never had under control – popped into the air.

Essex defensive back Steve White grabbed it and began a no-time-left, 103-yard desperation sprint for a touchdown that brought Essex an 18-14 homecoming victory – and brought him legendary status in a little town that has taken its football very seriously since early this century.

"I know I've never seen anything like it," said mechanic George Ross, who's missed only seven Essex games in 35 years. "Some of our people were already leaving, figuring the game was lost."

Essex coach Dave Jauron, 49, said he's "seen a lot of last-second shots in basketball and a lot of last-out hits in baseball in my career, but never something like this that turned a sure loss into a win. As Steve was running up the field, my assistant grabbed me and yelled, 'Are we seeing the real thing?' As he ran on down the field, he kept edging closer to the sidelines and I about had a heart attack thinking he might step out of bounds. It should have made the national TV news."

And get this: White, a 135-pound sophomore who played only sparingly until then, wouldn't even have been in the game had not another Essex player injured a hand. "It was my first touchdown for Essex," White recalled, "and I thought for a minute it might be my last one because after I crossed that goal line, all my teammates and a lot of the crowd piled on me. The weight was so bad I couldn't breathe."

Later that night, Steve White walked into the Gas Lamp, the restaurant and bar that is the local gathering spot. "I went back to the back room with the rest of the kids," he said. "This girl came back and said there were some people out front wanting to see me. I walked out there where all the adults were. They cheered and clapped."

He kept the football, which belonged to Hamburg. School finance being what it is, Hamburg later asked that either the ball be returned or Essex buy one in its place. "I don't think there'll be a problem in us coming up with the money for that," said Essex coach Jauron.

Has it occurred to young hero White that this is the play he'll be reliving decades from now?

"What do you mean?" he said.

Well, odds are that no matter what success you have later in life, you'll never be too far from thinking about this runback.

"Hadn't thought about that," he said.

Oh, but he will.

For the first couple of years after Steve White's dash to glory, when young Essex athletes were ordered by their coaches to run 100-yard wind sprints, the coaches often said, "Get out there and run your Steve Whites!"

And 18 years after his dramatic touchdown, nearly all sports fans around the small southwest Iowa community could still recall it. But the heck of it was, no one seemed to know whatever became of Steve White.

He left Essex High in the fall of his senior year, 1989. His family, which was split and blended after parental divorces and new marraiges, moved away a short time later. White himself hadn't had any contact with anybody around Essex for several years.

For six months from the late summer of 2004 into early 2005, I tried to find him. I made more than 70 phone calls. I wrote more than 100 e-mails. People who were charmed by the idea of trying to help chase down a small town Iowa sports hero were very willing to search school records, police records, postal records, even water department records in a half-dozen different communities. His common name made the searches all the more frustrating. I talked to at least nine Steve Whites in different cities across the nation without finding the one I wanted.

When I finally reached his step sister and step mother, they said Steve had fallen out of contact with most of the family. The last they knew, he was working as a firefighter in the Virginia Beach, Virginia, area. I called and e-mailed nearly 20 different fire departments in that area, without finding him.

Finally, I decided to try one last thing – buying a want-ad in the local newspaper – and if that did not lead me to White, I'd give up.

And so on January 21, 2005, readers of the Virginian-Pilot serving the Norfolk and Virginia Beach area saw this ad: "Essex, Iowa, football hero? Looking for the Steve White in Virginia Beach area that beat Hamburg, Iowa., in 1987 on 103-yard fumble return. Call Chuck Offenburger in Iowa (515) 386-5488."

The first call came four days later – from Jason Skog, a reporter for the Virginian-Pilot. "Tell me more about this story, and why it's so important for you to find Steve White," he said. And so I told him.

Skog put a story about my unsuccessful search on page one of the newspaper's next edition. My phone started ringing, and the e-mail messages began arriving, before I was even out of bed in the central time zone. Two dozen Virginian-Pilot readers responded that they knew a Steve White. I called three of the Steves and, by mid-afternoon, I was talking to the old Essex Trojan hero himself.

My first question to him? It was the same one I left him with back in 1987: Is the long-ago touchdown run something he's been reliving ever since?

"The play is still clear in my mind, but I really don't think a lot about it," the 34-year-old White told me. "I suppose there have been 10 or 15 times through the years that I've told somebody about it. Every once in a while, I'll be talking to a buddy about football, and I'll say something about it. Most people listen, look at me and say something like, 'Oh, really? That's cool.' I don't know if they think I'm pulling their leg or not."

When his mother-in-law and several friends saw the story in the Virginian-Pilot and started calling his home and workplace – a U.S. Navy firefighter training center – his wife Suellen McCubbin remembered an old football videotape the couple had in storage. By the time Steve came home from work, she and the couple's daughter Sarah, 7, and Steven Jr., 3, had watched the end of the 1987 game several times. Then they watched it several more times with Steve.

"I had actually forgotten we even had the tape," he said, "but Suellen knew right where to find it upstairs. When I watch it now as an adult, and think about it, it hardly seems real that something like that could happen. I get goose bumps. It's a pretty emotional thing."

Skog, the Virginian-Pilot reporter, wrote a follow-up story a day after I'd talked to White. In fact, the newspaper borrowed White's copy of the game tape and ran a video clip of the 103-yard touchdown run on the paper's Internet site. When Skog's story was picked up by the Associated Press, people across the nation were going to the Internet site to watch the play. At halftime of a basketball game that Friday night at Essex High School in Iowa, Trojan fans packed into the school office, where one of the coaches used a computer to go to the Virginia newspaper's Internet site and let them cheer their favorite sports moment again – and again.

So what had Steve White's path been from Essex to Virginia Beach?

After his big moment in his sophomore football year, he went on to have "a pretty good season" as a junior, when he was a starter at defensive cornerback. But then he "started getting involved in some bad stuff," and wound up dropping out of school three games into his senior year. "I'm one of those with a lot of lessons of life," he said, "and one of them is 'Don't do drugs.' They'll mess up your life, like they did mine."

School was not difficult for him, he said, and "when I dropped out, I went right to the community college, spent three days taking tests and got my GED." He joined the Navy on a delayed enlistment plan, "and that gave me enough time to get my act cleaned up." He said that Navy experience changed his life. "It did me a 180-degree turn-around," he said. "I did a heck of a lot of growing up in the Navy. It taught me discipline and responsibility and a lot of other things that I really needed to learn."

Serving from 1990-94, he did sea duty in the Mediterranean and Red seas, in the effort to enforce United Nations sanctions against Iraq. Then when he was based in the Norfolk area, he met Suellen. After they married, she became an Internet site designer and a bookkeeper who is also a stay-at-home mom. They live in a townhouse in a nice neighborhood of Virginia Beach.Steve not only works as a civilian contracted to train firefighters for the Navy, he does similar work as a senior enlisted man in the Naval Reserve.

White said he devotes as much of his time away from work as possible "to being with my family – while my kids still like me. When they get a little older, they might not like me as much." I asked him if watching his old football video made them even bigger Steve White fans than they were before. "Yeah, right now they are," he said.

He said his wife "gives me a hard time about not staying in better touch with my own family and other people I knew in the past. With all the problems I had, I fell out of touch, and it was easy for me just to disconnect from everybody and try to go on with my life. For me, it was the past – done and over with – and I wanted to be all about now and the future."

He added, however, that he planned to make new contact with his family, and with old friends and coaches in Essex. He said one phone call he would make soon was to his old football coach Dave Jauron. "I did Coach Jauron a bad way when I quit on him in my senior year," White said. "I'm going to call him up and tell him I know that now, and I'm sorry for it."

Part of the fun of finding White – and all the attention his story got after it was published across the nation early in 2005 – is that he is now back in touch with his former Essex High teammates. And he has also heard from Clay Boatman, the former Hamburg running back who fumbled the ball into the end zone back in 1987.

Boatman, 35 in 2005, lives and works in Urbandale on the edge of Des Moines. He is vice-president of a Missouri-based bank that does correspondent banking for financial institutions across Iowa.

So, the two principals in one of Iowa's wildest football plays ever had a good phone conversation. And Boatman pulled out his own copy of the game videotape and watched it several times with friends and co-workers.

"I'm going to appeal!" Boatman said, with a laugh. "I think I had possession of that ball going over the goal line. It's only been 18 years ago, can I still appeal?"

He said he remembers his fellow Hamburg Wildcats being as astonished in defeat that night as the Essex Trojans were astonished in victory.

"It was pretty quiet afterward on our bus as we were heading home," Boatman said. "I was in one of the back seats, and I remember that after a while, our coach Jim Zuck yelled my name out from up front. I said, 'Yeah?' He said, 'We should have knelt on the ball instead of trying to score – not your fault – it was a bad call by me.' That was pretty nice of him."

The Virginian-Pilot reporter Skog checked in with Boatman by e-mail, saying he "was just curious how things turned out for you" after that long ago fumble, adding, "Since you're a bank vice-president, evidently they're not too shabby."

Boatman's response to him: "Haven't had too many sleepless nights since then – just hundreds of thousands of dollars in psychiatric fees! Ha!"

And whatever happened to the historic game ball, the one that Essex High School had to pay for before White could keep?

"Sorry to report that the game ball is gone," Suellen McCubbin reported. "Steve said that he played ball with it until it fell apart. Who knew?"

IOWA'S MOST FAMOUS HIGH SCHOOL SPORTS EVENT. I

used to tell the editors at the Des Moines Register that they did not appreciate the task that their sportswriters were undertaking in their coverage of the annual Iowa High School State Wrestling Tournament.

It's more difficult, I told them, than covering the Iowa Legislature, the Iowa Political Caucuses, the Iowa State Fair, the state championships in other sports or any other big event that happens regularly in Iowa.

Why?

In recent years, 672 wrestlers have qualified. Nearly 90,000 fans buy tickets. Reporters, photographers and technicians come from 50 radio stations and more than 180 newspapers. There are 45 referees, 25 scorers and timers, a dozen directly involved in directing the tournament. It takes six just to supervise getting the winning wrestlers on and off the awards stand at the right times.

"To the uninitiated, it's a four-day car crash – used to be a three-day car crash – but now it lasts four days," said Dan McCool, the veteran wrestling reporter who has been covering the tournament for the Register since 1987.

Dave Harty, who in 35 years as tournament manager built the Iowa tournament into a national phenomenon, said "we have a saying that at the tournament that 'it's halftime all the time.' The crowd is always moving. It's a beehive."

Indeed, in Iowa, high school wrestling fans are devoted. Well, they're beyond devoted. They're just on the polite side of fanatical, actually. And at state tournament time, hundreds of these fans will come from the towns with strong wrestling heritages, if they happen to have even a single wrestler competing.

"It's amazing how many people live for that week," said McCool. "Unbelievable fans, great fans."

A little different from fans of basketball, track and other sports, too, said the IHSAA's Harty.

"The wrestling fan is a different breed, as are the competitors, coaches and officials," he said. "I call it 'blue-collar professional.' They might tell you where to go, but they're good people."

The tournament, as you can guess, receives tremendous media coverage.

113

When Sports Illustrated was celebrating 50 years of publishing in 2004, the magazine's writers fanned out across the U.S. to cover one favorite sporting event in each of the states. In Iowa, Kelli Anderson covered the high school state wrestling tournament.

"In late February, Iowa high school wrestling fans flock, like migratory fowl, to their traditional spots in Veterans Memorial Auditorium in Des Moines," Anderson wrote.

She noted that "even as wrestling is dying out in colleges around the country, the sport thrives in Iowa's high schools." She cited the state tournament's growth over the years from one class to three, and from being held in two days years ago to the four-day run now. "In the early 1960s about 100 Iowa high schools had wrestling programs," she continued. "Today 347 of the 402 schools in the IHSAA are represented on 300 wrestling teams."

Of course, Sports Illustrated does not cover the Iowa high school tournament every year, but the coverage by Iowa media far exceeds what the sport gets in any other state.

"When I go to the National Wrestling Rules Committee meetings, I always take along the sports pages from the Des Moines Register and other newspapers around the state, and show off the full pages of stories, results and photos," said Harty. "The wrestling coordinators from the other states are just shocked. They get nothing like that in their home states. On wrestling, from a media standpoint, we are blessed in Iowa."

And, get this: During the 2004 state wrestling tournament, the IHSAA's site on the Internet – where results of each match are posted – received two million (1,942,592, to be exact) "hits" over the four days.

Wrestling is as big on the college and university level in Iowa as it is in the high schools. Why did the sport become so strong in this state?

"I think it was the influence of our agricultural heritage, our small communities and the work ethic of our people," said Bob Siddens, the retired coach at Waterloo West whose teams won 11 state championships and whose individual champions included the legendary Dan Gable. "The sport really grew up in the northeast part of the state – in places like Cresco, Osage and New Hampton, right on down to Waterloo. The farm people were working class, and back then, it didn't cost much to have a wrestling program."

The more sophisticated the sport became, the more dedication it seemed to demand from its participants, he noted. And again, that fit with the farm work ethic.

Arlo Flege, of Waverly, who refereed wrestling for 40 years, gives credit to such early coaches as Finn Eriksen at New Hampton and Waterloo West, Fred Cooper at Fort Dodge, George Flanagan at Cresco, Howard Barker of Mason City, Dave Natvig at Waterloo East, Leon "Champ" Martin of Algona, Dale Brand of Clarion and others. Such coaches, he said, not only built strong programs of their own but also helped other schools start the sport.

"A whole lot of schools in northeast Iowa started wrestling in the 1940s," Flege said. "Then once the state tournament moved from Waterloo to Des Moines, it really spread to other areas of the state, too."

Another measure of the growth was the start in the middle 1980s of the "State Dual Team" tournament, which follows the state wrestling tournament by a week. At the "dual" tournament the top eight teams in each of the three classes compete for a team championship as opposed to individual championships.

Through the 2005 state tournament, there have been 16 wrestlers who were so dominant that they won state championships all four years they competed in high school.

It takes an extraordinary athlete to do that, of course, since it usually means changing weight classes as they grow, wrestling through minor illnesses and injuries. Those 16, with their senior years noted, are Bob Steenlage, Britt, 1962; Jeff Kerber, Emmetsburg, 1979; Scott Morningstar, Lisbon, 1980; Joe Gibbons, Waterloo Columbus and Ames, 1981; Greg Randall, Mount Vernon, 1982; Mark Schwab, Osage, 1985; Dan Knight, Clinton, 1987; Shane Light, Lisbon, 1990; Jeff McGinness, City High of Iowa City, 1993; Jason Keenan, Ogden, 1995; Eric Juergens, Maquoketa, 1996; Jesse Sundell, Ogden, 2001; Mack Reiter, Don Bosco of Gilbertville, 2003; C.J. Ettelson, Hudson, 2003; Daniel LeClere of North-Linn of Troy Mills, 2005, and Jay Borschel of Linn-Mar of Marion, 2005.

The robust health of the sport in Iowa was well-told after the 2004 state tournament, when the Mason City Globe-Gazette made it the subject of one of its unsigned editorials:

State wrestling tourney remains remarkable event

Iowa's wrestling tournament continues to produce special moments, special champions.

You do not have to be a wrestling fan, even a sports fan, to appreciate what a special event Iowa has in the state wrestling tournament.

Some say the sport is on the decline in other parts of the country. But not in Iowa. The sport's popularity was demonstrated again in the 2004 version of the state tournament.

A sellout crowd, of course, packed Veterans Auditorium in Des Moines on Saturday to witness yet another emotion-charged chapter in the long history of wrestling in Iowa.

There are the kinds of stories that can't be made up; the kinds of stories that truly would make good movie plots; the kinds of stories that will live as long as fans get together in gyms and coffee shops to talk about the ultimate one-on-one competition.

North Iowa proved its strength with 30 place winners emerging from among the 47 wrestlers that went to Des Moines. We detailed their accomplishments – and yes, heartbreak – on our pages throughout the four-day tournament.

Two wrestlers achieved the ultimate goal, with Belmond-Klemme's Jordon McLaughlin winning the Class 1A title at 189 pounds and Clear Lake's Nick Weber capturing the 160-pound title in Class 2A.

Speaking of remarkable stories, you have to look no further than Weber – wrestling for his father, Gary, the well-respected coach of the Lions; placing the previous two years and writing before going to bed every night for a year, "I will be a state champ, I will be a state champ..."

It is the kind of motivation that few of us can understand, and that even fewer of us are willing to allow to drive us.

Finally, that drive paid off. The elusive title was his. Appropriately, he celebrated by jumping into the arms of his father. Appropriately, the tears flowed.

He and McLaughlin achieved perfection with undefeated seasons.

It was, said McLaughlin, "a moment I'll remember for the rest of my life."

To Jordon McLaughlin, Nick Weber and all of you wrestlers who made it to Des Moines: You did it right; you made us proud, and set a high bar for others to follow in coming years."

THE GREAT SMALL-SCHOOL BASEBALL STORIES. In the home dugout on the baseball field where Spalding Catholic High School plays in the town of Granville in northwest Iowa, the sign painted on one wall says: "The Spalding baseball tradition will not be entrusted to the timid or the weak." Pennants above the scoreboard in the outfield signify seven state championships.

On the edge of New Albin in extreme northeast Iowa, the big town sign says: "Welcome to Kee Hawk Country – Iowa's Richest High School Baseball Tradition!" It goes on to list Kee High School's 10 state championship teams and eight more runners-up. The bottom line on the sign notes that coach Gene Schultz is "National Career Wins Leader – 1,250 & Counting!" (His total was an amazing 1,404 after the 2004 season.)

Meanwhile, on the edge of Norway, a town just west of Cedar Rapids in east central Iowa, the sign says: "Welcome to Norway – A great place to come home to," with two baseball bats shown crossed over a home plate. You don't have to be in town long before someone mentions the Redcaps' 17 state baseball championships, including the magical one in the summer of 1991. That was the last activity of Norway High School before consolidation with neighboring towns in the Benton Community School District.

And in little Bancroft in northwest Iowa, where the St. John's High School Johnnies ruled Iowa baseball for nearly 50 years, old timers fondly recall their great coach Vince Meyer saying, 'The only thing basketball is good for is to keep the boys in shape for baseball." He directed the Johnnies to six of their nine state championships before the school closed in 1989.

Obviously, in small town Iowa, high school baseball has been taken very seriously.

Oh, there have been some outstanding programs in the bigger schools, too – notably at Mason City High School, Council Bluffs Thomas Jefferson, Marshalltown, Valley of West Des Moines, Dowling Catholic of West Des Moines, Burlington, Decorah and others. But the small-school teams are the ones that have so often stolen the hearts of the state's fans.

How could they get so good?

In their heydays, many of the small schools in Iowa had no football or track programs, and instead played baseball in spring, summer and fall seasons. The IHSAA sponsored spring state tournaments from 1928 through 1972, state tournaments in the fall from 1939 to 1985 and state tournaments for summer baseball since 1946. So there was a whole lot of baseball being played in small towns in Iowa, especially from the 1940s into the '80s.

Jim Van Scoyoc, the legendary Norway coach for 19 years, remembers that Mike Boddicker, a 1975 graduate who was one of their all-time greatest, "played in 258 baseball games in the four years he played varsity for us. And that's not counting the American Legion games he played on Saturdays." Boddicker rang up 76 career pitching victories and struck out 1,122 – and he is still the state leader in both categories. He was so good he went on to become All-Big 10 at the University of Iowa, then had a 15-year major league career with the Baltimore Orioles, Boston Red Sox, Kansas City Royals and Milwaukee Brewers.

You forget just how good some of the old baseball stories are about these small-school powerhouses.

Bancroft fans say the reason St. John's High School developed such a strong baseball tradition was not because of Vince Meyer, actually, but rather because of Monsignor Joseph "Smokey Joe" Schultes, who was the Catholic pastor in the community from 1933 to 1967 – as well as a frequent pitcher on the town baseball team.

The monsignor's nickname, said former Bancroft mayor Paul Bernhard who was a 1946 St. John's graduate, "came from the fact that he smoked a cigar and he could throw smoke, too."

118

Schultes insisted his parish's high school would have good baseball. But in 1935, he was caught without a coach. In fact, the only available man for the job was his new English teacher Vincent James Meyer, whom he had just hired straight out of Columbia College (now Loras) in Dubuque. Meyer, a native of Elkader, had graduated from old St. Joseph High School in that community, but he apparently had not been involved in sports there.

"Meyer said later that he had never played baseball at all," said Bill Dudding, a semi-retired truck driver and a 1950 St. John's graduate. He is Bancroft's unofficial baseball historian. "And he'd never even been in a gym before he came here," Dudding continued. "But it turned out that what he was, really, was a great teacher. A lot of St. John's graduates will tell you he was the best they ever had. So, Monsignor Schultes taught Meyer what he needed to know about baseball, and then told him to teach it to the kids."

The monsignor also persuaded local grain elevator owner Art Murray to donate land and money to build St. John Athletic Field, the forerunner to beautiful Bancroft Memorial Park that is still in use today. Murray also occasionally coached the local American Legion team.

Meyer rounded up generations of the Vaskes, Hattens, Bernhards, Menkes, Schiltzes, Wesselmans, Elsbeckers and others, and turned them into an enduring baseball juggernaut.

And, oh, was he tough!

In the classroom, he was a taskmaster, one known for launching erasers at students across the classroom if they were not paying attention or misbehaving. In fact, in one of his first years of teaching, he threw an eraser at Mary Williams – who in 1943 became his wife.

He left St. John's to spend three years in the military during World War II.

"Meyer was pretty good at cussing before he went to the service," said Bernhard, "and he was a lot better at it when he came home."

The coach would occasionally turn that loose with the baseball players. "I don't ever remember him ranting or raving on the field, but he sure would in the dugout," Bernhard continued. "If you made a physical error on the field, it was no big deal. But if you made a mental error, oh! He'd chew your ass. But later he'd joke about it and refer to it as 'corrective criticism.' "

One of Meyer's best players was Denis Menke, a 1958 graduate who signed a professional contract with the Milwaukee Braves and had a 16-year major league career with the Braves, Houston Astros and Cincinnati Reds. He is one of two major league players the community produced, the other pitcher Joe "Lefty" Hatten, who spent seven years with the Dodgers and Cubs in the late 1940s and early '50s.

Eventually, government and economics were added to Meyer's teaching load. His economics class for years operated the St. John School Bazaar, which raised thousands of dollars for the school. And he was always a hard worker in the community. He wrote-up all the Johnnies' game stories for the Bancroft Register. For 25 years, he directed the community's summer playground program. For a dozen years, he managed the local swimming pool and the movie theater, too. His wife Mary would sell tickets to home games at Memorial Park, and the two of them even operated the concession stand occasionally. Meyer had the baseball players so well trained that they'd do the field preparation and pre-game warm-ups on their own. Then he'd slip into the dugout just before game time, always wearing khaki trousers, a white knit sport shirt and ball cap with St. John's logo.

He had great teams right through his final season in 1981. He died that October. He'd been having heart trouble for several years, and in his last two seasons, he was taking nitro pills and using oxygen in the dugout during games. The state championship game in 1980 surely tested his heart – the Johnnies lost 4 to 3 to Kee in 13 innings.

But Vince Meyer did not lose many. The man who knew no baseball when he arrived in Bancroft in 1935, directed his teams to 1,105 victories against just 179 losses – and that landed him in the National High School Sports Hall of Fame.

He was succeeded as baseball coach at St. John's by one of his former players, Gene Meister, who won two summer state championships with the Johnnies in the 1980s. After St. John's closed, Meister went on to build a great baseball program at Bishop Garrigan High School in nearby Algona, and eventually became superintendent there.

Even in 2005, 15 years after St. John's last played, baseball fans from around the state still show up in Bancroft to walk on the diamond at Memorial Park. Strangers often are in the stands watching the North Kossuth Cougars, the team from the public school in nearby Swea City that now plays its home games in Bancroft. They seek out conversations about Coach Meyer, the Johnnies and the great winning tradition in the community. I've done that many times myself.

In fact, in the fall of 1997, I had David Morain, then a junior at Jefferson-Scranton in west central Iowa, traveling with me while I was going to Ringsted, one of Bancroft's neighboring towns, for a column I was doing for the Des Moines Register. On the way up, young Morain was telling me that he was a baseball player, and I started telling him the story of Bancroft St. John's.

"Chuck told me how it had been the Mecca of high school baseball in Iowa for more than a generation," Morain later wrote. "He said that before schools were separated into classes by size, St. John's would challenge and dispose of teams from bigger cities with student bodies many times larger."

As interested as my passenger was, I decided we had to make a side trip to see the Bancroft ballpark.

"I was in love with the stadium before we even entered it," Morain wrote. "It was like something from a baseball time capsule, complete with wooden bleachers, cavernous dugouts and a tall, dark fence enclosing the spacious outfield. It was baseball at its purest. I could almost imagine the likes of Honus Wagner, Tris Speaker or Nap Lajoie taking grounders on a field much like it, a century ago. I didn't ask many questions as we stood behind home plate. I think Chuck was talking about some of the players who used to play there, but all I remember was feeling incredibly jealous of the high school team that got to play at a cathedral like this.

"I got my chance a year later. My baseball coach Jim Henrich at Jefferson-Scranton set up an early season game against North Kossuth in the Bancroft stadium. Even though it was a two-hour bus ride, and the day was cold and gray, playing there was one of the great thrills of my high school baseball career. We lost that day against North Kossuth, but I never regretted being able to experience the finest stadium in all of Iowa, even if it was only for one game."

As the St. John's tradition was winding down, it was almost like a handoff was made to the baseball programs at three other Catholic high schools in northwest Iowa – Spalding Catholic and Bishop Garrigan, which have already been mentioned here, and Remsen St. Mary's. The latter won three consecutive championships from 1983 to 1985 under coach Marv Thelen.

Meanwhile, the programs at little Norway and Kee High of Lansing and New Albin were also in full bloom.

"Norway had always been a good baseball town, and it was in the 1960s when the high school program really came along," said Van Scoyoc, who coached through the 1990 season. Then he coached three years in the professional baseball's minor leagues with teams affiliated with the Detroit Tigers. In 2005, he was working at a Cedar Rapids industry, coached pitching at Kirkwood Community College and was traveling the U.S. evaluating ball players for a major league scouting service.

Van Scoyoc credits Bernie Hutchison, his predecessor as Norway High baseball coach, with developing the program.

"One of Bernie's biggest assets as a coach was he could make amazingly quick decisions," Van Scoyoc said. "But he also really knew how to teach baseball fundamentals. He worked with three men in town – Lyle Kimm, Wayne Kimm and Gary Butz – on getting the little kids started on the fundamentals. Then by the time they got to high school, we could start them at a higher level. They already knew by then when to take a pitch, when to turn up the aggressiveness, when to lean into a pitch. That made it very easy on us as high school coaches."

Van Scoyoc says in the glory years in the town of 600, "we had about 140 students in high school, and maybe 60 of them were boys. Of those, we'd get 40 coming out for baseball. We'd run two complete programs, and keep as many kids playing as we could."

Every couple of years, the Norway Tigers – the "Redcaps" mentioned earlier was a more informal nickname they also used – would have a new star who would be the talk of the state: Bob Byers, Rick Ryan, Dick McVay, Bruce Kimm, Max Elliott, Steve Stumpff, Mike Boddicker. It seemed there were always Brechts, Schultes, Freses, Kuesters, Kims and Van Scoyocs in starring roles, too.

In the 1991 season, Norway's last with a high school team, the team won the championship with a first-year coach Kent Stock. That story is to be made into a movie "The Final Season" in the summer of 2005, shot on location around Norway by a Hollywood production company, with actors Sean Astin, Sam Elliott and Katherine Ross in starring roles.

Meanwhile, Van Scoyoc says it was good that the professional baseball job had lured him away from Norway for that final season.

"It saved me a ton of trouble because I have a big mouth," he said. "I was not the least bit in favor of closing our school." Now, more than a dozen years after the closing, he says he has "a mixture of feelings about it all. I'm proud, more than anything else, of the way the Norway kids played all those years, but I'm still sad that it's over."

In Iowa's northeastern most town of New Albin, pop. 600, they regard "Shooky" Fink Memorial Field as hallowed ground.

Lush farm fields ring the outfield, with the Upper Iowa River flowing just beyond them. Spectacular wooded bluffs, 300 feet high, nearly surround the valley in which the picturesque little ball diamond nestles with its small covered grandstand, press box and concession stand.

This is where Harris "Shooky" Fink for decades taught the kids of the community how to play ball.

"He'd start working with them from the time they could carry a glove," said Kee High baseball coach Gene Schultz, the nation's winningest high school baseball coach.

Schultz says he and Kee baseball are still benefiting from the tradition Fink established, even though he has been dead since 1988.

"Shooky" was a school custodian in New Albin, and the nickname came from the fact that "he talked so fast a lot of people couldn't understand him," said his son Dana Fink, now a newspaperman in Perry, Iowa. "He'd really get going."

Schultz recalled him as "a guy who'd talk a mile a minute. He'd start three sentences and never finish any of them. And, he wore these wire rim glasses. The frames had been broken so many times that they had a welded spot about every millimeter – and Shooky welded them himself. You'll never meet another one like him, I'll tell you that."

And what a baseball man.

"Every day in the summer, 11 a.m., Shooky would have practice and all the kids would be there," Schultz said. "Then he'd load them up in a couple of cars and take them to games all over the area. They always had a mix of jeans and T-shirts and maybe a few uniforms. Shooky didn't care how they looked as long as they played well."

And they did.

They were also just waiting for a high school coach like Schultz to come along. He arrived in 1969, fresh out of Winona State University in his hometown of Winona, Minnesota.

"The towns of Lansing, New Albin, Harpers Ferry and Churchtown had just consolidated their public schools, and there was still a rift – especially between Lansing and New Albin," Schultz said. "In fact, it took us another 20 years for people really to begin accepting it, and the fact that we were good in baseball helped. It was something that brought people together."

The school is actually Eastern Allamakee Community, but everybody has always called it Kee High.

Schultz was hired to coach baseball and basketball, and in August of '69, he arrived in Lansing, the town of 1,000 where the high school is located.

"After word got around that I was in town, the superintendent called and said the kids were waiting for a meeting to get the baseball season started," Schultz said. "I said, 'What? Already?' And he said, 'Well, you've got a game next week!' That was a shock to me. I'd never understood that we were playing fall baseball in addition to spring ball."

So he quickly launched his first team and they played 16 games that fall, 28 the next spring. Everyone around the area was shocked that the new coach wanted to play that many in the spring season – the norm had been about 15 or 16 – but Schultz was only getting started. By his second spring season, he had his team playing every day possible from April 1 to the end of May. In his third year, he added a summer season, and the Kee Hawks then

124

played baseball from April 1 into October. That continued until 1981 when the school abandoned fall baseball in favor of its then-new football program. One year, spring through fall, they played 69 games!

They also had some disputes with the IHSAA over how many games they could play and how many players they could carry on the squad. One of those fusses wound up in District Court before Kee High and the athletic association reached an agreement.

The Kee Hawks weren't big winners immediately. After all, the new Kee High in the fall of 1969 had only 119 students from kindergarten through high school. St. George Catholic School, just up the street, was still in existence and had a larger high school enrollment than Kee, but officials there knew the tough finances of private education were threatening St. George's future. It closed in the spring of 1973.

"By that time, we had a pretty good team," Schultz said. "We were undefeated that spring of '73 with our own kids, then we added the St. George kids for the summer season, and we wound up going 47-0 and winning our first state championship. After that, things really came together."

In the 1980s and early '90s, the Kee Hawks were flying high. They won four consecutive championships from 1989 through 1992, with summer records of 35-12, 45-2, 46-1 and 46-1. That four-year record adds up to 172-16, and that two-year record of 92-2 in the 1991 and '92 seasons sounds like fiction! But indeed it happened.

The names of the Kee players – Heiderscheit, Peters, Fink, Darling, Imhoff, Brennan, Shepard – could be quickly recalled by baseball fans across the state.

You can actually see the tradition now by walking into the front hallway of Kee High in Lansing. Schultz maintains a baseball record board there that has team and individual statistical leaders listed in 120 or more different categories – including some odd ones like "most runs scored with two outs." Of course, all the state championship and runner-up trophies are displayed there, too.

And at "Shooky" Fink Memorial Field, there is now what must be the largest scoreboard used by a high school anywhere in Iowa, maybe beyond. It was a computer-driven, $30,000 scoreboard when North Carolina State

University bought and began using it. In the spring of 2003, a Kee High alumnus Brad Wild spotted it for sale on the "eBay" site on the Internet for "$1,000 minimum." Wild got in touch with the equipment manager at N.C. State, told him about the Kee High baseball program and its interest in the scoreboard. The university then offered it for $100 if the Iowa high school could find a way to transport it. Kee High boosters eventually found a trucker with a 40-foot flatbed trailer to haul it to Iowa for $1,350. After investing another $850, they had it set up beyond the outfield fence and in use during the 2004 season.

Schultz, 58 years old in 2005, has continued as head baseball and boys' basketball coach at Kee High despite having retired from teaching physical education. In 2002, his alma mater Winona State asked if he'd be interested in returning as their varsity baseball coach.

"I've always pushed so hard on the fundamentals and discipline and being in shape, I think I'd have trouble with the college game," he said. "I'd especially have trouble recruiting kids. Today a lot of those college players ask, 'What are you going to give me?' I doubt they'd react real well when I'd say, 'Uh, laps and discipline.'"

How long does he intend to keep coaching at Kee High?

"I've always said I'd go until my younger son comes through," Schultz said.

That is Quin, a freshman at Kee High in the 2004-05 school year. He is a talented athlete who skipped baseball in the summer of 2004 after being injured earlier in the spring when he was struck in the face by a ground ball. But he will likely be back in the baseball line-up for the Kee Hawks with his brother Gabe, now a junior. Gene Schultz and his wife Julie also have daughters Courtney and McKenze, who are students at Iowa State University.

When the retirement question came up again in an interview during the 2004 season with the LaCrosse Tribune in neighboring Wisconsin, the coach mentioned that his sons are playing high school ball now, but then added, "I also have a couple of nephews in sixth and seventh grade."

So the lead that Schultz has on all other high school baseball coaches in the nation for career victories is likely to be extended considerably before he eventually retires.

Many of those other coaches probably doubt that Iowa is as good a place to be a high school baseball coach has Schultz has found it. It s the only state in which interscholastic baseball competition is held in he summer, a time when the weather is much nicer in Iowa and there is ess competition from other sports and school activities for the time and attention of athletes and fans alike.

"I think it's a model for other states to look at, especially northern states," Schultz said.

One thing he knows – it's hard to beat a summer night at a ball game on "Shooky" Fink Memorial Field in New Albin, Iowa.

ALL IN THE FAMILY. Is there a "first family of high school boys' sports in Iowa"?

If you were going to name one from the first century of the IHSAA, you would certainly have to consider the Breitbachs of Cedar Rapids Regis. Brothers John, Dick, Tom, Dan and Mike all played several sports at Regis in the 1980s, and their father Dick Breitbach was often their coach. In fact, the Breitbach boys were stars on their dad's teams that won three consecutive state basketball titles from 1982-84. In the fall of 1998, Regis High School became part of the new Xavier High School serving the Cedar Rapids Catholic community.

Also not to be forgotten are the Rubleys of Davenport Assumption and later Davenport West. Six of the seven Rubley brothers were outstanding quarterbacks – Tim and Ted for Assumption in the 1970s, and then Terry, Todd, Trent and T.J. for Davenport West from the mid 1970s to the late 1980s. Their brother Tom couldn't play sports because of a childhood illness, but he became the public address announcer for basketball games at Davenport West for 18 years.

But as best as I could determine, no family can match the record of the Tryons from little Glidden, pop. 1,250, in west central Iowa.

There were eight brothers and two sisters. The boys were all excellent athletes. The girls, in an era when Glidden offered no girls' sports, were both cheerleaders. With that many of them involved, there was a Tryon on the field or court for the Glidden Wildcats from 1946 to 1973.

But the real clincher for the Tryons being the first family of Iowa boys' high school sports is what they did as adults. Seven of the brothers became teachers and coaches in Iowa. And both sisters married men who taught and coached in Iowa. And all the Tryons have been as successful in coaching as they were when they were competing as athletes.

"We're proud of them in Glidden, I can tell you that," said Dick Onken, a 1952 graduate who was a teammate of several of the Tryons. "Every one of them was a good athlete, right on down the line, and they were good students, too. It seemed like we always had a Tryon as quarterback in football."

Bill Ferguson, 87 years old in 2005, and retired in Apache Junction, Arizona, was principal at Glidden High School when the oldest Tryons came through.

Then he left education and became editor and publisher of the Glidden Graphic newspaper. So he was involved in some of the coverage of Glidden High teams.

"When I look back on that, we didn't make much over them, really," Ferguson said. "Oh, I wrote about them some, of course, but it was more, 'Here comes another Tryon!' Now that I think back of how many of them there were, and how long they played, we probably should have made a little more out of them, you know?"

The Tryons are the sons and daughters of the late Clarence and Dorothy Tryon.

"We're told that Dad was an outstanding basketball, baseball and softball player while growing up in the small town of Defiance, Iowa," said Dale Tryon, who has retired in Ames. "When he was a senior, he was on the basketball team, and they had only one cheerleader – our mother, who was in the junior class at the time."

After he got out of high school, Clarence Tryon operated a combination feed store, hatchery and produce house for several years in Defiance, then in 1944 he and Dorothy and their growing young family moved to Glidden. They bought a feed store and hatchery downtown, and a house directly across the street from Glidden High School. Clarence served as president of the school board for more than 20 years, which covered most

128

of the time the Tryon kids were going through school, and in 1975 Dorothy was named "Iowa Mother of the Year."

Their oldest son Ray, who graduated in 1948, set the stage in sports, becoming an all-conference basketball player and turning down a chance to sign a professional baseball contract to pitch in the Chicago Cubs organization. Then came Bill, Dale, Gaylord, Larry, Jerry, Dick and Randy. Their sisters are Donna and Nancy. Most of the brothers made all-conference and several won all-state honors while competing in football, basketball, baseball and occasionally track. In the late 1940s and early '50s, they were joined on the Glidden teams by their first cousins Ken and Jim Hulsebus, who had moved from Cooper in order to play with the Tryons.

They all helped teach each other in sports.

"I can remember as kids, our first taste of backyard basketball consisted of putting a bottomless cardboard box about eight feet high on a tree," Dale said. "We would use a tin can of rolled up socks for the ball. We had no rules. We could push, shove, tackle and run around until one person on the team finally got the can through the basket. It was usually a three-on-three game, and we'd find a neighbor boy or two to help fill out the teams if we needed to. Mostly we got along great. However, I can remember one time that I got mad and threw the can at one of my brothers. It hit him right behind the head. When we'd have our occasional small fights, we would soon be back playing together again.

"The brothers always tried to help each other out. I remember one day, my older brother took time off his work and went to the baseball field to hit me about 100 ground balls. Another thing that we would do was pitch a ping pong ball, and somebody else would try to hit it with a board from an egg case, cut up to look like a bat. It really helped teach you to keep your eye on the ball, as you could make those light ping pong balls do strange things – curve, rise, drop. Another thing we did to help eye-hand coordination was play a lot of table tennis. We had a great room in the basement, where the table was set up, and all of us played. We would have serious competition every time we got together, even years later."

Their teammate Bill Weller lived on a farm, on the edge of Glidden, and the bar had a haymow that became a basketball court. "We put baskets at each end and had many good times playing basketball there, especially on winter days," Dale recalled. "More than once, a player would fall down one of the openings in the floor that were used to get up into the haymow."

Glidden High had a run of real sports success during the Tryon years, finishing second in the state baseball tournament in 1950 and enjoying an undefeated football season in 1953.

Most of the brothers went on to Buena Vista College, and several became stars for the Beaver teams.

When they went on into coaching, at one point, there were five Tryon brothers serving as head football coaches at high schools located on U.S. Highway 30 – Dale at Cedar Rapids Kennedy, Dick at Nevada, Larry at Ogden, Bill at Carroll and Jerry at Ar-We-Va. They were known then as "The Highway 30 Connection."

Brother Gaylord, after teaching and coaching at Sac City, became an administrator at Arthur and then Ames, eventually becoming executive secretary of the School Administrators of Iowa.

In the 2004-05 school year, one brother was still coaching – Randy at Adel-DeSoto-Minburn, where he has volleyball and girls' basketball.

When you tally up all the schools the Tryon brothers and their brothers-in-law Bruce Stevens and Warren Watson coached at, it is amazing – Sanborn, Storm Lake, Carroll, Denison, Manson, Audubon, Cedar Rapids Kennedy, Ames, Boone, Sac City, Battle Creek, Rockwell City, Perry, Spencer, Ogden, Pomeroy, Ballard, Alta, Jefferson, Ar-We-Va, Guthrie Center, Nevada, Meriden-Cleghorn, Interstate 35, ADM, Galva, Charter Oak-Ute, Lake View-Auburn, Atlantic, Elk Horn-Kimballton and the University of Iowa.

The Tryons' sons and daughters did well in high school sports, too, with 11 of them winning all-state honors in a variety of sports.

There were similarities in the teams that the Tryon brothers and brothers-in-law coached.

"It was always important to us that we were building character among our players," Dale said. "It was important to us that an athlete was a better person for having played sports on our teams. We also all believed that having a large turnout of players was important, and we made sure all kids got to play each week. We would find a spot for them, even if it was just being on the field goal team.

"We all tried to be 'positive' with our athletes. We'd spend a lot of time patting our players on the back and encouraging them. Being negative, swearing at players, putting down players in front of others – that was never part of our coaching philosophy."

They all stressed "making athletics fun, especially the practices," he said. "I would set aside about five minutes in practice to have a 'fun' thing to do. Sometimes it'd be having the team divide up for a tug-of-war contest, or a sack race, and the winning teams would not have to run sprints after practice. By including things like that, players would really look forward to coming to practice rather than dreading it."

All the Tryons were early believers in the value of lifting weights.

Dale said he thinks "that the former University of Iowa coach Forrest Evashevski had a lot of influence on our coaching style. We all owned Evy's book, and we all ran his 'Wing T' offense in football."

But the ultimate influence, he noted, was the credo the Tryon parents used with their sons – "faith, family, fun and football, in that order."

ANOTHER FAMILY ACT OF SPECIAL NOTE – THE PETTITS OF CARROLL. Todd and Pam Pettit have 12 children who, in the spring of 2005, ranged in age from 28 down to 2, "and they're all athletes, or look like they will be," Todd said.

"We're up to six boys and six girls now, and they all seem to be golfers and basketball players, with maybe a little baseball stirred in, too," said the proud dad.

The four oldest have certainly set a high standard.

Ben was the Class 3A state golf champion in 1994 for the Carroll High Tigers, then was a top golfer for Drake University and is now a professional golfer playing on the Canadian tour.

Tiffany, now living in Waukee, played on Carroll High's state champion girls' basketball teams in 1996 and '97 and was also a good golfer.

Nate won the Class 3A state golf championship in 2000 and was also a three-year letterman in basketball for Carroll High. He is now a scholarship golfer at Colorado State University.

Wade won the Class 3A golf championship in both 2004 and 2005. In his senior season of 2005, he got the chance to play with his brother Kirby, a freshman on the Tigers' team. Wade was also on the Carroll basketball team that finished third in the 2005 state tournament.

When Wade became the third Pettit brother to win the individual golf championship, the Carroll Daily Times Herald observed, "Once could be luck, twice a coincidence, but three times? That's a trend, or in sports, a dynasty."

There's little doubt where the Pettit kids got their athletic talent. Todd and Pam, both 46 in 2005, were classmates and good athletes at Carroll High. Todd was a four-year letter winner in baseball and golf, and Pam lettered in both basketball and track. "We got together our freshman year for homecoming, and she's been putting up with me ever since," Todd said.

They operate a car wash as well as a truck and trailer rental service.

"I guess people will be reading about Pettits playing in Carroll for a long time," Todd said. "And when we get to the youngest, we'll be doubling-up. We've got twins that are 4 and a half years old now (in 2005) and twins that are 2."

OUR ALL-TIME BESTS IN TENNIS. Forty years separated the two players who were probably the best singles players in Iowa high school tennis competition.

Art Andrews, of City High in Iowa City, won three consecutive state championships from 1953 to 1955. Tyler Cleveland, of the Maharashi School for the Age of Enlightenment in Fairfield, won three from 1995 to 1997. They're the only two players to win three state titles. Both went on to become the No. 1 player on teams at the University of Iowa, and both won Big 10 Conference championships.

Andrews, 67 when he retired from full-time teaching at the University of Arizona College of Law in late 2004, said that his success in tennis "was all due to Don Klotz, who coached me from the time I was a little boy, and to the fortuity of growing up in the same town where he happened to be living."

It's quite a story.

"My father died when I was six months old, and so my mother was raising four of us and doing whatever she could do to get by," Andrews said. "We lived across the street from the University of Iowa athletic facilities. Don Klotz, who was a young single guy coaching the university's tennis team, found the Andrews boys playing tennis in the street, took an interest and started coaching us. Our mother would rent out rooms in our house, so Don even roomed at our house before he got married."

Both Art and his older brother Jamie developed into terrific players. Jamie won two state singles championships at City High, including in his senior year of 1952, when Art was a freshman.

"You could play in either singles or doubles in that era, but not both," he said. "Because Jamie was playing No. 1 singles for us in 1952, I teamed up with Ted Dunnington in doubles for the tournaments and we won that title."

The next three years, Art won the singles championships. He played at 5 ft., 11 in. and medium weight, "and always was pretty mobile," he said.

"I suppose the strength of my game was back-court play," he recalled. "I was brought up playing on clay courts, so a big serve wasn't as much as an advantage as it is on faster courts. We played the state tournaments on hard courts, so my back-court play helped make-up for the fact that I didn't have a real strong serve."

He won a Nile Kinnick Scholarship for outstanding scholar athletes at the University of Iowa, graduated Phi Beta Kappa and had an excellent tennis career. At graduation, he was invited to try out for the U.S. Davis Cup team. He went on to law school at New York University, and in 1968 began teaching law in Arizona.

In his 36 years teaching full-time, Andrews was honored several times for his work with students. But the highest honor came at his retirement ceremony, when three former students surprised him by announcing they had raised $500,000 from other alumni and his faculty colleagues to endow a law school professorship in Andrews' name. In 2005, he continued teaching part-time.

Jamie Andrews, incidentally, served as a professor at the University of Iowa and in 2005, lived in retirement in Iowa City.

Art Andrews said he continued to play tennis into the 1970s when he "developed a bad hip and gradually quit playing. Now I just play a very mild form of the game occasionally."

Tyler Cleveland, the best athlete that the Maharishi School has produced in its first three decades in Fairfield, went on to become a financial broker in Chicago after his graduation from the University of Iowa in 2001. After two years in business, however, he decided to give professional tennis a try, and at age 26 in 2005, was playing on a tour in California.

In addition to tennis in high school, the 6 ft., 4 in., 175-pound Cleveland played basketball and baseball and ran cross-country.

The Maharashi School was established primarily to serve the children of Transcendental Meditators who began moving to Fairfield after Maharishi Mahesh Yogi, of India, established a university in the southeast Iowa community in 1971. The Maharishi University of Management now occupies the former campus of the defunct Parsons College.

The Maharishi School was established for children of elementary school age, with more advanced academic programs being added as they grew up. The first high school graduating class was in 1985. It quickly became known for its success in academic and fine arts competitions. Athletic success came later for the "Pioneers," as they are nicknamed, and frequently involved one of the Clevelands. Tyler's older brother Kyle and their sister Heidi both were good tennis players at Maharishi School, and in 2005 Kyle is a teaching pro in the sport in Fairfield.

Among several two-time state singles champions in IHSAA tennis competition is Roger Knapp, of Des Moines Hoover, who is also one of the best players the state has produced.

Knapp won the state titles in 1975 and '76. He was an outstanding all-around athlete as a youngster, then focused on tennis in high school and also played in national amateur competition. He won a tennis scholarship at the University of Southern California, where he was a two-time All-American doubles player. In the early 1990s, he came back to Des Moines, and for five years served as head coach of the Drake University tennis program. His men's teams there won Missouri Valley Conference championships in 1992 and 1993.

In 2005, the 45-year-old Knapp is involved in real estate development

---

in Sarasota, Florida, where he is "fading out of tennis and getting into golf more," he said. "The only tennis coaching I'm doing now is a little with my daughters."

Another individual player who deserves special mention – for tenacity as well as for his considerable ability – is Kirk Schuler of Red Oak. In all four of his high school years that he reached the state competition, he played the championship match in singles competition. And in all four years, he finished runner-up. Maharishi School's Tyler Cleveland beat him in 1996 and 1997, Dan Delorbe of Waterloo Columbus beat him in 1998 and Maharashi School's Naren Clark beat him in 1999. Schuler went on to have a good tennis career at Drake.

Des Moines Roosevelt has had one of the strongest tennis programs through the years, with 12 Roughriders winning singles championships. Maharishi School, however, has had seven win singles titles, and the school has only been in existence since the 1980s. Camanche has dominated team tennis, in which competition was initiated in 1983, winning nine championships.

THE GOLDEN BOY OF IOWA HIGH SCHOOL SWIMMING.
Mark Wagner, the veteran swimming coach at Valley High School of West Des Moines, is quick to tell you what it's like, as a coach, when you realize you've got a once-in-a-career caliber of athlete right in front of you, ready to compete.

"I was lucky to be there when Craig Oppel came through," said Wagner. "I'd just unlock the pool door, turn on the lights and get out of his way. It was one sweet ride. It really was."

When Oppel graduated in 1985, he owned the state records in five high school swimming events – the freestyle at 50, 100, 200 and 500 yards, as well as the 100-yard butterfly – "and no one else has ever come close to doing that," Wagner said.

His 200 freestyle record of 1:36.36 still stands in Iowa. It stood for six years as the national record before it was broken.

Oppel won a swimming scholarship in the powerful program at UCLA, won the 200-meter freestyle national championship in 1987 and was a 24-time All-American by finishing among the top eight in events in the NCAA championships.

Capping his career, in the 1988 Olympics in Seoul, South Korea, he was on the 4-by-200 relay team which won the gold medal for the United States.

Little wonder why Wagner is still talking about Oppel 20 years after the young swimmer graduated from Valley.

"I've had teams over the 20 years say to me, 'Are we ever going to hear about anybody else besides Craig Oppel?' " Wagner said. "I tell them, 'Guys, you get as good as he was and I'll talk about you for the next 20 years.' "

How does it all seem now to Oppel?

"Like it was a long time ago," he said from Muscatine, where he is a lawyer. "I look back on it as something I was lucky enough to do, with a lot of help – from my parents and good coaches. But honestly, it's not something I dwell on now."

Oppel gave up swimming after graduating from UCLA, although he "did play a little water polo when I was going through law school" at Drake in Des Moines. He also earned a master's degree in communications and business at Syracuse University in New York.

"I can't say that I miss swimming now," Oppel said. "I mortgaged my childhood to the sport, which I was willing to do in order to swim at the levels I did. But after college and the Olympics, I was ready to move on. I still like to watch swimming, but I got to the point where I wasn't interested in competing any more."

The Oppel family moved to West Des Moines from the Omaha, Nebraska, area, where Craig's father finished a career in the U.S. Air Force. He accepted a job with the Iowa Department of Transportation that brought the family to central Iowa.

The four Oppel kids were all swimmers. The oldest, sisters Sherry and Sandy, swam in college for Texas Tech and the University of California at Santa Barbara, respectively. When the Oppels moved to Iowa, brother Curt was a high school junior – he swam two years for Valley – and Craig was a sixth grader.

"You could already see Craig was going to be something special," Wagner, the Valley coach, said. "He'd been winning age-group trophies in swimming from the time he was seven or eight years old."

The Oppel parents, along with the families of some other promising swimmers, organized the Des Moines Swimming Federation to give their kids year 'round coaching and more opportunities to compete.mThe federation hired Mike Burton, who'd been a swimmer on the 1968 and 1972 U.S. Olympic teams.

"I was only too happy to have our kids getting help from Mike Burton," said Wagner. "Some parents thought I might be upset by the kids having another coach, but it didn't bother me at all. He'd been places in swimming I'd never been, and I learned a lot working with him."

Craig Oppel grew to 6 ft., 3 in. and about 190 pounds when he was competing in high school, so he was an unusually big and strong swimmer.

"You know, I don't think he ever won much as a freshman, but then when he started to mature more, he became the dominant force in Iowa swimming – more than anybody we've seen since then," said Wagner.

Oppel said after going to college on the West Coast, then doing part of his graduate work in New York, he decided Iowa "was more livable" and wanted to settle here. His parents had moved away, but his brother Curt was practicing law in Davenport, so Craig looked for opportunities in that area In the firm he joined in Muscatine, he spends most of his time representing financial institutions. He's married with two young children. "Neither of them is a swimmer," he said. "We're all snow skiers now."

After Oppel's era at Valley, four other Iowa high school swimmers have approached his level of dominance, although never equaling it. They are Chris Eckerman, of West Des Moines Dowling, who graduated in 1993; Ian Renner-Arjes, of Bettendorf, 1999; and Sean Osborne, of Cedar Falls, and Andrew Van Meter, of Ames, in 2003.

Osborne, Eckerman and Van Meter each hold two of the current state records.

Van Meter and Renner-Arjes are tied for most gold medals in state meets, with 10 each. Van Meter won eight in individual events and two in relays, while Renner-Arjes won seven in individuals events and three in relays.

Cedar Rapids Washington has the most team swimming titles, with 26, having had the state's leading prep program in earlier years, but the Warriors have not won one since 1997.

At the turn of the century, Cedar Falls High School came on strong, winning the titles in both 2004 and 2005 under veteran coach Richard Marcussen.

In fact, Marcussen himself won an honor that really signified a whole new level of recognition for swimming among the sports in Iowa's high school athletic program. That was in 1998 when the Des Moines Register named him the "high school coach of the year" in the state, an honor that has most often gone to a football or basketball coach.

Marcussen, a Cedar Falls native who joined the faculty at his alma mater in 1967, started the swimming program there. He coaches both the girls' and boys' teams. Both teams won state championships in 1993, and the girls' team has been dominating competition ever since. His boys' teams have come on strong in more recent years.

A fine arts teacher, Marcussen never was a competitive swimmer.

"I was coaching sophomore football and an assistant in wrestling and this opened up," he told the Register's chief prep sports writer John Naughton. "I thought I'd give it a try and have been at it ever since. I did a lot of reading. That was the only place I could learn swimming. Other coaches helped me out."

OUR MOST LEGENDARY COACH IN 100 YEARS? There have been thousands of good coaches in the 100 years of the Iowa High School Athletic Association, and dozens of great ones.

Anybody's list of the best would include Russ Kraai, of Holstein, who coached 45 years in both boys' and girls' sports.

When Kraai died late in 2004 at the age of 89, Sioux City Journal sports editor Terry Hersom recalled that in Kraai's 25 years as a football coach, his teams had 12 undefeated seasons. His boys' basketball teams in 16 seasons won eight conference titles. He coached girls' basketball 39 years, had 10 undefeated regular seasons and made the state tournament 11 times, finishing runner-up twice. He coached track for 45 years, Hersom wrote, "including 41 in which he ran what was once the largest track meet in the state – the Holstein Relays." He added: "Kraai's love for young people didn't stop at the end of the school year, either. For 50 years, he hired between 700 and 800 youngsters each summer, directing detasseling crews for DeKalb."

But there have been many others whose impact was also great:

Baseball coaches Gene Schultz of Kee of Lansing, Vince Meyer of Bancroft St. John, Bill Freese of Davenport Central, Jim Van Scoyoc of Norway and Dennis Olejniczak of Decorah.

Track coaches John Raffensperger of City High of Iowa City, John Sletten and Hiram "Hi" Covey of Ames, Mike Augustine of Des Moines East, Jesse Day of Davenport High School, Ira Dunsworth of Davenport Central and Dennis White of Mount Pleasant.

Wrestling coaches Bob Siddens of Waterloo West, Fred Cooper of Fort Dodge, Dave Natvig of Waterloo East, Leon "Champ" Martin of Algona, John Harris of Corning, Al Baxter of Lisbon, Bob Darrah of Dowling Catholic of West Des Moines, Dan Mashek of Don Bosco of Gilbertville and North Scott, and Brad Smith of Lisbon and City High of Iowa City.

Swimming coaches Jim Voss of Cedar Rapids Washington, Dave Linder of Des Moines Hoover, Mark Crouch of Dowling Catholic in West Des Moines, Mark Wagner of West Des Moines Valley and Richard Marcussen of Cedar Falls.

Basketball coaches Steve McGraw and Murray Wier of Waterloo East, Glenn "Shrimp" Strobridge of Waterloo West, O.C. "Pop" Varner of Diagonal and Mount Ayr, Al Comito of Des Moines Roosevelt, Larry Ireland of Ankeny, Eddie Colbert of Dubuque Wahlert, O.J. "Lefty" Cayou of Livermore, Alden Skinner of Palmer, Don King of Cedar Rapids Washington, Jerry Brown of Murray, Bill Fleming of Maquoketa, Dick Breitbach of Cedar Rapids Regis, Jerry Nikkel of Pella Christian and Marshalltown, Bob Hilmer of WACO of Wayland, Jim Squiers of Bellevue Marquette, Paul Loos of Newell-Fonda, Marty McKowen of Wapsie Valley, Dwight Gingerich of Iowa Mennonite, Mitch Osborn of Harlan and Jim Eekhoff of Western Christian.

Tennis coach Gary Foster of Camanche and Lawrence Eyre of

Maharishi School in Fairfield.

And in football Curt Bladt of Harlan, Ed Thomas of Aplington-Parkersburg, Jim Bellamy of Mount Vernon, Koy Goodchild of West Bend-Mallard, Bob Howard of Sigourney-Keota, Jerry Pezzetti of Ankeny, Butch Pederson of West Branch, Tom Stone of Pekin of Packwood, Ken Winkler of Treynor and West Marshall, Duane Twait of Emmetsburg, Merv Habenicht of Bettendorf, Larry Brown of Iowa City High, Reese Morgan of Benton and then Iowa City West, Walt Fiegel of Sioux City East, Jim Williams of Dowling Catholic of West Des Moines, Gary Swenson of West Des Moines Valley, Tom Good of Cedar Rapids Regis, Howard Vernon of Waterloo East, Jim Fox of Davenport Central, Harold Tackelson of Burlington, Bob Evans of Mount Pleasant and Dick Tighe, who in 2004 coached his 51st season at Fort Dodge St. Edmund after earlier career stops at Carroll Kuemper, Webster City and Iowa Falls.

But the most legendary of all Iowa high school coaches during the IHSAA's first century may well have been Paul Moon, who from the late 1920s to the early 1950s, turned old Davenport High School into the state's powerhouse basketball program. Today, older fans remember him not only for all the winning his teams did, but also for his fashion eccentricity – he was a sharp dresser when he coached, generally wearing business suits and white or gray "spats" on his ankles.

To understand what Moon was all about, we go to a story by Dearrel Bates, who for nearly 35 years has been covering prep sports for the Quad-City Times in Davenport. This story was published in 1988 when Moon was being inducted posthumously into the Times' Sports Hall of Fame.

PAUL MOON: Winning, winning, winning...with class
By Dearrel Bates
May 8, 1988
Quad-City Times

Some called him "Mr. Basketball." Others dubbed him "Mr. Spats." Paul Moon, by any name, was a winner on the basketball court in Davenport for 26 years.

Moon won 541 games, seven state championships and had a winning percentage of 83 at Davenport High School from 1928 to 1954. Remarkably, with all of that success, he never had an unbeaten team: 24-1 was the best. However, he also only had one losing season (9-13) among his 26.

He was also a winner off the basketball floor. A strict disciplinatian, Moon was considered an excellent teacher in office machines, bookkeeping and commercial classes for 45 years. In addiiton he taught Methodist Church classes for newlyweds and made countless speaking appearances before church and sales groups.

Moon, also an assistant coach in track and football, died in December of 1977 at the age of 84.

With his coaching record, it was easy to see why Moon acquired the title of "Mr. Basketball." No one came close to matching his feats in state tournament competition.

Besides capturing state titles in 1929, 1930, 1941, 1947, 1950, 1951 and 1952, how about these accomplishments? Moon has the most state tourney appearances (16), most consecutive state tourney appearances (6) and most victories at the state tourneys (36).

Born in DeKalb, Ill., Moon graduated in 1913 from a two-year teacher college in DeKalb, and later received a bachelor degree from St. Ambrose College in Davenport.

His first job was in 1913, coaching the girls' basketball team in Walnut, Ill. A year later, he moved to Peoria Manual High School where he remained for 10 years, although he took time out to serve three years as an Army captain during World War I. Moon came to Davenport in September of 1928 after coaching and teaching in Freeport, Ill., for four years. He was the coaching of the "lightweight," or junior varsity, team in Freeport. The varsity coach at the time in Freeport was Adolph Rupp, who later went on to collegiate basketball coaching fame at the University of Kentucky.

Moon succeeded Glenn Trumbo as the Blue Devils' head basketball coach at Davenport High.

Immediately, Moon became a success. He directed Davenport teams to state crowns with 21-4 and 24-1 records.

"I was fortunate to win two state championships in my first two years," he later said. "It got the parents to talking basketball, with the idea of having their boys in later years play on a championship team. Winning in basketball became a tradition after that."

He also attributed his coaching success directly to his teaching of commercial subjects, especially classes in salesmanship.

"I think, as a salesmanship teacher, I was able to sell my players better on playing the game of basketball the way I wanted to, even more than most coaches," he said.

Moon surprised people by announcing his retirement at the age of 61 just before the Blue Devils entered tournament play in 1954. He went on to teach until retiring in 1958.

Why did he retire from coaching in '54?

"It's not an easy decision," he said then. "But when it gets to the point where basketball interferes with your health, it's time to get out. After some recent defeats, I just couldn't sleep or eat.

"Some people may think you're silly with all the pressure in basketball, to get into the game in the first place, and at my age, it's silly to be coaching. The more I thought about it, the more I made up my mind to quit while I was still able to awake in the mornings."

After retiring as a teacher in '58, Moon and his wife Edna, who died in 1972, split their time between a cabin in Minnesota and homes in California and Florida.

They called him "Mr. Spats"

How did Paul Moon acquire the nickname of "Mr. Spats"?

Spats, for the younger generation, are cloth or leather covering for the ankle and the top part of the shoe, having buttons up the side and a strap under the instep. They were in style during the 1920s.

Back in his early years of coaching, Moon was weary of chilly, drafty floors in some gyms.

"I purchased a pair of spats because it was cheaper than long underwear," he once told a writer as to why he always wore them.

When he showed up at the state basketball tournament finals with one of his first Davenport teams, fellow coaches ribbed him as a "dude." Other coaches thought him to be superstitious while others thought Moon was using it as a publicity stunt.

"Truth of the matter is," Moon said at the time, "my ankles get cold."

Moon's '49-'50 teams may have been best

What was Paul Moon's greatest team at Davenport High School? Jerry Jurgens, retired sports editor of the Quad-City Times, and others feel it was probably his 1949-'50 squad.

Although the Blue Devils finished with a 24-3 mark, it was how they breezed through the state tourney to capture the title.

The group of Bill Stenger, Ken Buckles, Bob LeBuhn, Ed Lindsey, Willie Newman and Bob McKee won four games in the tourney by scores of 70-28, 78-15, 71-22 and 67-28.

Despite such success, Jurgens remembers Moon as the most gracious of coaches.

"Never did he alibi a defeat," Jurgens said. "He could lose as graciously as he won. But he actually hated to lose."

Moon was a disciplinarian

The first thing that pops into Ken Buckles' head when you mention Paul Moon is not winning basketball games, although he certainly did a lot of it. Rather, it's "disciplinarian."

Buckles, now a Davenport businessman who also serves as a volunteer coach with Davenport West's boys' basketball team, was a key member of two Blue Devils state tournament teams. One team that Buckles played on, the 1949-'50 group, won a state title.

"I remember Paul as a very fair person, but a strict disciplinarian," Buckles said. "We'd win a game and he'd walk right past you and not say a word because you were expected to do it right. He was such a perfectionist.

"As a team, we didn't run a sophisticated offense or defense. We ran a fast break offense and spent about 75 percent of our practice time perfecting it. No team could shut down that part of our game."

Buckles admitted he was in awe of Moon back in his high school days.

"I never took any business classes from him because I was afraid of him. When I first went out for basketball, I wasn't sure if he liked me or not; he had that type of presence surrounding him.

"No players or parents messed with Paul. He called the shots, and everybody knew it."

The Paul Moon heritage in basketball lives on today, with his grandson Denny Aye. In 2005, he was at Marshalltown Community College in Iowa after earlier coaching stops at old Palmer Junior College in Davenport, then at small colleges in Oklahoma and New Mexico. He went on to California, where he coached at Columbia College, Fresno City College and California State at San Bernardino before returning to Iowa.

And in the generation of great-grandchildren, Denny's son Tyson Aye is now in his second year as an assistant basketball coach at San Jose City College in California. Another son Dion Aye was a scholarship basketball player at Southern University in New Orleans before graduating in 2004, and younger son Devin Aye is now playing for his father in Marshalltown.

Denny Aye was a top scorer on Davenport Central teams before he graduated in 1969, and his younger brothers Dana and Bobby also played for the Blue Devils. Their sister Mary Jane was a cheerleader.

The Ayes' mother Jane Moon Aye is the youngest and sole survivor of Paul and Edna Moon's four children. There were three sons – Paul, Jack and C.A. "Ace" Moon – all of whom served in the Army Air Corps in World War II. The three brothers then settled out of Iowa.

Jane and her husband Duane "Bucky" Aye stayed in Davenport. Bucky Aye, incidentally, graduated from Davenport High in 1944 and had wanted to play basketball for Coach Moon, who eventually became his father-in-law, but it didn't work out. "My dad got cut from the squad by Grampa Moon for 'playing too much YMCA ball,' or at least that's the story they always told us later," said Bobby Aye, with a laugh.

Bobby is now a detective with the Scott County Sheriff in Davenport, and he and his wife bought the old Moon family home, which is a few blocks from the high school. It has "an attic stuffed with so much it's hard to tell what all is there," he said. One thing he knows is there, however, is a pair of the storied spats his grandfather wore while he coached.

"The ones we have are gray ones, I think," Bobby said. "But I know he had white ones, too. I think he had different ones to match different suits. He was always a pretty meticulous dresser. He took good care of himself through life, and he usually looked real sharp."

He said that his grandmother Edna Moon suffered from emphysema, and that's why the couple moved to California after Paul retired at Davenport High, "back before smog was a problem out there," Bobby said. After her death, Paul moved back to Davenport.

In those years in the early 1970s, Bobby played for his brother Denny's first teams at Palmer Junior College, and their grandfather would often attend the games. "Denny and I would both ask him about basketball all the time, but he'd never say much," Bobby said.

They've heard the stories passed down about what an innovative coach their grandfather was, in his use of the fast break, being among the first coaches in the Midwest to welcome African American players on his squads and in his uncompromising discipline with his teams.

"I think the whole community thought a lot of him, and I think they made sure they were taking good care of him and our grandmother," Bobby said. "I know the Davenport Chamber of Commerce bought them a car after one state championship. You still hear great stories about what a disciplinarian he was, too. If you were on his team, and he said the bus was leaving at 5 o'clock for the game, you better be there, and it didn't matter what kind of star you were. There were a few of them who got left behind because they were late through the years. It'd only happen once, because they'd be scared to death to have to go face him."

Denny Aye has little doubt that his grandfather's career inspired his own decision to go into coaching.

"In seventh grade in 1964, to satisfy an assignment in English class, I wrote my granddad who was living in California at the time," Denny said. "I asked him many questions about coaching. I knew then that I wanted to become a basketball coach. I'm sure grandad's legacy helped lead me into coaching, but I got my determination and competitiveness from my dad 'Bucky' Aye, who was a very good fast pitch softball and basketball player in his time.

"I never saw my grandfather coach," he continued, "but I heard many stories. As I approach and pass middle age, I begin to appreciate those stories even more. Most of them were about discipline and lessons taught to young men, and how years later they appreciated what he and the team had meant to them, both then and now."

Midway in the 2004-05 basketball season, Denny Aye had a career record of 610-279 in college basketball, where he's done all of his coaching.

He got his first head coaching job – the one at old Palmer Junior College in Davenport – when he was just 22 years old.

"I had graduated from St. Ambrose College in Davenport, and

went on to get my master's degree in one year from the University of Connecticut," he said. "I came back to Davenport and found out the Palmer basketball job was open. It really was a part-time position, and I got it kind of by default because nobody else wanted it. It also helped that the president of Palmer then was A.J. Stolfa, who had been a coach and then the athletic director for years at Davenport High School. So, of course, he knew my granddad."

In early 2005, as Denny Aye approached his 900th game as a college head coach, he said he couldn't have picked a better career.

"I am truly blessed to have coached all three of my sons and to have the good fortune to wake up every day and be in a profession that I wouldn't trade for anything," he said. "The most memorable thing I remember Paul and Edna Moon saying many times was, that they could have made more money doing something else, but the good times from coaching far outweighed the money. Or as I tell people, I put in a lot of hours, but have never worked a day in my life."

So, has he been any kind of fashion trend-setter among coaches?

"I've never worn spats, but my brother Dana gave me a pair for Christmas a couple of years ago, and I probably will wear them sometime to a game," Denny said. "I did wear tuxedos as a coach for about six years."

Huh?

"That was at Palmer," he said. "The first couple of years, just starting out, I didn't have any money for clothes, and my team was always giving me a hard time about wearing this same old sweater for every game. So one day I said, 'Well, next year, I'm going to wear a tuxedo when I coach,' and of course, they didn't believe me. And I did, too. I went to a tuxedo rental place there in Davenport and they donated a tux for me to wear every game, and I did that for a long time."

WE ALSO HELPED LAUNCH ONE OF AMERICA'S MOST FAMOUS COACHES – IN A VERY ODD SORT OF WAY. Interestingly, Paul Moon also had a connection to one of the most fascinating and quirky coaching stories in IHSAA history. The Quad-City Times story earlier in this chapter referred to it – that prior to Moon's coming to Davenport High School, he was an assistant coach from 1926 to 1930 at Freeport, Illinois, where the varsity coach was Adolph Rupp.

Rupp indeed went on to coach basketball at the University of Kentucky for 42 years, before retiring in 1972. He directed the Kentucky Wildcats to 879 victories against only 190 losses, including four NCAA championships and 27 titles in the Southeastern Conference. Interestingly, Rupp's biographies point out that his nickname of "The Baron of Basketball" started when he was at Freeport High School, not at Kentucky, where it evolved to become "The Baron of the Bluegrass."

It was also at Freeport where he started his habit of always dressing very fashionably when he was coaching – but always in brown suits. There is no record of him wearing spats, but perhaps his clothes consciousness inspired his young assistant coach in Freeport.

The Rupp connection to Iowa high school sports is even more fun than his link with Moon.

If you check the IHSAA's records, you'll see that Marshalltown High School won the first state wrestling championship that the association sanctioned in 1926. Note who the coach was of Marshalltown's wrestling champions: Adolph Rupp!

He had grown up in little Halstead, Kansas, then as a player helped Coach Forrest C. "Phog" Allen's University of Kansas basketball teams win national championships in 1922 and '23. He went on to teach history and coach both football and basketball at Burr Oak, Kansas, a town in the north central part of the state, then came to Marshalltown for the 1925-26 school year. The 1926 Marshalltown High yearbook lists Rupp as a social science teacher and "faculty sponsor" of the wrestling team. Russell Dickinson was the basketball coach.

Information about Rupp on the Internet site of the Naismith Memorial Basketball Hall of Fame in Springfield, Massachusetts, says that he was "a wrestling novice" when he got to Marshalltown. After being assigned to coach it, he "purchased a book about the sport and led his team to state championship."

However, his coaching role with that championship team is questioned today.

148

"The story the old timers were all telling when I came to Marshalltown was that Adolph Rupp was actually more of a chaperone for the team than the coach," said George Funk, the veteran Marshalltown High basketball coach, now retired after leading the Bobcats from 1963 to 1989. "Marshalltown had a great wrestler on those teams, Allie Morrison, and he supposedly did most of the real coaching."

Indeed, Morrison won an individual championship in that first sanctioned state tournament in 1926, and he'd also won a title the previous year in an unsanctioned meet. He is listed as "acting coach" of the wrestling team in the 1925 yearbook, and "coach" in the 1926 book. This is the same Allie Morrison who went on to win a gold medal in wrestling in the 1928 Olympics.

Marshalltown school officials today say they have no records indicating how Rupp might have found his way to Marshalltown in 1925. Indeed, most people today are unaware that the man who would become the most famous name in basketball helped lead an MHS team to the school's first sanctioned Iowa state championship – in wrestling!

TWO OF PAUL MOON'S BEST GOT AWAY. Davenport High School had a stable full of good athletes in the early 1940s, but two of the best were twin brothers Loran "Pee Wee" Day and Lawrence "Fats" Day.

Pee Wee, who was 6 ft. tall and 175 pounds, may have been the better natural athlete, and he is in the Iowa Hall of Fame in three different sports. But Fats had a tremendous size advantage at 6 ft., 1 in. and 230 pounds, and he came on like gangbusters during their high school careers.

In their sophomore year, 1940-41, they became key players on a football team that lost a close opening game, tied in its second game – both of those being against Illinois teams – and then never lost again. In basketball, they were both varsity players on the Blue Devils team that won the state championship. In baseball, it was another state championship.

As juniors, 1941-42, their football team went undefeated, and their basketball team finished runner-up in the state.

And then they moved!

As seniors, in 1942-43, they led Mason City High School's football team to an undefeated season, then helped the Mohawks' basketball season to an undefeated season and state championship (including one state tournament win over Davenport 50-36), then led the Mason City baseball team which lost only to the eventual state champions.

How did Paul Moon let two of his best get out of Davenport? And how big was the news about their departure?

"The boys' father Loran A. Day Sr. was an office manager for Standard Oil back in that time, and he was transferred often," said Marjorie "Midge" Day, Pee Wee's widow who lives in Davenport. "They were born in Wichita, Kansas, and I know they lived in Minnesota, Wisconsin and North Dakota before they came to Davenport when the boys were in eighth grade. I think they wound up going to 12 different schools before they graduated from high school. Dad Day kept getting promoted, and every time he did, it meant another move.

"So really, Coach Moon wasn't all that surprised when the family was moving to Mason City in that summer before the boys' senior year. I'm sure he wasn't happy about it, but he knew the reality was that they were going to go wherever their father had a job."

But it was big news?

"Oh yes, it sure was," Midge said, noting clippings in old family scrapbooks that showed that even the Chicago newspapers carried the story. "It was the talk of Iowa."

Some speculated that Mason City's own coaching legend, J.A. "Judge" Grimsley, was involved in some recruiting. The Mason City Globe-Gazette's headline on the story about the Day twins moving to town was: "Big Break!" The story led off this way: "Did Judge Grimsley, Mason City High School coach, look in a very happy mood to you? Well, he is and here's why..."

Midge Day said, "It was shocking to everyone who followed sports, of course. But Pee Wee and Fats were so used to moving around, it wasn't such a big deal to them – just Dad being transferred again. And there wasn't anything to the 'recruiting' stories. Grimsley was not involved."

All of that happened in a very different time. World War II was raging. Many boys were leaving school to join the military. In fact, the Day twins graduated from Mason City High on a May morning in 1943, and that same day got on buses with other recruits to go to Des Moines and be sworn into the service – Pee Wee into the Marines and Fats into the Seabees. Pee Wee, who served in both Guam and at Iwo Jima, was wounded but recovered. They both returned from their military duty in 1945 and both then accepted scholarships at Northwestern University in Evanston, Illinois, where they became major stars on the Wildcats' football teams. Indeed, they helped Northwestern beat California 20-14 in the 1949 Rose Bowl, with Pee Wee's interception stopping Cal's last drive, preserving the victory.

Both Days started their business careers with Standard Oil. Pee Wee went on to spend years in the concrete business, primarily in Davenport, where he eventually retired. He died in 2003. After Fats left Standard, he sold insurance and then joined Pepsi Cola for a long career in the Chicago area. He retired to Manhasset, New York, and in 2005 was living there at the age of 80.

Sports editor John O'Donnell, of the Davenport Democrat and Leader wrote that "as far as athletics are concerned, the Day twins were born with gold spoons in their mouths." Their prep careers "were a blaze of glory," O'Donnell noted in his tribute, which was published in the spring of 1943 as they neared graduation at Mason City. He said when it came to twin brothers who were good athletes, "I'll string along with the Day twins as the best 'repeaters' on championship teams the prep circle of Iowa has ever known." They still may be, more than 60 years later.

HOW DO GOOD COACHES BECOME GREAT COACHES?

I talked about that with five of the best in recent years – John Raffensperger, retired track coach at Iowa City High; Duane Twait, retired football coach at Emmetsburg; Curt Bladt, football coach at Harlan; Steve McGraw, basketball coach at Waterloo East, and Dennis Olejniczak, baseball coach at Decorah.

Having some sports heritage certainly helps you get started in a coaching career, but it's not essential to being a great coach. Having patience is very important. Having perspective is probably even more important at the high school level, where sports programs really are just a part of the larger and more important educational process.

And another characteristic of great coaches is that they tend to be innovators.

Raffensperger may have the best story about that.

He retired after the 2003 track season, but in his 36 years at City High he built the most successful track program the state has ever known – with 10 state team titles, 17 conference champions and 56 individual or relay state champions. He was named Iowa's track coach of the year eight times, and the City High track is now named after him.

"As we were developing the program, we always seemed to have a lot of talent and success in the running events, but for a long time we struggled in the field events – and especially in the throwing events, the shot put and the discus," Raffensperger said.

"I went through several different throwing coaches, and we couldn't seem to get to where I thought we should be. I finally decided I better learn more about it, so I could coach it myself."

He had been a four-sport athlete as he went through old University High School in Iowa City, and he played football and competed in track at the University of Northern Iowa. In track, he ran the 200 and 400 meters races, the low hurdles, long jumped and threw the javelin. But never the shot put.

"So I did a lot of research on the shot put," he continued. " I studied the technique, and then I realized that to be successful in coaching it, I was going to have to learn how to teach it to someone. So, for several nights, we'd pull the drapes at our house so the neighbors wouldn't think we were crazy, and I taught my wife Shirley how to throw the shot put in our living room."

Shirley was the ever-loyal, hardworking track statistician for City High during her husband's coaching years, but few know she was also the prototype shot putter for the Little Hawks.

The "shot put" the Raffenspergers used in their living room, incidentally, "was either a tennis ball or a softball," John said.

How was her form after his instruction?

"It probably wasn't Olympic caliber," the old coach said, "but that's how you learn things – by teaching someone else how to do it. It started helping our shot putters at City High, I'll tell you that."

152

Raffensperger had those other qualities of great coaches, too.

As for heritage, his father Leonard Raffensperger had been an outstanding football coach at Waterloo East during the 1930s and '40s, then was head coach of the University of Iowa Hawkeyes for two years. John's brothers were good athletes. Gene played quarterback for his dad at Waterloo East, later went into journalism and served as sports editor of the Des Moines Register. Paul excelled at University High School. Their sister Marsha, who graduated from City High, "could have been a great athlete if they'd had girls' sports when she was in school," John said.

As for patience and perspective, Raffensperger seemed to have the perfect mix for high school sports.

"I think one reason I've been successful is that I did try to keep it in perspective," he said. "We worked hard, and we won a lot, but I always believed that practices should not be overly long. We'd average having 90 kids out for track at City High, and the assistant coaches and I would structure our workouts so that we didn't have much down time. We also relied on our seniors a lot. We'd keep everybody moving and we'd generally be done in an hour and a half. We also tried to avoid having practices on weekends. I always thought kids needed time just to be kids when they're in high school. I'd tell them we were going to work hard but we were going to have a good time, too."

He said he "never took myself too seriously, and I tried to get the kids to be that way, too. As good as we were, I never allowed them to be too showy or cocky. We wanted to do things in a classy way."

Duane Twait was the head football coach at his alma mater, Emmetsburg High School, from 1974 through 2002, and in that time won seven state championships. His teams reached the playoffs 28 of his 29 years and they reached the finals 14 times. The E'Hawks overall record those 29 years was 280 wins and only 40 losses. They were 187-13 in the Lakes Conference and won every title from 1974 through 2002.

"Unbelieveable," I said.

"Yeah, you know, it almost is," said Twait.

So how'd he do it?

"One thing we did was run the same offense and same defense for our teams from junior high right on up through high school," Twait said. "So by the time the kids reached the varsity, they really knew the system.

"We were also well known for using the 'no huddle' offense. You know what? I don't know if that gives you a real advantage in the game, because your opponents get used to it and adjust their defense. But the advantage is that they all spend a lot of time before the game worrying about it and preparing for it, and maybe that keeps them from getting ready for other things we're going to try to do."

Having a coaching staff that stays together through the years may be one of the biggest factors in a team's success, Twait noted. Jim Willmore was his assistant for 28 years. Tom Steen, his successor as head coach, was an assistant for 13 years.

Of course, they also started and supervised a good weight lifting program.

"I really think the biggest factor though is that our high school football program got the support of the parents and the community," Twait said. "It's big here in Emmetsburg, no doubt about that. The kids really put forth the time and effort to become good players. They will do that because the program is solid, it's something that you're proud to be a part of, and they realize that if they stick with it, they will probably get to play as seniors if not before that."

After his retirement, Twait has served as an assistant coach to his own son Kevin Twait, who was the head football coach at Iowa Central Community College in Fort Dodge in 2005.

`It's almost hard to believe there could be a football program more successful than Emmetsburg's, but as fans of the game in Iowa know, there is one – Harlan's.

Curt Bladt, 60 years old in the spring of 2005, has coached the Cyclones to nine state championships, including the most recent two – in 2003 and 2004. In his 27 years as head coach, the team's worst record was 7-2, they've never lost a season opener, they've never lost two games in a row, and they've never lost a first-round game in their 24 appearances in the state playoffs. The Cyclones' record under Bladt: 288-31-0.

Everybody around Harlan, a southwest Iowa town of 5,300, and football fans across the state had Bladt and his family in their thoughts and prayers from December, 2004, through the spring of 2005.

A few weeks after his team clinched the state championship, he was stricken with "Miller Fisher syndrome," a rare condition in which Bladt "lost his senses of smell and taste, developed double vision and his once-sturdy legs became weak," the Des Moines Register reported. By mid-spring, rest and physical therapy had helped him recover to the point that he could help coach the shot putters and discus throwers in track. But his continuing vision problems and partial paralysis in his face kept him from being able to return to the classroom, where he teaches biology. In April, 2005, he told the Register that he hoped to be back on the sidelines of the Cyclone football team in the fall.

Updates on his condition were posted by his family and former students on a specially-designed site on the Internet, www.CoachBladt.com, and it had received 750,000 "hits" from around the world by mid-spring.

How has Bladt built such a successful program at Harlan?

"Well, first of all, I didn't start it," he told me in 2004.

Harold "Swede" Johnson won five conference championships with his teams from 1950 to 1962, the last of which was undefeated. He then stepped aside as head football coach, but served a total of 33 years as athletic director. In a 1967 school consolidation, Harlan took in most of the students from Catholic high schools that closed in nearby Panama, Portsmouth, Earling, Defiance and Westphalia, and that nearly doubled the size of the Harlan High student body.

Johnson then hired Terry Eagen, a native of Exira, as the head football coach, and Eagen's teams won 85 percent of their games, including the state championship the first year the playoffs were held in 1972. Eagen left in 1973 for Marshalltown, but in his Harlan years, he persuaded his bosses to hire another Exira native, Curt Bladt, who had just graduated from Morningside College in Sioux City. He was hired to teach biology and be an assistant wrestling coach. In 1968, Eagen also asked him to be the line coach in football. Ken Pap succeeded Eagen as head coach in the 1974 season, and then Bladt took over in 1978.

"So, I didn't have to start the program," Bladt said. "I just took the reins and tried to keep it going."

And, oh, has he ever!

"A lot of people use the word 'mystique' about the success we've had," he said. "But there's no mystique at all. We just get our kids to play hard. They invest a lot in our football program, and when you've invested a lot and build a winning program, it's hard to give it up."

From what you learned about the Emmetsburg program, it will be no surprise that Bladt has also managed to hold on to his assistant coaches.

"There are five of us who have been together for over 20 years," he said. "We don't have to spend a lot of time writing down what we're going to do. We all know each other and the system so well, we just go do it."

The four long-time assistants are Ken Carstens, Bill Hosack, Russ Gallinger and Al Simdorn. Carstens is one of the most respected defensive coordinators in the state, Bladt noted. "We've traditionally emphasized defense, and it's not very often that we have to outscore somebody to win," he said.

Another key: "We have never really focused on one person," Bladt said. "We never just feature one player. We try to have everybody be a team player and a contributor."

There is substantial pressure on Harlan players and coaches to continue the winning tradition, of course.

"But we try to make it as fun as we can," Bladt said. "We're always throwing some little game or gimmick into our practices, just for fun."

And, as serious and focused as he and his assistants are on the sidelines during games, many fans are shocked when they see Harlan's players arrive for state championship games at the UNI-Dome in Cedar Falls. It has become another Harlan tradition that if the team reaches the finals, the players do crazy things with their hair – wild braids, mohawks, handprints-shaved-on-their-heads and many different shades of red.

"I know they all love to do that, so I just tell them that if they want to do that, as silly as it looks, that's fine with me," Bladt said. "A lot of other things might upset me, but that doesn't. I do remember, though, that when my own youngest son was playing in his senior year, he came out with a handprint on his head, dyed red and I thought, 'Oh, God!' But, you know, if they have fun doing that, and it builds a little more camaraderie on the team, why not?"

One other thing has helped "sell" Harlan football in the Bladt era. Home games have become a wonderful spectacle, a total showcase of the high school and community experience. The Harlan High band is as good as the football team — they even march over and play the opposing school's fight song in their pre-game performance — and a color guard from local American Legion posts unfurls a huge American flag before the National Anthem is played. Crowds of 3,000 or more are not unusual. The home fans rarely ever leave unhappy. "It's a real show," Bladt said, "a big show, a whole lot of fun for people."

Year-in and year-out over the past quarter century, Waterloo East basketball coach Steve McGraw has done one of the finest jobs of coaching in all of Iowa high school sports.

He's had great success. After the 2004-05 season, he had more than 530 career victories, two state championships and 14 state tournament appearances in his 26 years at the inner city school.

All well and good, McGraw, who was 58 in 2005, will tell you. But the educating and mentoring he does is more important than the actual coaching.

"We all hope to make a difference with what we do in other people's lives," he said with remarkable calm one night, barely an hour before a mid-season game with rival Cedar Falls. "We get a lot of opportunities to do that."

The East High student body is one of the most racially balanced in a state that is overwhelmingly white. The school sits on the north edge of downtown Waterloo in a predominantly African American neighborhood. Many students come from tough circumstances — economically and sociologically. Over the past century, it has also developed one of Iowa's proudest athletic traditions. And the administrators and faculty members are some of the most impressive in the state.

"Some people probably think my job is tough, and it can be, but there are a lot of jobs tougher," said McGraw. "There may be others who think it's an easy job that I have, because we always seem to have a lot of talent."

McGraw admits now he was an unlikely hire for the position back in 1979, when he had so little experience with black students. His athletic credentials were strong enough. He had been an All-State football player and a good basketball and baseball player at Indianola High School, and he played basketball and baseball at Simpson College, graduating in 1969. In his first coaching job that summer, he took Sibley to the state baseball tournament. He taught a year there, but then left for six months of active duty and training as a member of the National Guard. In the late fall of 1970, he began nine years at Tri-County of Thornburg in southeast Iowa, where he taught and was a successful head coach in basketball and baseball and an assistant in football.

"As a young coach, you're always looking to move up," McGraw said. "I'd applied for a couple of different jobs over the years, but didn't get them. Then the East High basketball job became available."

Hall of Fame coach Murray Wier had stepped down from the head boys' basketball job after winning the state championship in 1974, but had continued as athletic director.

"East basketball had slipped a little from 1974, or I'd have never been hired," McGraw said.

He had little experience with African Americans.

"We had no black kids in Indianola when I grew up there," he said, "and we didn't at Tri-County, either, when I was there. But I worked the summer basketball camps at the University of Iowa a number of years, and worked with a few black kids there. One of them was David Cain, who came in from Milwaukee and told us he just hated where he was going to school. I worked with him some at the camp and got along well with him. Right before that next school year started, I got a call at Tri-County and it was David, saying he was in Iowa City and asking me to come get him and help him go to school where I was."

McGraw said he contacted Bernie Saggau at the IHSAA, explained the situation and young Cain was ruled immediately eligible. The coach said Cain "was a pretty good player – he could've played at Waterloo East or a lot of other schools – so he helped us at Tri-County that year. He was good enough that he made me kind of the scourge among some of the other coaches and fans around the area." McGraw said he regrets that he has had no contact with Cain in recent years.

Athletic director Wier at East High thought McGraw's teaching and coaching credentials merited hiring. Tom Thorson, then East's assistant principal, recalled "there wasn't any doubt we had some concerns about a guy coming in from Tri-County in Thornburg to East High in Waterloo.

"But of the six or seven candidates we interviewed, Steve definitely had the best presentation. He was very organized, and he was very definite about what he wanted to get done here."

Which was?

"I knew Waterloo East's tradition," McGraw said. "I also know that kids are kids. I don't care if they're blue or red or whatever color they are. Kids here wanted to play basketball, and I thought I could help them."

His first year, the Trojans "went about .500," he recalled. His third year, they went to the state tournament. They've been flying high ever since.

Through the years, McGraw has had such marquee players as Tyrone Scott Sr., Mike Davis, Sedric Robinson, Andre Galloway, Mike Henderson, Carlton Reed and Tyrone Scott Jr. Two of his assistant coaches Bryan Joens and Galloway played for him at East.

How has McGraw made it work?

"A lot goes into making a team," he said. "Certainly talent is a big factor, and we've got talent. But there are other important things. One of those that's made us successful is continuity in our coaching staff. We've been together a long, long time. We all get along, we're very dedicated to our program and we have an awful lot of loyalty. The kids see that closeness in the staff, and that helps, especially in this school. A lot of kids at East are being raised by one parent, or maybe no parents. They really want that feeling of closeness.

"We get 65 to 70 coming out for basketball, some of them just because they really want to have that feeling of belonging. I don't cut – I've never cut here. A lot of times kids will cut themselves if they're not going to get a lot of playing time. I feel it's okay if they make that decision, but I try to keep them all playing. We'll have two full groups, with 20 to 25 on the varsity squad. I don't mind having a larger group like that around if they play hard. We do a lot of full-court stuff in practice, so we need a lot of kids."

McGraw said there are two things he pushes hardest in his educational approach to coaching.

"I think the biggest thing is consistency," he said. "We try to maintain consistency in our whole program, and the players see that. They know they've got to be consistent in their lives if they want to compete consistently at the highest levels.

"And while winning is important to us, of course, it's more important to the coaches to put our kids in a position where they can be successful. First, we have to help them realize what it takes to be successful, then we help them take the steps to get there."

And those are life lessons, McGraw said, not just basketball lessons.

In Decorah in northeast Iowa, the basement walls in the home of Dennis and Paula Olejniczak are covered with sports memorabilia. A ping pong table is at the ready. The wallpaper in one room looks like the pinstripes on a baseball uniform.

Two signs on the walls say it all about the Olejniczaks. One is: "Live well, laugh often, love much." The other is: "Baseball! Baseball! Baseball!"

Dennis, who has coached the Decorah High Vikings in baseball for 41 years and is still going, looks around the basement and says, "Obviously, high school athletics has kind of been our life. We've always encouraged high school kids that if they want to get away from a party or something, to come on over to the Olejniczaks. They're always welcome here."

Five Olejniczak kids went through the Decorah schools, and they were all outstanding athletes. Sons Lon (a '79 graduate) and Jason (an '89 graduate) were both first team All-Staters in football and basketball, and Lon also received mention in basketball. Both went on to star in football at the University of Iowa. Daughters Lesly, Heidi and Lindy were all excellent softball players.

160

play-by-play, his post-game reports, interviews and high school scoreboard shows are excellent.

In Clinton, Determan has been broadcasting the games of the Clinton High School River Kings and other area schools for 30 years. His KROS predecessor Hank Dihlmann did the River Kings' football and basketball for 40 years and is still an active fan.

In LeMars, Callahan has been doing KLEM sports since 1973, after spending three years earlier with Mitchell at KGRN in Grinnell. "I figure I've done somewhere close to 5,000 sporting events and traveled close to 204,000 miles in my 34-plus years in radio," Callahan said.

In Waverly, Neff brings 32 years of experience to his KWAY game broadcasts, having earlier done them for KCFI in Cedar Falls, KWLO in Waterloo and KCJJ in Iowa City. He has battled back from two strokes that have interrupted his career.

In Forest City, Harris has been doing games since 1978 after earlier stops at KRIB in Mason City and KHBT in Humboldt.

Field, who has been at KJAN in Atlantic since 1988, and Hughes, who started at KMA in Shenandoah when he was in high school in 1969, are two of the state's busiest high school play-by-play broadcasters. During state basketball tournaments in recent years, their stations are the only ones that still do all, or nearly all, of the games – instead of just focusing on the games involving teams from their home areas.

Hughes continued a long tradition by KMA sportscasters that stretches back to 1955 when Veterans Memorial Auditorium opened in Des Moines and became the home of the state basketball tourneys. Rather than broadcasting from "press row," located on overhangs from the first row of the balcony, Hughes and his predecessors opted for a booth high in the rafters, on the balcony's back wall. Why? So students and other fans from southwest Iowa schools can make the long climb and "say hello" on the radio to the fans back home. During the 1992 girls' state tournament, Nikki Nelson, then a senior at Fremont Mills in Tabor, took advantage of the on-air opportunity to add, "And I still don't have a date for prom. I've available, and I'm very good looking."

In Mason City, the 48-year-old Fleming is so smooth and so good in his game broadcasts on KGLO that you wonder why he hasn't gone on to major college or professional sports. Oh, he's tried them, he explained, "but I never wanted to get away from the local sports. I enjoy doing the college sports. But when I go through the Hy-Vee checkout line, the kids bagging my groceries are also the kids who are playing for Mason City High School and Newman Catholic High School here. I like it when they say, 'Hi, Mr. Fleming, how are you doing?' That's important to me, and it always has been. There's a lot of 'community' reflected in that."

Coaches and athletes in the northern Iowa area know they have something special in Fleming's work.

"He's got a great radio voice," said Dan Delaney, the activities director at Mason City High and a member of the IHSAA Board of Control. "Some of the broadcasters are yellers, screamers. Compared to that, Tim's voice is like opera."

Fleming is a native of Dubuque who grew up listening to his father Pat Fleming do play-by-play on stations WDBQ and KDTH, and by the time he was 16, Tim was doing color commentary with his dad. After studying at Loras College two years and marrying Sue, his high school sweetheart, Tim began working full-time at KDTH. Then in 1977 he moved to Mason City.

"They hired me at KGLO as an afternoon announcer," Tim said. "I told them I just had to be doing sports, too, that if not, in a year I'd be looking somewhere else. Within 10 days, I did a North Iowa Area Community College football game, then they added a couple of Newman Catholic football games for me and before long, they told me I'd become the sports guy."

He followed Ken Kew, who eventually became the mayor of Mason City, and Tom Anthony as the KGLO sportscasters.

As they had done, Fleming not only did high school sports, but also community college games as well as the football games of the University of Iowa Hawkeyes – in the years before the university went to exclusive broadcast rights. "I'd do a high school game on Friday night, then we'd charter a flight out of Mason City in the wee hours of Saturday morning to get to the Iowa game," he said.

While he enjoyed doing those games, he knew his heart was in high chool coverage back in the Mason City area. He said one of his career highlights has been the ability to broadcast games in which his own three children were competing for Newman Catholic. They are Amy, now a news anchor at KIMT-TV in Mason City; Eric, who is now a deejay with KISS-FM radio in Mason City, and Kimberly, who has started working part-time at KGLO while finishing high school.

"Mason City has to be one of the best towns anywhere for high school sports," Fleming said. "We're big enough that our teams are playing the top competition, but we're small enough that games are still community events. The kids love to play, the coaches love to coach and the fans come out and make events out of them. It's still the thing to do in Mason City."

As his career has grown, Fleming has become KGLO's operations manager in addition to being sports director – and he's also host of the 5-to-9 a.m. morning show.

"I still do a lot of play-by-play, but I suppose at my busiest, I was doing 25 to 30 football games every fall, 80 to 100 basketball games, 15 to 20 baseball and softball games," he said. "Not bad for a guy who has a wake-up call at 3:25 every morning, huh?"

KGLO helped lead Iowa radio stations into the Internet era in the 1996 and the 1997 basketball seasons by becoming the first station to "stream" its game broadcasts on the World Wide Web. Those were the years when Dean Oliver was leading the Mason City High Mohawks to consecutive state championships. The station's news director Tim Renshaw, who was savvy about the new technology, figured out how to put the games on the 'Net, and former Mason Citians scattered around the globe listened in – then joined in e-mail "chat rooms" for post-game discussions. When Fleming began describing what the station was doing to his pals in the press room at the state tournament, no one could understand then what he was talking about. "I didn't really understand it myself," he recalled. "I just knew we had people as far away as Turkey and Japan listening to my play-by-play."

Television coverage of Iowa high school sports has grown considerably since the first, rough telecasts of state basketball championship games aired in the 1950s.

By the 1970s, some local stations began televising first- and second round state tournament games, if one of their local teams was playing. Coverage of the championships was packaged by the IHSAA and sold to a network of a half-dozen commercial stations across the state. For years, Iowa Public Television aired the football and wrestling championships, before that too, went to a commercial network. And expansion of cable television has enabled many schools to begin televising their regular season home games, generally on a tape-delayed basis.

Meanwhile, the number of television stations sending sports reporters to file reports from high school games has mushroomed, as has the amount of time the stations devote to prep stories.

Of all the television personnel who have been a part of that, four stand out for their consistent attention to high school athletics over the long haul – Heidi Soliday of KCCI-TV in Des Moines, John Campbell of KCRG-TV in Cedar Rapids, Tim Seaman of KCAU-TV in Sioux City, and Seaman's predecessor there, the late Gene Sherman.

Soliday, a native of West Des Moines and a graduate of Valley High School, started at KCCI as a part-time news and sports photographer in 1976 and has been there ever since. "My first glimpse of the state basketball tournaments was in March, 1978, and I've seen a bunch of them!" she said.

Campbell, a native of Oskaloosa, started his television career in Wisconsin as a news reporter and photographer, then moved to sports. In 1979, he became sports director of KCRG.

Seaman grew up in Forest City, Cherokee and Emmetsburg. His father Ron Seaman for years was managing editor of the Emmetsburg Reporter-Democrat, then helped launch radio station KEMB there and did play-by-play on it. So it was no surprise when Tim Seaman decided to go into the media, too. He became sports director at KCAU in 1989 and has anchored the sports news segments since. He has also anchored the network television coverage of state wrestling tournaments, and at state basketball tournaments he has done feature stories and interviews for the network.

Sherman was sports director at KCAU-TV from 1959 to '85, and during that same period, did a lot of play-by-play of high school games on radio station KMNS and others in the Sioux City market. He died in 2000.

Very few sports media figures through the years worked for both newspapers and radio. Mo Kelley did that early in his career in Boone with he News Republican and with KWBG radio, before he became publications director at the IHSAA.

Frank "Buck" Buckingham, of Cherokee, worked both at the Daily Times and KCHE radio during his career, which stretched for about 40 years. When he died in 2001, Sioux City Journal sportswriter Barry Poe saluted him this way: "His unmistakable voice was one you could never forget and nobody, I mean nobody, cared more about sports in Cherokee than Frank Buckingham."

Besides the longest-tenured sportswriters I mentioned earlier in this chapter, several others had careers that spanned decades.

Russ Smith, 80 years old in 2005, worked 42 years full-time in sports for the Waterloo Courier, and was sports editor from the late 1970s until his retirement in 1990. He covered college sports, too, of course, but stayed involved in high school athletics. He became known as the foremost writer about wrestling in the nation.

Following Smith as sports editor has been Kevin Evans, 57 in 2005, who has been working in the Courier's sports department since 1965 – and full-time since 1969. Evans, like Smith, has become known nationally for his wrestling coverage. In 2005, he noted, "I will be working my 40th straight state high school wrestling tournament."

Jim Rose spent 42 years as sports editor of the Mount Pleasant News before his retirement in 1991. Besides his excellent game coverage, Rose wrote a sports column – "almost every day, Monday through Friday, most of those years" – named "Sports Through Rose-Colored Glasses." In retirement, he has continued to write that column twice each month.

Phil Chinitz retired from the Atlantic News-Telegraph in 1995 after doing "sports and everything else, too," for 40 years. In 2005, he was still phoning in the scores of Atlantic Trojan games to the Des Moines Register, Omaha World-Herald and Council Bluffs Nonpareil.

Bob Brown made the Fort Dodge Messenger's sports section one of the strongest in the state, especially for high school coverage, during his full-time career of 38 years at the newspaper, most of them as sports editor but two of the years as editor in chief in the latter 1970s.

"It was a one-man sports staff for a lot of that time," said Brown, "but finally I convinced my bosses it was going to take another writer or tw if we were going to continue trying to cover 91 schools like we did. I think we were up to four on the staff when I retired," in 1991.

In retirement, he continues to write a column on fishing and other outdoor sports – "Inside on the Outside" – on a regular basis.

Jim VanHeel was sports editor of the Mason City Globe-Gazette f 42 years before his retirement in 1981. He died in 1988 of cancer, when he was 69 years old.

"Jim was a wealth of knowledge about high school and University Iowa sports," said Jeff Tecklenburg, who worked as an assistant to VanHee for four years and now is the editor of the Muscatine Journal. "He was a stickler for the basics, and he did things his way. His stubborn streak could rub some people wrong, but I learned to appreciate his character and learn a lot from him in my rookie days.

"During some road trips to state tournaments or playoffs, I was treated to a number of lively discussions between Jim and his longtime cohort at the Fort Dodge Messenger, Bob Brown," Tecklenburg continued "I'll just say that they were passionate when arguing their points but still managed to remain friends."

Tom Thoma, now an editorial writer at the Mason City newspaper, was a high school student when he started working part-time for VanHeel. "He taught me so much, and was one of the reasons I got into this busines said Thoma. "He was gruff at times, but would help you however he could

Jim Logan did sports and news for the Red Oak Express for 38 yea before he retired in 1984. In basketball, Logan was a fixture sitting on the Tigers' bench with the coaches and players, keeping score on his clipboard while generally wearing a bright orange sports coat.

The late Max Sandeman served as sports editor of the Creston Ne Advertiser for 31 years before he retired in 1979. He continued part-time a the newspaper until he died in 1989. "Max was one of the real icons in Iow prep coverage," said Larry Peterson, now a columnist at the News Advertis

George Kampling served as the Clinton Herald's sports editor for 25 years before retiring in 1995. And for 15 years earlier, when he was living in Iowa City, he was a fixture at high school games and other sports events, working as a "stringer" for the Iowa City Press-Citizen, Cedar Rapids Gazette, Quad-City Times in Davenport and Des Moines Register. Kampling now still works part-time for the Clinton newspaper, writing feature stories.

Jack Marlowe wrote sports for the Maquoketa Sentinel-Press for about 35 years. In 2005, in retirement, he continued to write his column "Sports Slants" almost weekly, and "occasionally takes a picture when we're short-staffed, and he has filled in with some regular coverage a couple of times when we've been between sports editors," said Doug Melvold, the editor of the Sentinel-Press. "He keeps up with his contacts and with the area teams on his own now, almost as much as when he was actively writing."

Howard Brantz had a 40-year career covering high school sports in western Iowa, from 1948 to 1956 for the Carroll Daily Times Herald and then at the Omaha World-Herald from 1956 until his retirement in 1988. Brantz, who died in 1996, was considered the authority on prep sports in southwest Iowa for years, always rating the teams during the seasons and then picking All-Southwest Iowa teams.

The Omaha newspaper for at least 50 years has had an edition serving southwestern, now western, Iowa and a string of good reporters have concentrated on high school sports for that edition. In 2005, that slot was filled by Kevin White, 36, a native of Minden, Iowa, who moved to the World-Herald in 2000 after starting his career at the Council Bluffs Nonpareil in 1990. He got his foot in the door at the Nonpareil in 1986 when, as a senior on the Tri-Center High School baseball team, he kept a diary for the newspaper while competing in the state tournament. Veteran sportswriters across Iowa now consider White one of the best of the younger people in the business.

Carroll, with both Carroll High and Kuemper Catholic High, is a great town for prep sports, and a sportswriter who helped make it so is Dennis O'Grady, a native of Des Moines who was sports editor of the Daily Times Herald from 1971 to 2001. The colorful O'Grady decided he'd had enough newspapering and moved back to Des Moines, where he began sporting goods sales – but he is still a regular in the press room at state tournaments.

Alex Stoddard served as sports editor of the Sioux City Journal for 32 years before retiring in the late 1970s.

His successor Terry Hersom, a native of Cedar Rapids, joined the Journal late in 1977 at the age of 27 years old, reportedly making him the youngest sports editor of a metro newspaper in the U.S. at that time.

It turned out to be a good hire, as Hersom was still sports editor in 2005. He and veteran sports staff member Steve Allspach, who joined the Journal staff in 1981, do an exceptional job on Iowa high school sports – and, of course, they also are keeping track of schools in northeast Nebraska and southeast South Dakota.

Hersom and Allspach also each write two columns per week, giving the Journal sports section more personality than most of their competition. They're both very well-read and have interests beyond sports – Hersom is a terrific singer – and that adds depth and fun to their columns. Another thing both of them bring to their coverage is almost encyclopedic knowledge of high school sports in Iowa. They know the territory!

Hersom, a graduate of the University of Northern Iowa, came to Sioux City after brief stints at the Waterloo Courier, Cedar Falls Record and Ottumwa Courier.

Allspach, a native of Baxter in east-central Iowa, started college at Wartburg in Waverly, went to the Army and then graduated from William Penn in Oskaloosa. He began his newspaper career at the Oskaloosa Herald, went to the Cedar Rapids Gazette and the Centerville Iowegian before joining Hersom in Sioux City.

In eastern Iowa, the Cedar Rapids Gazette has had an Ogden covering and/or supervising the coverage of high school sports for more than 50 years.

First it was Jack Ogden, who "walked the sidelines all over eastern Iowa from the 1950s on" and served as executive sports editor of the Gazette "for 30-plus years," said his son and successor J.R. Ogden.

In fact, it's a case of father hiring son.

"I was 17 years old, going to Washington High School in Cedar Rapids," J.R. remembered. "In my junior year, I decided not to play football and basketball, and Dad said, 'Well, then you're going to get a job.' "

J.R. became a part-time sports staff member at the Gazette, continued part-time through his college years at the University of Northern Iowa and the University of Iowa, then started full-time. Through the 1980s and into the early 1990s, J.R. focused on covering high school wrestling and track.

Jack Ogden died in the 1980s. Succeeding him as sports editor was Mike Chapman, and he was followed by Mark Dukes.

J.R. became sports editor in 1998. He heads a staff of 13 full-time and six part-time reporters and editors. The prep sports coordinator is Jeff Linder, who joined the Gazette in 1995, worked with veteran Bob Hilton on sports until Hilton retired, then became coordinator in 1999. Linder, a native of Stanwood in eastern Iowa, graduated from Drake University and then picked up experience at the Iowa Falls Times-Citizen, the Fairfield Daily Ledger and the Burlington Hawk Eye.

Also heavily involved in the Gazette's high school sports coverage are Jeff Dahn, Jeff Johnson, John Riehl and K.J. Pilcher. That's a lot of emphasis on coverage of the preps.

"In my opinion, behind our coverage of University of Iowa sports, our prep sports coverage is number two in importance here," said J.R. Ogden. "High school sports is the one thing we can give the reader things that they can't get off the Internet or in other places. Everybody on our staff has been involved in prep coverage at one time or another. I think that goes back to my dad's influence. High school sports were everything to him. He had a chance to cover the colleges, of course, but he always wanted to cover high school sports. He did a 'Meet the Preps' column for years, picked a 'Prep of the Week' and really became 'Mr. Preps' all over eastern Iowa."

Some veteran sportswriters, like Dearrel Bates of the Quad-City Times in Davenport, say they prefer covering high school athletes instead of those playing in the brighter lights.

"I'm sort of old-fashioned, maybe," said Bates, who has been writing prep sports for 41 years, "but I really look at high school sports as the last pure form of athletics.

"I also cover the small colleges and junior colleges now, and they're basically okay, although most of them do give their athletes some subsidies. I like the idea that high school kids are playing for fun and because they love the game."

Bates, at 63 years old in early 2005, is the dean of Iowa's full-time high school sportswriters as the IHSAA observes its one-hundreth anniversary. His reporting and writing are solid, efficient and authoritative.

He is a native of Muscatine and he began his newspaper career during his high school and college years working part-time at the Muscatine Journal for the veteran sports editor there, Frank Blake. So did Dearrel's brother Roger Bates, who is seven years younger, and now Roger is the Journal's sports editor.

Dearrel Bates' first full-time newspaper job was as the Journal's farm editor, the first two years he was out of college. What did he know about farming? "Nothing," he said with a laugh, "but my wife grew up on a farm. When I'd be out covering the farms and small towns around Muscatine, and doing the county fair, she'd have to help explain the difference between a sow and a boar. It was an okay job, but obviously I wanted to be back in sports."

That happened when he landed the sports editor's job at the Oskaloosa Herald in 1964. He spent two years there, then joined the Marshalltown Times-Republican as sports editor. In 1969, he joined the Davenport newspaper's sports department, and he's spent the rest of his career there. The staff includes 11 full-time editors and reporters, and with several part-timers, they cover high school and community sports in both Iowa and Illinois, as well as college and university teams in both states.

Bates has occasionally been summoned over the years to help with coverage of the Iowa Hawkeyes and Iowa State Cyclones.

"I enjoy sports at every level," he said, "but especially the high schools."

Another of the long-tenured writers still actively covering Iowa's preps is Chuck Schoffner, the Associated Press sports editor for Iowa, who i based in the wire service's Des Moines news bureau. A native of Ohio who finished high school in Indiana, Schoffner came to Iowa to attend Drake University and started his sportswriting career while he was still a student, working part-time for the old United Press International in Des Moines. He joined the AP in 1979.

"I probably covered a state basketball tournament for the first time in about 1972 for UPI," Schoffner said. "I guess I've been around long enough that maybe I shouldn't still be sitting on those planks at games."

By 2005 he wasn't doing as of that as he used to, because since 1994, he has also been the AP's national reporter for major college women's basketball. In that position, he covered many of the biggest games between the NCAA Division I teams, as well as the NCAA tournament.

In 2005 Schoffner said he still spends "a fourth to a third" of his work time covering Iowa high school athletes. His stories are distributed to more than 30 daily newspapers in the state, as well as nearly all of the radio and television stations. He also oversees the AP's weekly polls of the high school football and boys' basketball teams. He definitely does not consider it a come-down to do coverage of high school sports while he's also doing national stories on women's basketball.

"Prep sports are such a big part of life in Iowa," Schoffner said. "With the lack of major league professional sports here, there is still a lot of statewide interest in good high school teams, and the state tournaments are always huge attractions. They're still big news."

Of course, the Des Moines Register's coverage of Iowa high school sports, dating from the start of Jack North's career nearly 90 years ago, set the early standard for newspapers across the state. Both the Register and the afternoon Tribune circulated statewide until the 1960s, when the Tribune's focus was redirected to central Iowa. In 1982, it ceased publication.

The names of the Register's chief prep sportswriters ring as familiar to many Iowans as the names or former governors and senators. Following North and Brad Wilson, there was Tony Cordaro, Chuck Burdick, Randy Peterson, Dave Stockdale, Susan Harman and now John Naughton, Andrew Logue, Rob Gray and Dan McCool, the latter of whom you've already met in this book.

Burdick was the chief from the mid-1960s into the 1980s before handing off to Peterson, who covered the preps for more than a decade. In 1990, Peterson also began doing more coverage of major college sports for the Register, and Harman took over on the preps. She had practiced law for 11 years before she went back to college to study journalism and then began her sportswriting career. After leaving the Register, she worked briefly in politics and then became sports editor of the Daily Tribune in Ames for five years. In 2003, she joined the Iowa City Press-Citizen as its prep sports reporter.

Since 1993, the chief of the Register's high school coverage team has been Naughton, a Des Moines native who is now 43. He chips in with help on nearly all the high school athletic events, and takes the lead on girls' sports.

Logue, Gray and McCool have done more of the boys' coverage in the last few years. And as Logue has taken on more assignments in major college sports, more of the boys' coverage has been in McCool's hands, with Gray in support.

"Right now, Dan McCool is the best friend of Iowa's high school boy athletes," said Bud Legg, the information specialist at the IHSAA. "They may not know him, but he's their best friend. He also does a great job on major-college wrestling and small-college sports in general for the Register, but what he does for high school sports is so important. Coaches have a great deal of trust in him."

The 45-year-old McCool, a giant of a man at 6 ft., 6 in. tall and 285 pounds, seems almost a fashion counterpoint to Wilson, the nattily-dressed Register prep reporter of the 1950s and '60s. At games and around the Register's newsroom, you most often see McCool wearing jeans, a T-shirt from some wrestling tournament or boxing match, a ball cap and, on occasion, a pair of red high-topped wrestling shoes. He has a large, bushy mustache and seems perpetually in need of a haircut and shave. And yet, he's so good at his job that his bosses, coaches, athletes and fans don't seem to mind how he looks. He points out that he did wear a tuxedo when he got married in 1996. And he wore a coat and tie in 2001 when he and Kevin Evans, of the Waterloo Courier, were picked as the honorary escorts of the "Grand March" that starts championship night at the state wrestling tournament.

McCool is just as much a character as all of the above indicates.

He is a native of Clarion in north-central Iowa, the youngest of five sons of Dr. Robert and Kitty McCool, who often did medical missionary work in the Dominican Republic, St. Lucia and on Indian reservations in the American West.

"I was never much of an athlete," he said. "In fact, I was a bad one. I was a bad baseball pitcher and a bad center on the football team. I tried wrestling in junior high, but Clarion is a hotbed of wrestling, and I wasn't good enough to make it."

But he was a fine writer, from his earliest school years, and by high school, he was a regular in the office of the Wright County Monitor newspaper there in town.

"That got started because my older brother ran the little league baseball program in town, and I'd write up his results every Monday and take them to the paper," McCool remembered. "Eventually I moved into covering boys' basketball, baseball and the other sports."

After he graduated from high school in 1978, he joined the U.S. Navy, was out in three weeks on a medical discharge and then took a job as a sports and news reporter for the Knoxville Journal-Express. After two years there, he moved on to a sportswriting job at the Dickinson Press in North Dakota, the first daily newspaper he had worked for – and he was immediately hooked on journalism.

In 1982, he returned to Iowa and a sports job with the Cedar Falls Record. A year later, the paper was merged into the Waterloo Courier, and McCool was out of full-time work.

But Register sportswriter Burdick, who had come to know McCool and his work, suggested to his bosses at the Des Moines paper that McCool would be a good part-time "correspondent" to cover home football games at UNI in Cedar Falls.

"I did that, and then the next thing I knew, the Register was asking me to do basketball media day," McCool said. "Then they had me do more and more games at UNI and some high school stuff around the area. The UNI-Dome became like my home away from home."

That arrangement lasted a decade, with McCool becoming the Register's primary reporter on UNI sports, traveling with the teams, occasionally initiating other stories – and always trying to cut corners on his expenses in the hope that the newspaper bosses would not decide it was too costly having him around. He laughs now recalling how in 1988, he covered world championship boxing match at Caesar's Palace in Las Vegas involving fighter Michael Nunn of Davenport. "I stayed in a little place where my week's lodging was $125," he said. "I went out and bought a can of roach powder to sprinkle on the floor around the bed."

Eventually, McCool had become so valuable to the Register he was hired full-time. He then spent one more year based in Cedar Falls, then moved to Des Moines in 1994. He was thrilled.

"I grew up reading the Register and Tribune," he said, "and I was the kid in Clarion who called in our game scores to the Register and the Des Moines radio and TV stations. I always remember getting up on Saturday mornings in the fall, grabbing the Register and checking out whose name go mentioned in the football and basketball coverage. That was big stuff."

Does he perceive that it still is "big stuff," for young athletes in Iowa

"Oh, it's slipped a little, I suppose," McCool said. "In some places, high school sports aren't the end-all, be-all they once were. Kids want to do other things now. They want a car. They have to have a job.

"But, you know what? I always remember back in Clarion how everyone wanted to 'make state.' And the one thing that hasn't changed in my 26 years since high school is that kids still dream. They still want to be on a state championship team, or be a state qualifier in wrestling or run in the state track meet."

In 2005, McCool's "beat" included high school football, wrestling, soccer, baseball and some tennis, as well as major college wrestling and all sports at Iowa's small colleges.

He said while "the Register is a different paper now, high school sports is still regarded as being very important. It seems to be one part of the paper that still has an interest in all four corners of the state."

McCool said he enjoys "working with kids, and watching them go from somebody trying to find their way, to becoming somebody who can rule the roost. I'm finding now that I'm covering the second generation of athletes. I'll go to a wrestling tournament somewhere, see some good kid and realizing I covered his dad, too."

How does he get along with them?

"I think real well," he said. "I always want them to think they're going to get fair treatment by me. I see how hard most of these kids work, trying to get better, trying to win. They work too hard to get criticized, but sometimes they get that from the fans and the media. I think it's pretty tough to write something negative about a kid who is trying so hard."

THE BIGGEST AND LITTLEST OF OUR REGULAR-SEASON COMPETITIONS. Years from now, fans may wonder what the scale was of Iowa high school boys' athletics at the time of the IHSAA's centennial. So I thought it important to try to frame it up for them.

Among all high school sporting events that happen every year in Iowa, early in this 21st century, no regular season game or event is consistently as big a spectacle as the football face-off each fall between the Tigers of Valley High School and the Maroons of Dowling Catholic High School, both located in West Des Moines.

The littlest? It may well be a basketball game like the one I attended on a Monday night early in 2004, when the Rivermont Collegiate "Lions" were hosting the Scattergood Friends School "Crew" in Bettendorf in eastern Iowa. Not many fans noticed.

I'm going to take you to both events here.

For those living outside Iowa and unaware, Valley High School and Dowling Catholic are traditional powerhouses in nearly all sports, and they especially love their football. One or the other contends for the Class 4A state championship almost every season.

So, on a pleasant Friday night in September, 2003, I was among 10,000 fans who packed the beautiful, two-year-old, $8-million Valley Stadium. Everything about the game was big and grand, even the final score – Valley, 45-14. The Tigers' superstar running back Jason Scales had an amazing night, carrying the football 24 times for 274 yards and four touchdowns – and being crowned Homecoming king at halftime.

Let's look around.

Both teams suit-up 50 to 60 players. Valley head coach Gary Swenson has nine assistant coaches, five of them volunteers, and Dowling's coach then, Matt Dillon, has 10 assistants.

How many high school teams play games on artificial turf? They do at Valley Stadium. There is also a brick locker room at the north end of the field big enough to accommodate both squads.

The scoreboard is a tower more than 50-feet tall at the south end of the playing field, with brightly-lit orange and black letters arching above the board to spell out "Valley."

The marching band, the regionally-renowned Valley High School Marchmasters, must put 200 or more uniformed kids on the field, and they play as well as most big-time college bands. My goodness, the band hauls its instruments and other equipment to performances in a semi-trailer truck.

There were a half-dozen reporters from newspapers and other publications covering the game. Three radio stations were broadcasting it live. A cable television channel was taping it for replay through the weekend, and all three Des Moines network stations had video crews there to shoot the highlights for their Friday night sportscasts. And – the surest sign of a big event in urban America – one of the television stations had its news helicopter hovering over the stadium as fans were arriving.

There were 10 corporate sponsors of this game, and each time Valley scored, each of the sponsors would donate $25 to Valley High's "Dollars for Scholars" program that provides funds for college scholarships for the school's graduates – and not just athletes.

It was a great scene, well supervised and policed. Very enjoyable.

Valley's athletic program was named the best in the state in both the 2002-03 and 2003-04 school years in a survey by the Des Moines Register. The newspaper awards points to each school that finishes in the top eight in state competitions in all sports – boys' and girls' – and then totals them to determine the top programs. In the first of those two years, Valley's teams finished fourth or higher in the state in 14 of the 19 sports the school offers. In 2003-04, the Tigers won state championships in football and baseball and were among the top eight finishers in 11 other sports.

And yet, the focus of Valley's program is not on the superior athlete.

When Register columnist Nancy Clark asked Valley athletic director

Steve Duncan how many of the school's athletes would go on to compete in college sports, he said he had no count. "We don't figure that," Duncan responded, "because we know that 98 percent of high school kids end their athletic careers at the high school level. We're here for that 98 percent, to give them as good an experience as we can."

Duncan, a Burlington native who has been Valley athletic director since 1989, administers a program that operates on a $1.3 million annual budget, if you include the coaching salaries of 72 coaches. Transportation costs alone for Tiger teams range from $60,000 to $68,000 per year. But it's all to serve the 1,500 athletes who are members of the 50 or more teams, including varsity, sophomore and freshman squads.

"We're a little unusual for a 4-A school in that we have a no-cut philosophy throughout our athletic program," Duncan said. "For some kids, just being a part of the team is important, even if they're not getting to play as much as they might like, so we find a way to keep them involved. We've had kids go through all four years in a sport, never dress once for a game and yet never miss a practice."

Key to the Tigers' success in many of the sports has been the athletes' year-around dedication to workouts in the Valley fitness center. Duncan designed it in 1989, had it built for $60,000 and athletic officials from across the nation have used it as a model when they've developed their own fitness centers. It is directed by Gary Swenson, the football coach. "Obviously that has been very important to the success of Gary's football team, but he has been just as committed in helping all of our athletes."

Duncan pushes himself to maintain contact with all the coaches and athletes. He does a walk-through of nearly every Tiger practice session. He meets every Monday morning for 45 minutes with the group of head coaches whose sports are in season. And he meets twice monthly with the "Athletic Director's Advisory Council" – which includes 20 athletes selected by their teammates. "We meet for an hour at 6:30 in the morning on two Wednesdays each month, just me and the kids," Duncan said. "It's more of a discussion group than an action group, but it gives me a chance to hear directly from the athletes how they think things are going."

It may surprise many that Valley's athletes tend not to be one-sport specialists.

"I believe we have a very high percentage of multiple sport athletes, and we encourage that," Duncan said. "Many of our athletes are also involved in our music programs, which are very strong and other activities, too. We've got a very active student body"

He said three things are key to all of Valley's success in sports: 1) The longevity and like-mindedness of the coaches – all of whom Duncan has hired during his 17 years as athletic director; 2) outstanding facilities and equipment, and 3) the fact that "our parents have very high expectations for their children."

As I took it all in at the Valley vs. Dowling football game, I began wondering – what is on the other end of this? What regular season game athletic event would be as "little" as the Valley-Dowling football game is big?

That's what led me to a tiny gym in the eastern Iowa town of Bettendorf, high up on a bluff with a stunning view of the Mississippi River as it meanders through the "Quad Cities" of Iowa and Illinois.

I was there for Rivermont Collegiate vs. Scattergood Friends in a mostly-boys high school basketball game. I say "mostly-boys" because Scattergood did have freshmen Vicki Volk and Kathryn Gunderson on its squad, and the two girls more than held their own when they played.

These two private schools, both over 100 years old, are among the newest members of the IHSAA.

Rivermont, a college prep school in Bettendorf, was founded as Saint Katharine's in 1884 by the Episcopal Diocese of Iowa as a boarding school for girls. In 1968, the school dropped its boarding program, opened up to boys and re-named itself St. Katharine's-St. Mark's. In 1973 the school moved from a bluff top in nearby Davenport to Bettendorf – in fact, into the mansion and carriage house built in 1915 by industrialist Joseph Bettendorf. In 1980, the affiliation with the Episcopal Church ended and in January, 2002, the name was changed to clear up the frequent confusion over whether St. Katharine's-St. Mark's was a parochial school. "Rivermont Collegiate" seemed a good choice for a school that has long prepared its students for some of the best colleges and universities in the nation. When was visiting, there were 257 students in pre-kindergarten through 12th grade, with 48 in the top four grades of the upper school. More than 90 percent of the students come from the Quad Cities area, with a few driving each day from homes up to an hour away. Four students have come from Korea. High school tuition for the 2004-05 year was $8,700, excluding meals, and 40 percent of the students receive some level of financial assistance.

Scattergood Friends School, located 45 miles west along Interstate Highway 80, just east of the town of West Branch, was founded as a boarding school in 1890 by the Religious Society of Friends, known informally as the Quakers. It has a proud history of social compassion, hosting many refugees – sometimes whole families – from around the world. The actual school operates only on the high school level, with 54 enrolled in 2004 in grades 9-12. Total costs for boarding students is listed at $18,000 per year, or $10,000 for day students, with the school's average aid package at $5,500 per student.

Both schools have had limited athletic programs through the years, generally competing at the "club" level. In 1995, St. Katharine's-St. Mark's did play a year of interscholastic basketball sanctioned by the IHSAA, but after getting beat 115-15 by powerful Bellevue Marquette in the first round of the district tournament, they decided to stick to club competition a while longer.

But by early 2004, both had joined the IHSAA. Rivermont had decided to compete again in the basketball tournament, while Scattergood – while ramping up its level of competition – decided to wait another year or two for tournament play.

Their schedules include such church schools such as Tri-State Christian in Illinois, and from Iowa, Cono Christian of Walker, Iowa Mennonite of Kalona and Burlington Notre Dame. They play such public high schools in Iowa as Olin, Alburnett, WACO of Wayland, North Linn of Troy Mills and Bennett.

The Rivermont boys were a 69-29 winner over Scattergood in the game I saw. It was "Parents Night" at Rivermont, so the crowd was bigger than normal for a home game. In fact, there were 47 people – I counted them myself – sitting in the only bleachers, located on the stage that is the south wall of the gym built in 1976.

Although this basketball game couldn't have been any more different from the scene at the Valley-Dowling football game I had seen, it was just as enjoyable – maybe even more so. Every kid on the floor seemed to give just as much of himself (or, in the case of the two Scattergood players, herself) as Valley's superstar running back Jason Scales had that night.

Among the Rivermont Lions were brothers Adeel Yaseen, a senior, and Raheel Yaseen, a sophomore, the starting guards, quick as cats and deft with their passing. Their father, who is a physician, and mother came from Pakistan, settled in Arkansas and then re-settled in the Quad Cities. The Yaseen brothers were feeding the ball to, among others on the wings, Vishal Parihk and Ramana Gorrepatti, whose parents came from India. Pakistanis and Indians may not get along so well in the ol' home countries, but on the Rivermont basketball team, they were doing just fine.

Meanwhile, the Scattergood Friends squad included not only the two girls, but also three players from Rwanda in Africa – David Gatabazi, Chris Kayonga and Fabrice Musoni. They also had Edgar Weibe from Germany, Sagoshi Ishihara of Japan and perhaps the best player on the team Young-Bong Kim of Korea.

You know they have an interesting mix of home-grown kids playing, too, just by considering some of their names – Skyler McLean and Demario Davis of Scattergood, and Connery Kappeler and Axel Larson of Rivermont.

The coaches were as interesting as their players.

Scattergood coach Michael Watson, 27 in 2004, introduced himself to me as "head coach, assistant coach, athletic director, student manager and bus driver." He is an Iowa City native who was a good soccer and basketball player at West High School. Then he went on to Beloit College in Wisconsin where he majored in creative writing and education. Five years ago, he took the job at Scattergood, started the sports program and has stayed.

Why?

"Well, this is the place where I can be a head coach this young," Watson said. "I was also getting the opportunity to develop a program for a school. I thought that if I could do that here, then later on I'll be more like o get a chance to do it somewhere else, too. It's been a lot of work – a whole lot of work – but I love seeing it develop. We're still not real good, but we're eight years of where we were when I came to Scattergood."

That Scattergood team's nickname, the "Crew"?

"There's a decades-old system for getting chores done at Scattergood called 'the crew system'," said Watson. "It involves working together, helping each other. We thought it'd be a good fit for the nickname of our teams."

Since he's a creative writer, does he have any stories stirring about his coaching experience at the school?

"Oh, I've got several pieces I'd like to write," he said with a grin. "Finding time to do it is the problem."

Ed Knupp, then 42 in 2004 and the Rivermont head coach and athletic director, pointed out that while he did have a paid assistant coach, Dr. Laura Hechtel, and a volunteer assistant, Jeff Hasse, "I still am the one who washes the team uniforms and sweeps the gym floor after games."

Knupp grew up as a fair athlete in Vinton, Iowa, then went on to Iowa State University, where he didn't compete in intercollegiate athletics but did help Cyclone coach Johnny Orr with his summer basketball camps. That helped him after graduation, when he landed a job as an assistant men's basketball coach at Wartburg College in Waverly, where he served nine years with Wartburg head coach Buzz Levick. Incidentally, Rivermont was "still running Levick's offense," Knupp said with a smile, "even if it's a little old-school by today's standards."

Knupp later served two seasons as head men's basketball coach and athletic director at Mount Saint Clare College in Clinton, Iowa, and he's also had stops at two colleges that have since closed – Mount Senario in Wisconsin and Marycrest in Davenport. Besides coaching men's basketball, he has coached the women's game, served as athletic director and started/coached three college women's soccer programs. He thought he was done with coaching in 2001, when he opted to become general manager of the highly-successful Quad-City Steamwheelers professional football team in the arena league. He did two seasons with the Steamwheelers before happening into the opportunity at Rivermont Collegiate and making the move.

"I love it here," said Knupp, who served as athletic director in his first year at Rivermont and then took over the basketball program in his second year. "I'm divorced, but I have a three-year-old son and I want to b part of his life as he's growing up. I already knew how much time college athletics takes you away from home. Between recruiting, scouting and playing, you're on the road so much. Then with the Steamwheelers, I learn that management of minor league sports is a real labor-intensive business.

"So I found this job, which means my son will be able to go to sch here and I'll be able to spend a lot of time with him. Besides that, I get summers off, and I'm heading up a basketball program that has absolutely pressure."

Knupp was even living at Rivermont, holding the title "Mansion Master" What that really means, he noted, is that he was in charge of locki up at night after Rivermont or outside groups have used the facilities. And Knupp was allowed to live in an apartment built into the spectacular old home where the Bettendorf brothers once entertained the railroad barons America. They'd come to Davenport to buy the railroad car wheel assembl that the brothers invented and produced at their iron works.

That mansion now also serves as the administration building as wel as hosting some classes and the dining area at the school.

Headmaster David Stephens came seven years ago to St. Katharine St. Mark's after heading the Upper School at Worcester Academy west of Boston in Massachusetts. He was born and raised at Lawrenceville School i New Jersey, where his father was on the faculty. He became a good hockey goaltender, one whose services were sought by colleges throughout New England. He shocked his family by becoming its first male to opt out of Princeton University, choosing instead Hobart College in Geneva, New Yo where he thought he would get more time on the ice. He did, and now in h 40s, he's still playing the game – in the adult leagues around the Quad Citie

Stephens loves to point out that the Episcopal bishop who came to Davenport to establish the original St. Katharine's School came from Hoba College.

Stephens has had a major impact on Rivermont. Besides shoring up the academic programs, he also led an effort that raised $4.5 million and bu Becherer Hall, which opened in 2001 and is a major addition to classroom

198

facilities and also includes a nice performing arts auditorium. With the extra space, he has been successful in attracting more students. When he came, there were 198 in the pre-school through upper school, in early 2004 there were the 257 and "we're budgeting for 280, growing toward a goal of 300, in the next year or two," he said.

When you check Rivermont's list of major donors, you see such family names as Becherer, Waterman, Foster, Figge, Schermer, Adler, Van Duyne, Pray, Carver and more. Those are families that have long provided the business, industrial, medical and social leadership of the Quad Cities area. Most have sent children through Rivermont or its predecessor schools, too.

So, why has Rivermont decided to elevate the athletic program into interscholastic and tournament competition? There's now volleyball, coed soccer, golf, cross country and track. And in 2004, tennis was under consideration.

"Everyone around the Quad Cities knows we have outstanding academics at Rivermont, but some think we're a nerd school," Stephens said. "They forget that our students, while being very bright, are also normal kids who have interests in all kinds of activities. We've had some agreements with Bettendorf High and other schools to let some of our kids who have an interest play on their teams, but we've reached a point where there is enough interest among our students to have our own teams.

"In addition, one thing we've been focusing on is marketing ourselves better," he continued. "We've been doing a lot of really good things in academics and the arts, but a lot of the people in the Quad Cities just never thought about us. Now with our boys' basketball team playing an interscholastic schedule, there we are on the 'Highlight Zones' on the local TV stations on Friday nights. Our games are getting newspaper coverage. People are a whole lot more aware of us, and that's really helping us."

Coming away from Rivermont, I realized ever more the real value of a good high school sports program. And, you know, the number of wins and losses has little to do with it.

It's all about the kids, what they learn and how the experience helps them grow. The challenge is for coaches and administrators to keep that in perspective – whether the crowd is 10,000 in a major stadium or 47 in a crackerbox gym.

Of course, it's an even bigger challenge for us fans to keep that in perspective. Sometimes we're pretty good about that. Other times we need be reminded.

A ROLL CALL OF OUR MOST MEMORABLE TEAM NICKNAMES. You know, high school boys' sports in Iowa just haven't been quite as much fun since 1990. That's when the Everly and Clay Central schools in northwest Iowa consolidated. That meant a new nickname for the Clay Central-Everly teams: "Mavericks." Not bad, to be sure.

But Clay Central, which included the towns of Royal, Rossie and Greenville, gave up being the "Camanches."

And worst of all, there were no more Everly "Cattlefeeders" boys' teams or "Cattlefeederettes" girls' teams.

Because of changing times, shifting populations and consolidating schools, we've also lost the Churdan Gremlins, the Clutier Charging Czechs the Rockford Rohawks, the Sheffield Claydiggers, the Fox Valley Trotters, the Bancroft St. John's Johnnies, the Protivin Rudolphinum Rudohawks, the Loras Academy Gubs and – losing this one still breaks my heart – the Mallard Ducks.

The Ducks were the obvious and perfect nickname for a team from the northwest Iowa town of Mallard (pop. 600), where the town sign along Iowa Highway 4 is topped by a colorful mallard duck the size of a buffalo, and the billboard says, "Mallard – We're friendly ducks!"

It was not only a great nickname, the school had perhaps Iowa's greatest cheer. If the Ducks were leading going into the fourth quarter of games – and sometimes even if they weren't – the Mallard fans would stand tuck their arms like wings and chant together:

> *Black and gold!*
> *Gold and black!*
> *Mallard Ducks!*
> *Quack! Quack! Quack!*

One summer when RAGBRAI – that's the Des Moines "Register's Annual Great Bicycle Ride Across Iowa" – rolled through Mallard, more than 2,000 of the cyclists paused during their lunch stop and all did the Duck cheer together on the main street of Mallard.

All those nicknames – and that cheer – are a lot of lore to lose.

But the good news is that we are still pretty well-stocked in Iowa when it comes to colorful and fun names of our high school teams.

Iowa is known as the "Hawkeye State," you know, and we have several different kinds of hawks – the Kee Hawks of Kee High School of Lansing, the Go-Hawks of Waverly-Shell Rock, the Mohawks of Mason City and Moravia, the Redhawks of North Tama, the E'Hawks of Emmetsburg, the J-Hawks of Cedar Rapids Jefferson and Urbandale, the Tigerhawks of Colfax-Mingo, the Little Hawks of City High in Iowa City, the Warhawks of Southeast Warren and the WaHawks of Waterloo West.

We still have nicknames with a nice link to a community's ethnicity or a tie to its history – the Saints of Mormon Trail High School in Garden Grove, the Dutch of Pella High, the Danes of Elk Horn-Kimballton, the Gaels of Fort Dodge St. Edmond, the Norsemen of Roland-Story, the Cowboys of Sidney ("The Rodeo Town"), the River Kings of Clinton (located on the Mississippi River), the Admirals of Farragut (a town named after Admiral David Farragut), the Sailors of Waterloo Columbus and the Bloodhounds of Fort Madison (home of the Iowa State Penitentiary).

Some nicknames just roll off the tongue right – the Muscatine Muskies, the Rock Valley Rockets, the Clarinda Cardinals (you can rearrange the letters in "Cardinal" and get "Clarinda"), the Chariton Chargers, the Clear Creek-Amana Clippers, the Crestwood Cadets, the Starmont Stars, the Ballard Bombers, the Bedford Bulldogs and the Akron-Westfield Westerners.

From the dark side, we have the Washington Demons, the Albia Blue Demons and the Osage Green Devils, while both Davenport Central and Martensdale-St. Marys are the Blue Devils.

But we can answer with the Crusaders from Bishop Heelan Catholic in Sioux City, more Crusaders from Coon Rapids-Bayard, the Saints of Xavier High in Cedar Rapids, the Knights of Unity Christian in Orange City and the Warriors of Cono Christian in Walker.

Unique? We've got unique!

There are the Orabs of Sheldon (where the school colors are orange and black), the Midgets of Estherville, the Toreadors of Boone, the Crew of Scattergood Friends, the Wheelers of Audubon, the Polar Bears of Des Moines North, the Nikes of Burlington Notre Dame, the Roadrunners of Interstate 35 High School in Truro and the Lions of Des Moines Christian.

Meanwhile, Iowa Mennonite, of Kalona, and Western Christian, of Hull, have no nicknames.

St. Albert of Council Bluffs has two – the boys' teams are the Falcons and the girls' teams are the Saintes.

All well and good.

But it's hard to imagine we'll ever fully recover from the loss of the Everly Cattlefeeders.

Chapter Six

The organizational history of the IHSAA

Things were a little rough in Iowa 100 years ago.

High school sports teams were just starting to form – in track and field, basketball, baseball and football, a sport thought to be for ruffians.

There were no formal rules governing participation and scheduling, just somebody's general idea of how the games were supposed to be played.

Bernie Saggau, the executive director of the Iowa High School Athletic Association in its centennial year of 2004, said stories he heard from his predecessor Lyle T. Quinn indicated "it wasn't unusual to find kids playing five, six, seven years. Some 'high school' teams even had military veterans and school teachers playing for them. And they'd bring in players from other towns. There were stories about some communities hiring the freshman team at Iowa State College to come represent them in their high school games.

"So, a bunch of the principals at schools around the state decided that there just had to be some rules. Mr. Quinn told me the first rule was pretty basic – 'you have to be in school to play.' "

Those school administrators were already organized in the Iowa High School Principals' Club. That organization would meet periodically, and one of their meetings was always held during the state teachers' convention, generally held in Des Moines late in the first semester.

In 1903, that club "acted to end the jumble of regulations by appointing a rules committee to draft a uniform code," according to a five-page history of the IHSAA in a 1954 edition of The Palimpsest magazine, a publication then of the State Historical Society of Iowa. "Out of this action came one set of rules for all schools participating in Iowa scholastic sports.

"The first rules committee had two members – Forrest C. Ensign of Council Bluffs and Maurice Ricker of Burlington. Their labors resulted in the Ensign-Ricker report, which the principals adopted in 1904. Carrying out one of the recommendations on December 28, 1904, the superintendents and principals formed the Iowa High School Athletic Association. The idea that had been forming for years at state teachers conventions was now a reality."

In the century since then, the IHSAA and its programs have given us some great athletes and teams. More importantly, they've produced legions of young people whose lives have been forever enriched by the competitive experience. They've also given us a whole lot of wonderful entertainment.

The first sports sanctioned by the IHSAA were football, track, basketball, baseball and football. Schools set their own schedules within the designated seasons. IHSAA-sponsored state competitions and tournaments began with track in 1906, basketball in 1923, wrestling in 1926, spring baseball in 1928 and the others came later. The most recent addition was soccer in 1994. However, before those IHSAA championship events, it was common for teams in all sports to go to invitational tournaments, with many of those sponsored by the University of Iowa and Iowa State College.

The IHSAA has also produced several great leaders and grand characters.

There was no part-time or full-time executive in the organization's earliest years. The superintendents and principals from around the state who were on the Board of Control took care of all business and whatever coordination was necessary. Their terms ran two years, but there was no limit on the number of years they could serve.

The early board members, according to The Palimpsest story, included D.A. Thornburg, of Grinnell; George Edward Marshall, of Sioux City; Frank L. Smart, of Dubuque; A.V. Storm, of Cherokee; R.S. Whitley, of Sioux City; M.M. Bedall, of Boone; R.B. Crone, of Washington; Eugene Henely, of Grinnell; Seth Thomas, of Fort Dodge, and C. E. Humphrey, of Denison.

Marshall, who was principal at Sioux City High School when he served on the first board in 1904, went off in 1906 when he was moving to become principal at Davenport High School, then was re-elected in 1908 and served until 1932.

He was certainly one of the most influential persons in the organization's history. Harry Burrell, the well-known Iowa State sports publicist who wrote that IHSAA mini-history in 1954 for The Palimpsest, characterized Marshall this way:

> *George Edward Marshall – he was never just George Marshall*
> *– more than any other man gave of his time to the IHSAA.*
> *A member of the board for 28 years, his imprint on the high school*
> *athletic field went far beyond the confines of his state. He played*
> *a leading part in the formation of the National Federation of State*
> *High School Associations. That group, working with the various*
> *state organizaitons, has moved high school athletics to a leve of the*
> *highest ideals of play and sportsmanship. Marshall died in 1932, but*
> *the impact of th eman is still felt in the state and nation wherever*
> *high school athletics are conducted.*

Marshall also apparently made many of the decisions about eligibility and other issues. "Often…Marshall would simply explain the decisions by mail and that would end any problem," Burrell wrote. "School men…realized the need for organization and ethics, and accepted the early rulings most gracefully."

Among those other early board members, Grinnell's Henely served 20 years. Denison's Humphrey served 17. Eventually, the term for board members was extended to five years, and a limit of two terms was agreed upon. The last board member to serve longer than 10 years was R.R. "Red" Watson, superintendent at Sheffield and later New Market, who served from 1945 to 1965.

THE IHSAA'S FIRST EXECUTIVE – A GREAT LEADER, A GRAND CHARACTER. Another person who was apparently involved in the IHSAA founding and who later became very prominent in the organization was George A. Brown.

In 1904, Brown was an enthusiastic 22-year-old teacher and coach in Shenandoah in southwest Iowa who, according to newspaper stories, actively supported the idea of a new organization to sanction and control high school sports.

He had grown up in nearby Hamburg, and was still attending and playing football at Tabor College in Tabor, another town in that area. He was already certified to teach after completing a two-year education course at the college. Brown, in 1923, became the first executive secretary of the IHSAA, after it had grown to the point where it needed more management than the volunteer members of the Board of Control could give it. He worked part-time at it until 1927, when the board hired him full-time.

He was certainly one of those great leaders and grand characters in the IHSAA's history.

Brown drove the growth of the association to nearly 1,000 member high schools. In 1932, he directed a change in policy that for the first time allowed IHSAA member schools to schedule games against Catholic high schools. He was an innovator who encouraged an Iowa company to develop a new basketball when schools complained that the balls from the national chains were too expensive. In 1939, he founded the Iowa High School Insurance Company so that, in a time when many Iowa families were living in near poverty, athletes would indeed have health insurance in case they were injured during competition. He presided over the expansion of IHSAA programs from four sports to nine, adding wrestling, golf, tennis, cross country and swimming

But he was also in charge when interscholastic competition for girls was banned in 1926. That caused the schools that wanted to continue offering the very popular game of girls' basketball to form a separate sanctioning body, the Iowa Girls High School Athletic Union, in 1927. Brown briefly headed both the boys' and the girls' organizations, then devoted his full attention to the boys' association.

A very strong and forceful administrator, Brown's dealings with the Board of Control, the member schools, the public and the media became increasingly contentious through the 1930s and early 1940s.

Until 1936, there were annual meetings of the IHSAA member

chools, with nearly all of them sending representatives. Those big meetings
became "classics in riotous debates," the Des Moines Register observed.
They were discontinued in 1937 in favor of forming a "Representative
Council" to give the schools additional oversight of Brown's and the board's
operations. The council continues to be part of IHSAA governance today.

And talk about contentious! At the 1937 state basketball tournament
in the Drake Fieldhouse in Des Moines, Brown, then 54, got into a fiery
argument with one of his most persistent critics, Waterloo Courier sports
editor Ed Moore, who was 29. "Words waxed hot, and Brown, many years
Moore's senior, swung on the sports editor," the Register reported, "but was
prevented from following up his advantage by friends."

In 1938, Brown decided to run as a Democratic candidate for State
Superintendent of Public Instruction, which would have taken him out of
the IHSAA, but he was defeated by fewer than 500 votes in the primary by
Lucy Hall of Newton.

Once he had entered the public arena as a candidate, several
members of the Iowa Legislature began making calls for Brown's ouster as
IHSAA executive secretary and for various other reforms in the organization.
One such idea from legislators was to disband the IHSAA and turn control
of high school athletics over to the State Department of Public Instruction.

Brown also managed to turn aside a secession effort by some
member schools. In the late 1930s, that group announced plans to form a
new "Hawkeye Athletic Association" in protest of Brown's management
practices, according to stories in the Des Moines Register's archives. Among
the leaders of that movement was Manning Superintendent Amos Lee,
and Brown immediately suspended Manning from IHSAA membership
for "flirting with a rival organization," the Register reported. Then
Superintendent K.G. Vanorden, a member of the Board of Control from
Mapleton, briefly took over leadership of the schools wanting to secede.
But "threatened with expulsion" from the IHSAA, which would have meant
being banned from competition with other IHSAA member schools, "the
rebel organization dissolved itself," the Register reported.

In a more positive step, and in an attempt to improve management
of the growing workload, Brown recommended in February, 1940, that 33-

year-old Lyle T. Quinn, a Boone High School teacher and coach, be hired b
the Board of Control as a new assistant secretary of the IHSAA.

Brown, with Quinn's assistance, then came up with his last real
innovation for the organization. Between Christmas and New Year's Day in
1940, the IHSAA's first "Coaching School and Officials Clinic" was held fo
two days in Marshalltown.

But right after that, the most tumultuous period in IHSAA history
erupted. Here is how sportswriter Brad Wilson of the Des Moines Register
looked back on it, in a 1947 story written after Brown's death:

> *In February 1941, a routine board meeting held in conjunction with the state
> swimming meet at Boone was turned into a turbulent session by I. W. Edie,
> then a Board of Control member from Rudd, Iowa. Edie, newly elected by the
> old northeast district, presented photostatic copies of letters and briefs, which he
> said showed conclusively that the election of Superintendent Dave J. Robbins of
> Cresco to the (Representative) Council 'had been maneuvered by Brown.' The
> board adjourned in a hurry and raced back to the association's Des Moines
> headquarters in quest of a ballot, which Brown said would clear him of Edie's
> charges. The ballot was never found. But Edie produced photostatic copies of th
> original ballot sent to Loras Academy of Dubuque, which had never voted as
> Brown claimed... The election of Robbins, after many weeks of investigation,
> was finally declared void and a new one held. Shortly afterward in March, Brow
> was asked to resign in a dramatic midnight session of the board.*

Robbins had been a supporter of Brown, and after the first election
Brown reported that Robbins had won election to the Representative
Council, 9 votes to 7, over Monticello Superintendent A. B. Grimes, who w
a critic of Brown. In the new election ordered by the Board of Control in
early March, Grimes won by five votes, the Register reported on March 10.

Brown said through his friend O.C. "Pop" Varner, a board
member who was superintendent and coach at Diagonal, that he was being
"persecuted" by the newspapers and that he was the victim of a "frame up,'
the Register said.

Brown's resignation came on March 12, 1941, after the board agreed o pay him $5,000 in "cold cash," per his demand, covering half of what his salary would have been for the two and one-half years remaining on his three-year contract.

He issued a statement to the media, saying: "I have accepted the proposition made by the majority of the Board of Control of the IHSAA and I am asking to be relieved from further duties, but will be available to assist Mr. Quinn with the correspondence and completion of the (basketball) tournaments."

Quinn was immediately named "manager" of the IHSAA with a one-year contract. But just eight months later, in November, 1941, the Board of Control went ahead and gave him the title of "executive secretary" and a three-year contract.

At the time of Brown's resignation, the Des Moines Tribune reported that he had "accepted a position with a school supplies firm." It is uncertain how much longer he remained in Iowa before he moved to Aurora, Illinois, just west of Chicago, where he died at 64 years old on March 1, 1947.

The Des Moines Register reported Brown "had been in poor health for a number of years" and was living with his son Robert Brown. He was also survived by his widow Florence Brown, who soon moved back to Des Moines from Illinois, and another son George C. Brown, also in Des Moines. Both George A. Brown and Florence Brown, who died in 1988, are buried in Resthaven Cemetery in West Des Moines.

It is sad but true that in 2004, George Aretus Brown is nearly a forgotten figure in IHSAA history.

Some of that may be because of all the trouble late in his career with the organization. And there is a possibility that in 1944, when Quinn moved the IHSAA's headquarters to his hometown of Boone, where he still lived, some of the early records and newspaper clippings about the Brown era were simply discarded.

But deep searches by librarians at the Des Moines Register, the State Library of Iowa, in Des Moines, and at the Public Library in Brown's hometown of Hamburg finally led to records – and eventually relatives – that helped document what an unusual and strong person he was.

George A. Brown was born May 31, 1882, in a sod hut near

Phillipsburg, Kansas, to homesteaders Henry H. and Bettie C. Brown. They had met in her home area of Fremont County, Iowa, the southwestern-mos county in the state. An older sister Bertie was born in 1880 and a young sister Nettie in 1884. Their father Henry Brown died of pneumonia in 189 and Bettie Brown then moved with her three young children to be near her relatives in Hamburg.

All three Brown children graduated from Hamburg High School – George in 1901 – and all three continued their studies at Tabor College. After two years George received the credentials then required for teaching at the high school level, and he was hired by Shenandoah High School as a teacher and coach in 1903.

While working in Shenandoah, Brown also continued his studies at Tabor College and graduated with a bachelor's degree in 1906, whereupon h was hired as the principal at Shenandoah High. Using the title that back the went with the principal's job, he was known as "Prof. (or Professor) Brown.

The Browns' involvement at Tabor College is very intriguing.

That liberal arts college was founded in 1853 by a Congregational Church minister Rev. John Todd, who came to southwest Iowa with a group of settlers from the area around Oberlin College in Ohio. Todd was a stror abolitionist on the slavery question, which was alarming and dividing the citizens of Missouri, Kansas and southwest Iowa. The town of Tabor and i new college were founded on the principles of "equality, devout spirituality and abolition," in the words of Todd. And Tabor soon became the "most significant hub of the Underground Railroad in western Iowa," according to an Internet site of the National Park Service. That "railroad" was actually a network of secure hiding places used by abolitionists to shuttle slaves who had escaped from their owners in Missouri and Kansas, on to the east and north across Iowa, to freedom.

It is well documented in Tabor history that among the abolitionists accompanying the slaves through that area "many times" was John Brown, the fiery anti-slavery leader whose base during the 1850s was Kansas. He wa eventually arrested, charged and convicted of treason for an attack he led on the Federal Arsenal in Harper's Ferry, Virginia, where he was attempting to steal rifles and pistols that his abolitionist followers could use. John Brown, who had 18 children by two wives, was hanged in 1859.

George A. Brown, who would eventually lead the IHSAA, may have been a descendant of the abolitionist.

"We were always told that," said Gerald Brown, of Phoenix, Arizona, the grandson of George A. Brown. "I don't know we've ever been able to document it, but that is what our grandmother told us."

Gerald's twin brother Ross Brown, of Tulsa, Oklahoma, said their grandmother "always said there were no records about the connection to John Brown because they were 'burned, out of embarrassment.'"

Of course, as time has passed, many people have started to regard John Brown as a hero of the anti-slavery movement, even if he did violate the laws of his era. George A. Brown was an active member of the Congregational Church the rest of his life, his grandsons noted.

While little is known about him during his high school years in Hamburg, there are some interesting glimpses of young George during his Tabor College and early career years.

At the college, he was frequently kidded about his receding hairline. The college yearbook "The Cardinal" of 1906 noted, "When George laughs one would think the hens were crowing. They say he lost his hair in the war. George is the president's confidential advisor, also an honored member of the Howard household. He leads Y.M. when Elmer does not. It is hard to say much about George – he says it all himself."

George played right tackle on the Tabor College football team, which traveled on railroad trains to play such opponents as Tarkio College of northwest Missouri and Amity College of College Springs in southwest Iowa.

Tabor College, incidentally, closed after the 1927 commencement ceremonies, re-opened briefly in the 1930s and then closed forever.

At Shenandoah High School, Brown was well respected. The official school history says Brown "is given much credit for increasing interest and enthusiasm in the development of a better curriculum" during his years as principal.

In the summer of 1908, he began his studies for a master's degree at the University of Chicago. He did not return to that university until the summer of 1915, when he took several more courses, but he never did complete the advanced degree.

He remained as principal at Shenandoah High until 1910, records indicate, and then became principal and coach at Grinnell High School.

In that community he met and married Florence Rose Cunningham, of Brooklyn, Iowa, who graduated in 1912 from old Iowa College, later renamed Grinnell College, with a double major in history and economics.

"I remember our grandmother telling how our grandfather didn't get serious about her at first," said Gerald Brown. "But then when he was applying for a job some place, he found out that they wouldn't give him a re. look unless he was married."

So George and Florence were soon married, and they moved on to Burlington in southeast Iowa, where George became principal and coach at Burlington High.

At both Grinnell and Burlington, he apparently continued his interes and involvement in the IHSAA.

By 1920, Brown decided to leave high school administrative work to become a Des Moines-based inspector of consolidated schools for the State Department of Public Instruction. In that position, he traveled all over Iowa and became acquainted with even more principals and superintendents. Tha led to his hiring as the first IHSAA executive secretary in 1923.

The Browns raised their sons George C. and Robert in a home in the Drake University neighborhood of Des Moines. Both Brown boys went to Roosevelt High School in Des Moines in the 1930s and may have been tenn players.

George C. Brown, who spent his career in Des Moines as a social worker, and his wife Helen had three children – the twin sons Ross and Gerald and daughter Karen.

Ross Brown was a two-year letterman in wrestling for Roosevelt in the 1960s, and Gerald Brown was a breaststroker and medley relay participant on a state champion swimming team. Karen was not an athlete.

"When we were in high school, I don't think it ever came up that ou grandfather had been the IHSAA executive," said Gerald Brown, "but he'd been gone a long time by then.

"He died the year after Ross and I were born, so we have no direct memory of him. And our dad didn't really tell us much about him, although I do think it was clear to us that our grandfather had a tremendous passion for athletics. It also seems like our grandparents were fairly well to do, because they not only had the house by Drake, they also owned a farm somewhere.

"Our grandmother, Florence, lived until she was 99, and she was still in her own home when she was 93, so we knew her real well. She was really something. Of course, she was a college graduate and she'd been around education all her life. I can remember in later years she'd talk a lot about teaching, about all that had happened to the teaching profession, and how it wasn't nearly as good a career as it once had been.

"My only other recollection about our grandfather George A. is a story Grandmother used to tell about him. She said that when our dad George C. wanted a bicycle for Christmas one year, George A. thought it'd be unsafe for a child his age to have a bike. Instead, they gave him a .22 rifle! In present times, people would be horrified by the .22 rifle gift for a youngster rather than a bike, but it must have seemed somewhat normal back then. And based on what I've been finding out lately about our grandfather, it now seems to fit. I wish I could have known him."

Gerald Brown is now a hospital administrator working in Texas and Arizona; his twin Ross Brown is now a computer software entrepreneur in Oklahoma, and their sister Karen Brown Goulart, now 55, is a critical care nurse in San Diego, California.

Their uncle Robert Brown, who was an attorney in Illinois, did not marry until late in life and had no children. I think there's too much information in this section.I think it's all important, particularly because most of it really exists nowhere else and is important for historical purposes.

THE RIGHT MAN AT THE RIGHT TIME. Lyle T. Quinn, who succeeded George A. Brown as executive secretary of the IHSAA, turned out to be exactly the kind of person the organization needed to recover from the years of turmoil.

He had come on board as an assistant to Brown in February, 1940 and 13 months later, he was in charge. He continued as executive secretary until his death at 60 years old in July of 1967, although Bernie Saggau was essentially directing the IHSAA during Quinn's last illness of about 18 months.

Quinn was solid, practical and stern when he needed to be. He was conservative in his financial dealings, his appearance and his mannerisms. He was also something of a renaissance man – a scholarly sort who was a voracious reader, loved poetry and recited it often, coached both debate and tennis at the high school and junior college levels, and was also a great fan of football and wrestling.

Lyle Temple Quinn (that middle name being his mother's maiden name) was born in Carroll, Iowa, in early November, 1906, to Fred and Anna Quinn, who may have lived in or near Scranton, Iowa, at that time. He was their only child.

In his infancy, the Quinns moved to Boone, where Fred went to work with his father and brothers at their Quinn Wire and Iron Works, founded in 1900 to produce calf weaners, devices used to facilitate the weaning, or nursing, of calves. They soon added a foundry and started making hog waterers and chimney tops, then branched out into making concrete drain tile. That firm is still in operation as a division of Besser Company, based in Alpena, Michigan, and is the world's largest manufacturer of concrete products equipment. In 1998 Besser acquired the company in Boone.

Lyle Quinn was captain of the Boone High School football team in 1924, then went on to attend Boone Junior College and Simpson College, in Indianola, Iowa, where he received his undergraduate degree. He did graduate work first at the University of Iowa, then at the Drake University School of Law during a period when he was contemplating becoming an attorney. Then in 1937 he earned his master's degree in education at Iowa State College in Ames. By then he was on the faculty at Boone High School, where from 1933 to 1940 he taught history, government and vocational guidance in addition to his coaching.

He married Kathryn Zimbeck Quinn, who was born and raised in Boone, and they lived most of their married life on the eastside of town in an unassuming one-bedroom house on Linn Street. The home had an extra room upstairs, where the Quinns' two daughters Charlotte and Marilyn slept.

Lyle Quinn became a very good game official in both basketball and

Football, and that is apparently how he came to the attention of George Brown at the IHSAA. "Mr. Quinn had the rules books memorized, and he could quote them verbatim," Bernie Saggau said. "My memory of conversations with him is that George Brown had asked him to do some rules interpretations for coaches and officials."

When Brown eventually offered Quinn the job at the IHSAA, he accepted – but only with the provision that he could commute from his home in Boone to the organization's office, which was then in the Valley Bank Building in downtown Des Moines. Quinn, then 35 years old, married and with the two young girls, felt settled in Boone and did not want to move to the capital city.

"Dad drove back and forth every day," recalled his daughter Marilyn Quinn, 74 in 2005, and a retired teacher in Des Moines. "That road was real curvy from Des Moines to Madrid, and then it was a straight shot on north to Boone. There were probably a lot of times the drive was dangerous because of the weather, but Dad always claimed he could do it blindfolded."

In April, 1941, a month after Brown resigned, the IHSAA moved its headquarters to the Des Moines Building, also downtown.

By January, 1944, Quinn had convinced the Board of Control that the organization could operate more efficiently in Boone.

"The staff at that point was only Mr. Quinn and about three other employees in Des Moines, and there was a former bank building available in downtown Boone," Saggau said. "The other banks in Boone got the building and rented it to the athletic association for the first year, with an option to buy the building after a year. The other banks might've been trying to keep some competing bank from coming to town and moving in there."

That stately old brick building, which had been the Security Savings Bank at 809 Eighth Street, served as the IHSAA's home until May, 1975. That's when the headquarters building located near the south entrance of town at 1605 South Story Street was completed.

The former headquarters building downtown has, since the 1970s, served as the offices of the law firm now known as Doran, Anderson & Baltimore, which has long represented the IHSAA.

The Quinns, obviously, loved life in Boone. They spent most

evenings, at least the ones when Lyle was not working, at home with their daughters. All four would go to University of Iowa football games, spread a blanket on the hood of their car and have big tailgate lunches. Lyle and Kathryn followed the girls in all their school activities, which for Marilyn included playing "both forward and guard at different times" in the old six-player form of girls' basketball.

Both Marilyn Quinn and her sister Charlotte Quinn Chiles, 76 years old in 2005, and retired in the Des Moines suburb of Clive, recall their father working very hard in the 1940s. He traveled the state extensively, probably to re-establish the IHSAA's legitimacy with the member schools and the public.

"Being an old debater, speaking in public came very easy to him," Charlotte Chiles said. "He was a great organizer – always one to follow a regimen – and he was a good leader."

Marilyn recalled that her father would usually work on Sunday mornings, the only time he would go to the IHSAA offices dressed casually, "and we'd have to call him at noon to tell him it was time to come home for dinner."

Lyle Quinn did not miss many of Kathryn Quinn's dinners.

"Mother was a great cook," said Marilyn. "Her father had been a butcher, and she really knew how to cook meat. One of Dad's favorites was always beef tongue, which Mom fixed with a lot of spices. She'd make sandwiches with tongue, too, and Dad loved those."

But he was also a great one for mashed potatoes and gravy, pie and biscuits, his daughters recall. Eventually his weight became a real problem, soaring to more than 300 pounds and complicating his problems with hypertension.

But from the 1940s into the early 1960s, he was a dynamo. He stayed reasonably fit by playing golf and tennis regularly. During pheasant hunting season, he'd carry his shotgun with him during his travels around Iowa, Charlotte said, "and sometimes he'd even come home with a pheasant!"

Lyle and Kathryn also traveled extensively to meetings of the National Federation of State High School Associations. Bernie Saggau recalled how he and his wife Lois accompanied the Quinns on one of those trips soon after Bernie joined the IHSAA in 1963. "We were going to Jackson

Hole, Wyoming, and when we pulled out of Boone that morning, somehow the subject of poetry came up," Bernie said. "Mr. Quinn started quoting poetry, and he kept it up for eight hours – and he never repeated a poem!"

When public interest in high school athletics started growing rapidly after World War II, Quinn was ready. He began adding services and programs for the member schools, introduced many innovations to the state tournaments and began adding members to the IHSAA office staff, too.

In 1951, he hired an old friend Harold G. Schmickley as assistant executive secretary. Schmickley was very well known across the state, having taught in two small high schools, and then serving as high school principal in Scranton and as superintendent of schools in Lanesboro, Jordan, Lohrville and Dayton. He was also a coach and highly regarded as an athletic official, and Bernie Saggau has always said that Schmickley "had one of the best baseball minds ever."

Schmickley served 20 years before his retirement, and lived into his late 90s in Boone, where he was an active community volunteer.

Among Quinn's many innovations were the August coaching schools and officials' clinics, started in 1941 at the YMCA Camp near Boone but soon moved to the Iowa Great Lakes; the start of baseball tournaments in the fall, spring and summer seasons; regular publication and distribution of Board of Control rulings; overseeing the 1947 move to allow the 60 member schools of the Iowa Catholic High School Association to join the IHSAA and thus become eligible to compete in the IHSAA tournaments; classification of the state track meet in 1948 to make competition more fair; arranging the first television coverage of a state basketball championships in 1953; moving the state basketball tournament to the new Veterans Memorial Auditorium in Des Moines in 1955; classification of the state basketball tournament in 1956; ordering the use of teeth-protecting mouthpieces in football in the early 1960s; beginning in the 1963-64 school year to allow special education students to play on their high schools' teams, and in July, 1966, at Saggau's urging, welcoming the Iowa High School Music Association and its first executive Leo Grether, of Manchester, to share quarters in the IHSAA building, an arrangement that continues today.

As Quinn built the clerical staff to 10 or 11, among his hires was his own daughter Charlotte Quinn Chiles.

"That was from 1963 until 1970," she recalled. "I was married and had young kids, and it was a really good place to work. Of course, I'd grown up going to the state tournaments, so I loved the athletic association anyway, and it was fun working there because you got to do so many different things with the sports changing through the year. My regular job at first was on the wrestling program, and then later I was an assistant bookkeeper to Ruth Ingalls. And it was great getting to work for my dad because I always looked up to him so much."

She was also there when her father's health began to slip, and when he died.

"That was very hard on us all," Charlotte said. "He'd been such an active man, it was hard to see him slowing down like he did. He died way too young, that's for sure."

Ingalls, who was from little Fraser just northwest of Boone, set the IHSAA tenure record for employees with 51 years before she retired in 2003. Both she and her sister Shirley Ingalls Morgan, who worked 10 years for the IHSAA, were recruited by Lyle Quinn.

"Mr. Quinn would go over to the high school and find out who were the top students in the stenographic course and then try to hire them," Ruth Ingalls said.

Actually, she opted first for nurse's training in Chicago, but after injuring her back while working with a patient, she decided office work would suit her better. When Quinn learned she had returned to Boone, he recruited her again. This time she accepted the job at the IHSAA, initially with its Iowa High School Insurance Company.

"My first day of work was July 1, 1952, and I had to call in sick," Ingalls said. "I had strep throat, and I was so sick there was no way I could get there. I wondered if they even believed me when I called. I've always said I spent the next 50 years that I worked there, trying to prove to them that it was a good decision to hire me."

She said she remembers Quinn "as a serious man, very dedicated. He knew everything that was going on in his office. He'd come out and look over employees' shoulders and make suggestions about what they were doing. But he was really good to his people. Every two years, he'd trade office equipment so that his people had the latest machines. And he had real foresight about innovations. I remember him bringing in a card-punch system – kind of the forerunner to the computer – at a time when that was considered pretty high-tech."

She also recalls him as "very persuasive. We had a saying in our office that you could go into his office to talk about the differences between black and white, and by the time you left, he'd have you convinced that black was white and white was black!"

But he could also be very abrupt, generally more with coaches and athletic directors than with his own employees.

"He could make people angry, and a lot of people were afraid of him, but he was a great man who did so much for the athletic association," said Bernie Saggau.

"With schools, he dealt almost totally with the administrators and almost never with the coaches. Every once in a while, some coach or an athletic director would be upset about something and call him, and Mr. Quinn could be so hard on them. He'd say, 'Does your principal know that you're calling me? You get his permission first, and then you can call me back,' and he'd hang up.

"I was coming out of the business world, and I knew you couldn't treat people like that," Saggau continued. "So I challenged him on it. I said, 'Mr. Quinn, you can't put people down like that.' But by that time in his career, I knew he wasn't feeling very well, and so any time I could, I covered him on that kind of stuff."

Arlo Flege, of Waverly, who eventually refereed 30 consecutive years in the IHSAA state wrestling tournament, recalled that when he was a young official starting out, "I had worked the district tournament in Waterloo five or six years, and I thought I ought to be working the state tournament, too. So I ran into Mr. Quinn at one of the tournaments and asked him.

"I said, 'Mr. Quinn, how long before I get to work a state tournament?'" Flege recalled. "He looked at me for a moment and then said, 'Young man, you just wait your turn!'" He wasn't smiling when he said it, either.

Flege, incidentally, served 27 years on the school board at Waverly-Shell Rock, and from that position, he was appointed to the IHSAA Board of Control as a representative of the Iowa Association of School Boards, and served 10 years.

During Quinn's last year at the helm, his hypertension problems intensified to the point that he was seldom able to come to the office for more than a few hours a day, a day or two per week, and he hated being on the sidelines. Kathryn Quinn asked Saggau and Cheryl Kane, the veteran office manager, to take over as many of Lyle Quinn's responsibilities as they could – without him knowing about it.

Ultimately, he discovered what they were doing, and became very incensed, berating both Saggau, whom he'd hand-picked to be his successor, and Kane, his longest-serving and most loyal employee.

In one of those sad moments that happens occasionally in office situations like this, Kathryn came to her husband's office to get him, and, with Saggau and Kane there, told him she had asked them for their help. She told Lyle it was now time for him to remain at home to fight his illness. He objected, and in the month before his death, the IHSAA Board of Control finally had to put him on a leave of absence because of poor health. Stan Bowker, who was covering southwest Iowa high school sports for the Omaha World-Herald, wrote in a touching column that it was probably "the toughest decision the Board of Control…has had to make in a long time.

"If he had been a poor administrator or failed to gain the respect of the association's member schools, the task of asking him to step aside would have been easy. But for more than 27 years, Quinn has been a driving force behind the state's high school athletic program. True, not all of the decisions he has made have been popular. However, they all have been dedicated toward one purpose – providing Iowa with one of the top all-around programs in the nation."

Bowker reported the board had put the program "in good hands," with Saggau taking over. Then he went on with a tribute to all that Quinn had accomplished.

"When Quinn assumed the post of executive secretary in February, 1940, the association was not financially sound," Bowker wrote in his

220

June 21, 1967, column in the Omaha paper. "Through his efforts, the association has grown into a $300,000 operation with a net worth of around $500,000..."

He noted Quinn's many other accomplishments and concluded, "He will be missed..."

Lyle Quinn probably should be remembered as the person most responsible for saving the IHSAA, at a time when it appeared it might be disbanded by the Iowa legislature and/or the State Department of Public Instruction. And then he directed the high school sports program into a golden era.

Saggau said he "can say without any reservations that Mr. Quinn was the most important person during the 100 years of the IHSAA's history. He came along when they needed a man with his leadership qualities and the ability to bring integrity back to the athletic association.

"And I'll always be indebted to him for having the confidence and faith in me when he hired me without interviewing anyone else, and telling the Board of Control he had hired the next executive director," Saggau continued. "From day one, he let me grow and learn. He had a lot of patience. Every day he was in the office, we would spend an hour-and-a-half to two hours on rules and regulations history, why we do things and why we don't do things. I tested him every day only to get lots of answers."

Saggau said he "never hoped to be more important than Mr. Quinn because I recognized his ability. When we traveled together, I was always proud of how he was respected by all the other executive directors from the associations around the country. All this being said, he was a real friend whom I respected greatly."

In the 1970s, Kathryn Quinn gave up the family home in Boone and moved to Des Moines to live with her daughter Marilyn. Kathryn died in 1980. Marilyn, who never married, spent most of her career teaching physical education at Des Moines North High School before retiring in 1993. Charlotte Quinn Chiles left the IHSAA in 1970, after her own four children had grown up in Boone, and moved to the Des Moines area, where she worked several more years for Massey Ferguson before retiring. In 2005, she had six grandchildren.

Cheryl Kane, for so long the IHSAA office manager, served with such distinction in her 41-year career that in 1975 she was promoted to "administrative assistant," which placed her on what is considered the executive level in the organization. Just before she died in 1986, she was promoted again – this time to "Honorary Executive Secretary."

THE LEADERSHIP OF BERNIE SAGGAU. The stories of George A. Brown and Lyle T. Quinn – both of them grand characters in different ways – give you a good idea of the legacy of strong leadership that welcomed Saggau to his job as the IHSAA executive in 1967.

And as you've already learned in this book, Saggau added to that legacy, which was passed on to his successor Rick Wulkow on January 1, 2005. You'll learn more about Wulkow in the next chapter.

Saggau's leadership was steady and firm during his long career.

"He really personifies 'the iron fist in a velvet glove' – very benign – and always with the kids' best interests at heart," said Carol Greta, the Iowa Department of Education's representative on the IHSAA Board of Control in 2004.

His leadership has probably been most bold on two initiatives, one soon after he became executive secretary in 1967 and the other in the last years of his career.

The first was actually a loss, in the "Bunger case." That was a lawsuit challenging a "Good Conduct Rule" that the IHSAA had imposed in 1968 to try to do something about widespread alcohol use among high school students. The Iowa Supreme Court ruled against the athletic association in 1972, saying it was up to individual school districts whether they wanted to have good conduct rules and how they would enforce them. However, news stories from back then indicate that the IHSAA's stiff penalties probably did have an impact in reducing teen drinking, at least for a few years.

The second initiative on which Saggau's leadership was so bold was his long, hard-fought and ultimately successful campaign to build the Iowa Hall of Pride, which opened in Des Moines in late February, 2005, soon after his retirement. This $12 million project is fully discussed in Chapter 8. "Leadership," Saggau said in a videotaped interview to be used in that Hall

f Pride, "is being unafraid of telling the people there might be some bad
ews."

He certainly had to do that in 1967, after realizing something was
probably going to have to be done about excessive alcohol use by high school
thletes and other students.

"When I first came to the association, we'd get calls from the schools
sking for advice on the length of punishments for athletes who got caught
doing something against the law," Saggau said. "Up until the late 1960s, it was
usually, 'Bernie, we've got a kid who got caught stealing watermelons – what
do you think?' And I'd say, 'Well, hold him out for a game.' But then we
started getting more serious calls, the major issue that school people all over
the state were dealing with was beer and alcohol.

"After listening to a lot of that, I said publicly that 50 percent of
owa's high school kids were drinking, and I was criticized for even saying
hat. But then in Cedar Rapids, they surveyed the high school athletes and it
showed 68 percent were drinking.

"So the Board of Control went ahead and passed the Good Conduct
Rule, and we enforced it uniformly. It was a tough rule, but a fair rule.
Basically, it said that if you were an athlete in a car with alcohol in it, you
were ineligible for six weeks."

It applied, even if an individual athlete was not drinking himself
or had nothing to do with the alcohol being present. It did not apply if the
athlete was with his father or mother when alcohol was present, or with
his siblings if they were 21 or older. Also, if an athlete was in a group that
was stopped by an officer, and if alcohol was found that the athlete did not
know about, he could preserve his eligibility only in one way. If on the next
school day, or before the next game, he reported the incident to his school
superintendent, principal, athletic director or coach, and convinced them he
had no knowledge of the alcohol, he could still compete.

The rule was new, and it was complicated, but nearly everyone could
understand the rationale of why it had been invoked.

Even Supreme Court Justice Harvey Uhlenhopp, who eventually
wrote the court's opinion that went against the IHSAA, understood. Here's
what he wrote as background about the Good Conduct Rule:

"The member schools strongly oppose the use of alcoholic beverage by athletes. In recent years, the drinking problem has increased, particularly the drinking of beer. Attempts by individual school boards to deal with the problem proved unsatisfactory. School boards and administrators were sometimes under local pressure to play outstanding athletes notwithstanding infractions, and different boards had varying rules relating to similar violations. Largely at the behest of the schools themselves, a committee of IHSAA studied the problem and proposed rules which were adopted by a substantial majority vote of the membership."

The actual vote by the schools, the Des Moines Register reported later, was 403 to 28.

What happened when enforcement began?

Several thousand students were ruled ineligible. In fact, the Register quoted Saggau in March, 1969, saying that 3,500 had been declared ineligible since the preceding September when the rule went into effect. In addition, the newspaper reported, "Ten schools have forfeited a total of about 20 football games for using players involved in beer incidents."

There were similar news stories all across the state about the rule and its impact. Despite the controversy, "the board and the schools were really behind it," Saggau recalled.

In the late winter of 1969, the schools voted to retain the rule, although predictably, the margin of 230-143 was not nearly as lopsided as the vote for initial implementation had been a year earlier. When Saggau reported those figures to the Board of Control, according to a Register story, he told the board members: "You men set a precedent with this Good Conduct Rule. You really shook the tree. It shows the association expects athletes to be good citizens."

The strict enforcement indeed had an impact. During 1970, there were only 350 ineligibility rulings.

"I'm not so naïve as to think drinking among youngsters has dropped that much," Saggau told columnist Gordon Gammack of the Des Moines Tribune.

He conceded, Gammack reported, "that teenagers who drink, particularly athletes, are much more careful not to get caught. Another

224

probable cause of the low suspension rate is that the courts and public opinion, perhaps, have curbed the zeal of police in their severe interpretation – resulting in fewer arrests – of revised state beer statutes."

Indeed, resistance was growing.

One of the first public critics of the Good Conduct Rule was State Senator Bill Reichardt, the Des Moines clothier. He told a Register reporter that "only about one of every 30 of the boys affected by the rule was ever charged in court. I think the association believes the Iowa courts are inadequate with their punishment. The association members are thus taking the law in their own hands by establishing themselves as judge and jury."

Reichardt argued that the rule "is discriminatory against the athlete and is also breaking one of our inherent rights of being innocent until proven guilty." And he added, "It is grossly unfair to penalize an entire school and athletic team by forfeiting games because of the guilt of one boy."

On June 7, 1971, a routine arrest in Waverly in northeast Iowa sparked the legal dispute that eventually overturned the Good Conduct Rule.

William Hal Bunger, a 16-year-old Waverly-Shell Rock football player and track man "and three other minors were riding in a car containing a case of beer," Justice Uhlenhopp later wrote. "William knew the beer was in the car. An Iowa Highway Patrolman stopped the four minors, discovered the beer, and issued summonses to all four for possession of beer as minors. Three pleaded guilty. William pleaded not guilty, and the charges against him were subsequently dismissed by the county attorney."

Three days after their arrest, young Bunger – and that German name is pronounced "Binger" around Waverly – told his high school athletic director about the incident, and said that while he drank no beer, he knew it was in the car. He was ruled ineligible for the first six weeks of the upcoming football season.

Bill Bunger was the fifth of sixth children of William Bunger, a worker at Rath Packing in Waterloo for years, and his wife Vera, a homemaker. Bill was a good athlete, although not a great one, playing defensive back and wide receiver in football, a sport that meant a lot to him. The ineligibility was to be enforced in the fall of his senior year.

Bill's oldest brother Darwin Bunger, 64 years old in 2005, and a prominent attorney in Burlington, Iowa, was then a young, aggressive lawyer practicing in Carroll in western Iowa. Darwin had been a good athlete himself, in four sports, before he graduated from Waverly-Shell Rock in 1958 and then went on to Wartburg College, State College of Iowa (now the University of Northern Iowa) and law school at the University of Iowa.

"Either our mother or father, I can't remember which, called me a few days after Bill had gotten the possession charge and told me what happened," Darwin recalled. "I was told that the other three kids in the car said Bill didn't have any of the beer, and that the county attorney threw out the charge against him, but that he was still being suspended by the IHSAA.

"I looked at it, and my initial reaction was that there was some fundamental unfairness, that maybe the rule was just too broad. But then I thought maybe there was another issue – did the Waverly-Shell Rock school board really have the authority to delegate its authority to the IHSAA on a matter like this?"

He said he advised his parents and brother that they should file a lawsuit in Bremer County District Court in Waverly, and that he would represent them. That's what happened.

"What would they have done if there hadn't been a lawyer in the family?" Darwin Bunger said, pondering a question. "I don't know. They didn't have much money, that's for sure. Bill was not a defiant kid at all. He's always been relatively mild-mannered. But on this issue, he thought he was right. And our father felt what had happened to his son was unfair."

The attorney representing the IHSAA was Lloyd Courter, of Boone, the longtime general counsel to the athletic association, a man who would become one of Bernie Saggau's best friends. Representing the Waverly-Shell Rock School District was Ike Ackerman, who later became mayor of Waverly.

After the District Court trial on August 11, 1971, the judge ruled in favor of the IHSAA and school district, upholding the Good Conduct Rule and the ineligibility of Bill Bunger.

The Bungers immediately filed notice of appeal to the Iowa Supreme Court, and obtained a temporary injunction that prohibited the IHSAA from enforcing its conduct rule until the issue could be decided. Bill Bunger was hus allowed to go ahead and play his senior year of football.

"Bill took some heat about the case," Darwin Bunger said. "I drove over from Carroll for most of his games, and I remember one night in New Hampton. I was standing along the sidelines, and this guy next to me sees Bill out on the field and says, 'Give number so-and-so another beer!' I stood there and cringed. Waverly-Shell Rock won that game, by the way."

The Bunger case was argued in front of the Supreme Court in early spring, 1972. The 5-3 decision in favor of Bunger was announced May 11, 1972.

The court ruled that Waverly-Shell Rock and other Iowa schools did not have the authority to delegate disciplinary authority to the IHSAA or the Iowa Department of Education without a formal, legal agreement to do so being in effect, and there was none. Such agreements between government entities today are known as "28E agreements," after the section of the Iowa Code that authorizes them.

However, in the Bunger ruling, the Supreme Court questioned whether such an agreement would have been legal. The court declared that the IHSAA penalties for beer possession in the Good Conduct Rule were "too extreme," that the rule itself was too broad and "invalid as unreasonable."

Of course, that was big news across Iowa.

What was the reaction in Waverly? You really had two camps in our hometown," Darwin Bunger said. "There were the athletically-inclined, and some of them thought the rule was unfair, but there was a solid minority that felt that 'a rule's a rule.' So it was pretty divided."

The IHSAA gave consideration to contesting the decision, "but finally we decided to let it go," Saggau said.

Ever since then, good conduct rules have been in place in most of the IHSAA member schools, "but they're very different from school to school," Saggau said. "Those decisions about eligibility after somebody has broken a rule are all handled locally, and the inconsistency is unbelievable."

The Bunger case, which received national attention at the time, is still being cited in court cases across the country dealing with eligibility for participation in school activities.

Darwin Bunger, the attorney, went on to become mayor of Carroll and a two-term president of the I-Club, the booster club supporting University of Iowa athletics, while continuing his law practice in Carroll, then Iowa City and now Burlington.

And, Bill Bunger, the young athlete in the middle of the fuss?

As a 50-year-old in 2005, he lives in Indianola and serves as a "depredation biologist" for the Iowa Department of Natural Resources. In that position, he works to control the number of deer, Canadian geese and river otters when they proliferate to the point where they are damaging crops and causing environmental problems.

A soft-spoken and gentle outdoorsman, he said in 2004 that it had been at least a decade since anybody had asked him about the "Bunger case."

Is he glad now that he challenged the IHSAA Good Conduct Rule – and won?

"Oh, I don't know," Bunger said. "It's hard for me to say. It's not like I saved the world or anything big like that. Whether it was right or wrong, or whether we won it or not, I'm not sure it was worth what all it took out of me and my parents.

"It was pretty hard on us," he continued. "I remember going to the fall football meeting, when our parents would come with us to meet the coaches before the season started. People shunned my parents that night, and I was pretty much treated that way the rest of the year on that team. I was not so much a part of the team anymore. The other three guys who I was with when we got picked up, they'd pleaded guilty and sat out their time being ineligible. They seemed to be accepted more than I was. There was always kind of a stigma attached to me for taking it to court, I guess."

He said the night of the arrest, he'd "just been along for the ride, and didn't have any of the beer, but it was guilt by association, I guess."

He said "most of the people I ran into who were supportive of what I did were players on other teams who had been in the same boat I was in, and were getting to play because of my court case."

He said as a high school senior, he was not concerned about whether his case was going to force a big change in the way disciplinary penalties were handled for high school athletes in the state.

"I probably didn't understand how far it was going to go," Bunger said. "For me, I just wanted to play the game I'd always loved. I guess everybody else was in it to settle the bigger questions about the rules of the athletic association."

The experience changed his outlook on high school sports.

"I no longer had the enthusiasm for some of those things. I couldn't see the relevance of them anymore."

He skipped going out for track his senior year.

In later life, though, he's been supportive of his own children's participation in athletics. His daughter played high school volleyball and his son played soccer. He said he has taken time to explain the "Bunger case" to his daughter, and will eventually probably do the same with his son, who is younger. While "it may have been a horrendous thing for me at the time it happened, that was a long time ago, and I don't know that it'd be very important to my kids," he said.

Life since high school has been good to Bill, he noted. He attended the University of Iowa for a year, and then spent two years in the African nation of Zaire, where his older sister was also living. Her husband was the director of a school operated by the U.S. Agency for International Development, and Bill Bunger taught English to the local people.

He returned to finish his college work in biology at Iowa State University. "I'd always liked hunting and fishing," he said. "And so I decided to follow my heart and find something to do with wildlife and the outdoors."

Married and with the two children, he has been with the Iowa DNR for 21 years.

THE IHSAA STAFF AT WORK IN BOONE. There are three things you notice immediately when you visit the Iowa High School Athletic Association headquarters in Boone.

First, the one-story, white-brick building that is now 29 years old is still very striking in its appearance.

It has proven to be a great investment, with the original building and two smaller additions later costing a total of $1.3 million. The replacement cost today would be three or four times that. Steel wall sculptures across the front of the building portray athletes engaged in many of the sports the IHSAA sanctions. An oval-shaped area on the south end of the building contains a beautiful, wood-paneled meeting room used by the Board of Control.

But probably more striking than the exterior of the building is the beautiful landscaping on the 4.2-acre site. "As a non-profit educational organization, our property is tax exempt," Bernie Saggau said. "But we decided a long time ago that one way we can support the community, since we don't have to pay property taxes, is to make our grounds the showcase of the town." The outdoor lights at Christmastime are one of everybody's favorite displays in Boone.

The head groundskeeper in 2004 was Paul Whannell, an 82-year-old retired farmer who also helps stuff envelopes when the staff does occasional mass mailings to member schools. "Paul is also kind of our adopted grandfather," said 32 -year-old Chad Elsberry, who is director of communications.

The second thing you notice when you visit the IHSAA is a very pleasant work atmosphere. It's professional, but not stuffy. Most of the employees dress in "business casual," which is common all over Iowa. If staff members recognize you walking in the door, you're likely to get a big wave and a warm personal greeting. If you're a first-timer, you get a quick smile and a "welcome."

In an age when the pace of work in most offices moves awfully fast – too fast, in fact – there are still some charming small-town business practices at the IHSAA that wind up making for a happier staff. And it shows.

One of those is that they close the office during the noon hour, and everybody goes to lunch. Or, in recent years, some have started bringing their lunch, gathering in the break room and hoping that the old veterans Saggau and Dave Harty, 69 years old in 2005, who is semi-retired after serving as assistant executive director for 32 years, join them. When that happens, Saggau and Harty inevitably start spinning favorite old stories from all their years together, and the staff loves the tales.

The office is also closed for a week during the summer and again between Christmas and New Year's Day, so that everybody can get a break from working the odd, and sometimes long hours required during the tournaments and other busy times.

The third thing you notice when you visit, and once you start talking to the staff, is that their background and experience makes them exactly what Saggau has long contended, the strongest staff of a high school activities organization in the nation.

And the volume of work the 20 people get done is almost unbelievable. It's clear to me – and I've visited lots of offices over my career – that the member schools of Iowa are getting a bargain for what they pay the IHSAA staff.

You've already read about several of the employees in this book, and you'll read in more depth about two others in the next two chapters – Saggau's successor Rick Wulkow and Jack Lashier, the director of special projects who has coordinated the Iowa Hall of Pride.

Most senior among other key employees is Harty, a native of Iowa Falls and a graduate of Iowa State University, where he wrestled three years for the Cyclones. He taught biology and the physical sciences for two years at Postville and then 11 years at Eagle Grove before joining the IHSAA in 1970. He also coached wrestling, baseball, football and track. And he has become the person most responsible for making the Iowa High School State Wrestling Tournament the biggest and best in the nation. The summer baseball tournaments he directed rank almost as highly.

Joyce Lindahl, who is a native of Boone, served as Saggau's secretary for 24 years. She was an athlete herself at Boone High School, playing basketball for three years. She then went on to earn her associate degree at the Des Moines Area Community College in the academic program for executive assistants. What you notice about Saggau when you work as close to him as she has, Lindahl said, "is that he puts in very long hours, has a phenomenal memory and is very considerate of other people's time when he's asking them to do things." She took dictation from him for his many letters, and she also handled all his e-mail, since he was not adept at computer usage.

Janet Johnson, 35 years old in 2005, also a native of Boone, has been Wulkow's secretary for most of her 10 years with the IHSAA. In fact, she was a high school classmate of Wulkow's daughter Sally, his son-in-law Dan Dighton, Dave Harty's son Jeff and another IHSAA staff member Elisa Kahler, who heads the mailing team. Johnson continued her education in business at Des Moines Area Community College, then worked a year for a bank in Boone and three years as newsroom secretary at WOI-TV in Ames.

David and Sandra Anderson are one of two married couples working for the IHSAA.

David, 53 years old in 2005, a native of Renwick, joined the IHSAA in 1989. He came on board as a substance abuse coordinator, when the IHSAA started its first-in-the-nation program in that area, and he has also been coordinator of the state meets in cross country, track and field, and soccer. He serves as webmaster on the IHSAA's site on the Internet.

Anderson came to the association with unusually strong and varied credentials.

He was an excellent athlete in track, cross country and basketball at Boone Valley High School, then he went on to the University of Northern Iowa, where he earned bachelor and master's degrees. He ran track for four years at UNI, and in his senior year was an All-American and captain of the Panthers' team. He went on to teach and coach for two years at Sac City, before leaving in 1977 to join a struggling young company, Cookies Food Products, in Wall Lake. He was quickly appointed plant manager, at the same time Duane "Speed" Herrig, who owns the robust company today, was contracted to do the sales. A year later, Anderson was hired away by Wall Lake banker John Goodenow to become a partner in the bank's insurance business, and he stayed there until he joined the IHSAA.

He and his wife Sandra, who was the cashier at the bank, were very involved in community activities, including David's service for four years on the board of education of the Wall Lake Community Schools. And the Iowa Association of School Boards designated him as their representative on the IHSAA's Board of Control.

"I was on the Board of Control when we voted to create the position f substance abuse coordinator," David Anderson said. "Ever since college, 'd always wanted to work either at the IHSAA or the Girls Union. So one ime I mentioned that to Bernie Saggau, when we were riding home from meeting together, and he said, 'Well, when something opens up, be an pplicant.' After we created the substance abuse coordinator position, I did he honorable thing, resigned from the board, applied and got the job."

Hence, he has "had a lot of experiences with Bernie as his boss when was on the board," Anderson said, "and then I've had a lot of experience with him as my boss once I joined the staff. What I can tell you is that he is always ahead of the pending issues, and that never ceases to amaze me. He has a much broader perspective on things than anybody I've ever known."

When the Andersons moved to Boone for David's new job, "people n Wall Lake thought we were nuts," he said.

Sandra was not only cashier at the bank, but she also had become ts chief operations officer and compliance officer. A native of Odebolt, she was also a UNI graduate in education. When the couple moved to Sac City for David's teaching job, she went to work for an insurance company and became a licensed agent. After joining the bank in Wall Lake, she went through a short course at the Colorado School of Banking.

After they moved to Boone, Sandra went to graduate school and earned a master's in business administration. She became vice-president of sales for a bank in Boone for two years, then joined Redeker's Furniture & Carpets in Boone as the controller and business manager for five years. In 1999, she started work at Iowa State University as an accountant for the Iowa 4-H Foundation, and in September, 2003, she was asked to join the IHSAA as their controller to succeed Ruth Ingalls, who was nearing retirement.

"Ruth had started working here a month before I was born, so I put that in perspective and knew I could learn a whole lot from her," said Sandra Anderson, who is 52 in 2005. "Ruth was a perfectionist, and did her job immaculately at every level. The only real change that was needed was more computerization, but her accounting system was perfect – it really was. There really was no chance for error in it."

Sandra had helped out at the IHSAA before she became a full-time employee, working on the ticketing for reserved seats at the state basketball and wrestling tournaments. "I really knew everybody here when I started the accounting job," she said. "It was not at all like coming into a new work environment for me."

Alan Beste, a native of Sauk Centre, Minnesota, was teaching health and serving as athletic trainer at Pleasant Valley High School near Davenport in 1989, when his school principal gave him a flyer from the IHSAA about the new substance abuse coordinator position opening. He had done his undergraduate college work at St. Cloud State in Minnesota, then earned his master's in health at Northwest Missouri State. "I wasn't all that familiar with Iowa yet," Beste said. "When he told me there was a good job opening with the athletic association in Boone, the first thing I asked was, 'Where's that?' "

Beste applied for the job, which you've just read David Anderson was given. Saggau did tell Beste that the IHSAA intended to add another new position, "health and wellness coordinator," in the near future. A few weeks later, Saggau called and offered him the job.

It fit Beste's background well. He had not been an athlete in high school, but served as student manager in football, basketball and baseball for three years for the Sauk Centre "Main Streeters," as the teams were nicknamed there in the hometown of author Sinclair Lewis. In college, he was a student athletic trainer in four sports.

In the 15 years since he was hired, Beste, 48 years old in 2005, has developed one of the best wellness programs for high school athletes in the country.

He produces monthly wellness newsletters for the member schools, does presentations on wellness in the schools and works especially hard on weight control issues in wrestling. In 1992, he developed an informative video on the deadly HIV/AIDS disease, and groups around the world have contacted the IHSAA for copies. And he was also way out in front of most health coordinators with his warnings in 1991 about the dangers of anabolic steroid use.

"Our approach has been that besides giving our students the negatives and warnings about everything, we have also given them positive alternatives – with information on areas like nutrition, conditioning and eight training," Beste said. "We've come a long way in the programs and information we're getting out to our students now, and I think we've had real impact. I don't know if it's been good planning – or that things just happened the way they did – but we've been on the cutting edge with a lot of what we've done over the years."

He is always careful to document the sources of his information, both in his newsletters and programs.

"We cite the medical journals and other resources," Beste said. "We want to assure our schools about where this information is coming from, that it's not just Alan Beste holding forth Sometimes we're perceived as being alarmists, but we can back-up what we're saying, and that makes the program more effective."

In addition to his work as wellness coordinator, Beste is also in charge of the championships in tennis and swimming, assists with the wrestling tournament and directs the junior high sports programs.

Chad Elsberry has been director of communications and graphic design since the retirement of Mo Kelley in the summer of 2001. He had come on board as Kelley's assistant 18 months earlier.

A native of Boone and a golfer at Boone High School, Elsberry had been aware of the IHSAA as he grew up, but never really understood all that the association did until after he went to work in 1992 for the Boone Today newspaper and the Boone Shopping News. He did graphic arts, composition, make-up and darkroom work for those publications while working on his undergraduate degree at Des Moines Area Community College, Grand View College in Des Moines and Iowa State University. He eventually became a reporter, then associate editor and photo editor at the papers. In 1998, he moved to a newspaper and shopper in Waseca, Minnesota, and was commuting for weekend classes for a master's in business administration at Iowa State University.

He saw an ad for the assistant's job at the IHSAA, applied and accepted it, fully intending to go back into the newspaper field once he completed his advanced degree at Iowa State. But when Kelley retired as publications director, Saggau came to Elsberry and asked him to take over.

In his position, Elsberry oversees the preparation and printing of 15 to 20 publications a year, including the IHSAA Bulletin that comes out four times per year with 2,300 copies; an annual directory of member schools; a directory and rules guide for game officials, and state tournament programs. He also puts together the annual "sportsmanship posters," which feature well-known alumni who've gone on to success in college athletics and are distributed to all the state's high schools and junior highs.

Elsberry also serves as a staff photographer, and backs up Bud Legg, the IHSAA information specialist, in handling calls from the media.

Jim Wingfield, 63 years old in 2005, has been in charge of the IHSAA's in-house printing for 16 years. He came to the job in an indirect way. A native of nearby Ogden, he had worked 18 years as a meat cutter for the Fareway grocery store in Boone, and then five years at the former Quinn Machinery & Foundry. He also did some painting on the side, and in 1988 was hired by Bernie Saggau to paint the interior of the IHSAA headquarters.

"When I was getting near the end of the paint job, Bernie asked me one day if I'd be interested in a full-time job," Wingfield said. "I said, well, I might be, and he told me their printer Jim Duff was leaving. I told Bernie the only problem was I didn't know a thing about printing, but he told me Jim would teach me what I needed to know, and that's the way it worked out. I guess I'm still learning, too, with all the changes there have been in machines and technology."

He now operates two sophisticated presses and a very high-tech copying machine to handle most of the IHSAA's printing needs.

The pace of the publications work can get crazy.

"My busiest days at the association are akin to the adrenaline rush of a newsroom," said communications director Elsberry. "In the end, however, everyone at the association is willing to do whatever it takes to get the job done – period. That doesn't always happen in other work places."

Bernard Henry "Bud" Legg, 61 years old in 2005, who was already one of the most widely known sports figures in Iowa as a coach and commentator on radio broadcasts of basketball games, was offered a big challenge by Bernie Saggau and Rick Wulkow when they called him in the late spring of 2001. They asked if he'd be interested in taking over part of the work that Mo Kelley had been doing.

While Elsberry would handle the publications, they wanted Legg to fill a new position, "information specialist," to work directly with media around the state, as Kelley had done.

But, in an even bigger assignment, they asked him if he would also dig back through 100 years of newspaper clippings, microfilm and scattered other resources to come up with the IHSAA's first-ever "state records book." While newspapers and some schools around Iowa had kept pretty good records on their own athletes and teams, there was no authoritative set of state records. It would be, needless to say, a daunting task.

"They outlined the job, and then asked me what I thought," Legg said. "I said, 'I just wish this was 25 years ago you were hiring me.'"

He accepted immediately.

The job has taken him back into the field that was his first love and first job – sports reporting – back in his hometown of Anita in southwest Iowa in the late 1950s. He has done a whole lot since then, including being a teacher, a coach of both girls' and boys' sports, an athletic director, a school administrator, a radio sportscaster and even a member of the board of directors of the Iowa Girls High School Athletic Union for one term. Those positions took him from Oakland to South Hamilton and in 1977 to Ames, from where he took early retirement in the summer of 2001.

The IHSAA job came at just the right time.

"This whole position has re-energized me in a personal sense, and for that I'll be eternally grateful," Legg said.

While he was a three-sport athlete at Anita High, winning all-conference honors, it now turns out after all these years that his high school sports writing experience for the Anita High "Spy" and the town's weekly newspaper, the Anita Tribune, was just as important as his athletic experience.

Even earlier, as an 11-year-old newspaper carrier for the Des Moines Register & Tribune and the Atlantic News-Telegraph, and already a major sports fan, he began a practice he continues today – clipping out the All-State teams in football and basketball and pasting them in spiral notebooks. Those earliest notebooks are still an important part of his statistical resources.

He relied on them as he started compiling the new book of state records. He also began spending two nights a week at the Ames Public Library, reading back copies of the Des Moines Register and Ames Daily Tribune, making notes on all references to the best performances of Iowa high school athletes. He started compiling lists of what seemed to him to be records, then circulated them among sports media, coaches, athletic directors and longtime fans all over the state.

The result now is a credible list of state records – available at the Internet site www.iahsaa.org – that took an incredible amount of work to put together. He threw himself into the challenge with a wholehearted devotion and tenacity that Saggau and Wulkow never expected, nor would have dared ask, any employee to muster.

"My motivation in doing it," Legg said, "is a deep respect for what has taken place the last 100 years in boys' athletics. But even having said that, I think it's imperative for today's youth to see that there is a link to the past. We tend to forget what happened yesterday. If you don't capture it in context of what's happening now, it's forever lost."

His work has already been a tremendous contribution to the high school sports "culture" in Iowa, as Legg refers to it.

"There is a culture that exists in our state," he said, referring to a feeling of community that has grown up around prep sports here. "You can go to a high school ball game anywhere in Iowa, and you're not a stranger, even if you don't know anybody on either team. It's still like that here."

Roger Barr, who turned 54 in 2005, had been officiating football, basketball and baseball for 30 years by May of 2003, when he became the IHSAA's first full-time coordinator of officials.

He is a native of Algona who had spent those same 30 years in the sporting goods business in Storm Lake. School officials across northwest Iowa became very accustomed to seeing the van roll up with "Mr. Ref" on the license plates, carrying Barr on both sales calls and officiating assignments.

He became one of the most respected referees in the state, umpiring 16 state championship games in baseball, and officiating 11 title games in basketball and 10 in football. He also worked college games.

In fact, he was a second generatigame official, following along as a boy when his father Everett would do the same three sports years ago.

"In baseball season, I'd chase foul balls while Dad was umping, and when I could turn a foul ball in for a sack of popcorn, why, I thought I was king of the hill," said Roger Barr, who has had a nickname of "Smokey" since childhood.

Needless to say, it was a little difficult to think about giving up officiating to become the coordinator of officials for the IHSAA. In fact, he refereed through the state basketball tournament two months before he took the job.

"But there comes a time when all of us have to move on," he said, "and this job was an opportunity in which I feel like I can give something back for all that high school sports have given me over the years. And, really, I'd always thought, like a lot of officials, that it'd be kind of a dream to have a job like this."

The new position includes doing rules interpretations for officials and coaches in football, basketball and baseball; assigning tournament officials in those sports, evaluating the officials during games, developing training courses for officials, recruiting new officials, and organizing an "Officials Department" in the IHSAA.

Barr, who had sold his sporting goods store in 2001 and was a branch manager of a Storm Lake bank, was one of 70 applicants for the IHSAA job.

He now coordinates the 2,500 officials registered for basketball in Iowa, about 2,000 in football and 1,500 in baseball. About 5,000 officials are active in the state, but "we'll always be looking for more officials," he said. "You just never have enough."

The pay for calling games has increased through the years, to where in 2004 football officials commonly were paid up to $70 per game, basketball officials up to $80 and baseball umpires up to $75 for a doubleheader. But, of course, the officials more than earn that money.

"Kids are bigger, stronger and faster than ever before, so it's harder to keep up with them," Barr said. "And television plays a part in how difficult it is to call games now. With so many sports events being televised, people who watch the pros or college games, think they know the rules and don't realize the high school teams are playing by different rules. So you have a lot of fans wanting to straighten out the officials on their calls.

"But I really think officials in Iowa owe a whole lot to Bernie Saggau and the IHSAA. He and the staff have done a tremendous job in promoting good sportsmanship. If it wasn't for the job they've done on this, we'd all have a lot more problems."

In the 2003- 04 basketball season, the IHSAA began having the officials meet with both coaches at center court before the games began, and then one of the officials would read a "Sportsmanship Statement" printed on a pocket-sized yellow card.

"We want to take a moment to discuss good sportsmanship," it says. "It is a priority of the Iowa High School Athletic Association that all participants in this contest exhibit good sportsmanship. Your cooperation in role modeling sportsmanship will ensure that this contest displays the positive values of high school sports."

That is now also being read at meetings between coaches and officials before games in football, baseball and soccer, as well as wrestling matches and swimming meets.

Barr said the statement serves as a good reminder, especially being read right before the action begins. "Communication is a huge part of officiating," he said.

Barr is assisted in the new Officials Department by Laura Morlan, 40 years old in 2005, who registers new officials, keeps track of attendance at rules meetings and grades the tests they take for the five levels of recognition – "temporary," "approved," "recognized," "certified" and "superior."

It gets hectic during the tournament seasons when Barr is assigning officials and Morlan is chasing them down by phone to confirm them. "I get very stressed, but I also love doing that," she said. "Most of those tournament officials are ones we've worked with for several years, so for most of them, we have their home and cell phone numbers."

A highlight of the year for the officials is a year-end banquet every

The IHSAA through 100 years

Featured in this photo section are some of the people who have been memorable figures in the Iowa High School Athletic Association's first century. *Left:* Alden Skinner, who coached the Palmer Panthers to four state basketball championships in the 1980s. *Below:* Vince Meyer, whose Bancroft St. John's baseball teams won 1,105 games, four fall state championships, two in the spring and three summer American Legion state titles from 1935-'81.

Chuck Offenburger

Vince Meyer

Painting by Leanne Bednarz Castillo

Chuck Offenburger

Sports Information, University of Iowa

Above top: Representing the 5,000 officials in Iowa, Dan Rourke of Indianola and Randy Blum of Ankeny. *Directly above:* Dan Gable (left), after his Hawkeye wrestling team wins an NCAA championship, shares the moment with his high school coach Bob Siddens of Waterloo West. *Left:* IHSAA executives Rick Wulkow (left) and Bernie Saggau with Wapsie Valley's Brooks McKowen, Iowa's all-time leading scorer with 2,831 points.

IHSAA

The first two executive secretaries who directed the Iowa High School Athletic Association, and their years in charge, were (right) George A. Brown, 1923-41, and (below) Lyle T. Quinn, 1941-67

The two IHSAA headquarters buildings in Boone. *Inset photo:* A former bank building downtown served from 1944 to 1975. *Main photo:* The current headquarters was built on the south edge of Boone and opened in 1975. The front exterior wall showcases the American flag and wall sculptures representing several of the sports that IHSAA offers.

Chuck Offenburger

Familiar faces among the media covering Iowa high school sports: 1) John Jensen (white shirt, left) of the Oelwein and Independence newspapers and Jim Sullivan (right) of the Waterloo Courier interviewing Dunkerton basketball coach Justin Little after 2004 state basketball championship. 2) Tim Seaman (left) of KCAU-TV in Sioux City with wrestling TV commentator Jim Gibbons. 3) Lee Hughes of KMA radio in Shenandoah likes to broadcast state basketball tournaments from high above. 4) John Naughton (right) of the Des Moines Register and Scott Pierce (center) of the Iowa Prep Report, with Dunkerton star Brian Brungard. 5) Kevin White of the Omaha World-Herald interviewing Nick Siepker of Manning in 2004. 6) Two of the top writers about high school wrestling are Dan McCool (left) of the Des Moines Register and K.J. Pilcher of the Cedar Rapids Gazette. 7) Dennis O'Grady (left)

covered for the Carroll Daily Times Herald for more than 30 years, and often traded tips with Brian Lage, who writes for the neighboring Manning Monitor.

All Photos by Chuck Offenbruger

Right: Paul Moon, known for the gray spats he usually wore while he coached, directed Davenport High School to seven state basketball championships. With him in this 1948 photo are players Skip Greene (left) and Dick Keyoth. *Below:* Dick Tighe was coaching football for a 51st season in 2004, at Fort Dodge St. Edmond High School. His teams have won more than 70 percent of their games in his career stops at Hamilton Catholic in Ontario, Canada, then in Iowa at Carroll Kuemper, Webster City and Iowa Falls before taking over the St. Edmond program in 2003. *Far Below:* Among many special contributors to IHSAA programs are veteran public address announcers at the state basketball tournament, Don Uker (left) of Denison and Rev. Craig Collison of Sioux City.

Tom Vogt

Chuck Offenburger

Chuck Offenburger

At the 2004 state basketball championship, little Dunkerton won the Class 1-A championship, bringing to mind the school's 1933 state championship in a one-class tournament. Dean Holdiman, the last surviving member of that '33 team, and his wife Ruby were in the front row of fans during the 2004 tournament.

Chuck Offenburger

Two of the most recognizable publications of the IHSAA. *Left:* The calendar, which can be found in all schools and has not changed in appearance in decades. The date of December 28, 2004, is noted – that's the 100th anniversary of the IHSAA. The anniversary was also commemorated with a special seal, shown here. *Below:* A new poster each year features alumni of IHSAA programs who've gone on to distinguish themselves in academics, athletics and citizenship on the college level. The 2004 poster featured college basketball All-Americans Nick Collison, of Iowa Falls and the University of Kansas; Kirk Hinrich, of Sioux City West and Kansas, and Kyle Korver of Pella High and Creighton University.

The IHSAA staff in the summer of 2004. *Front Row:* Angie Kruse, Janet Johnson, Amy McNace and Elisha Kahler. *Middle Row:* Roger Barr, Donna Barr, Joyce Lindahl, Sandra Anderson, Laura Morlan and Paul Whannell. *Back Row:* David Anderson, Bud Legg, Jack Lashier, Alan Beste, Alan Greiner, Rick Wulkow, Bernie Saggau, Chad Elsberry and Jim Wingfield. A new employee since this photo was taken is Anne Jonotta.

All Photos by IHSAA

Among other longtime
IHSAA employees have been
(clockwise from upper left)
Dave Harty, the late Harold
Schmickley, Ruth Ingalls and
Mo Kelley.

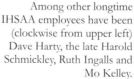

The Iowa Hall of Pride

Architectural rendering by HOK Sport+Venue+Event, Kansas City, MO

All Photos of the Interior by Architectural renderings by Synthesis Design, LLC., of Haddonfield, NJ

The IHSAA's boldest project, the Iowa Hall of Pride, is a $12 million, 26,000-square-foot celebration of the high school experience, opened in early 2005. It is part of the new Iowa Events Center complex, in Des Moines, with a new arena and additional convention facilities. In the Hall of Pride, the accomplishments of Iowa's students, athletes, musicians and alumni are featured, as well as the stories of the state's schools, communities and leading citizens. The hall has display areas – like the ones shown above for choir, football, wrestling and baseball – for all the high school sports and other activities. The displays are enhanced with interactive technology, high-definition video and original art. The exterior view shows that the Hall of Pride is located on the south side of the Iowa Events Center, on the lower level of the Hy-Vee Hall exhibition area. The Hall of Pride stretches from the vertical sign on the right to the west side of the building.

Succeeding Bernie Saggau as executive director of the IHSAA is Rick Wulkow, who has been a key member of the staff for 24 years. In the photo at the right, the two are shown at the 2004 state basketball tournament. Photos below are of Wulkow around his hometown of Lytton in northwest Iowa.

Chad Elsberry

Chuck Offenburger

Chuck Offenburge

Chuck Offenburger

Chuck Offenburger

Wulkow grew up on a farm southwest of Lytton. As a boy, he worked on his pitching ability by throwing baseballs at a small area on the side of the hog house, between the doors the pigs used, that was about the size of a batter's strike zone. In photos above and to the right, he's shown at his old school in Lytton, where he graduated in 1963 after an outstanding athletic career. He went on to star in three sports at Buena Vista College in nearby Storm Lake.

May that the IHSAA has been sponsoring for the past 10 years. Typically, 200 or more officials gather in either Ames or Des Moines at an event also attended by the members of the Board of Control and the IHSAA staff. The banquets have featured such speakers as wrestling great Dan Gable, college athletic directors and the executive directors of other states' high school activities associations. Then the veteran officials are recognized for 15, 25, 35 and 50 years of service. And five "new" officials, who have from five to 10 years of experience, are also recognized.

In 2004, Roger Barr's wife Donna also began working in the IHSAA building, as an assistant in the office of the Iowa High School Music Association (IHSMA), which is also headquartered there.

The IHSMA executive director is Alan Greiner, 41 years old in 2005, who has headed the organization since July, 2001. He is a native of Blairsburg and a graduate of Roland-Story High School and Iowa State University. Before he joined the IHSMA, Greiner taught instrumental music for 18 years, two years at Northwest Webster and 16 years at Prairie and then Prairie Valley of Gowrie.

He is the third executive director, succeeding Leo Grether, of Manchester, who served from 1966 until 1978, and Everett Johnson, who taught and coached in Sheldon before becoming the IHSMA executive from 1978 until his retirement in 2001.

There are about 390 member schools paying $25 each for annual memberships. The IHSMA is governed by its own board of directors, but the IHSAA assists the music organization by providing the office space and $5,000 of Greiner's annual salary. In exchange, Greiner and Donna Barr pitch-in and help with IHSAA events, including scheduling National Anthem singers and other music during the athletic association's state tournaments.

Greiner's route to IHSMA leadership came through his proficiency at music and teaching, of course, but also through his knowledge of technology.

"Everett Johnson and I began having a significant working relationship four to five years before I started this job," said Greiner. "He'd watched my band program grow, and we'd worked together in the Iowa

Bandmasters Association. I got into computers, so he asked me to become the webmaster for the IHSMA while I was still teaching.

"When I succeeded him, one of the biggest priorities I had was not to screw up a good thing," he continued. "It's a finely-tuned organization. The one thing I wanted to do was move us into the twenty-first century in terms of online registration for our contests and online distribution of our other information, and that's happening now."

The IHSMA now sponsors the All-State Music Festival, as well as state contests in marching band, piano, show choir and jazz band, with separate contests for solo, small-group and large-group performance in both vocal and instrumental music. More than 50,000 students are involved in IHSMA contests every school year.

You may not realize that those contests are evaluative rather than competitive, with trained adjudicators providing both oral and written constructive criticism.

"That's our board's philosophy," said Greiner. "We don't do a championship series, like they do in sports. We could probably create a real public following if we did, but why? Shouldn't this really be about educating young musicians?"

There are, of course, also competitive music events that schools enter, such as swing choir festivals sponsored by individual schools or by music boosters' organizations. While those are not sanctioned by the IHSMA, the organization does not disapprove of them, either. But it holds to its evaluative standard for its own events.

It's a system that works, because the Iowa high school music program is generally regarded as the best in the nation. Why is it so strong in our schools and communities?

"I think it goes back to our very roots," said Greiner.

From the start of the secondary education system in Iowa, vocal and instrumental music have been regarded as part of the educational curriculum, instead an extracurricular activity, and that has been extended to music teachers being able to give students private lessons during the school day. Also, early in the state's history, the Iowa Legislature passed the "Iowa Band Law," which allowed communities to levy a tax to equip municipal bands.

With those ideas "and some strong personalities," said Greiner, good music in the schools "became an Iowa tradition."

It certainly is a tradition in the Greiner family. Alan's wife Becky Greiner is high school band director at Jefferson-Scranton, and her brother Matt Schutt is the middle school band director there.

Elisa Kahler, who turned 36 in 2005, is a dynamo who is in charge of ordering the IHSAA's office supplies, supervises most of the mailings and, over her 10 years on the job, has become "kind of the go-to person when someone needs an extra hand," she said. That's not a problem with her. "My favorite times of work," she said, "are the busiest times. We put in really long hours during the tournaments, but I think all of us really enjoy that because we see the rewards of it all in how proud schools and towns are."

With calendars, posters, rule books, school directories, organizational handbooks, health and wellness information, and various forms all going out to all the member schools, the IHSAA is Boone's second largest mailer, she notes. An especially big bulk mailing is when "autograph" game balls – with a white leather panel for teammates to sign – are shipped to all squad members of the championship and runner-up teams in most of the sports, immediately after the tournaments. "That's been a real positive, real exciting addition to the awards we've always given," she said. "We hear back how much the athletes like those."

First cousins Angie Kruse and Amy McNace, 25 and 24 years old in 2005, respectively, joined the staff in July, 2003.

Kruse, an Ogden native and a graduate in accounting from Iowa State University, works in bookkeeping with Sandra Anderson. She said she went to an IHSAA staff picnic before she started work "and I felt like it was going to be like being a part of a big family here, and it has."

McNace is a secretary/receptionist, the person who most often answers the telephone when you call the IHSAA. "I call myself the 'Hospitality Committee' here," she said. "I'm very outgoing, talk all the time, and I think it's really fun to work here. Maybe that will get me in trouble some day. But I have the utmost respect for the people here. We have several who have worked here a long time, and that says a lot about a place, I think."

Morris "Mo" Kelley, who became one of the IHSAA's most publicly-recognizable staff members in his 30-year career as publications director, is now back doing the same job he started on in 1953 as a senior at Boone High School – writing sports for the Boone News-Republican.

"I'm really enjoying it," Kelley said when we talked in the middle of the newsroom in downtown Boone. "I'm usually here at 6:30 in the morning, get the sports done about 9:30 or 10, and then the rest of the day I look for feature stories. I try to write two or three features a week."

He retired unhappily at the IHSAA, he said, and then "did nothing for six months and found out that was not good – too much time for bad habits." That's when the News-Republican bosses welcomed him back as sports editor, and he says now it could not have worked out any better.

"What happened at the athletic association was that after the state basketball tournament in 2001, Bernie called me in and said they were changing directions in how they did publications and media," Kelley said.

Saggau said that Kelley had talked about retirement, and what he offered him was a phase-out plan. Kelley could continue working, but fewer hours during the week, over a three-year period toward full retirement. It turned out Kelley didn't really want to start into retirement.

"I was 66 years old then, and I didn't like the idea," Kelley said. "I had wanted to keep going. I felt like after 30 years, it ought to end a little better than that. But I was already eligible for the regular retirement package, and I decided rather than wait and risk being unhappy working, I might as well just go ahead and retire."

Kelley said while he was upset with Saggau at the time, "I'm fine with him now, I really am. He is a person who has had a tremendous impact on high school sports. He is one of the most forward-looking people I've ever met. He has an amazing ability to look ahead and see what's going to happen five years down the road.

"And, personally, Bernie gave me a lot of opportunities, and I had a real good run at it there. It was an excellent place to work, in terms of equipment, pay and benefits, especially in a community this size. Besides that,

ne Iowa high school athletic program is just tremendous. I can't say enough
ood things about it. It's a top-class organization, and it has been ever since
've known about it."

That was back in the early 1950s when Kelley was a four-sport athlete
t Boone High School Late in his senior year, he was offered a sports writing
ob at the News-Republican, and soon after that, he also started doing a
norning sports report for KWBG radio, which had the same owners as
he newspaper. He worked 17 years for both of them – and for eight of
hose years he was doing double-duty as the newspaper's sports editor and
he radio station's sports director. For a time he was manager of the radio
tation, and at the time he joined the IHSAA in 1971, he was managing
ditor of the newspaper.

He had also been a youth baseball coach in the community, and
ne directed a Babe Ruth team in 1962 that Boone people still talk about
or its state and regional championships and qualification for the national
ournament. That same group of players won a state high school baseball
hampionship for Boone in 1965 and anchored a program that became
 perennial powerhouse. He "met Bernie soon after he moved to town
n 1963," Kelley continued. "We were at a lot of the same functions and
ecame friends. He told me he always liked how I used so many names in my
ports stories and columns, and how that was good for the athletes. I think
hat's what led to me getting the job at the athletic association."

Kelley not only did the IHSAA publications work, but he also
ecame the media contact. He also did commentary with broadcasters Frosty
Mitchell and Mark Zelich on television coverage of the state basketball
ournaments, and was generally the public address announcer for all awards
eremonies at the IHSAA tournaments.

Saggau helped Kelley become the announcer for the Hall of Fame
eremonies at the annual conventions of the National Federation of State
High School Associations. Kelley says it was great to announce the induction
of such notable sports figures as football coach Tom Landry, golfer Arnie
Palmer, basketball coach John Wooden and broadcaster Pat Summerall.

THE IHSAA'S BOARD OF CONTROL. It says a lot that many

of Iowa's most respected high school administrators, at retirement, often cite service on the boards of either the Iowa High School Athletic Association or the Iowa Girls High School Athletic Union as one of the highlights – if not the highlight – of their careers.

And those board members who have served as representatives of the athletic directors/coaches, the Iowa Association of School boards and the Iowa Department of Education say the same thing.

Why is that?

"If you truly believe that athletics is an extension of teaching, this is where you want to be," said Mike Billings, 46 years old in 2005, the superintendent at Roland-Story who is chairperson of the Board of Control of the IHSAA as the organization starts into its second century.

Billings has taught, coached, served as a principal and a superintendent, but he says his service on the IHSAA board "is the best thing I've done educationally. A well-run athletic program like this makes such a big, positive difference in the lives of kids.

That's what it's all about."

Board member Dan Delaney, 58 in 2005, the activities director at Mason City High School, said he is "a firm believer that if they're run right, athletics are our best at-risk program for kids. We keep them occupied and on the right track. Of course, you need good coaches who, besides knowing sports, are good role models. Athletics – and the same thing is true of music and other activities – can build tremendous pride, not only in the individual student, but also the school and community. It's fun to be a part of that."

Dennis Presnall, 51 years old in 2005, the board member representing Iowa's school boards, says he always recommends community volunteer work to his employees at the Iowa Farm Bureau Federation, where as organization director he is one of the top executives. "My theory is that if you're going to spend time volunteering, you can't go wrong doing something for kids," he said. He's spent more than a decade on the board of education of the Ankeny Community School District, and he came to the IHSAA board in 2001. "It's been a positive experience for me being around these people," Presnall said. "I get excited just listening to Bernie Saggau and when I'm with the board at the state tournaments. I always ask myself, 'How can I take the things I'm experiencing here and instill them in my own children, and at work?' It helps me, even on my job, I know that."

Carol Greta, 49, of the Department of Education, sits on both the IHSAA and IGHSAU boards, and says her service on those boards "is my therapy" after dealing with the matters she handles as a legal consultant and administrative law judge for the DOE.

"My dad Frank Munch was a teacher and coach at Ar-We-Va, I-35 and then Forest City as I was growing up, so I've always had an interest in athletics, and I've got two kids in high school now," said Greta, who lives in Newton. "It's very interesting in my position to be on both boards. They have very different corporate personalities, and yet both overwhelmingly have students' interests at heart. It's significant, I think, that both organizations detest the term 'student athletes,' because both are very clear that these are students we are dealing with, and that athletics is just another part of their education. It's a subtle way the associations impact the culture of the high school experience in Iowa."

In the last year of the IHSAA's first century, those four board members served with Bob Tesar, principal at Cedar Rapids Jefferson High School; Steve Waterman, superintendent at Clarke of Osceola; Dave Sextro, superintendent at Albia; Robert Busch, superintendent at Riverside of Oakland; Ron Sadler, president at Crestwood of Cresco, and Dwayne Cross, superintendent at Rockwell City-Lytton and Southern Cal of Lake City.

In that year, the chairpersonship passed from Tesar to Sadler in November, 2003, then to Billings in November, 2004.

That same month in 2004, three newly-elected board members began their five-year terms – Dave Harris, superintendent at Sigourney-Keota; Deborah Menke, principal at Pleasant Valley High School just west of Davenport, and Brett Nanninga, superintendent at Tri-Center of Neola.

They join Billings, Sadler, Delaney, Cross, Greta and Presnall to make up the board that started IHSAA's new era, when Rick Wulkow succeeded Saggau as executive director.

All of those recent board members, like so many before them, not only use their school administrative experiences to help the IHSAA, they also add perspective from their interesting and varied life experiences.

For example, Albia's Sextro, retired in 2004 after 25 years in education, during which he taught, coached and then served as a principal and ultimately a superintendent. But even earlier in his career, he was an Air Force drill instructor and then a licensed mortician and funeral director.

"I also have farmed and helped lay I-29, so I know what it's like to have a scoop shovel in my hands," he said. "You know, I really think every teacher should leave the profession every five years, and work another job for a year, just to realize how life is in regular jobs. I think it would make for better teachers."

Sextro and his wife Anne were also one of the few husband-wife refereeing teams who did basketball, baseball and softball together.

Cross, 55, of Rockwell City-Lytton and Southern California, earlier served three years as principal at Prairie City-Monroe, and during his time there, he dealt with a huge unexpected problem – the high school burned to the ground one January night. "Within four days, we had all students back in school in temporary classrooms with new schedules, teachers and texts," he said. "That's something you never forget going through."

Greta, 49, of the DOE, earlier was in a private law practice in Newton, and also served as a district associate judge for five years in Jasper, Polk and Marion Counties.

Sadler, 61, of Crestwood, was a basketball star at little Grand Meadow High School in northwest Iowa, and in his senior year of 1961, he led the Larks and the whole state in scoring with a 36 points-per-game average. He was also one member of the three-member graduating class, which was the last one before Grand Meadow consolidated with Marcus.

He was also a hard-throwing pitcher on a junior high baseball team, when he was in eighth or ninth grades, and the home plate umpire for one of the games was young Bernie Saggau, who was then in the insurance business in nearby Cherokee.

"I threw very hard for somebody that young," Sadler recalled. "A pitch skipped and hit Bernie in the chest. He umped the rest of that game from behind the pitcher. We have discussed that several times over the years."

Through his career Sadler has taught, coached, farmed, went broke in the Farm Crisis years of the middle 1980s, worked in agriculture sales,

248

ubstitute taught, went back to college when he was 48 to earn his master's, nen began his administrative career.

He has been a real innovator at Crestwood, which is the name of the iigh school in the Howard-Winneshiek Community School District. He led n effort in which his school district's patrons authorized an agreement with Northeast Iowa Community College, then built a new attendance center for he college near the high school in Cresco.

"We now have 75 percent of our seniors and 55 percent of our uniors taking college classes while they are still in high school," Sadler said. "Our goal is to have students graduate from high school and at the same ime get their associate of arts degree."

Mason City's Delaney brings the perspective of having been a star athlete at Iowa City Regina High School, then was a three-year football etterman at the University of Nebraska.

He taught and coached at Fort Dodge and his alma mater Regina before taking over as Mason City High's activities director in 1985. The athletic program there is one of Iowa's largest and best, with 560 athletes in 22 sports that include – are you ready? – dance, bowling, hockey and even trapshooting!

"And music is huge in this town," Delaney said. "The kids all want to be involved in it, so we sit down and plan the calendar very carefully to eliminate the conflicts, so the students can be in sports and music."

Board members from the past two years say that the condition of the IHSAA and its programs is as strong as – actually probably stronger than ever. But all foresee serious challenges in the years ahead.

Tesar, 55, the Cedar Rapids Jefferson principal for 16 years, articulates it well.

"From a kids' participation perspective, it's never been better," he said. "We're offering more kids more opportunities to compete in more sports. I think coaches are much better prepared in college – and not just in the nuts and bolts of the sport but in things like human growth and development. I'm not knocking those coaches from earlier years, but the training now is better – the same as it is for teachers in general.

"The opportunities for high school athletes to have exposure and

249

recognition are also much greater now. In my era, you got a school letter and maybe a banquet. In football back then, there were no playoffs, no state championship. And look at how much coverage those events get now."

But among the challenges, Tesar said, are "so darned many competing interests" for the time and attention of high school students, parents and other fans.

"There are so many more opportunities away from school for kids than there used to be," he said. "Today our students are a little less willing to be a part of a sports program if they're not going to be an integral part of it and get a lot of playing time. They're a little less likely to want to continue going to practice, just to be part of the program."

Concerning the fans, Tesar said, "We've done surveys, and there's a big change we've seen from 30 or 40 years ago. In the 1960s and '70s, we had more casual fans coming to the games. High school sports and activities were more of a community event than they are now. What we're seeing now is that most of the fans have a direct connection to the players or performers. There aren't so many casual fans anymore."

Tesar's point is generally accurate, especially for large schools, although most of the smaller schools do still command the whole community's attention for their events. If those teams from small schools are not winning, however, their following will decline faster than it used to.

The result? Financial strain.

In the 2002-03 school year, Tesar noted that of Jefferson High's 19 sports, "three operated in the black and the rest were in the red." The $80,000 annual contribution from the Jefferson booster club saves them. He said school officials across the state "try to hold the admission costs as low as we can, but we all know that we've got a growing issue of how we can decrease our expenses and increase our revenues. I think what you'll see is that business partnerships will become much more important."

Other big issues in the future?

"Eligibility of athletes will always be an issue," said Sadler. On one hand, the eligibility questions are about what level of academic achievement that sports participants must maintain. "But that may change the more the state legislature talks about standards," he said.

Chapter 6

There are also eligibility questions arising from athletes wanting to move to school districts that have stronger programs in certain sports. IHSAA officials say they have seen "sham divorces" in which married couples have split, with one parent moving with the athlete to the distant school district with the stronger program, while the other parent remains in the original home with other children and maintains the family's business.

"Until I got on the Board of Control," said Sadler, "I didn't realize there were so many eligibility problems, that there'd be the number of people who try to circumvent the rules to try to gain for themselves. We spend a lot of time on that."

Added Albia's Sextro: "One growing problem we have is that parents have found ways to cheat other kids – phony divorces, phony addresses, manipulating the rules. Our job has been to try to keep the playing floor and the playing field equal for everybody. Having not been such an angel myself when I was growing up and in my younger years, I look at these cases and can't help but think these people are modeling poor parenting for their kids."

Cross, the superintendent serving both the Rockwell City-Lytton and the Southern California school districts, has spent much of his career working in schools that were going through, or just getting accustomed to, new consolidations or other forms of program sharing. "We're going to see more of that, especially in the rural areas," he said. "We may be moving toward each county having one high school with the traditional educational programs and one high school emphasizing vocational education. But whatever happens, reorganization will have a big effect on our sports and other activity programs."

Presnall, the school boards' representative, says "the continuing consolidation of small schools" specifically means "rising costs of transportation and real logistical problems in scheduling games with other schools in your same class."

There are also drugs, steroids and other performance-enhancing supplements to worry about, all the board members said, "and the problem of alcohol will never go away," Presnall added. "You can never do enough about those problems. The neat thing about our association is we always seem to be ahead of the game in those areas. Our substance abuse and wellness programs have been models."

On another matter which was new at the start of the new century, Greta of the Department of Education noted that "with the advent of coed state meets in cross country and track, if they prove successful, we could see more events becoming coed."

And that means "bringing the Girls Union and the IHSAA closer together," said Sadler. "I think there's a place for both organizations, but we've already started working closer with each other, and there will undoubtedly be even more of that."

Roland-Story's Billings said "the continued growth of club sports – and the leadership those organizations and teams have – is going to be a huge challenge." Club sports are for the most part not sanctioned by any education-based organization, and there are few requirements or standards for their coaches.

And Albia's Sextro said he will not be surprised if the IHSAA eventually expands its program to include statewide competition in other sports. He noted that bowling has already been considered, and he thinks there could eventually be boys' volleyball and softball, too. But none of the problems and challenges is enough to diminish the enthusiasm of the board for what the IHSAA is doing – and can do – for the state's young people.

"Research tells us that the more students are involved in activities in high school, the more successful they are as students," said Sadler. That's true of band, chorus, drama, cheerleading – many things beyond athletics. The students manage themselves better. They learn to deal with loss and with success in appropriate ways. They become well-rounded. They become real 'do-ers' – people who can get things done. They learn how to put people together, strategize and make everybody in the group more successful.

"And it's these involved students who will become your community leaders a few years later."

That's why so many other IHSAA board members – present and past – look at their service like Sadler does.

"It's been tremendous," he said. "Beyond my expectations. For me, it's the culmination of my experience as an athlete, teacher, coach and administrator."

Chapter Seven

Rick Wulkow's route to IHSAA leadership

After 37 years as executive director of the Iowa High School Athletic Association, Bernie Saggau retired on January 1, 2005. Rick Wulkow, who is no stranger to the job, or to Iowans, took over the position immediately. For 24 years, he had been a top assistant, in later years becoming the likely successor to Saggau.

So tell me, I said in a private moment with Wulkow, who turned 59 in 2005, what will that really be like?

"Scary," he answered, without hesitation. "Following a legend is probably not the ideal situation."

He even looked a little rattled as he said it.

Our conversation occurred in late April, 2004, in the quiet of the city clerk's office in his hometown of Lytton in western Iowa. We had borrowed the office for several hours earlier in the day to talk with townsfolk who've known Wulkow his entire life.

In their minds, he's a legend, too – probably the best athlete and one of the most successful people the community ever produced.

"I'll tell you, Rick was a model student athlete," said Bob Williams, who was 77 years old in 2005, and has been city clerk for 43 years. He coached Wulkow in youth baseball. He umpired many of the games Wulkow pitched in his high school years – "he had a pretty good curve ball."

But Williams remembered something else that impressed him more.

"You know how some of those good athletes have kind of an edge to them, maybe think they're a little better than other people?" he said. "That was never the case with Rick. He was always nice to everybody, and he had time for everybody – a real All-American boy, to tell the truth. He'll be a good one to come in behind Bernie."

Wulkow faces great challenges, of course – tight school budgets, declining student numbers in rural Iowa, likely school consolidations, competition from "club" and other non-school sports programs, the tenuous public understanding and practice of good sportsmanship, and more.

And yet, what needs to happen on his watch is really quite simple. If he can somehow help all kids in the state have the same quality of high school experiences that he had in the early 1960s in little Lytton, they will be well-served, indeed. And so will their schools, communities and Iowa itself.

Wulkow had an almost idyllic childhood, growing up on a farm four and one half miles southwest of town.

As an aspiring baseball pitcher, he learned to hit the strike zone by winding up and throwing balls against the exterior wall of a brick hog house, and he wouldn't count it as a strike unless he hit the 18-inch space between the little doors the pigs used. He would stack up hay bales as "the defense" in football, "then I'd run by, give 'em a shoulder and dive over the 'goal line'," he recalled. In basketball season, he would get the milking machines attached to the cows, then duck out the side door of the barn to shoot baskets, but there was a risk. "If I forgot what I was supposed to be doing and I'd go back in there to find the cows' bags shriveled up or milk spilled all over the floor, I'd catch holy heck from Dad," he said.

He would frequently "do play-by-play broadcasts" of his imaginary ball games out around the farmyard.

Wulkow went on to win 15 letters as a Lytton High School athlete. He was the star quarterback in football, once throwing a 99-yard touchdown pass to help beat rival Lohrville. He was a 20-points-per-game scorer in basketball during his last three seasons. He was a middle-distance track man, and a frequent winner in track's old "football throw" event. In baseball, he was the ace of the pitching staff. And he was a pretty good hitter, too, one who met "the measure of real home runs here – hitting a ball out on, or over, U.S. Highway 20," his brother-in-law Greg Williams, a farmer who turned 52 years old in 2005, remembered.

But sports wasn't everything.

He also played tuba in the school band. He sang in the boys' glee club but didn't always get selected for the mixed chorus. He served as president of the student council one year. He held down a part-time job at Mac Fagan's Sinclair service station. He showed the champion Duroc gilt at the Iowa State Fair, and he earned the Future Farmers of America top award for Iowa members.

His four years at Buena Vista College in Storm Lake were just as dreamy as his high school experience. And after graduating he married his sweetheart Barb Kreft, who grew up on a farm three miles east of Wulkows' farm outside Lytton. He then moved into a career of teaching, coaching, school administration and officiating before joining the IHSAA in 1980.

Times are much different now, of course.

It will be almost impossible for a twenty first century Iowa kid to repeat the Rick Wulkow experience.

Is there a young athlete anywhere in the state now learning to pitch by throwing at a spot on a hog house wall? It's doubtful, given the rapid disappearance of family farms, and the revolution in the scale and methods of hog production.

Somewhat related to that, towns the size of Lytton, with a population of 310, no longer have their own high schools. Would-be Lytton Bulldogs of today are now Rockwell City-Lytton Wildcats. "I didn't think I'd ever see the day I'd root for Rockwell City – we hated their guts," said Ron Dettmann, 76 in 2005, and one of Wulkow's biggest admirers. He spoke while wearing a "RC-L" ball cap and acknowledging he's one of the Wildcats' biggest fans.

Oh yes, times and things are different. More Iowa youngsters are growing up in larger towns and cities, and in that environment, high school games are not generally the community events they once were in smaller places.

And fewer athletes play four sports, like Wulkow did. They don't have time – or maybe just don't make time – for as many activities as Iowa teens once did. Cars, expensive entertainment and saving for college require almost all of them to have jobs.

But Wulkow comes to the IHSAA's executive job energized by his belief that young Iowans today have needs, dreams and potential as big or bigger than he ever had.

We'll get to what he thinks the future holds. But first, let's explore where he's coming from.

"You know," he said, as we started walking around the old Wulkow farmstead and into his past, "if it weren't for athletics, I'd probably be farming this land today. I loved the farm. It makes me sad to be out here now and see how much things have changed."

Rick is of the second generation of Iowa Wulkows, after his German Lutheran grandparents who came from Minnesota to Iowa and bought two farms near Lytton. Rick's father Delmar Wulkow, who was adopted, eventually took over ownership and operation of the home place, and Delmar's cousin Reinard Wulkow took the other farm.

They were hardy, resourceful people. Delmar had only an eighth grade education, but he knew where to find information he needed and he could figure out how to use it. He valued education, serving eight years as a member of the Lytton school board, and in 1988 when he was 65 years old, he was proud to earn his high school General Education Development (GED) diploma. The story of how the still fine-looking Wulkow house was built tells you even more about Delmar.

"When I was six years old, my dad and mom decided they wanted to build a new home out here," Rick said, as we walked around the farm. "So Dad went to the library in town, got books on construction, electrical wiring, plumbing – everything he'd need to know to build a house – and studied them. Then he and Reinard went to work on it. They dug the basement and built the whole thing themselves. For a long time, we lived in the basement part of it, which they finished off first. It took them six years to get the whole house done, but it was a nice one."

There Delmar and Flossie Wulkow raised Rick; younger sister Patty Wulkow Hogan, 57 years old in 2005, and a nurse in Carroll, and younger brother Dennis Wulkow, who turned 52 in 2005, and in a nursing home in Carroll because of the multiple sclerosis he's battled since his early 30s.

Rick, his sister and brother still own 160 acres of the farm operation. They recently sold another 100 acres and the homestead to help take care of their parents, who are now both living at a nursing home in nearby Wall Lake.

In the 1950s and '60s, the Wulkow farm was a busy place, with all the typical row crops of the era as well as fruit trees, milk cows, beef cattle, hogs and a chicken operation in which they raised Hy-Line laying hens. All the Wulkows were involved, as was hired man Bill Jarvis, who had a small house on the farm.

Rick learned even more about farming by joining the Coon Valley Coons 4-H Club, named after Coon Valley Township where the farm is located, and then the Future Farmers of America when he got into high school. He showed purebred Duroc hogs and Hereford baby beeves at the Sac County Fair, winning several championships there, and then won that Iowa State Fair championship with a Duroc gilt.

FFA was particularly strong at Lytton High. Besides his livestock projects, Wulkow was also a dedicated member of the teams his chapter sent to competitions in parliamentary procedure and milk-tasting. He wound up as chapter president, and earned the coveted "Iowa Farmer Degree."

His vocational agriculture instructor Chuck Schmidt "was a great ag teacher, but he really was a great teacher, period – one of the best. He taught me a lot about agriculture, but he also taught me so much math and science."

Wulkow continued his own livestock operations right on through his college years – selling boars with ads he placed in area newspapers – and indeed he was able to pay all his college expenses beyond the small athletic scholarships he received.

The family was active in St. Peter Missouri Synod Lutheran Church, located in the country just southeast of their farm. They made a decision to send their sons and daughter to Lytton for school instead of enrolling them at a one-room country school, which was also located in the rural neighborhood.

And that's when Rick Wulkow began falling in love with the town that, then and now, bragged on itself as the "Hottest Little Town for Business in the State."

In his boyhood, he recalls, "it was six square blocks with 375 people," and he ticks off the businesses downtown – the Lytton Co-op Creamery, a milk bottling plant, grain elevator, hatchery, hardware store, implement dealership, grocery, drug store, barbershop, several service stations, a tavern and the very popular Lytton Café on the corner. The creamery and bottling plant were known well beyond Lytton for their "Dairy Maid Milk" and "Lytton Maid Butter." A branch line of the Milwaukee Railroad helped move the farm produce to markets.

The town was in its heyday as Wulkow was growing up.

"Wednesday night was 'Town Night,' and all of us on the farms would come to town," he said. "We didn't have a movie theater – except for special showings at Christmas time at the Legion Hall – but we'd all go to our town friends' homes and walk all over town."

Once Wulkow got involved in the youth baseball program, people started talking.

When Wulkow's talent and enthusiasm became clear, Elmon Meyer took a special interest. Meyer had been a great pitcher in his prime in the 1930s, one who starred for years for the Lytton town baseball team after deciding against trying professional baseball. He was such a devotee of the game that when he died, he was buried with a baseball in his pitching hand.

"A lot of people thought Elmon Meyer might have gone to the professional leagues, but he decided to get married instead," said Gerald Kreft, who is Rick Wulkow's father-in-law. "He knew pitching inside and out, and he had a great knuckleball."

Meyer watched Wulkow playing ball on the youth league teams, and then "he got me started pitching," he said. "He'd come up to me and say, 'Let me show you something,' and he knew what he was talking about. He came to all of the baseball games, and he'd let you know how you were doing, too."

Wulkow's sports interests began to broaden as he reached his junior high years, when he started playing football and running track in addition to playing baseball and basketball.

Nobody argued with the fact that young Wulkow had natural ability, but everybody wondered if he was ever going to grow.

Donna Ditzel Rauch, who had a long career as the school secretary and always a special friend to Wulkow, recalled him about that time in his life as "a really cute kid, always with a crewcut, and a little Butch Wax on it."

And let Don Klink, Wulkow's coach through high school, complete the picture. "He was an eighth grader, and a scrawny little kid when I first saw him," he said. "But I was amazed at his ability. And he really knew about the games."

A native of Maxwell, Iowa, Klink arrived in Lytton in the fall of 1958, straight out of Iowa State Teachers College, ready for his first teaching and coaching job. He was hired as the high school football and track coach, but he also had eighth grade basketball that first year, and young Wulkow was one of his top players.

The following autumn, freshman Wulkow was the starting quarterback on the Bulldogs' varsity football team, which was going through what can only be called a "rebuilding" period. In fact, everybody who went out for football – all 17 of them – made the varsity squad.

"I weighed 115 pounds, and I was the starting quarterback, and we got the heck beat out of us regularly that year," Wulkow recalled. "I think we might have gone winless that year. Coach finally moved me back to a shotgun quarterback so I wasn't taking quite so much of a beating."

Lytton played in the BoCoon Conference, which took its name from the Boyer and Raccoon Rivers, and other member schools included Schaller, Early, Nemaha, Wall Lake, Newell, Battle Creek, Lohrville, Lake View and Odebolt.

The squad grew the next three seasons – numerically, physically and in ability. The turn-around was happening for Lytton High football. The post-game gatherings in the café side of the old Tu-Mar bar and grill in nearby Sac City became especially fun. Players, fans, coaches – they'd all get together there, with their counterparts from other area schools, too.

"We never won the conference, but we went 7-2 one year – I think it was my senior year," Wulkow said.

By that time, Coach Klink knew he had a great passer in Wulkow, who had grown up to 5 ft., 11 in. and 145 pounds and was all-conference his last two seasons. He was filling the air with passes to Denny Hinrichs, Dale Ross and a couple of other good receivers. Ross had moved into Lytton during his high school years and was the strongest and fastest player on the team.

"Rick developed into such a good passer that in his senior year, we opened every game the same way," said Klink, who retired in Armstrong,

Iowa, after spending the last 30 years of his career teaching and coaching at Armstrong-Ringsted. "Rick would roll out, throw a little flair pass to Dale Ross and we'd let him run with it. We'd almost always pick up a pretty good gain on that first play, and that's a nice way to get your passing attack established."

In the game against Lohrville, the Bulldogs found themselves on their own one-yard line.

"I was on the sidelines talking to Coach, and he said, 'Well, what do you think we ought to do?' " Wulkow said. "I said, 'Heck, Coach, they're certainly not thinking we'll pass – let's do that!' "

Standing in his own end zone, he hit Ross and the play went for 99 yards and a touchdown – the longest pass-play in Iowa that whole season, Klink recalled.

Basketball was Wulkow's favorite sport in high school, and he turned into a prolific scorer, averaging 20 points per game and once scoring 37.

"I lettered four years, but we were never very good," he said. "We had no size. I was playing in the middle of our zone defense, and I don't think we had anybody on the squad who was even 6 ft., 2 in."

He said one fond memory he has of his basketball games is how his mother Flossie Wulkow and Mary Lou Klink, the coach's wife "would sit together at games, and they'd wind up getting real excited and getting into trouble. She's always told the story of how I came home from high school one day, and the principal had talked to all of us about improving the sportsmanship at our games. I told her, 'Mom, I think he was talking about you!' "

In track, Wulkow ran the 440-yard dash, the 880-yard run, some relays and threw the football. His senior year he qualified in four events for the state track meet, and the team was second in the mile medley relay and Wulkow was fourth in the football throw. In baseball, the Bulldogs "were always competitive," he said, "and in my senior year, we got beat one game short of the state tournament." Wulkow and Fred Wise were the battery – they'd alternate pitching and catching – and in that critical tournament loss, "my arm just ran out of gas," Wulkow said.

One of the baseball stories he remembers most fondly is how

"when we'd have the 'Gala Day' town celebration in June, the old farts in the American Legion would put together a team and play the high school team." They're all still arguing and kidding about those games.

Ever since, Coach Klink has looked back on those happy times, knowing that he ran into something special in his first teaching and coaching position.

"I had such a good bunch of kids at Lytton that they became the benchmark for how I measured my students and athletes the rest of my career," he said. "And I was always hoping my own son would grow up to be like Rick Wulkow."

In that summer of 1963, after his graduation, and in his first college summer, besides working on the farm, Wulkow also worked for Mac Fagan at the Sinclair station on U.S. Highway 20 along the south edge of town. It was "a full-service station," Fagan recalled. And back in that era, "full-service" meant providing a place where the high school kids could hang out until 9 or 10 at night, playing cards and drinking pop.

"Mac taught me how to change oil, grease cars, fix tractor tires and those damned tires on the trucks from the creamery," Wulkow said. "Those big tires had the compression rings on the rims, and they were really hard to handle. Mac always told me it was helping me get stronger for football, and I guess it did. He'd also give me an extra hour off at noon so I could run and work out."

Wulkow remembers his boss Fagan "straightening me up a couple of times. Once was when one of his best customers came in for gas. I washed the windows and left a couple of smears on them. Mac let me know that we didn't turn the cars loose with smeared windows. The other time was when he took a weekend off and left me in charge. A couple of my friends came by and talked me into closing up a couple of hours early and going to the Calhoun County Fair in Manson with them. I thought I could probably get by doing that without anybody noticing."

Of course, there was a veritable line of customers waiting to tell Fagan when he got back to Lytton from his weekend away.

Rick Wulkow and Barb Kreft never dated in high school. They knew each other, of course. Everybody in Lytton knew each other – his Class of

'63 was typical in size with 21 students. And Barb was in the Class of '65 with Rick's sister Patty. She made a name for herself in high school sports circles by starting three years as a forward in basketball.

When Rick was working at Fagan's Sinclair station the summer after his freshman year of college, "Barb would stop by and get gas, and we'd start chatting." Their dating started "while both of us were dating someone else," Rick recalled. "After our dates, then Barb and I would meet."

As his college career continued at Buena Vista in Storm Lake, he'd see Barb frequently – "I made a lot of trips home because I still had my livestock projects to check on" – but after her graduation she decided to go to Drake University in Des Moines.

In the summers after his sophomore, junior and senior years at BV, Rick was also home working as a custodian at the Lytton school and directing the youth baseball program. That gave him more time close to Barb. And, in a way, both jobs helped shape his future.

"I took gum off desks, scrubbed floors and would go into the boilers and clean the pipes – I'd come out of there all black from the soot," he said.

That gave him an understanding and appreciation for the resources, hard work and time required for maintenance of school facilities. And the baseball job definitely enhanced his interest in coaching.

By the start of Rick's senior year, he and Barb were serious enough that she transferred to BV. They married in the summer of 1967 after he graduated.

"I always kidded Barb that I couldn't understand why somebody would want to transfer to little old Buena Vista after they'd been two years at Drake," her father Gerald Kreft said. "But I'd known Rick his whole life, and his parents, too. We were glad to get him into the family."

Wulkow's BV experience, as I indicated earlier, was nearly as ideal as his high school years in Lytton.

He'd been recruited by both football coach John Naughton and basketball coach Merritt Ewalt, who made trips to Lytton to see Wulkow play during his senior year.

"I recruited around this area for 25 years, and Rick was the best athlete ever to come out of Lytton that I know of," said Ewalt, who retired n Storm Lake.

Northwest Missouri State College in Maryville also recruited Wulkow, and he made a visit to the University of South Dakota.

"On the way back from South Dakota, we stopped at BV to see if Coach Naughton happened to be in, and he was," Wulkow recalled. "I told him that I kind of liked South Dakota, but I said, 'You know, they want me to pick one sport to play in college.' Naughton said, 'If you'll come here, you can play all the sports you want to play.' "

BV gave him a $300 annual scholarship, but it was that opportunity to be a multi-sport athlete that really won him over.

Wulkow played football and basketball for four years and baseball for three years at BV, winning nine varsity letters and becoming one of the most respected athletes in the Iowa Conference.

In football, he set several conference passing records, often throwing to his roommate, classmate and great pal Johnny Peterson, who had come to BV from Missouri Valley, Iowa.

"Rick was the real-deal, prototype quarterback," said Peterson, who has gone on to coach 19 national champion tennis teams at Tyler Community College in Tyler, Texas.

"He had a good head on his shoulders. He didn't get rattled in the pocket. He had a gun for an arm. And he could take a hit, too.

"Plus, he was a real field general. He even had the audacity to tell me to 'Shut up!' in the huddle a few times, when all I was doing was offering some suggestions that I felt should be made. I didn't really take that very well, but I suppose that as quarterback, Rick was just doing his job."

What kind of suggestions?

"It was usually, 'Throw it to me, Rick – I will be open!' " Peterson said with a chuckle. "He threw a lot of touchdown passes to me because I'd tell him to."

In basketball, Wulkow and Peterson teamed in the guard court for the Beavers, although Wulkow missed their entire junior year after breaking his leg late in the football season.

"That injury kept us from getting as much out of Rick in basketball as we probably would have otherwise," said Coach Ewalt. "He was a tremendous shooter. Oh, what a nice shot!"

Wulkow had skipped baseball as a freshman, wanting to make sure he'd have time for his college coursework. But he "missed it so bad that year, I went back out as a sophomore and played three years," he said. He roamed the outfield for Coach Jay Beekmann's teams, which were really strong in that era. Two of his teammates went on to play in Major League Baseball – Larry Bittner of Pocahontas, who played for the Washington Senators, Chicago Cubs and four other teams, and Dan Monzon, a native New Yorker who played for the Minnesota Twins. A third teammate, pitcher Bill Drummond of Council Bluffs, was drafted by the New York Yankees.

Ewalt said Wulkow's strength as a baseball player was that "he was quick, but even more important, he had one of those things you can't coach – instinct. He was off and running at the crack of the bat, and he would get to where the ball was going. And he had the real good arm, too."

The coach said that Wulkow, Peterson and other athletes were frequent dinner guests in the Ewalt home, which "would always thrill our own sons, Steve and Darrell. They were 9 or 10 years old then, and the BV athletes were like heroes to them: real role models. I had this theory that if you want your kids to turn out well, get them around good kids who are just a little older, and that's how it was for us, getting Steve and Darrell around Rick, 'Johnny Pete,' as we called him, and a few others."

Wulkow became especially close to the family.

"My wife Mareda always called him 'my brown-eyed boy,' " Merritt Ewalt said. "Besides being a good athlete, he was a wonderful person, too, and a really good student. The fact that he is where he is today is of no surprise to me. Rick had it all."

There was little doubt in Wulkow's mind that he would become a teacher and coach.

"I really wanted the opportunity to be around kids, and after all those years of playing ball as I grew up, I guess I looked on teaching physical education and coaching as a way that I would be getting paid to play ball!" he said. "But, more seriously, I had watched my high school and college coaches real close. They were really a great influence on me, and I think deep down, I wanted to be that same kind influence with young people."

Wulkow's career stops on the way to the Iowa High School Athletic Association were in Radcliffe and Denison in Iowa, the University of South Dakota, and then Paullina and Jefferson back in Iowa.

At Radcliffe in central Iowa, from 1967 to 1970, he taught elementary and secondary physical education and coached the football, track and baseball teams. His football team "only lost twice in three years, but really, I inherited that program," he said. "Track was probably a better test of my coaching ability. They were only getting 10 to 12 boys out for track before I came, but while I was there, we got 30 to 40, and we won two conference championships."

At Denison in west central Iowa, from 1970 to 1975, he taught high school physical education, coached football, track and baseball, and eventually served as athletic director. "I took over a football program that hadn't had a winning season in 11 or 12 years, and the year I left we were 8-1, and the next year they made the playoffs," he said. His baseball team in his final season there was eliminated one game short of the state tournament.

In 1975, Beanie Cooper, who had been a real success as football coach at Sioux City Heelan High School, was hired as head coach at the University of South Dakota, and he hired Wulkow as one of his assistant coaches. Wulkow was also an instructor in health, physical education and recreation, and in his two years there, he also earned his master's degree in secondary school administration.

"I liked college coaching, and I've always been glad I did it, but I just couldn't see it for my career," he said. "By that time, Barb and I started having kids, and the time available for my family was almost nothing. I'd take my daughter to school in the morning, and then I wouldn't see her until the next morning. I wanted more family time than that.

"And, to be honest, I wanted to be working with that high school age. I guess I was surprised to realize that on the college level, we really had to supervise and babysit the college kids more than I'd ever had to do with the high school kids I was coaching. On the high school level, the athletes go home to Mom and Dad after practice. At the college level, the coaching staff had to spend more time watching them than I would have guessed."

As he was coaching at USD and earning the master's degree, Wulkow was also becoming increasingly involved as a basketball official on both the high school and college level. He decided to give up coaching and classroom work to become a school administrator, and his first position was as junior high and high school principal in Paullina in northwest Iowa.

He was there a year when he had the opportunity to become principal at Jefferson High School in west central Iowa, and he was there from 1978 until he joined the IHSAA in 1980.

"When I got out of coaching, I wondered how much I'd miss it, and what I'd miss about it," Wulkow said. "I realized how much I had loved practices and, as I thought about that, I realized what I missed most was the teaching aspect of coaching, and it's at practice that you do most of that."

He said he "really enjoyed being a high school principal, and I think a lot of things I learned as a coach helped me in my relationships with the staff and students.

"I let the teachers know that they had the expertise in their subject areas, and that I wanted to be their support person, their leader, and that if they had a problem, my door would always be open. I learned quickly that the thing to do is surround yourself with good people and then let them do their jobs."

He said to enhance his relationship with the students, "every time the bell rang, I'd be right out there in the hallways with them. And I'd tell them that if they were coming by my office and my door was open, to come on in and say hello. I tried to connect with all the kids that way. I knew if I didn't reach out like that, I'd spend 95 percent of my time working with five percent of the kids."

Wulkow became one of the most respected basketball officials in the Midwest during his 31 years of doing games. He started out working high school games, then moved on to do NCAA Division I games for 17 years. His major college refereeing started in the Big Eight Conference, and eventually included the Big Eight, Big Ten, Western Athletic Conference, the Missouri Valley and Conference USA.

"I stayed pretty busy with it for a long time," he said. "I think the heaviest schedule I ever worked was about 50 games in 1997. I'd almost always drive to the games, and I'd generally be back in the office by 8 the next morning. I'd be behind the truck drivers all the way home from wherever the game had been."

Wulkow also eventually became an "observer of officials" in football and basketball for the Big Twelve, director of officials for the Iowa Conference and he served an interim term as Iowa Conference commissioner.

It was through his officiating that Wulkow actually came to the attention of Bernie Saggau in the 1970s, when Saggau was seeing a need to expand the staff at the IHSAA.

Saggau, who was also a graduate of Buena Vista, was certainly aware that Wulkow had been an outstanding athlete at Lytton High and BV, as well as a successful coach. With Wulkow's school administrative experience and his growing reputation as a game official, Saggau figured he was a good candidate.

There's a fascinating story about the first time Saggau and Wulkow met.

"I had seen Bernie when he'd be out doing rules meetings for officials around the state," Wulkow said. "But the whole time I coached and was a high school principal, I don't think I ever called the IHSAA office, so I had never personally talked to him. I did go to the office in Boone one time to take a baseball umpire's test, but I didn't see him that time."

Then late in the 1974-75 basketball season, Wulkow and a partner were officiating a girls-boys doubleheader between arch-rivals Wall Lake and host Lake View in northwest Iowa.

"All through the girls' game, there was this fan who thought my partner and I couldn't get anything right," Wulkow recalled. "He was really on us. I looked over there and I recognized him as Lowell Fullmer, the superintendent from Wall Lake, who was sitting up in the bleachers. I knew him pretty well, from working games at Wall Lake, and I'd never had a problem with him, so I was a little surprised."

Two to three minutes into the boys' game, the barrage of loud criticism continued. Finally, Wulkow said, he'd had enough.

"I stopped the game and went right up in the bleachers, and I told Lowell we were not going to continue the game until he left," Wulkow said.

"I told him I'd go stand down by the scorer's bench and if he was not out of the gym in one minute, I'd have him removed."

He got up and left.

Fullmer was no rookie when it came to high school basketball games, dealing with referees or the need for proper decorum by fans in the stands. After all, earlier in his career he had coached Lake Park's girls' basketball team to the state tournament. And he was now a school superintendent.

What Wulkow did not know was that Fullmer was also a member of the Board of Control of the Iowa High School Athletic Association. In fact, he served a dozen years on the board, from 1965 to 1977, first filling out an unexpired term, then running and being elected for two full, five-year terms.

So anyway, after the game, Wulkow called the IHSAA offices in Boone to report that he had ejected a fan – such calls were protocol for officials at that time. He heard nothing more about it until a month later, after a game he officiated in the boys' state basketball tournament at Veterans Memorial Auditorium in Des Moines.

"When I got to the dressing room after the game, one of the guys working back there handed me a note," Wulkow recalled. "It said something like, 'Please drop by Room A upstairs and see me before you leave,' and it was signed by Bernie Saggau.

"I showered, and then ran right up there. I shook hands with Bernie, and that was the first time I'd ever really met him or visited with him one-on-one. He said he wanted me to tell him about the basketball game at Lake View where I'd put Lowell Fullmer out of the game. He wanted to know what led up to the ejection, how it all precipitated and whether, if I had it to do all over again, would I do anything differently. I don't think he said anything about Lowell being a board member. He just wanted to know what happened."

Wulkow said he explained it all and told Saggau, "Under the circumstances, the way things developed in that game, if it came up again, I probably would handle it the same way. He said that was fine, we shook hands again and that was the end of it, as far as I knew."

Wulkow said he "didn't feel intimidated by Bernie asking me about that. Looking back on it, I think he wanted to see if I could defend my position on it, and I think I satisfied him that I could."

In the next couple of school years, Wulkow again received top officiating assignments from the IHSAA, Fullmer continued his long service on the board and Saggau said nothing more about what had happened.

"I didn't talk to Bernie again on anything until the fall of 1978, when all of a sudden, he stopped in my office at Jefferson High School one afternoon in October," said Wulkow. "He asked if I'd be interested in helping him out by conducting some rules meetings for other officials. It had always intrigued me the way Bernie did those meetings – he was really good at it – and so I said, 'Yeah.' I thought I could probably learn a lot from him.

"Lo and behold, I think that turned out to be the opening of the door for me. Later, like early in 1979, he came back through Jefferson one day, stopped and said he was going to start a new position at the IHSAA and encouraged me to apply."

Six people were interviewed for the new position of administrative assistant, and in July, 1980, Wulkow got the job.

Saggau has often said the key interview that was conducted "was when I interviewed Rick's wife, Barb. Once I talked to her, I came back satisfied in my own mind, and told the board, 'Yeah, we can hire him.' "

Saggau explained that he not only liked Barb Wulkow, but from a more practical standpoint, the IHSAA administrative jobs have always required some long and odd working hours, and he has learned that if a spouse doesn't understand that, it can be difficult later on for the employee.

Back in Lytton, the homefolks started conjecturing immediately what the future might hold. "I started calling Rick 'Little Bernie' as soon as he got the job, and I've been calling him 'Little Bernie' ever since," said Ron Dettmann, Wulkow's old friend and admirer. "I even ask for him that way when I call him up at the office in Boone."

So, in mid-2004, after it had been announced that Wulkow would indeed be the successor for the retiring Saggau as the IHSAA executive director, I reached Lowell Fullmer, who retired at the Iowa Great Lakes, to ask if he was aware of his niche in Iowa sports history.

"I guess not," said Fullmer who turned 81 in 2005, and completed his career as superintendent at Graettinger after he was at Wall Lake. "What would that be?"

I told him it was in a conversation over his ejection from that basketball game in Lake View in 1975 that Saggau first met Wulkow.

"Well, is that right! That's fine, I guess," Fullmer said, then adding that he, Wulkow and Saggau have long since made peace over the incident. "I've got no problems with Rick at all. I've gotten to know him well over the years, and he just did what he thought was right at that game.

"Really, though, the deal was that I wasn't the noisemaker that night," he continued. "I was sitting right next to the guy who was doing all the yelling – a friend of mine named Wid Ransom from there in Wall Lake. But Rick did think it was me. When he came up there and told me to get out, I just got up and left. There was no reason to raise a stink, because he sure could have had me physically thrown out."

Wid Ransom died in 1982. His widow, Lucille Ransom said she "wasn't there at the game that night, but I heard a lot about it. From what I remember, I think probably both Wid and Lowell were yelling. They were good friends, and they'd get kind of noisy when they were together at games. I will say my husband was a real fan – I don't think he ever missed a Wall Lake game, home or away. And he would get pretty excited at games."

Fullmer said that being on the board of the IHSAA was "a real highlight of my career," and that it was especially interesting being involved during the transition from Lyle Quinn as executive secretary to Saggau.

"Bernie has been an excellent leader for the athletic association," Fullmer said. "Rick is going to have a lot to live up to, that's for sure, but I think he'll do a good job. He's been well trained."

Wulkow said when he joined the IHSAA staff, "Bernie's instructions to me were right to the task.

"He gave me an office, told me to read a lot of printed material – the constitution of the association, the by-laws, the manuals for the various sports. He wanted me to get very familiar with the operation. He said at first, if I was making a decision in dealing with one of the schools, to review it with him. That wasn't like he was trying to control what I was doing. It was like mentoring, and I'd have to say he was an excellent mentor."

Saggau was also "a calming influence" for the whole extended

Wulkow family in October, 1982, when first Rick's father Delmar and then
Rick himself were hurt in separate, serious accidents in the same week on the
family's farm outside Lytton.

First, just as the harvest was starting, Delmar Wulkow took time to
do some repair work on the roof of his machine shed. He lost his balance,
slid down the roof and fell to the ground, landing on his shoulder and
injuring it badly enough that he was unable to get up into, or down from, his
combine.

So Saggau told Wulkow to take three-day weekends from his IHSAA
work during the harvest season, so that he could go back to the farm and do
the combining on Fridays, Saturdays and Sundays.

That's what was happening in the late afternoon and early evening
of Saturday, October 19. Rick had already put in a long day on the combine
when it broke down. He drove it into the farm yard, made a quick repair
and was starting to drive out again when his mother Flossie Wulkow yelled,
"Richard! Come on in for supper – that's enough for today!" But he yelled
back that he wanted to make a few more passes in a field and drove away.

Once back out in that field, "the combine clogged," Rick said. He
took it out of gear but left it running, jumped down "and I reached up in an
area underneath it, trying to unclog it – and I should have known better."

He caught his right hand in the combine's drive belt, which pulled
his hand into a pulley – that is where he lost his index finger and half of his
middle finger.

Oddly, in his memory, "it never really hurt. I just remember a burning
sensation, and I knew I had to do something fast."

He "kind of tucked my fingers and everything into a fist, put my
handkerchief over it, climbed up into the combine and turned it off, then
started walking and jogging to the house," he said. "It was about three-
fourths of a mile, and I had to climb over a fence or two to get there."

He said "the minute I hit the house, I kind of went into shock."

Barb Wulkow, who was at the house, managed to get him into the car
and drove quickly to Loring Hospital in Sac City, where Rick was treated and
stabilized. He was lucky, he knew, that only his hand had been caught, and
that he was in good enough condition to make it back to the farmhouse to

get help. He could easily have been hurt worse and bled to death in the field.

News of Rick's accident stunned the community of Lytton.

"Of course it did," said Donna Ditzel Rauch, the retired school secretary. "It happened to one of our boys."

His brother-in-law Greg Williams organized the neighboring farmers to complete the harvest at the Wulkow farm.

"I'm really fortunate the way it turned out," Wulkow said. "I lost the index finger, but I still have my writing stroke. The only thing I had to change was which pants pocket I keep my change in, because it's hard pulling out a handful of coins without that index finger."

When Greg Williams heard him say that, he added, "I was worried how you were going to be able to call the one-and-one free throw in basketball officiating."

Meanwhile, Saggau told Wulkow to take as long as he needed to recover before he resumed his duties at the IHSAA.

Working so closely with Saggau for so long, Wulkow said, "has been just amazing for me. Bernie is a visionary. He responds to situations so quickly, with such ease and common sense and good judgement. It's been really inspiring to be around that kind of leadership."

When Saggau was honored for his long career by the National Federation of State High School Activities Associations at their annual convention during the summer of 2004, he told them Wulkow will be a more than credible successor.

"I'm so pleased our board in Iowa has chosen Rick Wulkow as the next executive director," Saggau said. "Twenty-four years ago, I selected him, and while he learned from me for the first five years, I have learned from him the last 19."

Wulkow said he will start into his years as executive director realizing that "everything is running real well, so my first job is to maintain the philosophy and programs that have made us successful.

"What we're really all about is education-based sports. We do a whole lot more than just run tournaments. Our basic philosophy, as far as athletics goes, is participation for students and that through their participation, we have the opportunity to educate them in the core values we think are mportant – citizenship, sportsmanship, leadership, understanding the dangers of substance abuse, and improving health and nutrition.

"The club sports programs are really more about taking just the best athletes and seeing how far you can go. That's not us. And one thing we must do, as finances continue to be a problem for schools and as club sports grow, is we have to continue selling our program to the public – convincing people of the importance of having education-based sports programs."

Life has changed for Wulkow since January 1, 2005.

His salary has increased – to $130,000 per year, up from the $113,000 he had been earning as the top assistant.

The responsibilities have increased also.

Since he takes over at the age of 59, how long does he anticipate heading the association?

"Barb and I have talked about that, and I'd like to work at least 10 more years, if my health is such that I can still make good decisions and if my work is satisfactory with the board," Wulkow said.

He said his health is "excellent" as he takes over, "although I could lose 10 to 15 pounds and it wouldn't hurt a thing." He golfs occasionally, but "I'm not as avid about it as I once was." For exercise, he and Barb "walk every night that we can get it in" around Boone.

They live in a two and a half story home, built in 1931 on beautiful, tree-shaded South Story Street, just south of downtown Boone.

Barb for 20 years has worked at the "Pumpkin Patch" children's book and clothing store in downtown Ames, just east of Boone, and the last 10 years has been the manager.

They have three daughters, Sally Dighton, an elementary teacher in Boone; Wendy Postel, an obstetrics nurse at Iowa Methodist Medical Center in Des Moines, and Holly Anderson, a teacher and coach at Ankeny Middle School. The Wulkows have five grandchildren.

Rick Wulkow has long been active in church and community affairs in Boone. He is currently the chairperson for the congregation of Trinity Lutheran Church, and he led a recent financial campaign to build a major addition to the church building. He also serves on the board of the Boone Education Endowment Fund, and he is a member of the Iowa

Schoolmasters' "Walt Whitman Club," a 110-year-old organization promoting "a spirit of camaraderie among Iowa's school leaders engaged in creating quality educational opportunities for Iowa's citizens."

What is Wulkow like to work with?

"He is very, very organized," said Janet Johnson, who was 35 in 2005, and had been Wulkow's secretary for much of her 10 years at the IHSAA. "He takes on multiple tasks and can manage them very well."

His temperament?

"I don't think I've ever seen him get overly mad about anything," she said. "He is very easy going, very easy to get along with."

So, what will it be like for Rick Wulkow – besides "scary," as he said – in following a legend?

He can find good advice about that from Troy Dannen, 38, executive director of the Iowa Girls High School Athletic Union, who in 2002 succeeded E. Wayne Cooley, who had been in that position for 49 years.

"One thing Rick should remember is that nobody expected me to be Wayne, and nobody expects Rick to be Bernie Saggau," Dannen said. "Guys like Wayne and Bernie come around only once in anybody's lifetime.

"So the first thing I'd tell Rick is to be your own man. Go your own direction."

Dannen said that Wulkow "is a much different person than Bernie Saggau, just like I'm a much different person than Wayne Cooley. That's neither good nor bad. Just different. When you think about it, in age, I'm two generations removed from Wayne, and Rick is a generation removed from Bernie. We're bound to see things differently from Wayne and Bernie."

Naturally there are some challenges when leadership changes after a long tenure, but those can be healthy, Dannen said.

"After I took over, every time anybody on the staff said, 'We've always done it that way,' I would tell them they have to stop and explain why we've done it that way," he said. "That's really a healthy thing to do because it makes everybody evaluate the ways we have been doing things, and to give some thought to whether there are better ways to be doing them now. I was amazed at how many new ideas the people in our office would come up with, and the positive things that have come from doing that."

274

Dannen said he "first met Rick Wulkow when I was 19 years old and a student at the University of Northern Iowa, and I went to an officiating camp. Rick was one of the evaluators, and he evaluated me. I've still got that evaluation, too. Ever since then, I've admired him. He always holds himself well. He treats people right.

"In fact, I've yet to talk to anybody who doesn't like him."

Wulkow was the unanimous choice of the IHSAA Board of Control to succeed Saggau. The decision was made when the board met in June, 2004, in Ames.

"Basically, Rick had been preparing for this position for years," said Ron Sadler, the superintendent of schools at Crestwood of Cresco and the chairperson of the Board of Control then. "I don't know if there's anyone anywhere who would be better-qualified to be the successor to Bernie Saggau."

Sadler said the board considered Wulkow's "past experience as an official, not only at the high school level but also on the major college level; his interaction on the national level through the National Federation of State High School Associations, and his interaction with other executive directors of athletic associations in our surrounding states."

Wulkow's experience as a school administrator early in his career was another asset, Sadler said. So was the fact that Wulkow "is well-known and well-respected" across the state, after his 24 years at the IHSAA.

"Rick has the experience and the maturity we need at this time," Sadler said. "He is also an aggressive person who likes challenges, and he'll meet this challenge of succeeding Bernie. Someone that was not as knowledgeable might have trouble doing that, but the board has confidence in Rick."

Board members have already discussed the fact that Wulkow will not put in 37 years as executive director, as Saggau has done.

"The challenge to the association now is to be training somebody to follow Rick," he said. "Maybe that person is on staff right now, maybe not. But we've got to think 10 years or so ahead, and make sure we are identifying and developing someone who will eventually succeed him."

Meantime, Rick Wulkow's deep belief in — and enduring loyalty to

– the Iowa High School Athletic Association is being rewarded.

He takes over a position that only three others have held in the one hundred year history of this organization that nearly everybody in the state has had a tie to, at one time or another. There will be wide public interest in how he handles it.

He's ready.

Chapter Eight

Signature of a career: The Iowa Hall of Pride

Years from now, when Iowa high school alumni and others are browsing in the Iowa Hall of Pride in Des Moines, their focus will rightfully be on the stories and the talent portrayed there.

They will undoubtedly be inspired by the accounts of high achievement by Iowans in sports, the arts, education, religion, business, government and other fields.

They will learn how Iowa evolved, through the first one hundred years that the Iowa High School Athletic Association had been in existence.

A 12-minute, high-definition video "Tribute to Iowa" rolls in the "Iowa Experience Theater," telling the state's story – and glory.

In another area, lights on a large Iowa map mark the locations of the 967 member schools of the IHSAA in 1940, and then the changing numbers are shown in 20-year increments, to the 399 member schools as the 2004-05 school year began. You can hear the fight songs and experience the lore of those schools, including many schools that are no longer in existence.

Visitors learn about the teachers, coaches, directors, game officials, administrators, media and others who have served Iowa's students so well.

There is "a real 'Wow!' factor," the designers say, with the interactive technology, innovative video, and original works of art and sculpture in the building.

One example of that is a video, "Spirit of Competition," which in 15 minutes takes viewers through a year of some of Iowa's best-known "competitive" events – as seen through the eyes of the competitors and participants. The action surrounds the viewers on wrap-around screens. They experience the Iowa State Fair, the high school state wrestling tournament, the All-State Music Festival concert, the Drake Relays, the high school state volleyball tournament, the high school state cross country meet and the Des Moines Register's Annual Great Bicycle Ride Across Iowa (RAGBRAI).

It sure seemed spectacular at its opening in early 2005, and updates in the years ahead are expected to keep it that way.

But what I suspect will be forgotten is the story of just how the Iowa Hall of Pride came to be, and the almost decade-long struggle required to take it from dream to reality.

It has been an effort that occupied the time and attention of two governors, dozens of state legislators, several state boards and commissions, hundreds of donors, a small army of information gatherers, designers, videographers, architects, builders, economic development officials – and one man who put his planned retirement on hold for almost a decade because he promised he wouldn't bow out until the front doors of the project opened to the public.

That man, of course, is Bernie Saggau.

The Iowa Hall of Pride is "the signature of Bernie's career," said Jack Lashier, who came aboard in 1996 as the IHSAA's director of special projects to work directly with Saggau on the project.

The $12-million, 26,000-square-foot facility opened during the 2005 state wrestling tournament.

How tough was it to make it happen?

"We had some heartbreaks," Saggau said. "Whooo! Some real heartbreaks"

But they had a lot of fun, too. They were operating in places and with people they were unaccustomed to being around.

And it got wild.

First of all, the proposed location bounced from adjacent to the IHSAA headquarters in Boone, to three or four different spots on the State Capitol complex in Des Moines, back next to the IHSAA in Boone, then finally back to Des Moines. It ultimately became a part of the new $217 million Iowa Events Center built on the east and south sides of Veterans Memorial Auditorium.

Meanwhile, Lashier, who was 57 in 2005 and whose career had been n education and later business, spent so much time at the State Capitol in Des Moines over a two-year period that he had to register formally as a lobbyist. And when the member schools were slow to start gathering and submitting their information for the Hall of Pride, Lashier knew what was needed was a good sales job. So he hit the road starting in October, 2001, and by early June, 2002, he had traveled 87 days and 37,000 miles visiting all 403 schools. He successfully sold them on getting involved.

Then there's the unusual story of the lead interior designer Jason Ramos, of Haddonfield, New Jersey. He was in his mid-30s when he went to work on the Iowa Hall of Pride in 1999, after he was recommended by the OPN Architects firm in Cedar Rapids. Ramos right then was the talk of American architecture and design, after he'd spent a year studying in Italy in the prestigious "Fellows of the American Academy in Rome" program. When he started making monthly and eventually bi-weekly flights to Iowa during the key planning phases of the project, Saggau got nervous about him traveling so much – where would they be if there was a plane crash? So Saggau took out a million-dollar insurance policy on him. "No one had ever done that before on one of my projects," Ramos said, with a laugh. "Usually people don't care that much about what I'm doing."

And, in another very interesting sidelight, the Iowa Hall of Pride project played a significant role in helping convince Iowa natives Mark and Jeanne Bogenrief, nationally-acclaimed stained glass artists, to keep their headquarters and production facilities in Iowa. The Bogenriefs, who by early 2004 had outgrown their founding location in the northwest Iowa town of Merrill, were being heavily recruited by the states of Kentucky and South Dakota to move there. South Dakota offered a big-dollar commission for a new work of art by them. When Saggau, who is an admirer of fine art himself, learned that one of the new locations the Bogenriefs were considering in Iowa was the town of Cherokee, where he started his teaching and coaching career, he took an interest. State officials were already arranging a $1 million commission for the couple to do a major piece of stained glass art, and Saggau volunteered the Iowa Hall of Pride as a perfect, high-traffic display place for it. He also committed $100,000 to make sure it would be displayed properly. The agreement was announced in a press conference in Des Moines in late April, 2004. The Bogenriefs said they were thrilled that their work would be included in the Iowa Hall of Pride and that they appreciated their home state's effort to keep their headquarters here. They began work on two stained-glass panels, each 12-by-24 feet, to help tell the story of Iowa. "It will be quite a billboard for us," Jeanne Bogenrief told the Sioux City Journal. "Our ultimate goal is to get more projects like this." They now have studios, showrooms and offices in downtown Cherokee with additional facilities in the nearby town of Sutherland. Meanwhile, Saggau said, "to have a nationally renowned piece of art in the Hall of Pride truly will promote the cultural environment of our state."

After you consider all of the above, you can begin to understand why, as Jack Lashier said, "when the executive directors of the associations in other states hear about the Hall of Pride, they love the idea but then they just check out. They say 'no way' would they put that on their plate with everything else they already have going in their states.

"The difference is that Bernie really believed in the project," added Lashier. "He has seen it as a way to help Iowans feel good about themselves. I don't think he's done any of it from a selfish standpoint. And when we've hit the low points, the few times when it looked like it wasn't going to happen, he's too much of a competitor to say, 'I'm giving up.' "

So where did the idea come from, and how did it grow?

At one time, Saggau said, "The IHSAA board had considered building a hall of fame on our grounds in Boone, but I never felt that was quite right. It was going to just be for boys' sports, and I felt like if we were building something, it needed to be for all the kids and all the high school programs – not just boys' sports."

He remembered seeing a "Hall of Pride and Honor" within the offices of the New Mexico Activities Association in Albuquerque. A small display area there contains memorabilia from the state's high schools, put together "to give people who visited a feel for what the place was all about," Saggau said. He liked the name, especially the "pride" part of it.

It made him start thinking about the larger Iowa story, how the state was pioneered and built, and the experience of growing up here.

"I thought back about how our people originally came here for agriculture and religious freedom," he said. "They immediately started building little schools and churches, then communities. Those are our roots. And it's our work ethic. A value system grew up emphasizing discipline, determination, courage, teamwork, loyalty and pride.

"Now, we in Iowa have never been very good about bragging. But the time does come to brag. When you ask young people who've left Iowa and then come back here, why they've come back, it's not 'to make money.' What they come back for is quality of life, 'a great place to raise kids.' You hear that over and over. That's what I wanted to showcase in the Iowa Hall of Pride. I wanted to have Iowa's quality of life on display.

"Visitors will come to the Hall of Pride and see what kind of people have come out of Iowa, and they will see what the Iowa schools and communities have given to those people. It will be a good reminder for all of us who are Iowans. And people who are strangers will be shocked at what kind of state we've got — what kind of quality of life we've got here."

Saggau took his general idea for the facility to the IHSAA Board of Control in January, 1995, and they voted unanimously to undertake a study whether they could, or should, build such a structure.

But they started encountering some skepticism, too, as more people became aware of it.

"When he'd float this balloon, some would say, 'Oh, Bernie, another museum?' " Lashier said. "At that point, the idea was for it to be more of a collection of artifacts and records. It didn't evolve into using all the technology until later."

Still, the idea of displays — even static ones — that featured Iowa heroes, Iowa values and would be a central gathering point of information and records about all of Iowa's schools, seemed to have wide appeal.

In April, 1995, the board decided to poll the member schools on the idea of building the Hall of Pride in Boone, and the response was 258-58 in favor of the project.

That's when the first architects were engaged to design a structure, and a consulting firm from Kansas was hired to do a feasibility study of 63 Iowa businesses and individuals on whether sufficient money could be raised to pay for the project. Armed with generally positive responses from the study, IHSAA staff and board members visited the Rock 'n' Roll Hall of Fame in Cleveland, Ohio; the Pro Football Hall of Fame in Canton, Ohio, and the NCAA Hall of Champions, then located in Kansas City. Later there would be visits to other similarly-themed attractions around the country.

Then in April, 1996, the board voted to proceed and committed $2 million toward what was then expected to be a $7.8 million project.

In August of that year, they hired Jack Lashier.

"I had known Bernie Saggau my whole life," Lashier said. "Our paths have crossed many times."

His father Dick Lashier, of Clear Lake, a retired superintendent of schools, had served on the IHSAA Board of Control when he was in Jefferson, and he and Bernie had officiated games together. Dick had been a Buena Vista College roommate of Lois Saggau's brother Ronnie Kretzinger, and he hired Lois after she graduated from BV as a teacher at Lytton.

Jack Lashier spent his high school years in Jefferson, where he was a good athlete, and then went on to the University of Northern Iowa, where he earned a degree in business education. After teaching four years at Marshalltown High School, he went into insurance sales for eight years. He also served as president of the local United Way board for a time, and then became the organization's executive director for three years. Lashier went on to work 13 years as sales manager with Marshalltown's RACOM company, a highly successful locally-owned wireless communications provider, selling to schools, farmers and trucking companies, as well as selling "9-1-1" systems used by law enforcement.

By 1995, he found himself wanting a new challenge. His wife Kathy Lashier, a veteran kindergarten teacher in Marshalltown, had launched a highly-successful line of "memory journal" books – "Grandma, tell me your memories," "Grandpa, tell me your memories" and the like. Those books have now sold in seven figures worldwide. That eased some of the family's financial pressure in sending two sons through college.

In October of that year, Jack Lashier asked his old friend and mentor Bernie Saggau to come to the First Congregational Church, where the Lashiers were members, to speak at their stewardship service. Afterward, over lunch in the church basement, Saggau told him, "Jack, before I retire, want to build a building we're calling the Hall of Pride. We're going to have to raise some money. I could go somewhere and get a professional fundraiser, but I'd rather hire an Iowa kid. I've watched you a long time, and I want you to think about it."

Lashier pushed him for a few more details.

"That was on a Sunday," he said. "On the following Wednesday, I drove over to Boone and told Bernie, 'If that happens, I'd like to do it.'"

Ten months later, he took the job.

"Bernie said then that he expected in two to three years, we'd have the building built and operating, and he'd be retired," Lashier said. "I never dreamed I'd wind up with eight years invested in this. And I never even gave a thought to any possibility of it being a controversial project. That never occurred to me."

The first disappointment they encountered on the project was an unexpected turndown from the Iowa Girls High School Athletic Union, the organization that administers girls sports in Iowa, and its executive secretary then, E. Wayne Cooley.

The development of the plans had been covered by the newspapers in Boone, but the first time it drew attention in the media beyond Boone was when I wrote a column about it in the Des Moines Register in the fall of 1996. In an interview then, Saggau said he had discussed the project with Cooley, and said he was anticipating that the Girls Union and Cooley would be making "a large donation." When I checked with Cooley for comment, he said there would be no involvement by the Girls Union because "we didn't think our bylaws would allow us to be involved financially." And he said he was declining making a personal contribution "because he has other commitments that are more important to him," the story back then said. Cooley also said he thought "museums are out of vogue now."

Saggau was stunned, but marched on, saying that the Iowa Hall of Pride would continue its plan to feature girls' sports and other activities right along with the boys', no matter whether the Girls Union participated financially or not.

That was just the first of several disappointments and major challenges that the project would weather.

In the next three and a half years, fundraising for the project proved much more difficult than they'd anticipated.

"We had a ton of passion, but I'm not sure we had the technique we needed," said Lashier. "We were selling a dream, and it's hard for people to get their arms around a dream."

In the spring of 1997, they got their first big break when the Iowa Farm Bureau Federation board voted to donate $500,000 – and it came with a suggestion that the IHSAA consider moving the project to Des Moines.

"Their thinking was that so many more people would have access to the Hall of Pride if we built it in Des Moines," said Lashier.

That was initially hard for Saggau to swallow.

"I'd always wanted it to be in Boone because that's where our headquarters is," he said. "But the more I thought about it, I realized they were right – it needed to be in Des Moines."

Three different locations were considered. The first was land on the Farm Bureau campus in West Des Moines. But then the Hall of Pride idea came to the attention of Des Moines and Polk County officials who were working on a huge "Gateway East" development project just down the hill west from the Iowa State Capitol. They convinced Saggau and Lashier that would be the ideal location, and that became the plan – until January of 1998.

Then Governor Terry Branstad, Speaker of the House Ron Corbett and other members of the legislature conceived an idea to build the Hall of Pride on the northwest corner of the Capitol grounds. It would be just across the street east from the State Historical Building, and across the street west from a new State of Iowa parking ramp that was proposed as part of the project. Branstad arranged a $100,000 cultural grant from the state to assist in the planning.

As the idea went through the legislative process during all of 1998 and into the early fall of 1999, some objected that a new building on the corner of the Capitol grounds might block the grand views of the Statehouse. That led to new plans that would have all but the entrance of the Hall of Pride being constructed below ground level.

284

At one point, the state budgeted $3 million for the project, but then a legislative committee whittled that in half and, in September, 1999, tabled the whole idea.

In October, 1999, the IHSAA board, weary of the controversy, voted to end the effort to build the project at the Capitol complex. There is one standing legacy from all that effort – a much-needed new state-owned parking ramp was indeed built across the street from the State Historical Building and in the vicinity of other state offices. It would probably not be here today, had the corner of the Capitol grounds never been considered as a possible Hall of Pride location.

In November, 1999, another delegation from the City of Des Moines asked for an opportunity to make a new proposal to the IHSAA board, and so did the community leaders in Boone. In January of 2000, both groups made presentations to the board, and in February, the board voted 7-1 to locate the project in Boone.

And?

"Then we got hammered in the Des Moines media," Lashier said.

Nevertheless, the board proceeded with its plans, hiring OPN Architects of Cedar Rapids to design the building, The Weitz Company of Des Moines to be project managers and do the construction, and Jason Ramos' SynthesisDesign firm of New Jersey to do the building's interior.

Saggau looks back on that as a turning point, because it is when Jim McCulloh from The Weitz Company's Capital Resources subsidiary came on board as project manager for the Hall of Pride.

"Jim probably became the most important guy among all of us who were working on it," Saggau said. "I've relied on him in all our dealings with subcontractors, designers, the bids process, buying all the equipment – every phase of it. We'd heard good things about him, and I hadn't known him 30 days when I had complete trust in him."

McCulloh, who turned 52 in 2005, is a landscape architect and project planner by education, training and experience. He has put together major new developments all over the U.S., including golf courses, parking facilities for major stadiums, office projects and condominiums.

He also understood Saggau's mindset about Iowa pride.

"My wife and I both graduated from DeWitt Central High School over in eastern Iowa in 1970, and we grew up like most Iowa kids do – being involved in sports, 4-H and all the other activities that are available here," McCulloh said. "When you've grown up like that, I'll tell you, later in life you have an absolutely special feeling about Iowa being your home.

"And I think almost everybody who is from Iowa feels it," he continued. "I've seen it all the time in business. It's sort of amazing, but every major project I have done – and I'm talking about ones outside Iowa – it seems like there's always an Iowa connection. Somebody else I'm working with on the project has also grown up here, and there's an immediate trust."

After graduating from Iowa State University, McCulloh has used the Des Moines area as his base. Through commercial development projects over the years, he came to know real estate consultant Randy York, who heads The York Companies, headquartered in West Des Moines. York is also one of the top high school football officials in the state, as you read in Chapter 5, and thus has known the IHSAA administrators for years. When York learned that the Hall of Pride project was at such a key point, with a real need for expertise and experience in the final planning and construction phase, he recommended McCulloh and The Weitz Company to Saggau and Lashier.

Meanwhile, fundraising continued.

It got a good boost from businesses, organizations and individuals in Boone that came forward with $1 million in contributions.

"At that point, we had raised $5.5 million of what was by then going to be an $8 million project," Lashier said.

Two things had changed in the five years since the conception of the idea.

First, the State of Iowa had created two programs – the Community Attraction and Tourism ("CAT") Grants and the Vision Iowa Program – that would use proceeds from the gambling industry to help fund new projects in the state. Eventually, more than $250 million in projects, small and large, were proposed and funded, including the "America's River" project on the Mississippi Riverfront in Dubuque, the Iowa Events Center arena and convention complex in Des Moines, and smaller projects like community centers and enhancements to parks. Both programs were administered by the

Vision Iowa board, appointed by new Governor Tom Vilsack and chaired by Des Moines business leader Michael Gartner.

Second, and probably even more profound in its impact on the Hall of Pride project, telecommunications technology had taken the great leap into the Internet era. The possibilities for gathering, transmitting and displaying data and video advanced to levels that had been beyond most people's understanding, even beyond their wildest dreams.

However, the New Jersey designer Jason Ramos, then 35, looked at the rapidly changing technology and saw it for exactly what it could be – a wonderful new tool to convey ideas to people in this new age of video and instant communication.

"Steve Knierim, who is one of the partners with OPN Architects in Cedar Rapids brought me into the Hall of Pride project," said Ramos. "Our companies had done some work together in Cedar Rapids, and he called and asked me to take a look at the Hall of Pride. He sent me some material, and then he told me a group of them were going to Mississippi to look at a hall of fame, and asked me to come meet them there."

To turn to someone like Ramos, and ask him how best to present the stories of Iowa and its young people in a new Iowa Hall of Pride, was perhaps a leap of faith. Maybe you could have searched America and come up with a less-likely candidate to be the designer of this project. But it's fair to say that Ramos was a surprising choice to make for a fellow like Bernie Saggau.

"He didn't know a thing about Iowa high school athletics," Saggau now says, almost proudly.

Honestly, Ramos knew very little about high school athletics anywhere.

"Because of where I grew up, on Staten Island, New York, I really never had much of a brush with sports, other than a little tennis and swimming maybe," Ramos explained. "I went to the High School of Art & Design at Fifty-seventh Street and Second Avenue in the heart of New York City. You don't find any 'Fields of Dreams' there. I never saw a yellow school bus. I commuted two hours each way to go to school – just like businessmen commuting to their jobs – by train, ferry, subway and a walk."

He went on for his architecture training at Cornell University in Ithaca, New York, and was about to start graduate school when an opportunity for one of the much-sought-after positions as Fellows of the American Academy in Rome came up in 1991. He was the youngest architect ever selected for one of those fellowships, and he spent a year in Rome studying among 100 select artists and scholars from several different disciplines. Then he came back to the U.S. and in 1994 formed his company in New Jersey, just outside Philadelphia, Pennsylvania. It's a small firm – five people full-time – with other necessary services contracted. Ramos said the company's one venture into any sports-related project had been "helping develop the idea for the ESPN Zone" sports restaurants and bars later in the 1990s.

"We're known, I think, for being very specific on our projects," he said. "We don't do just anything, and we try not to take on more than we can handle. Then we give it everything we've got. We put a whole lot of our staff focus on any project we do, and that's how we've approached the Iowa Hall of Pride."

So that's the background and outlook Ramos brought to his first ever meeting with Bernie Saggau.

What did Ramos think of him?

"Well, the first time I met him, I knew instantly that I could not risk disappointing him on this project," Ramos said. "I knew I could not fail on this, that he would not accept that. I came to see him as a father. When he speaks, you're totally attentive, and you can see and feel his passion in all his presentations."

He said he told Saggau "that I was going on this project not for financial reasons, or because I had some specific design in mind that I wanted to use somewhere, but because this was something I wanted to see done the right way."

That fit precisely with what Saggau said he expected.

"He told me there were two things he wanted in this," Ramos said. "First, he wanted to make it a project that would be unique to Iowa. The second, he wanted to make sure the IHSAA's pride in Iowa showed through."

Ramos and his staff of designers, with a lot of input from the

IHSAA staff and many others in Iowa, began coming up with ideas that had never been considered, and enhanced other ideas that had already been included:

- High-definition video and audio of the All-State Chorus singing the "Battle Hymn of the Republic," with visitors being able to sing right along with Iowa's best.

- Video of a pitcher throwing 80-to-90 mile fastballs and sharp-breaking curves, shot from the home plate umpire's perspective, allowing visitors to play "You Make the Call!"

- Same sort of idea, with closely-focused video of a high school wrestling match, with a challenge for visitors to make the referee's decisions.

- Besides inclusion of all the sports that Iowa's girls and boys are competing in today, it seemed only natural to have an exhibit about the late, great game of "Six-on-Six" girls' basketball, for which Iowa was known nationally for decades.

- And, of course, earlier ideas would be incorporated, like life-sized bronze statues by sculptor Christopher Bennett, of Keosauqua, of three or four of Iowa's greatest high school athletes – initially football great Nile Kinnick of Adel, basketball/baseball great Gary Thompson of Roland and wrestling legend Dan Gable of Waterloo West. There are video interviews with 90 key figures in Iowa high school sports and the fine arts, past and present. In a "Hall of Heroes," the stories of 30 of the state's highest-achieving citizens are told in text, photos and video. There is a 20-foot-by-8-foot clay wall sculpture of children frolicking at play, titled "Recess at a One-Room School" by Des Moines artist David Dahlquist. Also there is the sculpture that Saggau most wanted to see in the Hall of Pride, "The Real Heroes," portraying a contemporary American family of mother, father, son, daughter and pet dog – rendered by sculptor Nick Klepinger, of Reasoner, Iowa,

The design work started and was progressing throughout 2000 and 2001. Meanwhile, over three months from November, 2000, through January,

2001, the IHSAA staff, board and others went to work on the necessary 650-page application for a "CAT" grant from the Vision Iowa board. There was positive reaction and encouragement from Vision Iowa officials throughout the process.

The application was to be presented on February 12, 2002, and just prior to that, the IHSAA staff was surprised when Vision Iowa officials asked that Saggau himself make the presentation. He was in Arizona on vacation at the time, but flew back to Des Moines for the session.

"We thought we were going in there with a slam-dunk success," Lashier said.

But the board was involved in a long discussion before Saggau, Lashier, Ramos and the project manager McCulloh were finally invited into the meeting room to make the presentation, about four hours later than they had been told to be there.

In seven minutes of remarks, Saggau described the project and asked the board for $2.67 million.

"The whole time I was talking, the board members were all looking at the floor," he said. "I've spoken to a lot audiences, and I can read them pretty well. I knew something was wrong."

When he stopped, he asked if the board had any questions.

As the Des Moines Register reported, board member Brad Parks of Dubuque asked, "Why would you build this anywhere but Des Moines?"

Then another board member, Shenandoah Mayor Gregg Connell, said, "Our problem is, we see the project as bigger than Boone, and you see it as Boone."

Saggau answered that "we tried to make it happen in Des Moines, but got turned down."

Board chairman Gartner then "suggested that the Hall of Pride would fit well with a proposed arena in Polk County," the Register story said.

Whereupon, the board rejected the request for the $2.67 million and encouraged Saggau to explore other options.

When Saggau and Lashier left that meeting, "it was like our worst moment," Lashier said. Saggau told the Register's reporter that he was "surprised and shocked" at what had happened.

"We were like whipped puppies," Lashier said. "We went to a restaurant, and both of us were saying, 'I can't believe this – I can't believe it happened!' I think those few moments were the lowest I've ever seen Bernie in my whole life."

The next morning at 8 a.m., when Lashier got to work at the IHSAA headquarters in Boone, Saggau was already there. He'd been in his office since 4 a.m., Lashier learned.

"I went in to see him, thinking it was all over for the project," Lashier said. "But Bernie had already turned it around in his mind. He'd already hit bottom and was on the way back up. He is amazingly resilient – he bounces back like that. He is a passionate, emotional guy, and the passionate part has been what kept this project alive."

Saggau said to Lashier, "What were they telling us? That they didn't like our project? No, they said it was one of the best, most visionary projects that they'd seen. What they were telling us was that it might be better in Des Moines, that more people would see it there."

Lashier's conclusion? "Bernie was ready to go again," he said.

About 9 a.m. that same morning, Saggau got a phone call from Angela Connolly, a member of the Polk County Board of Supervisors and one of the key supporters of the Iowa Events Center arena project that was being planned. "She said, 'Bernie, I've read the story in the paper this morning, and I think we ought to talk,' " Saggau recalled.

She said she thought the Hall of Pride could be included in the arena project, "but I told her we were talking about needing a larger space than just a room," Saggau said. "She asked how much space I was talking about, and I said our design in Boone was for 25,000 square feet. She said she had 26,000 square feet available in one part of the Iowa Events Center."

She went on to tell Saggau that the arena project "needs you worse than you need us." She explained that critics were charging that "the arena was just for Des Moines or Polk County, and that there wasn't statewide interest in it," he said. Having the state high school tournaments in the new building would certainly help answer that criticism, and so would having the Iowa Hall of Pride headquartered there. "Having the Hall of Pride as part of the project would be icing on the cake," the Des Moines Register said later in an editorial.

Within days of Connolly's call, Saggau and Lashier began meeting with the Polk County government and other development officials working on the arena project. And over the next six months, Saggau met 58 times with them, "and that doesn't count all the meetings Jack Lashier had with them on his own," Saggau said.

The agreement negotiated was that the IHSAA would pay $3 million for the 26,000 square feet of space in the Events Center, and an additional $350,000 to have a large sign outside on the building marking the location of the Hall of Pride.

Polk County officials developed an application for $70 million for the arena and other new facilities to take to the Vision Iowa board, and if it was approved, the IHSAA was to receive $5 million for the Hall of Pride. The $70 million also included partial funding for four other new projects planned in downtown Des Moines – the Science Center of Iowa, Des Moines Public Library, a continuing-education center and a headquarters for the World Food Prize in the old library building.

On July 9, 2001, the Vision Iowa board indeed approved the application.

Saggau and Lashier realized the dream was going to become reality.

"We were just giddy after that Vision Iowa decision," Lashier said. "We finally knew the Hall of Pride was going to happen."

Meanwhile, Governor Vilsack hailed the whole Iowa Events Center package and said, "Never before in the state's history have we had this sort of collaborative effort. That is what Vision Iowa is all about." The Des Moines Register editorialized that "this sort of state and local partnership has never before been seen on such a scale in Iowa. This should be just the beginning."

But one tough task still faced the IHSAA officials.

They had to square up with the 44 donors from Boone who had contributed $1 million with the understanding that the facility would be built in their community.

"We returned every penny of it," Saggau said. "There was no other way to handle it."

Only three of those 44 decided to leave their original donations in the new Hall of Pride project.

"There were some hard feelings in Boone, just as you'd expect," said Saggau. "But we really had done everything we could to try to build the Hall of Pride there. I had always wanted to build it next to our headquarters, but it just wasn't going to work there."

In the years that have passed since then, "Boone has probably healed up over this," Saggau said. "I went around and talked to four or five good friends in the community, and they understood we'd done everything we could to try to make the project happen in Boone."

In the 18 months after the Vision Iowa board's decision in July, 2001, Polk County developers withstood several legal challenges to the decision. But work on the interior components of the Hall of Pride was well underway by the time the last of the legal hurdles was cleared in late 2002. The first payment of Vision Iowa money to the IHSAA was made in January, 2003.

A total of 95 Iowans – coaches, teachers, game officials, school administrators and media representatives who expressed an interest – were formed into 19 different committees, to make final plans and preparations for what information and displays should be presented in the Hall of Pride. Centerville High School media coordinator Marcia Meller wrote 30 biographies of leading Iowans, with 35 students from the school working as researchers. Lead designer Ramos and two of his associates from New Jersey, Andrew Long and Laura Schetzsle, came to Iowa in the summer of 2002 and rode bicycles for three days and 211 miles of the route of RAGBRAI. "We did that to get a feeling about the "specialness" of Iowa, the feeling of community that is so strong there," Ramos said.

There was a contagious feeling of enthusiasm about a project that was finally a certainty.

For as long as the struggle had gone on – both to find a site for the building and to find the funding – it all came together rather quickly during 2003 and 2004.

Besides $5 million from Vision Iowa, the IHSAA Board of Control increased the association's financial participation to a total of $3 million. The Iowa Farm Bureau added $1.5 million to its initial $500,000 for a total of $2 million. Prairie Meadows Racetrack and Casino agreed to donate $750,000. Allied Insurance donated $300,000. An individual who requested anonymity donated $250,000. The Iowa Bankers Association contributed $100,000 for one of the works of art. There were several other contributions of lesser amounts by companies and individuals. The smallest has been for $5, an individual donation someone made to one of the five memorial funds directed to the Hall of Pride by the families of deceased IHSAA supporters, including a couple of coaches and game officials.

In the spring of 2004, two of the most surprising donations – and major ones at that – came from the board of the Iowa Girls High School Athletic Union (IGHSAU) and from its now-retired Executive Secretary E. Wayne Cooley, reversing their turndowns eight years earlier.

"A long time ago, Bernie Saggau had approached Wayne Cooley about the Hall of Pride project and had been turned down," said Troy Dannen, now executive director of the IGHSAU.

"But you know, the project changed a lot over the years. My position all along was that it was always going to be a good project. The later versions moved it to being a great project. In my own mind, I thought it was something the Girls Union should probably be getting involved in, and I did express that to Bernie later on.

"So in the fall of 2003, Bernie approached me about it, and I told him he really needed to come to talk to our board about it, and not just me," said Dannen, who succeeded Cooley in September, 2002. "I told him that we were coming off kind of a tough year financially, in the transition from Dr. Cooley's leadership to me, and I wanted to get through the state basketball tournament in the spring and make sure we were in good shape. He said he'd come talk to our board whenever I told him the time was right."

That was at the IGHSAU board meeting in April, 2004.

"At every board meeting for several months before that, I spent a few minutes talking about the Hall of Pride and what the progress on it was," Dannen said. "Then in April, Bernie and Jack Lashier came before us. Bernie Saggau is the classic, ice-to-Eskimos type of salesperson. He made a presentation of about 10 minutes, very candid, laying out the finances of the project, and then he left.

294

"I think within a minute of discussion, our board was unanimous in wanting to give Bernie an assurance that we wanted to be involved. And after about 30 more minutes of discussion, they had agreed on the amount. Ultimately, they gave him $600,000, which was $100,000 more than he had asked for. Bernie had said there needed to be some kind of foundation set up to cover operations of the Hall of Pride in perpetuity. So I had suggested to our board that we earmark the money we were giving for that endowment. But they said, no, they wanted to give him $500,000 to help finance the project, but give an extra $100,000 for seed money for the foundation."

Interestingly, Dannen said the board told him to inform Saggau, then adjourned and they all went to lunch. Dannen said when he got back to the IGHSAU offices in Des Moines, Lashier called asking what the Girls Union board had decided "but I didn't tell him. Instead I sat down and wrote a letter to Bernie for the board, telling him what their decision had been."

When he was ready to leave the office that afternoon, Dannen telephoned Lois Saggau "and she said Bernie wasn't home yet from Boone. I told her to tell him I was coming over with something he'd want to see. I stopped on the way, bought a bottle of wine and went out to Saggaus' house. I handed him the letter, asked Lois to pour the wine and said we had something to celebrate. I think Bernie was stunned."

Dannen said he decided to handle informing Saggau that way "because I've really grown to think of Bernie Saggau as a friend since I've been in this position, and I wanted to handle this like friends would, instead of like a business transaction."

He said the two talked "about how the Girls Union didn't want to be considered another one of the sponsors of the Hall of Pride but more as a partner," Dannen said, a few months later, "although to this day I still feel a little bit guilty about coming into it at the end."

He said the Girls Union board "didn't want a lot of recognition for getting involved."

There was some discussion about the Girls Union money being used to sponsor an exhibit about the old six-on-six basketball game that Iowa had been famous for, before the complete switch to five-on-five was made after the 1993 season. "I told Bernie I thought our contribution should go with all the other donations," Dannen said, "but I suggested he might find a sponsor for the six-on-six exhibit from some of the companies that helped sponsor the television coverage of the tournament back in those years. I was surprised later when I heard he'd gone back to for that. And I was really surprised – and delighted – when I heard that Wayne said yes."

How did that happen?

"Bernie called me and asked," Cooley said.

Actually, there's a more fun story to it than just that.

In May, Saggau and Cooley had been together in Storm Lake for a meeting of the Board of Trustees of Buena Vista University, the alma mater for both of them.

"During a break from our board proceedings, Bernie and I were visiting," said Cooley, "and I happened to make a remark about how, 'I'm getting mighty tired of people calling and asking for money. Between the political races and other charitable concerns, I am just getting tired of it!' We talked a little more about other things, then went back into our board meetings.

"So it was rather ironic that less than a week later, Bernie wrote me a letter and asked me if I would be the sponsor of the six-on-six girls' basketball exhibit in the Hall of Pride. He did apologize at the start of the letter, saying he remembered my remark at the Buena Vista board meeting about being tired of getting asked for money. But then he said he had to ask me for some money anyway. So I said yes."

How much?

"A certain amount of money, that I don't want to say," Cooley said.

"But the reason I said yes, after thinking about it, is that really, no one walked through those years with those girls in six-on-six as closely as I did. I thought, why should I leave it to someone else to sponsor that exhibit? I couldn't leave those girls in the company of some other sponsor when I'd been so close to them all those years."

It was a very nice resolution to an old fuss, one that was no longer a fuss at all, with all that had changed.

There was peace in the Iowa high school sports family.

"The two organizations were working well together before, on matters of concern to both of us," said Dannen, "and this puts us together in a whole new way. We're so much stronger at times when the organizations can act together."

So, all of that is the long, tangled story that will probably be forgotten in years to come, when the Iowa Hall of Pride is being heralded as the nation's finest showcase of the high school experience.

Bernie Saggau said he's been happy to have helped make it happen.

"It's our gift," Saggau said. "We put eight years and a lot of work in this baby. And it's our gift to the state of Iowa."

Chapter Nine

Iowa's athletes at the IHSAA's 100th

In the end, it's really all about the kids.

We can talk about the Iowa High School Athletic Association and its proud history. We can talk about the organization's executives, staff and board members who've provided outstanding leadership to high school boys' sports, both in Iowa and nationally. We can talk about the administrators, coaches, officials, media and fans who've been a part of all this for 100 years.

But it's really the athletes who matter most.

The whole program operates for them.

So, what do *they* think of high school sports in Iowa now? What kind of kids are they? How different, or how similar, are they to the high school athletes of 20 years ago? Of 50 years ago? Or even those who were competing way back in 1904 when the IHSAA was founded? Is it difficult to be a high school athlete in today's culture? And what ideas do they have about the future of high school sports in Iowa?

We had a group of six athletes come together from around the state between Christmas and New Year's in 2003, when they agreed to pose with IHSAA Executive Director Bernie Saggau for the cover of this book. In conversations that began that day, and continued for several months during personal visits, phone calls and e-mail exchanges, I learned a lot.

The six come from all over the state. City kids, small town kids, farm kids. They were a senior, four juniors and a sophomore when we first met them. Two come from large urban schools. One was from one of the smallest rural schools. Some were from families that have been known in Iowa athletic circles for decades and generations. One was an Iowa newcomer who arrived as a refugee from the ethnic and military carnage in the Balkans.

Three of them played in sports programs that are currently among the strongest in the state – Tyrone Scott Jr., a basketball player at Waterloo East, Blake Schoh, catcher on the Kee High baseball team from the northeast Iowa towns of Lansing and New Albin, and Max Orsborn, a running back for Emmetsburg's football team.

You might say that Mike Whisler is of "the wrestling Whislers" of Centerville, since his extended family has had somebody involved on nearly every Big Reds team since the school started its program 36 years ago.

Eric Westerberg is a four-sport athlete in Saggau's hometown of Denison.

Enes Elezovic, an outstanding soccer player at Des Moines Roosevelt before his graduation in the spring of 2004, was the Iowa newcomer, having arrived in 1999 by way of Germany after he and his family fled the terror in his native Bosnia in 1992.

Let's meet them all individually, and through their stories, learn what life is like for rather typical Iowa high school boys competing in the programs of the IHSAA as the organization turned 100 years old.

Then we'll close this chapter with all six of them in dialogue on a set of 10 questions.

Enes Elezovic, the graduated Des Moines Roosevelt soccer star, can tell you about living through war in the blunt, direct way that all refugees know and understand.

"War sucks," he said, in lingo understood internationally by young people in 2004-05.

He was six years old, living in Mostar, Bosnia's largest city other than the capital of Sarajevo, when the war broke out in 1991.

The Elezovics were living a comfortable, affluent life. Enes' father Sedat had been a helicopter pilot in the Bosnian army for 10 years, while living at home with the family. His mother Ljubica, or "Lu" as most know her, was a psychiatrist. His brother Semir, a junior in 2004-05 and a soccer player at Des Moines Roosevelt, was an infant back then. Life was good in a country that was crazy for soccer and, more recently, basketball.

The Elezovics were a mixed family, by religion, with Sedat being Muslim and Lu being Catholic. But for a long time, families could live with no fear of oppression for either religious or ethnic reasons.

And then?

"The war started in Croatia, and the Serbs and Croats were doing the 'ethnic cleansing' you heard about," Enes said. "We knew they were going to come to Bosnia because the Serbs and Croats wanted land. Many people thought it was a religious war, but it was really the Serbs and Croats wanting more land."

The bombing would start "every day at about 6 in the morning. A bell would ring, and we'd all have to go to the basement. Planes would be bombing all around us. There was gunfire all the time. I was very frightened, and it was all so fast-paced it was hard to understand what was happening.

"Somehow we lived a half a year with the war going on all around us, but then we were told we had to get out. We had to pack and leave in one day. There was no time to even think about it. We had to leave behind almost everything we had and get out. From what I remember, we had no idea if someone was going to try to capture us, or if they'd let us out of the country, or if we could even get into another country. We just had to leave."

An uncle, who had relocated to Achen, Germany, told the Elezovics to try to make it to that city located near the point where Germany, The Netherlands and Belgium meet.

"We had to leave Bosnia without my dad, and we didn't really know if we would see him again," Enes said. "I have a lot of friends who lost their dads in the war."

After three days, Lu Elezovic and her two young sons made it out of the country and arrived in Achen. Six months later, Sedat made it out of Bosnia and joined them.

The family went about the business of rebuilding their lives in Germany, hoping that after being there six years, they would qualify as German citizens.

"But then Germany kicked us out – that's what really happened," Enes said. "When we went there, the rule was you had to be there six years to become a citizen. But then Germany decided there were too many refugees coming, so they changed the rule that you had to be there eight years for citizenship. Those who were living there with less time than that had to leave.

"We wanted to stay in Germany, we definitely liked it there, but were told we either had to go back to Bosnia or find another country."

Hugo Smaljovic, a Bosnian friend who had settled in Iowa, contacted the family and suggested they join him. He volunteered to "sponsor" them in the U.S. After an interview at the U.S. Embassy in Germany, the Elezovics were told they would be welcomed to the U.S. as refugees, and so on February 16, 1999, they arrived in Des Moines to become part of the community of nearly 3,000 Bosnian people who had re-settled to Iowa's capital city.

Enes enrolled in the Des Moines schools as a second-semester seventh grader with a whole lot of global experience, and a lot of it not very happy. He was fluent in the Serbo-Croatian language the people had spoken in Bosnia and in the German he had learned in Europe, and he was fairly comfortable in the English that he had studied for four years in Germany.

He also knew another form of communication, one that is understood and loved around the world: Soccer.

He had just started playing the game as a 6-year-old in Bosnia, when the war broke out, then he played for the next six years when his family was in Germany.

He quickly became a part of the Amateur Athletic Union teams in the Des Moines area. And during his high school years, he also played for an adult Bosnian team that traveled to cities all over the Midwest and in Canada.

At Des Moines Roosevelt, he became a four-year starter on the varsity at the center-midfield position. He grew to be six feet tall and weighed a trim 155 pounds, and he became one of those players who can seemingly run all day long without tiring. Before his graduation in 2004, he played at Roosevelt during a real run of soccer success – including a third place finish in the state tournament in 2003.

His ability to kick a ball also came to the attention of the Roosevelt football coaches, and they made him the place kicker on the football team his senior year.

In his senior soccer season, Elezovic was an All-State first team selection, and he was recruited by several Midwestern colleges before choosing Grand View College in Des Moines, where he planned to study international business.

"If I get the opportunity, I would like to try professional soccer, but I probably would not play pro for very long," he said. "That's why I plan my career being in business."

His parents, now both 43 years old, have made the transition to American business very well. Sedat is now a supervisor in a manufacturing plant making doors. Lu is a successful Realtor. They own three houses, so they have rental income. And the whole family works together in their own company, Tip Top Cleaning, which does home and office custodial work and also cleans construction sites.

Does Enes ever long for Bosnia?

"I think about it, because we still have relatives there and in Croatia – grandparents and cousins," he said. "I went back in the summer of 2003, and Bosnia is still rebuilding after the war. There's no way to find a job. Nobody has any money. It's going to take a long, long time to rebuild the country.

"I hardly think I will ever live there again, although I will visit sometimes."

The Enes Elezovic story is one that reminds us all of just how inconsequential sports can be in the larger game of life. It also is testimony to what many of our newcomers in Iowa – people who have come from difficult situations in many different areas of the world – have gone through to get here.

But there's another lesson in it, too. As this fine Iowa athlete is quick to tell anybody, his sport of soccer has sustained him through some very difficult transitions.

Max Orsborn was the big, quick and rugged running back on the Emmetsburg E'Hawks football team. It's been a thrill, of course, being on a team that won consecutive state championships in Class 2A, and being in a program that has rung up eight state titles in its 29 appearances in the playoffs.

What Max was just starting to grasp, after the championship in his junior year, was that for the rest of his life, whenever he mentions that he was once the running back on an Emmetsburg E'Hawk football team, good sports fans in Iowa will react.

"I think all of us who are on this team are proud of being E'Hawks, proud of being part of the tradition," he said. "You think about it all the time when you see all the trophies in the school. And then kids from other · teams ask about the program. They wonder what it's like being in it."

It is a program built by Duane Twait, who coached the E'Hawks to eight of the championships before retiring after the 2002 season and turning the reins over to his assistant for 13 years, Tom Steen. Players like Orsborn begin learning the E'Hawk offensive and defensive systems when they start playing in middle school, and that is the same system they play under right on through their high school varsity years.

They grow up knowing the importance of lifting weights regularly, taking part in the agility camps and improving their speed.

"What I like most about playing football," Orsborn said, "is the idea of playing with 10 other guys as a team — on offense or defense — and working together as a team all fall, trying to get better. And I also really like the contact part of it."

By his junior year, he'd become well-equipped physically for that contact, having grown to six feet tall and 195 pounds, and he had sprinter's speed. In his junior season, he had just under 1,000 yards rushing for the season. And while "the highlight" of his whole football playing career was "winning the state championship" in the fall of 2003, he can point to one play as "the best single moment" for him. Oddly, it did not involve him crashing through the line on some important running play.

Rather, it was a crazy play the E'Hawks put together especially for the state championship game against Solon.

"We'd never run it before in a game," Orsborn said, "and we practiced it only one time, right before that last game. We used it right before halftime, when we were in a fourth-and-goal situation and we were down by seven points."

Orsborn took a pitch from the quarterback, ran to his right and then threw a pass "right into triple coverage," he said, with a smile. "It was a pretty bad pass, too. The Des Moines Register reporter who covered the game described it as a 'flutterball.' "

But in the end zone, his first cousin Jon Lapczenski, a senior on the team, leaped high over the defenders, caught the wobbly ball and held on to it as he fell for a touchdown!

It was a moment that almost certainly will be discussed – if not re-enacted – for decades to come at Orsborn family reunions.

Max is the son of an earlier E'Hawk football player, Melvin Orsborn, who is a farmer, and an E'Hawk golfer Mary Kay (Gappa) Orsborn, who is now a librarian in the nearby West Bend-Mallard Schools. His older sister Maureen is a musician studying at Luther College in Decorah, Iowa, and Max is a singer, too, performing with the Emmetsburg High choir.

He played basketball his first two years of high school, but in his junior year opted out in order to begin focusing more on football by increasing his weight work, speed and agility training. In elementary school he also wrestled, played baseball and was on the local swimming team.

Orsborn continues to compete in track, running sprints and sprint relays as well as long jumping, an event in which he qualified for the state track meet as a junior.

He has also worked at the local Fareway supermarket two to three mornings per week, from 5 to 8 a.m., unloading groceries and stocking shelves, and for five years he has worked two weeks each summer detasseling corn. "I don't like detasseling," he said. "For two weeks, it's your life. But it is good money."

He said he is grateful to have grown up in a small town.

"Sometimes we think it's pretty small and that there isn't much to do," he said. "But for sports, it's great, because you go out for about as many of them as you want to. You can try everything.

"What I notice about that is that during a season when I'm out for a sport, I feel a lot more focused – on practice, on games, on getting my schoolwork done, everything. I think I do better when I have more of a routine to follow. The other thing about it is that when I get in shape and am working out all the time, I feel better."

His goals?

"College football, if I get the chance," he said. His career, he imagines, is "something in business."

Blake Schoh, catcher for the baseball team at Kee High School in northeast Iowa, seems like he was born for the position.

"I'll play anywhere they put me – and I think I've played everywhere but first base," he said. At 5 ft., 4 in. and 135 pounds, Schoh (pronounced "Show") would not be a big enough target at first base for infielders' throws across the diamond.

"But my main position is catching," he continued. "I got my first set of catching gear when I was in T-ball, so I've been catching at least 10 years."

Why does he like it so?

"Catching is a good position for a control freak, and I love being in control," he said. "Somebody like me, just has to be behind the plate. Pitchers have some control of the game, but as a catcher, you know every situation, every pitcher, every batter.

"The other thing is that I've always been a guy who likes to get sweaty and dirty, get down there rolling around in it, you know? And the sweatier and dirtier, the better. I love it."

Oh, the glory of not only being a control freak, but also being a baseball freak, and also being the catcher for the Kee Hawks.

Their baseball program, as you read earlier, is arguably one of the most storied high school sports programs in the state. Coach Gene Schultz came to the Eastern Allamakee Community Schools in 1969. That's the formal name of the school district serving the towns of Lansing, New Albin, Harpers Ferry and Churchtown. But everybody locally and across the state knows the high school by its nickname – "Kee" High. In his 35 years there, Schultz has coached the Kee Hawks to 1,404 victories, 10 state championships and eight second place finishes.

You can imagine the hold that baseball tradition has on the imaginations of little boys growing up there.

"I've played baseball since I can remember," said Schoh, who in the fall of 2004 began his senior year at Kee High. "In fact, there's a picture of me when I was about three feet tall, with my baseball bat and our Lab retriever. Last year when my aunt got married, we decided to have my senior picture taken that day wearing a tuxedo, with my baseball bat and our Lab retriever. It's not the same dog, though."

Blake is the son of Scott and Jana (Henkel) Schoh, who were both Kee High athletes in the early 1980s. With younger son Maison, 14 years old in 2005, whose major sports interest so far is more football than baseball, they live on a 17-acre dairy and beef farm three miles south of Lansing.

"So I've grown up working on the farm, driving tractors, milking cows and all that fun stuff," said Blake. "I'm pretty much the farm boy – love my truck and at school I'm usually wearing work boots and jeans."

In his later high school years, he has also clerked at the Kwik Star convenience store and done small engine repair work at Big River Forge, both in Lansing.

He played football in junior high and sophomore year, and basketball as a freshman, but he gave those up along the way to focus on baseball during the summer and snowmobile racing during the winter. He races on a team with 12 drivers, based in Lino Lakes, Minnesota, and they compete across Minnesota and Wisconsin in 10 to 15 amateur races each year.

But it's baseball that is his first love.

"Kee High baseball is all it's said to be," said Schoh. "Home games are just crazy, and the night games at home are the best. The towns really turn out for us. Everybody will be there in New Albin at the field, and we'll get done about 9 o'clock. Then it's not unusual for us to sit and visit with people until 10 or 10:30 at night. The little kids come up and get your autographs. I did that myself when I was little. You build this relationship between the kids, parents, the older people – everybody loves baseball here."

The Kee Hawks typically play 40 games a summer, with about 20 of those at New Albin.

And they know they are playing for a legendary coach who is known across the nation.

"You hear stories about Coach Schultz – how tough he is – and he is tough, but he knows what he's doing," said Schoh. "He gets your respect, and once you get it, he gives you his respect, too."

Practices are no-nonsense, with no idle time and an emphasis on repetitive practice of good baseball fundamentals.

"Fundamentals are the most important thing to Coach – like bunting, especially squeeze bunting," Schoh said. "Not very many teams squeeze bunt a lot, but we do. And in practice, we've got this '5, 5 & 5' drill we do – five drag bunts, five sacrifice bunts and five squeeze bunts – and we might do that twice or three times during a practice."

Everybody knows how the program works.

Schoh said that "by the time you're an eighth grader, and you're getting a chance to make the varsity, it's like, 'Wow! This is awesome!' You really want to get that uniform and warm-up jacket. I made it as an eighth grader, and I could hardly believe that I was getting to play with some of the great athletes we had. Several of them were 18 years old, and I was 14."

That team went 33-7 and made it to the state tournament. Schoh lettered as an occasional designated hitter, utility player and pinch runner. The team was back at state in his freshman year, lost in the sub-state his sophomore year and got beat in the first round of tournament play in the summer of 2004 by arch-rival Valley of Elgin. Everybody on that Kee Hawk squad was going to return for Schoh's senior season.

Though he is small, especially for a catcher, he has made himself a strong hitter, averaging over .400 through his high school years and setting a record for extra-base hits in his sophomore season, with 16. He and the meat of the line-up during the 2004 season – Dan Mohn, Jordan Duffy, Gabe Schultz, Andy Beck and Clayton Welsh – started calling themselves "The Bomb Squad" because they fancy themselves as good hitters.

Schoh said the personal highlight of his high school career "is being all-conference since my freshman year." He won honorable mention then in the Upper Iowa Conference's selections, and he has been first-team since then.

His goal?

He said he hopes to play baseball in college, "but I'm not going to rely on baseball to get myself through." He said he wants to study mechanical engineering and use it to work in the snowmobile industry.

But actually, there's a more immediate goal.

"I want a state championship," he said.

He is, after all, a Kee Hawk.

Tyrone Scott Jr., basketball player, is from a family that for three generations has helped build the grand sports history at Waterloo East High School.

His grandfather James Henderson was an outstanding track man and football player in the 1960s. His grandmother is Ida Roby Henderson, and most Iowa sports fans know the Robys of Waterloo East as a family of great athletes. His father Tyrone Scott Sr. was an all-state basketball player at East before graduating in 1982, and went on to stardom at North Iowa Area Community College in Mason City and then at the University of Texas-Pan American. His mother Stacy Cole was a good track athlete at East.

Now comes Tyrone Jr., who knows the story about how his father bought him a full-sized basketball soon after he was born. He was a member of the Trojans team who won the state championship in 2003 and finished runner-up in 2004.

"Being on the team that won the championship was the greatest feeling in the world, and it probably didn't mean as much to me as it did to the players who were starting and playing a lot," he said. "But we're always known for winning in men's basketball at East High. It's a tradition. That means we're a target for everybody else, too. Every game we lose, the players and fans from the other school run out on the court in a big celebration, just like they've won a big tournament game or something."

There haven't been a whole lot of those losses in the 25 years that Steve McGraw has been the head coach at East. They've won two state championships and they've qualified for the state tournament 15 times.

McGraw has enjoyed having Tyrone Jr. emerge as a top player, particularly because Tyrone Sr. was on his first team in 1979-80 as a sophomore. Then in his senior year, 1982, Tyrone Sr. was a mainstay on McGraw's first team to go to the state tournament, and they finished third.

How does the coach feel, seeing a second generation of players come along?

"Like I've been coaching for a long time," he said, with a smirk.

Can he compare the two Tyrones?

"Tyrone Sr. never saw a shot he didn't like, and his son is just like him," McGraw said when we talked early one evening, midway through the 2003-04 season, "except that his son it not quite as good a shooter, yet."

But later the same evening Tyrone Jr. scored his varsity career high of 31 points in leading the Trojans to a 78-45 romp over Cedar Falls in the packed and raucous East High gym – and the coach was plenty happy!

Both father and son say they've loved playing for McGraw, although both said it took some getting used to before they started to enjoy it.

"He's a great coach, but he can make you feel bad," said Tyrone Jr. "It took me a while to adjust to that, and to understand that he's pushing you because he wants to help you do your best. He wants the best for us, on the court and in school, too. He checks our grades all the time. He talks to us. He keeps us focused."

Tyrone Sr. says if his son thinks McGraw is tough now, he should have seen him 25 years ago.

"McGraw has gotten soft now – I tell him that all the time," he said.

"But seriously, I played basketball at every level, and he's one of the best coaches I ever played for. The number one thing he cares about is his kids. He's well respected in the community, too. Everybody knows he's going to play the best kids, no matter who they are, and you've got to respect that."

Tyrone Jr. is growing up right around the corner from East High. His older sister Blaine Scott was not an athlete in high school, but younger sister Finesse Scott is a basketball player and track athlete at East. Younger brothers Trice Scott and Dejoni Norris, "look like players," Tyrone Jr. said.

Tyrone Sr. works with specially-challenged children and adults in the "Exceptional Persons, Inc." program in Waterloo and also helps coach junior high girls and boys basketball at an intermediate school in the community. Stacy Cole is the human resources manager of the Boys & Girls Club of Black Hawk County.

Tyrone Jr. got his own start in organized sports in youth basketball leagues when he was in third and fourth grades. He played football in junior high "and liked it better than basketball then," but he gave it up after giving the sport a try in high school. He ran track for a year at East, and showed promise as a sprinter, but he hurt an ankle and decided to give it up rather than risk injury and also so he could focus on basketball year 'round.

He grew to 5 ft., 11 in. and 170 pounds by his junior year and became a starter. He averaged 12 points per game, but he scored in the 20s on a few occasions and had that one 31-point game.

He played AAU ball after the high school season ended, and planned to start participating in camps and clinics with other top high school players, hoping to win the attention of college coaches.

As he's become more serious about having a future in basketball, he has also dramatically increased the attention he gives to his classroom work.

"I was an average student my first two years of high school, but I'm picking it up now that I know I need good grades," he said.

He also has increased his off-season weight lifting – "I still don't do that during the season because I'm afraid it'd throw off my shot" – and his nutrition. "It's a lot of water, fruits, breads, vegetables, salads, a lot of meat and I take vitamins, too," he said. "I notice that when I'm doing all that, I feel stronger and I've got more energy."

His commitment to his game is obviously strong.

"Athletics are very important to him," said Tyrone Sr. "They're probably the most important thing to him about school. But he has seen now that if he's going to have a chance to go Division I for college, then he has to improve his grades. And he's doing that. He's taken his grade point up from a 2.4 to near a 3-point in the past year, and that's going to really help him no matter what happens in basketball."

The father has seen his son's game improve, too.

"He has come a long way," Tyrone Sr., said. "He's always been able to score – in a sophomore game one time he got 49 points – but to be really good, he had to improve his defense, and he has. He's much more intense now on defense. He's learned how to play hard all the time."

Tyrone Jr. said "like any kid my age playing in a program like this, I'd like to play in the NBA if I ever get the chance. But if I can't make that, then I'd like to coach because it'd be a way to stay in the game and learn more."

Meantime, as a high school player, he has helped stir up a lot of wintertime fun for basketball fans, especially in the Waterloo-Cedar Falls area.

"Our crowds are always good, even on the road," Tyrone Jr. said. "People want to see us play. And I think the whole town of Waterloo likes the Trojans." Tyrone graduated from high school in 2005.

Eric Westerberg can look across the street from Denison-Schleswig High School, see the town's water tower standing right there on the hilltop and read this slogan under the name of the community: "It's a Wonderful Life."

That's up there, of course, as a salute to Denison's most famous native daughter Donnabelle Mullenger, who became Donna Reed, the Academy Award winning actress. She starred in the movie "It's a Wonderful Life" with Jimmy Stewart.

But you've also read Bernie Saggau's comments in this book, about how wonderful life was when he was growing up in Denison in the 1930s and '40s. And it's still that way today for kids like Westerberg, now a 16-year-old junior in 2005, at Denison-Schleswig High, renamed years ago after a neighboring town became part of the Denison school district.

He is a four-sport athlete who has been able to develop his athletic skills while participating in freshman and junior-varsity competition, going on up to the varsity in track, which has been his strongest sport. He also plays drums in the marching and concert bands. There are organizations for him to be actively involved in, like Teens Against Tobacco Use and the Fellowship of Christian Athletes. He's a member of a class of 180 students – more than twice as big as when Saggau was in school – and the student body is very diverse, with many Latino and southeast Asian families having moved to the community to work in meat plants.

But one thing has not changed about being a high school athlete in the 60 years between the time Saggau was there and in young Westerberg's time: Harlan is still the great-rival.

"Everybody gets up for the games whenever we're playing them," Westerberg said.

Indeed, he said the highlight of his first two years of high school sports competition "was beating Harlan in freshman football, 20-14" in 2002.

And his worst moment? "Getting beat by Harlan in JV football

10-7," in the fall of 2003. "It came down to the last play of the game. We threw a pass – to me – that would have been about a 30-yard touchdown to win the game, but it was batted away at the last minute."

Eric is the son of Steve Westerberg, the principal at Denison-Schleswig High, and Nancy Westerberg, who teaches in the "Open Arms" pre-school she operates at Our Savior Lutheran Church, which the family attends.

In the spring of 2005, an older son Scott was a sophomore at the University of Northern Iowa, and younger daughter Amy was an eighth grader. For most of Eric's life, the Westerbergs have also been a host family for court-placed foster children.

"We started taking in kids 12 or 13 years ago when a friend of ours at church who worked for the Iowa Department of Human Services asked us if we'd consider becoming 'emergency care' foster parents," said Steve Westerberg. "He said that was an area of their greatest need – somebody who can help when they get the 2 a.m. distress call – and we said we'd give it a try. We've been at it ever since. Early on, we had teenagers coming to live with us, but by now we've had kids of all ages.

"We think it's probably been a good experience for our own kids because it makes them more aware and understanding the underdog. It's also a good learning situation for them. Recently, we had two 1-year-olds, a 2-year-old and a 3-year-old all living with us, and on one weekend, my wife and I had a school obligation for a couple of nights. So the first night, Eric and three of his buddies took care of the little ones, and the next night Amy was in charge. In the long run, experiences like that will probably do them all some good."

Eric, 5 ft., 10 in. tall and 135 pounds in 2005, is a receiver in football, a good defensive guard in basketball, an outfielder in baseball and a 400- and 800-meter runner in track. He saw his first varsity competition in track as a freshman, and he has normally been a member of the distance medley and the 4-by-800 relay teams.

"I really think football could turn out to be my best sport," he said. "I hope I can be rotating in and out as a receiver."

He said being involved in sports "has kept me out of trouble, and it

lso keeps me in shape. But I really think the best thing about being in sports
s that you get to meet a lot of new friends.

"You also learn a lot. I've really liked learning about how the different
offenses work in basketball, and how plays work in football. And you learn
bout sportsmanship, and how if the other team is talking trash, you ignore
t, play your game and don't get caught up in the crowd. All of that helps."

The "pressure to win" sometimes is too intense, he said, "and since I
play all the sports, by the end of the school year, all the time you have to put
nto it starts to get a little tiring. It's two or three hours after school almost
every afternoon, but I enjoy it. I wouldn't be going out for everything if I
didn't like it."

Mike Whisler, who started wrestling when he was in kindergarten,
said during his senior year at Centerville High School that he'd "wrestled for
so long that it just seems like what you do in the winter."

It certainly hadn't made him love the sport any less. What is it about
wrestling that hooked him?

"It's just you out there," he said. "There are no excuses if you lose.
If you win, you don't share the glory. And when you're successful, you feel
great."

It's also a Whisler family thing.

His late grandparents Don and Leora Whisler, who died in 2000 and
2001 respectively, were such fans that "they never missed a wrestling event,"
Mike said.

They ran a trucking company in Centerville, and later operated
a mobile home park, and they loved high school wrestling. In fact, they
endowed a "Don and Leora Memorial Scholarship," which each year is
awarded to a graduating senior associated with the Centerville wrestling
program, and the winner can be a wrestler, student manager or cheerleader.

Among Don and Leora's sons, all were wrestling fans, but only Mike's
father Kevin Whisler was a wrestler in high school, "and that was just for one
year," Mike said. "It's kind of amazing we all came from that."

The "we" he refers to includes his two older brothers, Mark and Matt
Whisler, who graduated in 2000 and 2002. Both were four-year wrestlers

who attended college at Northwest Missouri State University and Kirkwood Community College. Their cousins Mason and Adam Whisler also wrestled all the way through Centerville High before graduating in 2002. And three other cousins were good wrestlers for the Big Reds in the early 1990s – Joe, Danny and Ryan Stephens.

In fact, the family is very proud that in the 36 years of Centerville High School wrestling, there have been 13 wrestlers who have had 100 career wins, and six of them have been Whisler grandsons.

Mike picked up his one hundreth win right after Christmas in his senior season of 2004-05, wrestling at 125 pounds. He was 41-5 as a junior, wrestling at 119, and he qualified for state at that same weight as a sophomore.

Kevin and Marsha Whisler live just outside Centerville with Mike and daughter Jill, a fifth grader in 2005, who earlier served as a "mini-cheerleader" with the varsity wrestling cheerleaders. Kevin is a trucker for Flywheel, Inc., a Centerville motor freight company, and Marsha is a partner with her sister Jane Whitney in a catering company.

Mike considers himself a "seasonal wrestler," since he also made time to participate in football all four years. He was a 5 ft., 10 in. starter at strong safety on defense. And he's in Centerville High's strong band program, playing drums in the jazz, concert and marching bands. He is also an Honor Roll student and for two years has worked part-time at the Fareway grocery store in town.

During wrestling season, he would increase his workouts. Besides the team practices of two to three hours after school every afternoon, he devoted two early mornings each week to hour-long workouts with his teammate and state champion T.J. Sebold and other local wrestlers at the Sebold's family gym. They frequently all gathered there for extra practices on Sundays, too.

They all were pushing hard to maintain a record that, for 30 years, has had at least one Centerville High wrestler qualifying for the state tournament. In that time period, two wrestlers have won two state championships each – Sebold, who is now a junior, and Justin Brown. Two others, James Lange and Jason Halupnick, have won one championship.

314

Mike Whisler, of course, had a goal of winning a state championship himself, but as a senior, he knew just how stiff the competition would be. Is all the time he invested in the sport still worth it?

"Oh, definitely," he said. "Sometimes it can be a little much – when you get into the season you can start feeling like you've got no time for anything else – but it's still fun. And it helps you out, too. It makes you better at balancing your time, getting the school assignments done, holding a job."

He says there is one thing he'd do differently about his high school sports career if he had it to do over it again. He'd add another sport.

"Now that I look back, I wish I'd gone out for another sport – maybe tennis," he said. "The reason I say that is that you've only got four years to do high school sports, and most of them, you'll never do again in your later life. Football and wrestling are my favorite sports, but I won't be doing them later. So if I had it to do over again, I'd play tennis, too."

But he said there are two carry-overs he's sure he'll have from his years wrestling. He'll always be a fan, of course, "and I'm sure I'll keep lifting weights and doing some kind of training the rest of my life, just to try to stay in a little better shape and stay healthy."

He said he is considering going to chiropractic school.

"Both my mom and my aunt have had back problems, and that's gotten me interested in chiropractic medicine," he said.

Now that you've met them, these six rather typical Iowa high school athletes at this 100-year point in the history of the IHSAA, let's talk.

1. What do you think, generally, of the high school sports program in Iowa?

Enes Elezovic, Des Moines Roosevelt soccer player: "I think the program has improved greatly in the last couple of years, especially in soccer, because now people take pride in it."

Max Orsborn, Emmetsburg football player: "I think it is organized very well, especially the way the schools are put into classes where they can be competitive. Many schools also have freshman and junior varsity teams, so you can compete all the way through high school."

Blake Schoh, Kee High of Lansing baseball player: "I think that the Iowa sports program has continuously grown for the better. I pretty much only focus on my one sport, so I don't really know a whole lot about anything but baseball. But having athletics in high school is so important. Lately, having money is such a huge factor, and then you have to get a job to have that money. Really, the kids need to relax while they are in high school, and be kids. Athletics gives them a way to do that, to have fun doing what they like to do, with their friends."

Tyrone Scott Jr., Waterloo East basketball player: "I think that the program has improved through the years. The competition is getting better every year. We are having better players from all types of schools that are showcasing their talent with the best in the country in AAU tournaments. The players in Iowa are starting to become known more now than in previous years, so it's growing pretty fast."

Eric Westerberg, Denison four-sport athlete whose earliest success has been in track: "I think it's great, because it is really fun. But people need to realize that sports are made to have fun, and not to win, win, win. Even though you should try to win, that's not what it's all about."

Mike Whisler, Centerville wrestler: "It's good. I wouldn't change a thing. There's a lot of tradition that I would like to see carried on."

2. What's the best thing about high school sports in Iowa?

Elezovic: "Its tradition and the self-respect it gives us."

Orsborn: "Being able to compete against surrounding towns, and then to compete against teams from across the state in the post-season."

Scott: "The best thing about it, for me, is the state (basketball) tournament. It's a college-like environment. There are a lot of people from each school on opposite sides of the floor, cheering for their team, and it's just great. It prepares you for the college life after high school."

Westerberg: "The best thing about Iowa high school sports is that I get to meet new people and I have fun playing."

Whisler: "The traditions – like how the events are run and how the ceremonies occur. I especially like the ceremonies like the Grand March at the state wrestling tournament."

3. What could be better?

Elezovic: "Newer stadiums and better equipment."

Orsborn: "It would be better for multi-sport athletes if there was more time between seasons. There are many one-sport athletes who get to work at their sport year 'round, and it is harder for someone to be competitive with them when you have just finished one sport and then have to start practicing the next one immediately."

Schoh: "There are a lot of things I'm sure the athletic association hears about that they should fix, but I am going to say them anyway. Tournament brackets need to be thought over a little more. There's no reason to get rid of one of the top teams in the first round, which doesn't just happen in baseball. Second, the way that teams are ranked during the season doesn't give enough credit to a team from a smaller school that is playing larger schools. Also, I would like to mandate that coaches keep better statistics. Talking with players from other schools, I know that some coaches don't even keep stats, and when it comes time to report stats for the conference and state, they guess!"

Scott: "Nothing. I understand things get better with time, and Iowa sports are already growing very fast. I think the program will get better as the players get bigger. Colleges are going to be looking at Iowa much harder because of the talent, and the program will most likely grow more because of that. Plus, the new facility (the Iowa Events Center arena in Des Moines) is really special to the state's players. I know it will be great to play there."

Whisler: "Make it possible for more schools to have sports like wrestling and football. In our county (Appanoose) alone, there are schools that don't have opportunities for students in those two sports."

4. From conversations you have with your parents, older relatives and friends, as well as your coaches and teachers, do you think athletes today are much different than they were 20 years ago? Fifty years ago? Maybe even 100 years ago? How? What do you think those older athletes and teams must have been like?

Westerberg: "I think athletes are different today than back then, only because back then, athletes were the coolest people and were the most popular. Nowadays, it seems like you don't have to be an athlete to be popular. If you're in a band or something else, you can still be popular."

Elezovic: "I think that 20 years ago, the athletes were working much harder, trying to get scholarships and play in college. Now our athletes just don't really care because there are a lot more options for us out there. Those older athletes and teams were much more competitive than we are."

Orsborn: "I think athletes today are much different. We spend much more time practicing the skills, in and out of season. I don't think athletes years ago spent money on camps and traveling teams like we do today."

Schoh: "I think that kids these days are bigger and stronger."

Scott: "It's very different. Kids now have gotten a lot better than 20 years ago. Also, there are more things to be involved in than back when there wasn't any AAU program in Iowa. Kids back then couldn't showcase their skills to coaches or anyone else outside of Iowa. We have way more opportunities, and it's our job to take advantage of them. And, it must have been crazy with little shorts in basketball, and all the other old-school looks!"

Whisler: "I believe there is a lot more intense training, with the technology and the longer sports seasons There's a big difference in the way we train and compete year 'round in comparison to the way my dad and his generation competed."

5. Are athletes held in high regard in your school and communities? Do you see much difference between young people who are athletes – and you can include kids who are real involved in other activities like music, drama, etc. – and those who are not involved in athletics and other school activities?

Schoh: "Being from a small school, and such a baseball town, you can tell the difference between athletes and others. The town is totally behind the athletes. Because we are athletes, we try to hold ourselves to a higher standard than others, to stay out of trouble, to help others and be all-around good people. In return we get backing from the community at game time."

Whisler: "Yes, because you get your name out in the community, and the people in the town get to know about you and who you are. I believe that kids who are not involved in sports or other activities have a harder time etting connected to school."

Elezovic: "Athletes are held in high regard because everybody loves ports, and it doesn't matter which one. Not as many high school students ill go see a music event that they're not performing in."

Orsborn: "Yes, students who are involved in things – sports or other ctivities – are the leaders in their grades and are successful in many areas."

Scott: "Yes, athletes are looked up to by everyone, especially the ttle kids around the community. You have to be on your best behavior at all imes, because everyone is watching you."

Westerberg: "I guess athletes are held in a little higher regard than ther people. That's probably because athletes are representing the school, nd people who don't play sports want to be represented well."

6. Do high school athletes read newspapers more than non-thletes? Are they more aware, or less aware, of non-sports things that re going on in their schools, communities, state, nation and world?

Orsborn: "I think most athletes read newspapers because they are nterested in what is going on in sports around them and at the upper levels f their sport. I think they become aware of other things in the world just by icking up the newspaper."

Schoh: "I would say that we don't get involved in non-sports stuff nore than anyone else. Being an athlete, I guess, doesn't change whether I ead the paper or not."

Elezovic: "My personal opinion on whether athletes read more, I hink that it might be true. But I don't think that we are more aware of what s going on out there beyond sports."

Scott: "I can't say for other athletes, but I read a lot of newspapers nd magazines, and I get on the Internet almost every day to see what's going n in the high schools around the country. I look at rankings and players' ommitments to colleges. So, in my eyes, I think athletes are more in tune vith the news than non-athletes are."

Westerberg: "I don't really think it makes a difference if high choolers are in athletics or not, on whether they pay attention to the news. t just depends on whether you really care a lot about what is going on in the world. I think athletes probably are more aware of sporting events than non-sporting events in the world."

Whisler: "I believe so personally. I'm always trying to see how my opponents in the past and future are doing, and that always lead me to read other things in the paper."

7. Is it difficult to be a high school athlete in today's fast-paced culture? As I ask this, I think of the pressure to win, the temptations about performance-enhancing substances, so much of the public's focus being on pro and big-time college sports, the financial need of making some money for college, cars and to help your families, etc.

Elezovic: "Yes, it is difficult because you are expected to win no matter what."

Orsborn: "Yes, because a lot of athletes feel they need an extra edge on their opponents to be noticed, and many athletes want to make it to the next level any way possible."

Schoh: "It is very tough, especially with getting school work done, having time for the practice schedules and still trying to hold a job so you have the spending money you want."

Scott: "I think it's a lot of pressure, especially for the top guys around the country. I look on the Internet all the time and see guys going for the NBA draft, and there is more pressure on them. But for kids in Iowa, it's not that harsh. It is important to win, though. I can say that if you don't win, the community may turn on a team and not come to the games. So I think there is a 'must-win' attitude with every athlete, especially me."

Westerberg: "I think it's really difficult to be an athlete because there is a lot of pressure to be good, especially if you don't do as well as people expect. Also, because there are a lot of substances that could enhance your performance, it's really hard to stay away from those temptations."

Whisler: "Sometimes being in sports can be a little much, but without sports, I'd be lost."

8. What do you think about "club sports," played away from school, compared to school sports? Which do you prefer competing in,

f you've had experiences in both? Why?

  Elezovic: "I prefer competing in school sports rather than club because there is just more tradition and willingness to win."

  Orsborn: "School sports, because you have your school and community to support you."

  Westerberg: "I would rather play school sports because of the memories and going to state and things like that. But I think that club sports are also good because they let you just play for fun, with not as much pressure put on you to win."

  Whisler: "I prefer school sports because it gives people a chance to be part of something during their high school years."

  9. What ideas to you have about the future of high school sports in Iowa? What would make it better for athletes who are coming along behind you?

  Elezovic: "High school sports are going to be expanding, no matter what, so what they (school and IHSAA officials) should do is to prepare and not let Iowa get behind what other states have."

  Orsborn: "I think that as schools in rural areas are getting smaller, there will be fewer and fewer towns to compete against, and teams will have to travel much farther to play. Something will have to be done about that."

  Schoh: "I have my brother and younger cousins who are coming up after me, and I hope that they realize that they need to play sports in high school. You're only in high school once, and everything you don't try, you regret the rest of your life. So my biggest hope is that they have the opportunity to participate in sports."

  Scott: "Just make it bigger throughout Iowa. They did that a little the last couple of years, with Mediacom televising some high school games, and interviewing the top athletes on teams after a good win. Most of the big games should be televised, just to get it out there so people who can't make the game can still watch. That would get more people in tune with sports."

  Whisler: "To ensure that smaller schools, if they have to join with the bigger schools, can still fund their own sporting events and teams."

10. Anything else you want to say about being a high school athlete now, in 2004, that you think the public and I should know?

Elezovic, after his graduation in the spring of 2004: "Now that I am an ex-high school athlete, I want to say that the times I was competing in sports during my four years were my best times in school. And being involved made high school go by fast."

Orsborn: "I am very glad to be playing for a school that has such a great tradition. It makes me feel proud to be from Emmetsburg. I can be in a different part of the state wearing an Emmetsburg shirt, and have a stranger say something about our football tradition. I think Iowa high school athletics are very successful now and will stay that way in the future."

Whisler: "In the past 35 years of Centerville wrestling, there have been 19 years that a Whisler family member has been a part of the wrestling program – an uncle in the first year of '69, my dad, five cousins, two brothers of mine, a girl cousin who was a student manager, and my little sister who was a mini-cheerleader for about three years. It's been a good thing for our family. And now I'm the last Whisler – until the next generation starts."

Schoh: "When I think about the things that make high school sports great, one of the biggest is when the community backs the athletes. I know in some towns people just don't get involved as much as they should with the school and kids. They have to remember that these are the adults of the future. Plus, for a kid playing ball, there is nothing better than having a big crowd that isn't afraid to have their voices be heard. It's really like being at a big league game. The more fun that the fans have, the more fun the games are for the kids, win or lose."

Westerberg: "I would say that high school sports are the biggest part of my life besides school. Lots of people should take the opportunity to play high school sports because if you don't, then you're missing out."

Scott: "The Iowa high school sports program is just great now. It gives us so many opportunities. You just have to grab them and make the best of them and work hard. And you have to stay focused on your goals for what you want to accomplish in your sport. That's what I say to young kids coming up in Iowa. Just stay focused. No distractions. Keep your mind toward your goal, and you will go anywhere you want."

Bernie Saggau & the Iowa Boys

Part II

Their sports experience
serves them well

They are 15 alumni of the programs of the Iowa High School Athletic Association, but none of them is generally recognized today for being a former athlete.

That's because each has gone on to significant achievement beyond sports in later life.

One is a Nobel Peace Prize winner, credited with saving millions of lives across the world. Another wrote the biggest-selling novel in history. Several operate at the highest levels of government and international business. One is among the world's greatest opera singers; another's piano recordings have sold more copies than any popular pianist ever. The list also includes a nationally acclaimed artist, two highly respected athletic administrators, a coach who overcame long odds and now heads a top college track program, and an American soldier who helped capture Saddam Hussein.

And interestingly, all 15 believe that their Iowa high school sports experience has been important to their success.

I asked them about it. And what follows here are some of their reflections, reported in the order of their high school graduation years.

Norman Borlaug, a 1932 Cresco graduate, talked about his high school wrestling experiences in Chapter 1, and how the "confidence" he gained as a wrestler has helped him over and over as he's worked, often in lonely situations, to initiate programs that have helped ease world hunger.

His work in increasing wheat production in very poor areas of the world led to him being recognized as "Father of the Green Revolution" and winner of the Nobel Peace Prize in 1970. And later he founded the World Food Prize, now based in Des Moines.

He was very successful in high school wrestling, placing fourth in the state at 145 pounds in 1932 under coach Dave Bartelma, an Iowa State graduate "who came to Cresco when I began my junior year, and who I learned all my wrestling from."

His only other interscholastic sport was football, which he played in his junior and senior years at Cresco High School.

"There was quite a gang growing up in the countryside around the little village of Saude, about 15 miles south of Cresco, but until some of the older ones became old enough to drive, we didn't have a way to get back and forth to practices," Borlaug recalled.

He was a guard on the football team in his senior year, and "it was one of the poorest teams in years in Cresco. We had several of our best players go down with injuries, and we took a beating that whole year. There were only four of us who were seniors on that team, and the next year, they won all their games, so maybe we helped set the stage."

Borlaug noted that his teammate Robert Smylie, a tackle, went on to earn a law degree after college, moved to Idaho, went into politics and served three consecutive terms as governor of that state from 1954 through 1967. Smylie died in the summer of 2004.

Baseball may have been his best sport, Borlaug said, "but Cresco had no team when I was in school. So I played second base on the team from Saude village, which played teams from other farm neighborhoods.

He and a Cresco classmate Irv Upton went on to the University of Minnesota, and both became leading wrestlers. After their sophomore year, the Golden Gophers' coach left. "The two of us from Cresco were instrumental in getting Dave Bartelma, our old high school coach, hired as the new Minnesota wrestling coach," Borlaug said. "When he came up there, the first thing he did was start high school wrestling programs in Minnesota, and the sport really took off up there after that."

Borlaug moved to Mexico in 1944 to establish an agricultural research and experimental station about 25 miles outside Mexico City, and later it became the headquarters for the International Maize and Wheat Improvement Center. He has spent the 60 years since then living at least half the year there. At 90 years old, he was still active there in 2004, as well as continuing to teach fall semesters at Texas A&M University as a visiting professor of international agriculture.

He has always stayed in touch with American sports, too.

In 1955, he and a scientific associate John Niederhauser "organized and introduced the first Little League baseball in Mexico, so that our sons could participate, and I coached Little League teams therefore six years," Borlaug said. The two later organized older age division teams there, too. He also has been a frequent visitor to wrestling tournaments at both the high school and major college levels in the U.S.

The farm where Borlaug and his two sisters grew up has now been donated to the Norman Borlaug Heritage Foundation, which is restoring it to its 1930s appearance and will operate it as a living memorial and interpretive center.

Roger Williams, a 1942 graduate of Des Moines North, was using his real name Louis Weertz when he was growing up in Des Moines. He was the son of prominent Lutheran pastor Rev. Frederick J. Weertz and his wife Dorothea, who was a music teacher.

"At age 3, the lad could play piano by ear," the Des Moines Register reported. "He could play 12 more instruments by the time he was 12."

He started performing professionally in high school, when he'd play piano for dinner at Babe's Restaurant and lunch at Younkers' Tea Room, both in downtown Des Moines. He's still playing in 2005, at 80. On his concert tours, he packs halls across the nation, and he also continues to record, adding to his 115 albums over the past 50 years. He's used the "Roger Williams" name professionally since a record producer assigned it to him for his first album in the early 1950s. In 1955, he recorded the song "Autumn Leaves," and it's been gold record after gold record, ever since.

"I'm a great pianist," Williams said, "and outside of that, I'm really pretty lousy at almost everything else. I was a lousy athlete in high school, and I was a lousy golfer later on."

But he did compete in high school, going out for baseball as a freshman at North High School, although he didn't play much. He also played as a reserve on the basketball team in his senior year. "I won a letter that year in basketball," Williams said, "and I've still got it on my wall at home, and I've still got my North High letter sweater, too."

In Williams' middle high school years, his father had a siege of bad health, and the family moved temporarily to the warm weather of southern California. Roger spent his junior year at Los Angeles High School, the oldest one in the city, and was on the basketball squad. He was back in Des Moines for his senior year at North.

"I was a reserve guard a little guy, 5 feet, 9 and a half inches and maybe 152 or 153 pounds," he said. "I sat on the bench, and played a little bit with a bunch of other bums late in the games."

He said he loved the camaraderie on the basketball teams he played on, and being involved helped him in another way.

"The combination of being in music, like I was, and being a preacher's kid, or 'P.K.' as we were known, spelled s-i-s-s-y back then, so I was always looking for ways to be a big man and I was always interested in sports," he said.

His father had been a boxer, and taught him some about that sport.

"Boxing became my big thing later," he said. "When I was in the Navy during World War II, I was a boxing champion," not thinking then that he was risking injury to the hands that would make him world famous as a pianist.

He said the physical demands of a lifetime on the road have been a constant reminder to him to stay in reasonable shape.

"I jog five days a week – about three miles – running in place in my rooms," he said. "It's the most boring thing in the world. I hate everything about it except the last step."

He also makes sure he gets his vegetables, just like his mother always insisted.

"When I was a kid, my mother made me sit at the table until I finished my vegetables, and I hated them," he said. "So now, every week, I go to the grocery store, buy my least favorite vegetables, grind them up in a juicer, pour them into a glass, hold my nose and drink the damned stuff. And then I don't worry about eating vegetables the rest of the week."

Williams' wife actress Louise DiCarlo died in 2003. He has three daughters from an earlier marriage.

One way he stays connected with the high school scene today is as an advocate for school activities programs, especially music, which have been drastically reduced under budget pressure in many parts of the country.

Former Iowa Governor **Robert Ray**, a 1946 graduate of Des Moines Roosevelt, was a two-year starter and then captain of the Rough Riders' basketball team in his senior year. He was also a tennis player, and probably would have played baseball and football, except for two broken noses.

"I broke my nose as a sophomore playing baseball and then I broke it a second time before the first break really got set," said Ray, who turned 75 in 2005. "I have a tendency to put my nose in the wrong place, I guess."

Doctors told him immediately to give up football rather than risk further nose damage, and so he became a "limitedly acrobatic" cheerleader during the fall seasons. It also let him focus on basketball.

"I was one of two sophomores who also played with the varsity team, and then I started in my junior and senior years," said Ray. "I was a guard, and not much of a scorer, but then none of us scored a lot of points in those days. My recollection is that we were better than average, but we never made it to the state tournament, and that was a disappointment."

In tennis, he "almost won a city championship one time," he said. "A person I was supposed to play was late and had to forfeit. I was packing up to leave when he got there, and I said, 'Well, heck, since you're here we might as well go ahead and play.' He ended up beating me. So much for being a good guy!"

Ray entered military service straight out of high school at 17 years old, and he played military football in Japan. He returned to enroll at Drake University, eventually earned his law degree and entered private practice. He served 14 years as governor of Iowa from 1969 to 1983. Later, he headed the Life Investors insurance company in Cedar Rapids, Blue Cross & Blue Shield in Des Moines and served interim terms as mayor of Des Moines and president of Drake University.

He and his wife Billie have three daughters who were all swimmers when they attended Des Moines Roosevelt.

"The thing I've always appreciated about high school athletics is the

329

way it develops a healthy competitive spirit," said Ray, a lifelong tennis player. "You learn to concentrate, to focus and to work with other people. You learn to create an environment in which people can succeed together, and it's important to learn how to do that."

Wayne Duke, a 1946 graduate of Burlington High School, served as the No. 2 person at the National Collegiate Athletic Association for 11 of its formative years, then as commissioner of the Big Eight Conference for eight years and commissioner of the Big Ten Conference for 18 years. His direction helped make the NCAA basketball tournament the great television success that it is. And there have been many other important assignments he's handled in his long career of athletic administration.

But listen to this bit of personal perspective about all that.

"I wrote a little thing one time a few years ago, and I wanted to have it put on a plaque and donate it to Burlington High School, but then I felt it'd be presumptuous on my part to do it," the 76-year-old Duke told me in 2004 from his Barrington, Illinois, home. "The plaque would read something like, 'I've been fortunate to have been involved in collegiate athletic matters of great importance, such as chairman of the NCAA Final Four, member of the Rose Bowl Management Committee, the College World Series. But none supercede the importance of my participation in interscholastic athletics at Burlington High School.' I really plan to do that eventually."

Duke, son of the Burlington fire chief, grew up loving sports in the southeast Iowa city. Chances are he would have become an excellent high school athlete, too, except that "I got all wound up in a pick-up neighborhood football game and dislocated my knee," he said.

But he still went out for football and baseball. Legendary football coach Harold Tackleson "found a big old brace he put on my knee, and I got to play a little in several games," Duke said. In baseball, his considerable size and lack of mobility made him a natural as a catcher, and he turned into a good receiver and hitter. In fact, he was the starter and catcher on Burlington High's 1946 baseball team that won Iowa's first summer championship.

And he helped the team another way – covering the games for the Burlington Hawk-Eye Gazette.

Here is how the story he wrote about the championship game began in the August 7, 1946, Hawk-Eye Gazette:

WATERLOO – Burlington's Purple and Gray banner waves high and mighty over the high school baseball realm of the state of Iowa for the first time in BHS athletic history. Coach Lloyd Haberichter's fighting Greyhounds copped the state-wide diadem here Tuesday night, dropping a win-determined gang from Stanhope by a 7-2 count...

Later in that story, it was noted that winning pitcher Gene Taylor, "who leaves to join the Marines Thursday, and Wayne Duke, this year's captain, will be the only boys lost via graduation."

Duke chokes up when he talks about that team, and that story.

"I'm a corny guy, and things like that get to me now," he said. "We were a bunch of ragamuffin baseball players who got the idea that if we'd work hard enough, we could win the state championship – and we did."

When Duke retired from the Big Ten job, he was named Indiana Sportsman of the Year, an honor that also has a $10,000 cash award to the charity of your choice. Duke directed the money to Burlington for renovation of the high school baseball field, and it was renamed in his honor in 1989.

There is little wonder about his great loyalty to Burlington. His wife Martha Buesch Duke grew up in the same South Hill neighborhood he did, and his high school experience was almost ideal. He served as president of the senior class and editor of the "Purple & Gray" student newspaper, in addition to writing for the Hawk-Eye Gazette and working at radio station KBUR. His radio work, which extended from high school into two years at Burlington Junior College, had him serving as host of two quiz shows for young listeners, "The Kiddy Quiz" and "Jackpot Jamboree."

He graduated in journalism from the University of Iowa, and while there he wrote for the Hawk-Eye and the Iowa City Press-Citizen. He also worked in the university's sports information office. After graduation, he spent a year doing sports information at Iowa State Teachers College, and then a year at the University of Colorado before joining the NCAA in 1952.

331

U.S. Senator **Chuck Grassley**, a 1951 graduate of New Hartford High School just northwest of Cedar Falls, went out for basketball for four years in high school, "did all the practices, but only suited up for a few games. I was never much of a player because I was so awkward," he said.

He had more success as a first baseman in baseball, although it did not come until his senior year.

"I lettered just the one year, because Jack Hovelson was a year ahead of me," Grassley said. "He was a first baseman, and his dad was principal so he got to play all the time, and I just got to play that senior year."

The senator, who was 71 years old in 2005, said that matter-of-factly, and then he laughed and began introducing an argument that has been going on for decades with his friend Hovelson, who retired in Cedar Falls after a career as a Des Moines Register news reporter.

And what does Hovelson have to say about it?

"Chuck Grassley, after all these years, continues to fantasize that he would have played first base at New Hartford High School for three years if my dad hadn't been the school's principal," said Hovelson. "All I can say is that Chuck is correct when he says he was awkward. If Coach (Bob) Fromanek had put him on first base before me, I think I would have stripped off my baseball uniform in broad daylight at home plate and never put it on again.

"But Chuck has to be credited with persistence," Hovelson continued. "He worked hard at baseball, much like he does in the Senate. Another parallel is that he waited three years to play first base, and he waited a long time to get the chairmanship of an important committee in the Senate. Patient fellow, that Grassley."

There were five Grassleys growing up on a farm outside of New Hartford, and Chuck decided to become a first baseman after his brother Bud played that position. "I suppose I was trying to follow him," Chuck said. "He was the first star in my eyes."

So how was Chuck, as a player? He says he was about 6 ft., 2 in. and 140 pounds as a senior.

"I wasn't an outstanding performer, that's for sure," Grassley said. "I was not a good hitter – I don't want to tell you how bad I was as a hitter

- but I was a good fielder."

The New Hartford Hawks were playing in the old Butler County Conference against such rivals as Shell Rock, Clarksville, Allison, Parkersburg, Aplington, Dumont, Bristow and Greene, and there would be non-conference games against Dike, Hudson and Janesville.

"I think the best thing I got out of high school sports was that it taught me patience and stick-to-itiveness," Grassley said. "It taught me to have the long view to get things done, and that's been important particularly in the Senate, where it can take a little more time on things. If you don't get it done today like you want to, well, then try again tomorrow.

"The other thing about it, the competitiveness of high school athletics is akin to the competitiveness of politics, even though what we're dealing with in politics is usually a lot more important than a game."

Grassley gives the former coach, Bob Formanek, who retired in New Hartford, credit because "he encouraged good performances. He had a way of making you want to do it, just for him and your teammates."

Grassley also played trombone in the school band, but he never sang. "Oh no, I can't sing at all," he said. "I don't even sing in church today because I'm so bad. Everybody turns around and looks at me."

He has been a loyal sports fan all his life, closely following the teams at his alma mater, the University of Northern Iowa and at New Hartford and then Dike-New Hartford high schools where his kids and grandkids have grown up. He, his wife Barbara and several other family members have been front-row spectators for 25 years on the championship nights at the girls' state basketball tournament.

Chuck still farms actively with his son Robin Grassley, but he has been a public official since 1958 when he was first elected as a Republican to the Iowa Legislature. He was elected to the U.S. House in 1974, then the U.S. Senate in 1980 and he's been in the Senate ever since, becoming one of the most powerful and respected figures in the nation's government.

U.S. Representative **Leonard Boswell**, a 1952 graduate of Lamoni High School on the south central Iowa border, is a decorated combat pilot, a farmer who survived the farm crisis of the early-to-mid 1980s, a 12-year member of the Iowa Senate and a U.S. Congressman since 1996. He has seen and done a lot.

But one of his favorite stories – and one he can tell so thoroughly it's like hearing a radio play-by-play of it – is how the Lamoni Demons in his senior year won over Osceola in a battle of unbeaten football teams.

"That old game still comes up," Boswell who turned 70 in 2005 said. "A year or two ago at the Iowa State Fair, I ran into Jim Zabel, the WHO broadcaster. The first thing he said to me was, 'Boswell, have you ever got it straightened out yet whether you watered that field in Lamoni to slow Osceola down?' "

Boswell was a 6 ft., 190-pound lineman that fall, playing with only grudging consent from his father, who'd kept him out of sports until his junior year. "My dad was one of those farmers who had only an eighth grade education from a country school, and he thought it was silliness to be playing high school sports," he said. "He thought if you had that much time, you ought to be doing more chores."

Both Lamoni and Osceola put together fantastic seasons in the fall of 1951, so pride and bragging rights were on the line in the final game, which was played on the field that Lamoni High shared with Graceland College.

"We'd already had an early frost, and then it went out of the ground," Boswell said. "That left the field pretty soft, and it was getting worse as the game went on. It was really close all the way. The Osceola team was not having any luck, but they all figured that sooner or later their speedster Gary Lutz, their school's first-ever All-Stater, was going to break loose and nobody would be able to catch him.

"Well, he did, and he was off and running. But we had our own speedster, Don White, who had moved in from California. He was playing defensive halfback on the other side of the field, but he came all the way across, caught Lutz from behind and tackled him. They did not score, and we won."

Boswell broke his ankle in the last quarter of that game, but the pain was salved by victory.

"A week or two after the game was over, our coach Bill Robinson was at a banquet, where somebody from Osceola got up and said, 'It's pretty bad hat Lamoni was so intent on winning that they had to hose down the field to stop Lutz,'" Boswell said. "Our coach stood up and said, 'You shouldn't be saying that because, first, we didn't do it, and, second, why would we do that when we had the faster man?' And that argument goes on today!"

Boswell also ran track. "I was pretty good for about five steps," he said. So he switched to distances, ran the half-mile and a leg on the two-mile relay. "We made it to the Drake Relays where we ran without distinction," he said, "but at least we participated."

Lamoni had no wrestling or baseball in that era, and Boswell's basketball was limited to some local tournaments with a team from the Future Farmers of America chapter. He was also in the school plays and "a little bit of music, but as a farm kid, I was always limited by having to get home and help with those chores."

Boswell went on to Graceland College, meeting his wife Dody there, graduating in business administration and playing football. He was drafted into the U.S. Army as a private in 1956, served 20 years and retired in 1976 as a lieutenant colonel. He became a top army pilot of both fixed-wing aircraft and helicopters, and did two tours during the Vietnam War piloting an assault helicopter. He became active in Democratic Party politics during the tough farm crisis years, when he was not only struggling on his own farm but guided the local farmers' cooperative and grain elevator as chairman of its board of directors.

The long-ago high school sports experience "served me well, especially in the army," the congressman said. "Learning about teamwork, and about how with practice you can get better, those are valuable lessons. And I got a lot from the arts, too. All those activities just add so much to life. You can overemphasize them, sure, but generally they're good for anybody."

Simon Estes, a 1956 graduate of Centerville High School who is known worldwide as an opera singer, has often shocked local coordinators of his concerts by asking if they can arrange for him to get into a high school gym and play a little basketball. Even in his 60s he has made this request!

That love of competition, fitness and relaxation goes back to Estes' high school years, when he was a very average four-sport athlete for the

Centerville Big Reds.

"Let's see," Estes recalled, "I high jumped in track, and I finally made 6 feet.

"In basketball, I was usually like the No. 6 player, although I got a few starts. I never scored much, but I do remember one night when I started and made my first three shots. Man, I thought I was ready for the Lakers! I was much better on defense, because I'd been taught by our football and track coach Bill Jerome to anticipate where the ball was going to be, and I could do that pretty well."

He said he still is replaying the final minute of one Centerville High basketball game "when we were behind by a point. Coach Jack Edling turned to me on the bench and said, 'Estes, get in there and get that ball!' I went after it, and I did knock it away. My teammate Bob Warren grabbed it and threw it to John Bruckshaw, who was running down the floor. John jumped up, shot it – and missed! We lost, and I was heartbroken. I not only still remember it, I can still feel it!"

In football, he played offensive and defensive end, "but I never weighed more than 140 pounds back then, and besides being so little, I really wasn't very good. In practice, I remember we had a lineman Frank Sconzo – a big mean guy who played pulling guard – and I remember he'd come down that line and wipe me out!"

In baseball, he pitched "but it was nothing to write home about, either," he said.

Of course, Estes was already excelling in vocal music. After he sang in public for the first time in church as a young boy, he entered the Bill Riley State Fair Talent Searches and in high school he became an All-State singer – initially in the soprano and alto ranges before his voice began changing to the booming bass baritone it is today.

Estes said his sports involvement in high school "really taught me to prepare," and working out all the time "definitely helped my lung capacity."

But maybe the best thing sports did for him was give him real friendship with his teammates. They were all white. He's African American, the grandson of a slave, the son of a coal miner who became a porter at the old Continental Hotel. Those friendships carried him through a lot of racial strain in the community and the area as he was growing up. In fact, many of those friendships among the old Centerville pals endure today.

Estes' professional development is well known. He went to the University of Iowa, planning to be a physician, singing in the Old Gold Singers and other groups. Music professors encouraged him to major in music performance, and he eventually followed his favorite professor Charles Kellis to the Juilliard School of Music in New York City, where he completed his opera training and later taught himself.

At the start of the new century he had been performing for five decades in the major opera houses and concert halls around the world. He has also always used his talent to provide and often pay for educational opportunities for young people growing up in poverty, in the U.S. and around the world. In 1996, he founded and continues to fund the Simon Estes Music High School outside Cape Town, South Africa, for musically talented young people from the black townships surrounding the city. His humanitarian and philanthropic work has resulted in him being referred to as "Iowa's Ambassador to the World."

In recent years, Estes has joined the music faculties at both Iowa State University and Wartburg College in Waverly, working directly with students and performing with their choirs. "I really love working with the college students," he said. "I enjoy being able to show them some of the things I've learned along the way."

Estes has three teenage daughters from an earlier marriage, and he remains very involved with them in Switzerland, where they live. He and his wife Ovida Stong Estes now have homes both in Zurich and in Waverly.

Among his many honors are receiving the Iowa Award – his home state's highest acclamation – and having the Simon Estes Riverfront Amphitheater in Des Moines named after him.

Robert James Waller, a 1957 graduate of Rockford High School in north central Iowa, is of course most famous for authoring the novel "Bridges of Madison County." That Iowa-based novel, published by Warner Books in 1992, was No. 1 on the New York Times Bestseller list for 38 weeks, remained on that Times' list for 150 weeks and has sold more than 12 million copies in 36 languages.

But many Iowans remember that, before Waller became the literary sensation of the world, he was a professor and dean of the business school at the University of Northern Iowa. And he was an occasional contributor of very popular non-fiction essays that were published on the editorial pages of the Des Moines Register.

One of those essays was "Jump Shots," published in the Register in 1986. It is the finest thing I have ever read about the experience of becoming a good high school and college athlete. Waller indeed was one, first at Rockford High School and then later at the University of Iowa, where he spent two years, before transferring and finishing at old Iowa State Teachers College, which is now UNI.

That essay has been such a favorite of mine that, with Waller's help, I arranged permission from Warner Books, Inc., for the Iowa High School Athletic Association to republish the essay in this book. You will find it reprinted on page 342 within this chapter.

It will come as a surprise to many what a fine athlete Waller became in high school.

In fact, it surprised his parents and him, also.

"I was an only child in a family that really had no athletic history at all," said Waller, who, at age 65 was living in Texas in 2005. His father Bob Waller operated a produce business in Rockford, a town of about 900 then, and his mother Ruth Waller was a housewife. They lived in "just a little old house," Robert said, with a basketball backboard and hoop on the garage.

"Junior high and high school were very traumatic and stressful times," Waller said. "Just why I decided to make it my goal to make that varsity basketball team, I still don't know. As a little boy athlete, I was a joke. I always tell how high school girls would walk past me and rub my butch haircut.

"I was so small, and Rockford was full of German and Scandinavian people, so most of the boys were really big by the time they were 14. I remember a night when I was probably about 13, and I was crying and crying because of how small I was. My dad looked at my feet, then about size 10, and he said, 'You'll grow into your feet.' "

About that time, he said, "my parents decided I wasn't eating enough breakfast. So my mother started fixing me pancakes, sausage and eggs every morning. I don't know that it was all because of the big breakfasts, but the fact is I grew eight inches in one year!"

You can read in "Jump Shots" about the glory that "Bobby" Waller and the Rockford Rohawks reached during his four years as a varsity basketball player. As a senior, he was fourth team All-State, one of only five players from small schools who made the five honor teams picked by the Iowa Daily Press Association.

He also was a standout in track, running the 440 and 880, anchoring the sprint relay teams and he placed second in the long jump at the 1957 state track meet.

He played shortstop and third base in baseball, which he "really liked," and played football in his sophomore year before giving it up to concentrate on basketball.

Waller said he and his teammates in high school "really weren't very strong athletically, but we were a bunch of modestly-talented guys who loved to play."

He is genuinely grateful for the opportunities they had.

Proof of that is that he has stayed in touch with his old coach Paul Filter, of whom he writes so fondly in "Jump Shots." Filter, who lived in Taft, California, in 2005, "is one of the people who made a profound difference in my life," Waller told me.

"He'll probably tell you things about me shooting baskets in a blizzard until I about froze my hands, and about how I went home after the prom and shot baskets. I'm an obsessive person. Anyone who knows me will tell you that. It's that way for me now with fly-fishing. I'm reading everything I can get my hands on about fly-fishing."

The overall high school sports experience "was probably positive in certain ways," Waller continued.

"First of all, school just bored the devil out of me, so being involved in athletics might have kept me from getting into trouble. It gave me a focus, something to live for.

"Second, to be honest, it was a confirmation of masculinity, which probably was important at that age.

"Third, and this is most important – something I've reflected a lot on over the years – high school sports taught me the value of discipline."

Waller went on to say "there's a phrase I've invented, 'the value of the small increment,' and some day I'm going to write an essay on it. I probably began to absorb and understand that phrase in high school basketball. What it amounts to is this: If you just do something enough, you'll get better at it.

"In basketball, you start shooting, and at first you can't make very many baskets. You practice a while, and then you can make a few. Then you start believing that after six or eight months, you might get better. And by God, I did! After two years, it got a lot better, and it went on from there.

"I've learned that same lesson in investing money. There's always a tradeoff between consumption and investment. Speaking as an economist for a moment, everybody wants to consume now, instead of investing for the future. But if you're going to be successful, you have to delay consumption for investment.

"You do it a little at a time, and you build a life, piece by piece. That's my 'value of the small increment.'"

Following his undergraduate years, Waller stayed in Cedar Falls and earned his master's degree from State College of Iowa, as Iowa State Teachers College had been re-named. He then went to Indiana University's School of Business, where he received his doctorate in 1968. He returned to Cedar Falls to join the faculty of the business school at the University of Northern Iowa, as the school had been re-named, again.

He concludes "Jump Shots" talking about how he moved on from his obsession with sports, especially late in his undergraduate years. He has maintained that separation since then.

"I only went to one basketball game the whole time I was on the faculty at UNI," he said. "I just grew out of that at 19 or 20 years old, and it never really interested me again."

However, he let his life-long interest in music grow, playing guitar and singing, performing frequently in bars and restaurants around the area, sometimes with UNI faculty friends and other local musicians.

Waller's writing bloomed during those years, especially in the middle 1980s when his essays began appearing frequently in the Des Moines

Register. They were later re-published in book form by Iowa State University Press.

The story line for "Bridges" began forming in his mind when he was on sabbatical from teaching at UNI. The Iowa Legislature recognized his rare combination of expertise in economics, keen eye for opportunities and writing ability, and decided to commission him to travel the state for a year, think about its future and come back with a report on his observations and conclusions. It was while he was working on that project – which Waller turned into a 1991 book "Iowa: Perspectives On Today And Tomorrow" – that he stayed overnight in Winterset. He visited the historic covered bridges of Madison County there, and felt a love story stirring in his soul.

After the unanticipated, huge success of "Bridges," Waller went on leave from UNI, and then moved to a ranch near Alpine in extreme southwestern Texas. He went through a divorce, moved to a smaller place near Fredericksburg in south central Texas, and now lives there with his wife Linda Bow Waller. He has one daughter from the earlier marriage.

U.S. Representative **Jim Leach**, a graduate of Davenport High School in 1960, was a state champion wrestler at 138 pounds in his senior year and an injury-plagued fullback and linebacker on a good Blue Devils football team. He went on to success as an athletic at Princeton University, where he was a varsity wrestler and rugby player and captain of the team in "sprint football," in which players had to be lighter than 160 pounds.

That considerable athletic success is all the more admirable when you learn about Leach's first real brush with organized sports.

"I started wrestling in junior high, and in a classic way," said the 62-year-old congressman. "I was convinced I was the best basketball player in the school, but I was the first guy to get cut.

"So I went out for wrestling. I was a 75-pounder as a seventh grader. We had four junior high schools in the city, but only one other had a 75-pounder. I defeated him, went home and told my parents I was city champ!"

As he went on to Davenport High School, his class of 850 members was designated to become the last to graduate in a system that had had only one public high school in the city. Old DHS would become Davenport

(Continued on page 347) 341

Jump Shots

Robert James Waller

In a Dakota February, the wind never rests. Neither do the basketball fans. Both are howling as I bring the ball up court in the North Dakota State University fieldhouse. Old patterns before me. Stewart shouting instructions from the sideline. Holbrook loping ahead and to the right. Spoden, our All-American center, struggling for position in the lane. Head fake left, and the man guarding me leans too far. Dribble right. Double screen by Holbrook and McCool. Sweat and noise, smell of popcorn. See it in slow motion now. Behind the screen into the air, ball over my head, left hand cradling it, right hand pushing it, slow backward spin as it launches. Gentle arc.. . .

The ball just clears the telephone wire and bounces off the rim of the basket as I land on hard-packed dirt in the silence of an Iowa summer evening. Miles from the wind, years from the Dakotas. Bored with school and small-town life at 13, I have decided to become a basketball player. Absurd. Five feet 2 inches tall, 110 pounds.

I am untroubled by the impossibility of it all. Day after day, night after night in the weak glow of the back porch light, the ball goes up. One hundred more shots, and I'll quit. Maybe 200. Can't stop until I have five straight from 20 feet.

Freshman year. I try out for the high-school team, which is just not done by freshmen. Freshmen are supposed to play on the junior-high team. That's understood. I take a pounding, mentally and physically, from the upperclassmen. Yet, into the evenings, wearing gloves in late autumn, I work jump shots around the telephone wire. Merlin, the school janitor, ignores the rules and lets me in the gym at 7 a.m. on Saturdays. I shoot baskets all day, with a short break for lunch.

The Big Day. Twelve will be selected to suit up for the games. I feel that I have a chance. I have hustled and listened and learned. But about 20 people are trying to make the team, a lot of them are seniors, and there is the whole question of whether a freshman even ought to be out there. At the end of practice, the coach has us informally shoot baskets while he walks the gym with a list. Studying it, he begins to call out names, slowly, one every minute or so: "Mehmen"... "Clark"... "Lossee"...

Eleven names have been called; 11 have gone to the locker room to select their uniforms. I can hardly make my shot go up, or dribble, or even think. The coach paces the gym, looks at his list. Three, four minutes go by. He turns: "Waller."

There is silence; I remember it. A freshman? Wait a minute! I trot to the locker room with a feeling that comes only a few times in a life. The locker room is silent, too. I am not welcome, for all those complex reasons having to do with tradition and adolescence and the 1950s' definition of masculinity. Even Clark, the thoughtful one, shakes his head.

The remaining uniform is the largest of the entire lot. The pants can be cinched in to stay up, but the shirt is so big that the arm holes extend down into the pants when it is tucked in. If it weren't so funny, it would be grotesque. But nobody is laughing.

Running through the darkness of a 1953 November evening, squeezing the neatly folded purple and white jersey, I explode through the back porch and into the kitchen. My parents are stunned. They have humored me through all of this, knowing how sensitive I am about my size. But they never expected success.

My dad is concerned for my safety. "Those big guys will make mincemeat out of you." My mother is worried about my schoolwork. But I care only about getting that damn suit to fit. Mother takes enormous tucks in the shoulder straps until the arm holes assume somewhat normal proportions. The armor fits. The warrior is ready.

Our yellow bus rolls through a midwestern winter with Hank at the wheel. St. Ansgar, Greene, Nora Springs, Riceville, Manly, and on and on, through the Corn Bowl Conference. I ride alone in my jeans, green checkered shirt, and engineer boots, ostracized. A good friend of the seniors has been left home because of me. On the bench, I watch closely. The season is not going well.

Gradually, and mostly out of desperation, the coach looks down the bench and says, "Waller, get up here." Occasionally there is a chance for the long jump shot that arcs into the bright lights of a dozen high-school gyms, slicing the net on its way through the basket. The other players are a little kinder to me. By the final game of the season, I am there. I start. We pound up and down the floor at Nashua, winning. I score 12 points. Merlin lets me in the gym the next morning at seven, grinning, with news of the game from the café. "Twelve points, huh?"

More time on the dirt in the summer. "Ya, I'll be in for supper in a minute." Can't quit until I hit 10 in a row from 20 feet.

Sophomore year. It's a winning season. I start every game. We upset Rudd, a powerhouse, in the county tournament, and the world is colored good. Merlin shows up smiling when I rattle the gym doors on Saturday mornings.

The back-porch light burns late in warm weather. Can't quit until I hit 15 in a row from 20 feet. My dad has taken an interest in the whole affair by this time and has the telephone wire moved out of the way. Mother worries about my schoolwork and cooks as if I am a one-man harvest gang. I am 5 feet 10 without warning.

Junior year, new coach. Paul Filter has a low tolerance for dolts. He smiles a lot, but his starched white shirts and neatly pressed suits give him away. This is a serious guy. Serious about teaching history, serious about getting young boys in short pants ready for basketball and for life beyond, a life I cannot conceive of.

We have lost most of our starters and struggle through a break-even year, improving as we go, while Filter lovingly calls us "clowns." But the jump shot is there, game after game, in the hot gyms. On some nights, 20 of them go in from far outside.

Paul Filter begins to see what I am up to and designs a training program for me in the off-season. Roadwork and push-ups (no high school weight-training programs around in those days). I do 140 push-ups at one time and grow to 6 feet. It's getting serious.

Something, though, is at work that I do not completely understand. This is more than a game. I think deeply about the art and physics of the jump shot and ponder these while I practice. The search for perfection, the ballet-like movement, soft release, gentle arc, the reward.

My last year rolls up, and I ride the momentum of years of steady practice. The jump shot floats through the Iowa winter nights. The points mount up game by game – 39, 38, 45, 34. I play with two people guarding me in most games, three one time. But the roadwork, the push-ups and, of course, the jump shot are there with enormous force. The other teams are not prepared for someone training at a near-professional level. Mo Parcher and Bill Mitchell grab rebounds, Tommy Ervin sets screens for me, and we win our first 23 games.

Filter keeps teaching. He has long conversations with me about getting athletics into perspective. He is aware that I will have offers to play college basketball, and he is trying hard to get me ready for something more. I sulk when he takes me out of the St. Ansgar game at the end of the third quarter. I have 39 points and have just hit nine out of 10 shots in that quarter as we bury the Saints. I want to stay in and break my own single-game scoring record. Filter moves me far down the bench and refuses to even look at me as he coaches nervous and eager sophomores. The next morning he talks long and hard to me about sportsmanship, perspective, and life.

It ends against Greene in the tournaments. We have beaten them twice before, but they dig in and go at us. My long jumper goes in and out with no time left. Over.

A few days later, a letter comes from Bucky O'Connor, coach at the University of Iowa. Can I come to the campus for a visit and see the Fabulous Five play?

My dad and I spend the day with Bucky, go to a game and exist in the realms of the privileged. Bucky will recruit four players this year, and he wants me to be one of them. My dad soars. He has spent a lifetime of evenings listening to the Iowa ball games.

We sit at the kitchen table and fill in the scholarship forms. Dad and I laugh and talk about jump shots in the Iowa fieldhouse. Mother says only one thing: "I think this boy should go to college to study something, not to play basketball." What? We verbally abuse her, and she stops talking nonsense.

My first jump shot at Iowa is a memorable one. Early-season scrimmage, and I confidently move downcourt. All the old rhythms are in place. I stop, go into the air, perfect timing, great release and the tallest person I have ever seen knocks the ball over my head to the other end of the court. Some adjustments will be necessary.

I don't know much about playing defense or even team basketball. The kids from the cement playgrounds of Chicago and Louisville do. "Okay, Waller, you don't get to play on offense anymore until we say so. Whenever the ball changes hands, you go over to the defensive side."

The jump shot is silenced for a while. Nonetheless, the coach says I am the greatest natural shooter he has ever seen. I grin at the world "natural" as I think of those seven o'clock mornings in the gym. Somewhere, Merlin the janitor also grins.

There is, however, something more going on in my 18-year-old head. The feelings are not clear, but they have to do with the words of Paul Filter and my mother. I like Tom Ryan, my humanities teacher, and also a strange little man who teaches literature. I do poorly in school, though, and blame it on basketball. My freshman year drifts by. Everybody exclaims about the jump shot while waiting for me to develop other areas of the game. And Bucky O'Connor is killed in an auto accident.

A ruptured appendix in the summer, a broken finger and a nasty knee injury early in the fall get me off to a slow start the next year. I am now haunted by these other feelings. I am close to falling in love with a young woman whom I will marry eventually. And the old curiosities from my boyhood, when I read most of the books in the Rockford library, are surfacing.

Other things bother me, too. Somehow a boy's game has been turned into something else. Grown-ups outside the university actually care about our sprained ankles and the quality of our man-to-man defense. I cannot attach the level of importance to winning that seems to be required. Practice and films and practice and films. Locker-room talk in which women fare poorly leaves me cold. The special study sessions for athletes where amazingly accurate information about upcoming examinations is handed out are repugnant. On principle, I refuse to attend these sessions and am laughed at for it. There is something wrong, deadly wrong, and I know it.

I drop out of school. My father is disappointed and hurt in ways he cannot even express. A few months of menial work, and Iowa State Teachers College takes me in. No scholarship, no financial aid. My parents send money, and I work at a local bank. Good basketball in a lower key.

Norm Stewart comes to coach. He teaches me more about defense in three weeks than I have learned in a lifetime. Mostly, aside from keeping your rear end down and staying on the balls of your feet, he teaches me that defense is pride and gives me tough assignments in the games. I like that. It fits the way I am starting to think about the world.

The purple and gold bus rolls through the Midwestern winters with Jack at the wheel. I stand up front in the door well and gather images for the songs and essays to come. I am studying literature, playing the guitar, spending Saturday mornings reading Clarence Darrow's great closing arguments to his juries, and wallowing in all the things that college and life have to offer.

I am so deeply in love with a woman and with music that basketball becomes something I do because people expect me to do it. Seldom do I reach the levels I know I can touch with the jump shot. Oh, there are nights, in Brookings, South Dakota, and Lincoln, Nebraska, when 25 feet looks like a lay-up, the way it used to look in Riceville and Manly, and the baskets are there for the taking. Mostly, though, the old magic is gone.

Still, my dad drives down from Rockford on below-zero nights to watch what is left of it. He sits along the west sideline in the old teachers college gym, and, moving downcourt, I can pick his voice out of 4,000 others, "Go get 'em, Bobby." He was there with the same words, years ago, on winter nights in all the Corn Bowl Conference towns.

He calls on a March morning to say that I have made the All-North Central Conference first team. He heard it on the radio, he is pleased, and I am pleased for him. I ignore my remaining eligibility, take some extra courses and graduate.

There is one final moment, though. The University of Iowa seniors barnstorm after their season is over. Another player and I team up with a group of high school coaches and play them at the Manchester, Iowa, gym for a benefit. It's a good game. We are in it until the last few minutes when our big center fouls out, and I am forced to guard Don Nelson, later of the Boston Celtics. And, for one more night, the jump shot is there, just as it once was. Twelve of them go down from deep on the outside.

The jump shot, with some 2,500 points scribbled on it, has lain unused for over 20 years. It rests in a closet somewhere, with my old schoolbooks and Flexible Flyer sled. I got it out once to show my daughter, who asked about it. It took a few minutes to shine it up, and she watched it flash for a little while in the late-afternoon light of a neighbor's back yard. I put it away again. It was a boy's tool for a boy's game, for growing up and showing your stuff. Merlin knew that.

More than anything, though, and I understand it clearly now, the jump shot was a matter of aesthetics, an art form for a small-town kid – the ballet-like movement, the easy release, the gentle arc over a telephone wire through the summer nights of Iowa, while my mother and father peered out the back-porch screen door and looked at each other softly.

Central as West High School, and eventually North High School, opened. And everybody knew that would weaken Davenport's 30-year domination of Iowa high school sports – and most other activities, too.

"I don't think there was ever more celebration in Iowa high school athletics than when they split up our high school and started the new schools," Leach said. "We'd been such consistent winners in almost everything. It had been an exceptional high school for extra-curricular activities – sports, band, choir, fine arts – probably as good as there was anywhere in the nation."

In the fall of 1959, Leach was a starter on defense and a back-up on offense as the Blue Devils went undefeated in football, including knocking off undefeated Dubuque Senior in the final game, to tie Burlington for the mythical state championship. Then came Leach's individual state championship in wrestling for coach Jim Fox, followed by his acceptance at Princeton – it was quite a senior year.

His experiences forever shaped his thinking on the importance of involvement in athletics and other activities.

"I have a view of the benefits of participating in athletics that isn't exclusively about athletics," Leach said. "I think anytime you work at anything that requires teamwork and encourages you to excel – whether it's wrestling, football, band or the class play – it's a good thing.

"But sports culture, in particular, is deeper and more profound in America than is often understood. The values you learn are fundamental to the American way."

Leach remains a great wrestling fan and advocate, and he spoke eloquently about the sport when he was inducted into the National Wrestling Hall of Fame in Stillwater, Oklahoma, in 1995.

"Wrestling is a pursuit that shares with all sports elements of competition – in this case nakedly individualistic – and elements of team companionship," Leach said. "From the retrospect of having last wrestled competitively 27 years ago, what strikes me is how much tradition, individual discipline and equality of opportunity is involved in this benchmark sport…

"As different as the likely participants are, in no place does it matter how rich, poor, black, brown or white a wrestler is. There is no more equalitarian circle than a wrestling mat."

He went on to say that "while all sports involve God-given athleticism, wrestling eliminates advantages of size and accentuates experience and conditioning. The talented, unschooled athlete simply cannot prevail over the dedicated plugger. Wrestling imbues discipline. It also teaches individual limits. All experienced wrestlers pretty well know the structure of all moves. Indeed, the sport is devoid of tricks, emphasizing meat-and-potato repetition over saucy innovation…"

Leach said every wrestler uses "a limited number of moves which best reflect his nature, physique, and ability as adjusted to his opponent's." He said that in his 130 matches from high school through college and during his graduate studies, he "seldom utilized much more than a well-nuanced duckunder and half-standing inside switch. Both moves were hallmarked by going with, rather than against, the opponents' momentum and strength.

"In wrestling, brute strength is, of course, an asset, but it is by no means determinative. The best wrestlers are generally strong of arm but use strength in unnoticed ways with moves refined to fundamental simplicity, optimally using the momentum of an opponent to advantage.

"A successful wrestler must know his opponent's strengths and weaknesses, but most of all he must know himself, his own limits and capacities. Not everyone matches up the same way. For instance, I always welcomed the chance to take on an overly-muscled opponent and was apprehensive if a tall strapping type appeared opposite me. Raw strength in others I felt confident I could counter or use to my advantage; long-legged wile I had more difficulty with."

And finally, Leach said, "As for rules, wrestlers learn to live within disciplined limits. Life is that way. Or at least it should be."

After graduating from Princeton in political science, Leach earned a master's degree in Soviet politics at Johns Hopkins University and then did research in economics and Soviet politics at the London School of Economics. Meanwhile, he was already becoming involved in public affairs in a career that has now stretched 40 years. It began in 1965, serving on the staff of U.S. Representative Donald Rumsfeld, the U.S. Secretary of Defense under President George W. Bush. Leach later served in the U.S. Foreign

Service, worked three years in business in Bettendorf, Iowa, and then was elected in 1976 as a Republican member of the U.S. House. He's been in the House ever since.

He has always been one of the regulars in the House Gym in Washington, D.C.

"I used to pride myself on my free-throw shooting in basketball, but partly because of arthritis, I've sort of lost my rhythm for it," he said. "And you know how in athletics, you develop your peripheral vision? I've got none. But I do a lot of exercise, partly because I have to with my arthritis."

Besides their home in the Washington area, he and his wife Deba, also live in Iowa City. They have a son and daughter.

Bruce Stevens, a 1960 graduate of Shenandoah High School in southwest Iowa, since 1985 has been president and chief executive officer of Steinway & Sons, the makers of fine pianos and other musical instruments.

Back in the old hometown in the late 1950s, nobody would have been surprised if they could have known that "Buck" Stevens, as many called him, would eventually head some major company. He was a bright kid, after all, and he was a heralded four-sport athlete for the Mustangs. But, president of Steinway & Sons? Did he even play piano in high school?

"I took piano lessons as a little kid, didn't enjoy it, fought it and I guess I 'won' because I gave it up," said Stevens, 62 years old in 2005, speaking from his office in Waltham, Massachusetts. "I tried trumpet, French horn and drums in band. I did sing in mixed chorus. But all I ever wanted to do back then was sports.

"My sister Barbara is very musical – played a Steinway through high school and college, became an opera singer and has been in a lot of Broadway shows. So, she puts in all this time in the music business, and then I come along, not very musical, but become president of Steinway. Right away, I'm getting invited to the White House for concerts, meet the presidents, know and work with a lot of artists. Barbara says, 'That's just it! There is no justice!' "

Bruce Stevens, who was 5 ft., 10 in. and about 165 pounds in high school, was a regular in the line-up in football, basketball, baseball and track.

The football, track and baseball teams were all very successful.

"In basketball, we were a disappointment," he recalled.

He said now he realizes that some of the best lessons he drew from his sports experience came from that disappointment.

"When I was a sophomore, the varsity team was struggling, and near the end of the season, our coach Ed Farnum decided to start four of us sophomores with a senior, Ray Lutz, who was our tallest player," Stevens said. "So Doug Olson, Glen 'Cookie' Rogers, Jack Millikan and I played with Lutz and we did pretty well the last three or four games. In fact, Red Oak was leading the Hawkeye Eight, and in our last game, we beat those bastards.

"But the expectations we created for ourselves – in our own minds and with all the fans – were that we were going to do some unbelievable things the next two years," he said. "And you know what? We never really achieved much in either of those two years, and none of us could ever figure out what happened. I learned a whole lot about expectations through that."

Other lessons from his high school experience?

"Being involved in sports gives kids a tremendous opportunity to focus, to put attention on getting in shape, to learn the teamwork concept that is so important in the rest of your life," Stevens said. "The things you gain by playing in games are invaluable – play by the rules, be gentlemen, be respectful of your opponents, learn how to win, learn how to lose. Sports are a magnificent vehicle to focus the energies of younger kids and teach them some real values."

The Stevens family in Shenandoah was a talented, hard-working bunch. Bruce's father Don Stevens and uncle Wayne Stevens had farming interests, ran a road construction business and Don was a hog buyer with his own stockyards on the edge of downtown Shenandoah. Bruce spent time working in all those businesses. His mother Jenny Stevens was society editor of The Evening Sentinel. His sister Barbara, five years older, was the obvious musician, and her parents bought her a used, 1933 Steinway piano for practices at home. Barbara still has that piano, incidentally, and her brother had it rebuilt in the Steinway factory 10 years ago. She graduated from the Indiana University School of Music, performed on the "Perry Como Show" on network television, toured with Broadway shows and also performed in rofessional opera. In 2005, she lived in New Rochelle, New York.

Bruce Stevens spent two years at Iowa State University – and played reshman basketball for the Cyclones – then transferred to the University of 'ennsylvania to study at the Wharton School of Business. After graduating 1 1964, he joined the floor makers Armstrong Cork Co., went through the ompany's excellent marketing training program, and was then assigned to sales district in Boston. After three years with Armstrong, Stevens joined 'olaroid Corp., "which was about as hot then as a company can get," he aid. He spent the next 18 years with Polaroid, winding up as director of the nternational marketing division and heading their operations in Japan.

In 1984, he joined several other entrepreneurs in the Robert Williams Co., a plastics reformulating firm in Boston, and soon learned that the partners were negotiating to buy Steinway & Sons. They asked Stevens to lead the new acquisition, and he has ever since.

He and his wife Teri have two grown daughters. Stevens has stayed ctive physically, playing golf, tennis and riding a bicycle as much as he can vork into his schedule – including a few days on the Des Moines Register's Annual Great Bicycle Ride Across Iowa one summer when the big ride vernighted in Shenandoah.

David Stead, who graduated from Monticello High School in astern Iowa in 1961, had what now seems nearly an ideal high school career. He won 12 athletic letters, participated in six state tournaments, was an All-State singer for four years, played trumpet in the Monticello concert band, vas active in drama and musicals, and was a class officer and a member of he National Honor Society.

Little wonder he believes so strongly in the importance of the high chool years.

He has also been able to turn that belief into a career.

In 2005, the 61-year-old Stead has for 16 years served as executive lirector of the Minnesota State High School League, which is the IHSAA's quivalent organization in the neighboring state. And in the summer of 2004, 1e began a one-year term as president of the National Federation of State High School Associations.

In many ways, he is a protégé of Bernie Saggau. And he's had another good mentor for his administrative career in his father Vance Stead, who was principal at Monticello High when David was in school there and who later became superintendent in LeMars.

"When I went to work for the Minnesota organization, it was great having the Iowa connection with Bernie," Stead said. "He was very kind to introduce me to other colleagues around the country, and that really helped me get involved in the National Federation."

During his career, Stead's understanding of the Iowa organization and its programs has of course deepened, and as it has, his appreciation for having grown up in it has increased, too.

"Iowa has developed a very stable program, and part of the reason is that Bernie has had such a long tenure there," Stead said. "I'm sure there have been bumps along the way, but Bernie has always known how things are, and how he thinks they ought to be, and he's never been hesitant to stand up for that. The citizenship thing has always been a big focus for him, but then at the same time, he's always been willing to listen to the ideas of other people and to be able to change his mind on things when it's for the good of the program. So it hasn't been stuck in one mode and become inflexible."

And, as Stead said in Chapter 1, the support of most Iowa communities for their school programs is amazing. He realized that before he ever left Monticello High.

"Right across the street from the high school building was an eight-plex apartment building, and the mostly-older people who lived there all came to our games," he recalled. "A group of the women came to be known as 'The Grandmas,' and they had specific seats in the gym that everybody else stayed out of. My own two grandmothers – Iva Rodman and Anna Stead – were among them, so I was especially aware of them. But the whole town would turn out for the games, the concerts and everything else at school."

Stead played pitcher, catcher and third base in baseball. He was a forward in basketball. He was the quarterback and middle linebacker in football. In track he ran the sprint relays, threw the shot put or discus and went to the state track meet for four years in the old football throw.

"It was a good time to be a high school kid, and a great opportunity for a bunch of kids to play sports together," he said. "It took all of us to make a team back then, so nobody was specializing in one sport like you see today. We found out that being involved in high school programs, gives you the skills and traits that will help in whatever you go into for your career."

Stead went on to play college football, first at the University of Northern Iowa, and then transferred to Morningside College in Sioux City. He began his career as an English teacher and coach of multiple sports at Rockwell City, then Manchester, both in Iowa. In 1973, after earning his master's degree at the University of Wyoming, he began his administrative career as assistant high school principal in New Ulm, Minnesota, later rising to principal. In 1986, he joined the Minnesota State High School League as associate director, and then became the director in 1988.

He and his wife Cathy, who in 2005, was teaching at Bethel College in the Twin Cities, have two grown daughters.

Clyde Duncan, a 1964 graduate of Des Moines North High School, is a legend among track fans in Iowa. He was state champion in three events for three consecutive years – the 100-yard dash, 220-yard dash and 440-yard run. That career total of nine individual championships is still the Iowa record for most championships by one athlete.

Maybe even more amazing was his performance at the 1964 Drake Relays during his senior year. Duncan ran a :09.3 time in the 100-yard dash, setting a new national record for high school sprinters. He also anchored the winning Polar Bear teams in the 880-yard and one-mile relays.

He was the runaway favorite athlete of the thunderous Drake Relays crowd of 18,000 – not only their favorite among all the excellent Iowa high school athletes competing, but also among the nation's best college, university and post-graduate amateurs who were there.

It was one of those rare moments when the whole state stood in awe of a high school athlete.

But the best story of all about Clyde Duncan is what he overcame.

And 40 years later, in 2005, very few people know anything about it.

Clyde was enrolled in special education classes from the seventh grade on through his high school years at North.

He was among the first special education athletes allowed to compete for their high schools in interscholastic competition, once the state Department of Public Instruction changed its rules to permit it. (That agency was the forerunner of today's Iowa Department of Education.) Making the argument for that change in the rules was Bernie Saggau, then the new assistant executive secretary of the IHSAA.

Duncan made such a name for himself running for Des Moines North in the Drake Relays, especially in his junior and senior years, that the big time college track coaches were all buzzing about him. But when they learned that he was a special-needs student, most didn't give another thought to recruiting him.

Except for Stan Wright, a track legend himself as head coach at Texas Southern University, a predominantly black school in Houston. The coach was African American, and so is Duncan.

Wright asked young Duncan to have breakfast with him during the Drake Relays weekend. Because Duncan's North High track coach Jimmy Lyle was tied up getting his team ready for the day, Duncan asked North's football coach Ray Pugh, whom he liked and trusted, to go along.

"I sat there and listened mostly," said Pugh, now retired after a long career as a professor at Drake University. "Coach Wright talked to Clyde about the help they could give him at Texas Southern, and then he turned to me. He told me that he'd spent time talking to Clyde, and to Jimmy Lyle, and he was sure Clyde could do college work. He said he wanted to reassure me they'd do everything they could to give him a chance to get a college degree."

Did that seem preposterous to Pugh, the idea of a special education student from Iowa going off to a college in Texas, where he would know no one, and have a chance at succeeding? It was practically unheard of at that time for such students even to consider post-secondary education.

"Not at all," Pugh said. "I knew Clyde Duncan would make it. People who doubted just didn't know what kind of young man he was. They did not know his desire. And they did not know that Clyde was – and still is today – the most respected kid ever at North High School, and I'm talking about being respected by the white kids as well as the black kids. Everybody loved

Clyde Duncan, and there was no doubt in any of our minds he was a young guy who was going to make it in life if he could get the right help."

Years later it is clear. Coach Stan Wright of Texas Southern University was right. Coaches Jimmy Lyle and Ray Pugh and all those students at Des Moines North High – they were all right about Clyde Duncan. Were they ever!

It turns out that Duncan was not even a special education student.

He had a speech problem of stuttering – his father had the same problem – but there was nothing wrong with his intelligence. The Texas Southern faculty helped him understand why and when he stuttered, and how to control it better. And they taught him how to study, a skill he hadn't needed in the special education classes.

The result? Clyde Duncan became a dean's list student, and earned a bachelor's degree in physical education in 1969. He was also an All-American in track and ran on three Texas Southern relay teams that set world records. He continued his education, earning a master's in physical education in 1972.

"And I earned both those degrees," Duncan said proudly. "Neither one of them had anything to do with track and field. I didn't get any special breaks."

As a 59-year-old in 2005, he is in his tenth year as the highly-successful head track and field coach at his alma mater, which has an enrollment of 12,500. He coaches both the Texas Southern men and women, with a total mixed squad of 75.

Duncan has been coaching at the college level since he completed his undergraduate work, with stops at Wylie College in Texas, Grambling, University of Houston, University of Washington, Arizona State and since 1995, at Texas Southern.

How does he feel now, looking back on what happened? Is he at all bitter about having been directed into special education classes in junior high and high school, when what he probably really needed was speech therapy and counseling?

"I don't fault anyone," Duncan said, in a soft, confident voice – and only stuttering occasionally. "I've always focused on how blessed I am to have moved on, to have received the right help when I needed it.

"As a student at North, sometimes I would wonder why I wasn't allowed to be in classes with the regular students," he continued. "But you know, I used to be kind of shy, and I just accepted that those special classes were probably where I was supposed to be. Now I think it was probably 100 percent because of my speech problem."

Interestingly, with his sports success in high school came many requests for interviews. "I don't remember Clyde stuttering in those situations," Pugh said. "Maybe it was that he'd respond to the pressure of the moment," just like starting a race. However, Duncan now says he "usually tried to give one and two word answers in those interviews. I tried to avoid doing much talking, especially on television"

Neither his stuttering, nor his being enrolled in special education classes, was ever mentioned in newspaper stories, radio or television.

Around his family at home, Clyde never stuttered as much as he did at school. "That's probably because of all the love that was there," he said.

Clyde comes from an amazing family.

His father, the late Earthol Duncan, was a well-liked custodian at the Des Moines Register & Tribune. His mother Marie Duncan "stayed at home," Clyde said. "Her job was us."

There were 14 of "us" – all the Duncan kids – Sequoia, Chiquita, Earthol Jr., Quintheta, Marcelline, James, Malvin, Clyde, Synthia, Jonathan, Omar, Lolita, Rosita and Ricardo.

The whole family was faithful in attending Corinthian Baptist Church, and later Shiloh Baptist, both in Des Moines.

Clyde began to get a sense, as a little boy, that he was fast.

"We used to line-up in our neighborhood – boys and girls together – and race down the street or around the block," he said. And he won some of those? "Well, to be truthful, yes," he said. "But my three older brothers were faster than me. They all went to North, too, but I was the only one who pursued the sport."

Duncan has been involved at the Drake Relays since he was in second grade at old Nash School. The Des Moines elementary and junior high schools back then would put together "shuttle relay teams" that would race on the infield at Drake Stadium, as sort of a novelty race during the big meet.

356

When he got to North High, he was initially as excited about football as he was about track.

"I had Clyde starting on the varsity as a free safety on defense in his sophomore year," said Pugh, the old football coach. "He was a tremendous player, because of that speed. He was still learning the game, and sometimes he might be way out of position, but when the ball would go up in the air toward one of the receivers, Clyde could usually get there in time to break it up or intercept it. I remember one night we played Dowling at Sec Taylor Stadium and Clyde intercepted five passes. He was doing incredible things."

But by his junior year, it was clear to the coaches that Duncan was so promising in track that he should not risk injury in football.

Five years later, when Duncan was graduating from Texas Southern, there were professional football teams contacting him to see if he was interested in returning to the game, even though he'd never played in college.

Of course, Duncan's old coaches, teachers, teammates and especially his family were all thrilled when he made such progress during college.

"Mom and Dad had just told me when I left to go down there to make them proud," he said. "They were very thankful that I was getting the opportunity, and you know, they always thought I was going to make it. I think they saw something in me that I didn't. The same thing with Coach Lyle and Coach Pugh – they were telling me in high school that they thought I could do something in college if the right situation came up."

He said his own experience makes him more open now when he sees special needs students enrolling at Texas Southern.

"I know how easily they can just get lost along the way," Duncan said. "That could have happened to me, except for the way I was raised, with my mother and father and my brothers and sisters all looking out for me. So now when I see students coming in with some special challenges, I like to get with them and tell them it can be done. I can truthfully tell them, 'If I can do it, you can do it, too.'"

Clyde and his wife Juanita Duncan live in Kingwood, Texas, about 20 miles from the Texas Southern campus. They have two grown daughters, and their son Clyde Duncan Jr. is an assistant coach to his father at the university. Clyde Sr. also has three step-sons.

Former Iowa Governor **Terry Branstad**, a 1965 graduate of Forest City High School in far north central Iowa, was quick with a highlight from his prep sports career.

"In football," he said, "I had a 10-yards-per-carry average."

But wait, I said, don't I remember you were a lineman?

"Well, yeah, that is right," Branstad said. "But one of the last games of my senior year, we were playing Lake Mills and we were way ahead in the fourth quarter. All of a sudden, our coach yells, 'I need a fullback!' So I stepped right up there and told him I was ready, even though I always played guard on offense and line or linebacker on defense. But he sent me in as fullback. I carried the ball once and ran for 10 yards. Ever since, I've been telling people I averaged 10 yards per carry."

Branstad lettered just that senior year in football, in which Forest City "had a winning season – maybe 5-3 in the North Iowa Conference, but we couldn't handle Belmond. They were the power."

He said one of his favorite football moments actually came over 30 years later. That was in November, 1996, during a huge party at the Surf Ballroom in Clear Lake celebrating his fiftieth birthday. The Forest City team of 1996 showed up and presented their famous alumnus a new team jersey, with "Branstad" across the back above his old number, 64.

He had more success in high school baseball, lettering three years while playing the outfield.

"I usually batted second in the line-up, and I was a pretty fair hitter – probably about .300 or close to it," he said. "But on defense, I made it exciting. I had a teammate Mark Lund who always said he hated to see a fly ball headed my way. I'd usually catch the ball, but I'd run around a lot before I did. I made them all look difficult."

Forest City played both spring and summer baseball in that era, and the Indians made it to the state tournament in the spring of 1963 before Davenport West beat them. "There were seven of us who were sophomores on that team," Branstad said, "we were really proud because we had to beat Bancroft St. John's, which was always tough, and then we were at state with Des Moines Roosevelt, Dubuque Wahlert and Davenport West. That was pretty fast company for us coming from a smaller school like Forest City."

In the spring of 1964, Bancroft St. John's beat Forest City in the district tournament and then went on to win the state championship over Waterloo West.

"It was really a thrill for us anytime we could play Bancroft St. John's and be around their coach Vince Meyer," Branstad said. "They had the best program in the state at the time, and Meyer was already a legend. I'll tell you though, that we never won much when we were playing in Bancroft."

In 1998, when Branstad was governor, Bancroft completed a renovation of its historic ballpark and invited him to come speak at the rededication ceremony.

"I told them I always enjoyed representing Bancroft in the legislature and as lieutenant governor and then governor, but that I had some bad memories of playing baseball on that field," he said.

Following high school, Branstad went on to the University of Iowa, getting a degree in political science. He served a two-year hitch in the U.S. Army, then went to law school at Drake University. While a student there, he ran for the Iowa Legislature and won the first of his three terms there. In 1978, he was elected lieutenant governor, then in 1982, he was elected to the first of his four four-year terms as governor. He left office in early 1999, having never lost an election and having served longer as governor than anybody in the state's history.

Subsequently he taught leadership in public affairs at the University of Iowa, served as a financial advisor, briefly worked with a public policy firm in Washington, D.C. and in August 2003 was named president of Des Moines University, the osteopathic college in the capital city.

Branstad, who has been a genuine fan of high school sports throughout his adult life, said the competitiveness, teamwork and desire to win that the Forest City coaches taught him long ago have proven to be important over and over in his career. Those coaches included Jim Redel in football, and Herb Konigsmark and Fred Smith in baseball.

"High school athletics are so important for kids," he said, "and one of the best things about it is being around coaches who are motivators. You never forget a lot of the things they tell you." He and his wife Chris, who have three grown children, now live in rural Boone County.

Mark Bogenrief, a 1968 graduate of LeMars Gehlen Catholic High School, has developed a national following as a stained glass artist, and in fact, has done a major piece for the new Iowa Hall of Pride that the IHSAA is opening in Des Moines. You read about that in Chapter 8.

Bogenrief Studios, which Mark owns and operates with his wife and fellow artist Jeanne Bogenrief, has done many lampshades, windows, ceilings, glass walls and more. But the glass panels they are doing for the Hall of Pride will be their first work with a sports theme and, at $1 million, one of their largest commissions.

So, was Mark Bogenrief an athlete?

"One year of football for the Gehlen Jays," the artist who turned 54 in 2005 said. "I started out as a halfback, but then went to the line and middle linebacker. There were so few of us out for football – maybe 18 or 20 – that you played everything.

"On defense, I was pretty decent, because of my size. I was 6 ft., 1 in. and about 210 pounds. On offense, my coach thought I'd be a good ball carrier, hard to bring down, so he had me at halfback to start the season. But the very first play of the very first game, the quarterback handed me the ball and I ran into the line. Somebody tackled me and when I went down, somebody else speared me with their helmet on the side of my knee, and it blew out my knee. So much for carrying the ball."

The team went on to "a dismal 1-7 record," Bogenrief recalled. "The only game we won was the one I sat out with the injury. Should that tell me something?"

He had planned to play basketball his senior year, too, "but I didn't have a car, and I was usually hitchhiking home to Hinton – about 15 miles from school – after all the practices." That wasn't too difficult in the fall, when it was still light into the early evening, but the rides became more difficult to find as basketball season and winter approached.

So he gave up his sports career.

"I wish now I'd have started earlier in sports," he said. "It's something that really teaches you discipline, and that's crucial later in life."

His wife Jeanne was probably the better athlete, he acknowledged. As Jeanne Stoltz, she was a star guard on two Hinton girls' basketball teams that made it to the state tournament in 1972 and 1973.

The Bogenriefs may be the most unlikely people ever to take-up the artistry and craftsmanship of designing and building stained glass. They taught themselves the craft and founded the business 25 years ago – when both were on strike from the meat packing jobs they had for then-IBP, Inc., in Dakota City, Nebraska.

Mark, a Vietnam veteran, had worked in a military morgue during the war, and then found himself working on the kill line in a meat packing plant.

Between the war and the packing plant, "I decided I'd had all the death I wanted," he once told me. "I became a complete pacifist, and I decided I was going to spend the rest of my life doing only beautiful things."

His first stained glass work was repairing some old windows his father had in his antique shop. As he began experimenting with other work with the glass, he discovered he was a natural at it.

And as his talent and skill grew, so did the business in little Merrill, Iowa, 18 miles northeast of Sioux City. There, Bogenrief Studios eventually took over six buildings in the heart of the small business district – a full block and a half. They employ about 20 people, including their sons Jesse, a glass blower, and Seth, who does odd jobs and set-ups. Their commissions have ranged from the lamp shades, worth a few thousand dollars, to the huge windows and ceilings which have sold for $500,000 and above. Their work is built into homes, businesses and galleries from coast to coast. Until three years ago, they had never sold a piece of their work in Iowa, but that has changed rapidly as their reputation and story have become publicly known.

In 2003 and 2004, the couple became the targets of an intense recruiting effort by the City of Paducah, Kentucky, which has an innovative "Artist Relocation Program." More than 40 artists have been given financial incentives to move their studios and galleries from across the U.S. to an old neighborhood in Paducah – and it's already become a national attraction. The Kentuckians came after the Bogenriefs at a time when they were outgrowing their facilities in Merrill.

Other Iowa cities got into the bidding, too, and eventually Bogenriefs decided to relocate their headquarters and gallery to Cherokee in northwest Iowa. Their new production facility was established in Sutherland, 15 miles northeast of Cherokee, and another gallery has been opened in Spencer, another 15 miles northeast. They made the move in the fall of 2004.

Mark Bogenrief said one reason he was enthused about the new facilities "is because the building we got in Sutherland is the former school, and a beautiful gym comes with it." He said he immediately began imagining how he and the employees would take breaks from the painstaking work in stained glass and blown glass, to shoot baskets. "We're also getting the old football and baseball fields," he said, "so we hope to work with the city of Sutherland to allow some continued public use of all those facilities."

Aaron Helmrich, a 2001 graduate of North Linn High School in Troy Mills, north of Cedar Rapids, is young enough that he has not had as many experiences in life as most of the other alumni we've visited in this chapter. He was a state wrestling champion at 112 pounds in his senior year, but others we've met here were champions in their sports, too.

However, all those alumni and lots of other people would line-up to hear about the experience Helmrich had on December 13, 2003.

Then a 20-year-old U.S. Army private first class, he was on the raid that found and captured Saddam Hussein, the fugitive president of Iraq, who was hiding in a "spider hole" in the small town of Adwar north of Baghdad.

"I didn't see him up close personally, but I was close enough to see him through a 'Scout Surveillance System' we use," Helmrich said. "He looked like a green person with a long beard, being escorted by our troops."

His unit, the 80-member "Golf Troop" of the Tenth Cavalry in the 4th Infantry, had been based in Hussein's home city of Tikrit from April, 2003, and remained there until March of 2004. On the strength of intelligence reports, they had been searching an area about 10 miles north of Adwar for any of the deposed Iraqi leaders.

About 7 p.m. on that night late in 2003, "We got an intelligence report that said we were going to be doing a raid 'on the No. 1 guy,'" Helmrich recalled. "So about 150 of us – our unit and some Special Ops soldiers – linked up at headquarters, and about 10 p.m., we left on a half-hour drive that took us to the area where we found him. It was a beautiful night, 55 degrees with a big moon out. We did the raid about 10:30 or 11. I was one of the guys securing the area, but we got word right away from Special Ops that they had someone who matched the ID for Saddam Hussein. We stayed in place, and about four hours later, we got confirmation it was him."

His immediate feeling?

"You know, we'd been in a lot of danger in Iraq, and in our little unit we're all real close, so you worry more," Helmrich said. "The first month we were there, we had seven windshields shot out of our trucks. And then we had three of our soldiers die on September 18. So my first thought after we knew we captured him was that our efforts hadn't been in vain."

He said the raiding party stayed in the immediate area until about noon the next day.

"That next morning, we all went into the house where we found him, crawled down in the hole he'd been in and it was amazing to see," Helmrich said. "He had electricity and a fan down there, running water. He had more comforts there in that hole than most Iraqi people had in their homes around there. The guy was living better in that hole than 75 percent of his people."

Another young Iowan, 23-year-old Sergeant Daniel Saffeels, of Truro, was also on the raiding party.

The news that two Iowa soldiers had been involved swept across the state, of course. At the 2004 state wrestling tournament, Helmrich's photo and a story about his role in the capture were featured in the program.

His first visit back to Iowa after his hitch in Iraq was in May, 2004.

He told me then how his parents Tony and Joellyn Helmrich had raised him, his two older brothers and a younger sister on a farm near Ryan in southwest Delaware County. He and his brothers started youth wrestling programs when they were 5, 6 and 7 and stayed with it through high school.

Aaron had the most success on the mats. In addition to his state championship, he had a 134-20 record over four years, setting school records for most career wins and for most pins, at 84.

His high school wrestling coach Brad Bridgewater said he thinks "much of Aaron's success is in direct correlation to the family's beliefs that anything is possible.

"As a wrestling coach, I have our wrestlers write personal goals starting with the words 'I am,' " Bridgewater continued. "Aaron's senior year, he wrote the goal, 'I am the 112-pound state champion.' He repeated this goal often, posted it above his bed, in his locker and on the mirror in his bathroom. Through hard work, dedication and a bit of luck, this goal became a reality, even though he was ranked sixth heading into the state tournament.

"I always tell kids that wrestling has a lot of 'life lessons' in it. As you know, sometimes in life you work really hard for something but come up short or lose out to someone else. But the relentless dedication that wrestling instills helps people, like Aaron, persevere against great odds."

Helmrich also played football for three years in high school, ran cross country one season and competed for a year in track and baseball, "but wrestling was always my main thing."

After graduation, he enrolled at Ellsworth Community College, and was on the wrestling team there, "but I decided pretty early that college wasn't really for me right then." He said he and other students were shocked, like everyone else, on September 11, 2001, when they watched coverage of the attacks on the World Trade Center and Pentagon and learned of the crash in Pennsylvania of the airplane that had been hijacked by terrorists.

"We took the whole day to watch the news on television" Helmrich said. "And it wasn't long after that, I started thinking I might as well go do something for my country while I was deciding what to do in life."

Helmrich enlisted in the Army in May, 2002.

Two years later, he said, it's turned out to be a good decision.

"I love being in the Army," he said. "I know it scares Mom and Dad, but I really do love it. I've grown up a lot. I've seen some changes in myself."

After Iraq, his unit was assigned back to Fort Hood in Texas in the spring of 2004. By then holding the rank of specialist, he had two more years on his enlistment, and said he would ponder extending his service while welcoming whatever new assignments come his way. He said if he does not continue in the military, he wants e to complete college, teach at a high school and coach wrestling. In the fall of 2004, he was still a bachelor.

And he was still grinning and complying when he was frequently asked to again tell the story of December 13, 2003.

According to his former coach, Aaron is "a small town farm boy who became a great wrestler and was part of a very big moment in history."

364

The 25 greatest athletes and
Centennial Honor Roll

Oh, we remember them. Do we ever.

Just the mention of someone who was a good high school athlete, even years ago, will still bring smiles in most Iowa communities.

And then there are those few great ones, who in their time had the whole state talking, whose names became as familiar as those of our governors and senators, often more so. Years later, visitors continue showing up in those elite athletes' hometowns and at their old high schools, wanting to re-live the stories.

In the Monroe County Historical Museum in the town of Albia, there is a whole trophy case dedicated to the athletic exploits of Kenneth "Moco" Mercer, who played high school sports there 83 years ago.

Gary Thompson, a superstar in basketball at little Roland High School in the early 1950s, said even now, at 69 years old, he gets a kick out of beingmentioned or greeted as "The Roland Rocket." It's almost like people forget that he went on to become a two-sport All-American at Iowa State University, a highly successful businessman in Ames and a commentator on televised basketball games. "Some guys say, 'You still like being called that – 'The Roland Rocket'?" he said. "I do, I really do, because I like the way it ties me back to my hometown."

In Waterloo, Jerry Moses was telling me that at 52 years old, he really can't remember much about his statistics at East High School there in the late 1960s and 1970. His thought was interrupted by his son J.J. Moses, the kick return specialist of the professional Houston Texans in the National Football League, who was home visiting. "Oh, come on, Dad!" said J.J., 25 years old in 2005, who had a brilliant East High and Iowa State University career himself. J.J. went right into the litany he's heard all his life from fans around Waterloo about what his father did at East: "Thirty-seven touchdowns in your senior year, 1,500 yards rushing, almost never played in the second half!" He could have added state indoor track champion in the high jump and hurdles, All-State in basketball with a 19-point average as a senior, president of his senior class, and more. Amazing!

Casey Blake, who was All-Everything at Indianola High School from 1988 to 1992, went on to become a baseball All-American at Wichita State University. And, in 2004, he had a terrific year as the third baseman for the Cleveland Indians in Major League Baseball. With so many thrills in later years, can the thrills he had in high school possibly compare? "My high school sports experiences must measure up pretty well against what I've done later, because I still have dreams about big games at Indianola," Blake said. "Playing in high school, I guess, was the last time I played with friends as teammates – people who really cared about each other – when placement of self wasn't even a factor. All we cared about was the team. I miss that. You don't find that much in pro ball."

With those thoughts as a primer, welcome now to conversations with and about Iowa's greatest schoolboy athletes from the past 100 years.

In interviews with more than 250 people around the state over a year's time, I kept asking everybody to give me their list of Iowa's 20 or 25 all-time best. These were current and former coaches, athletic directors, game officials, school administrators, sportswriters and broadcasters and, yes, many rank-and-file fans.

They'd immediately ask what standards they should use to make their selections.

So I imposed these qualifications: 1) Multi-sport athletes had to be given extra consideration, 2) if a person was a one-sport athlete he had to be so dominating that there could be no argument about his ability, and 3) nominations should be based on what the athletes did in high school, more than what they did or didn't do later in the collegiate and professional ranks.

Eventually I compiled a list of 125 outstanding athletes from over the decades. Those names are listed together at the end of this chapter as a "Centennial Honor Roll" of the 125 best athletes.

Put that in this perspective: A million boys – maybe more – have played high school sports in Iowa since the IHSAA was founded in 1904. Being among the 125 best is fast company, indeed.

Then I sent that long list of names back out to many of the same people I had originally talked to. This time, I asked them to pick 20 or 25 whom they'd identify as the greatest. A consensus began to build.

Three names were mentioned most often – Gary Thompson, Jerry Moses and Tim Dwight, the great City High of Iowa City track and football star from 1990-94 who went on to a great career at the University of Iowa and was playing professional football in 2005.

Those three and 22 others have become my picks as the 25 greatest athletes in the IHSAA's first 100 years.

And now let's take a stroll with them back through a lot of great triumphs, a few stinging disappointments and ultimately great memories for us all. Here are those 25 greatest, presented in the chronological order in which they played and with their high school graduation year noted.

Kenneth Ernest "Moco" Mercer, Albia, 1922.

He was a four-sport athlete, "perhaps the greatest athlete that Monroe County will ever produce," as it says in the historical museum in this south central Iowa town.

Kenneth Ernest Mercer grew up tough in the coal mining town, prefering to be barefooted whenever he could, usually carrying a slingshot and playing sports at every opportunity. He was a scrapper then as a young boy, later in high school and college, and for the rest of his life, actually. That's what his unusual nickname was all about. He picked it up in college.

The Albia High School yearbook from that era, "The Screech," notes that in his senior year of high school football, Mercer was "playing either quarter or fullback," and was "probably the star of the team. His exceptional ability to run, plunge, kick or pass made him a marked man in every game. Critics were unanimous in his praise."

He won All-State honors in both football and basketball.

He was captain of the Albia basketball team as a senior. "His rare dribbling, his speed and accurate passes and a thorough knowledge of the game marked him as one of the best," the yearbook noted. His "loss to Albia will be as keen in basketball as in football. This spring he will have ended three years of exceptional athletic service for his school."

He is also described as a good pole vaulter on Albia's earliest track teams. Mercer was also very involved in other school activities, performing in the play "Home Came Ted," being active in the Science Club and Hi-Y and serving as "athletic editor" of The Screech when he was a senior.

Interestingly, each senior's graduation photo in the yearbook was accompanied by a "motto," likely written by another member of the staff, and Mercer's was: "Would that men would know how truly great I am."

In the "Last Will and Testament" of the senior class, his classmates willed "Kenneth Mercer's ability to play everything to Fred 'Peck' Geneva," an underclassman who became another of Albia's great multi-sport athletes, according to Dave Paxton, the editor-publisher now of the Albia Union-Republican newspaper.

All of the above is a good deal more than Mercer's grown children have known about his early sports history.

"My dad never talked about any of his accomplishments in high school, or when he was playing at Simpson, either," said Melinda Mercer Blok, his daughter, who lives in Dubuque. "I do remember him telling how he probably never would have gone to college because he couldn't have afforded it, but some local men in Albia thought he should go. So evidently they raised some money and sent him to Simpson with some clothes they packed up in cardboard boxes and tied some rope around."

It didn't take long for the 5 ft., 9 in. 177-pound Mercer to make his mark at Simpson. He became the first star of the new Iowa Conference, in which 14 of the state's small colleges then competed.

Museum board member Sonny Williams said records indicate that Mercer won 17 letters at Simpson, excelling at football, basketball, wrestling, track and perhaps baseball. He was, as always, a feisty competitor.

In Des Moines Register sportswriter Buck Turnbull's 1961 book "The Iowa Conference Story," he writes that "after a rough basketball game at Parsons College, in which Mercer was ready to mix it up with the whole Parsons squad, his teammates tagged him with the nickname Moco from a Des Moines Register comic strip, 'Battling Moco.' "

When Mercer was inducted into the Register's Iowa Sports Hall of Fame in 1964, executive sports editor Leighton Housh wrote that "in four years of football at Simpson, Mercer scored more points, 348, than any Iowa college player ever has – or ever will." His last three years of football there, Simpson won two conference titles and tied for the other, with Mercer as a halfback, occasional passer and receiver, as well as a defensive back, place kicker and punter.

In the Turnbull history of the conference, he was described as "a drop-kicking artist," and he is quoted saying, "I used to stand on the 50 and drop kick over one goal, then turn and kick over the other. I also could hit a tub punting at 50 yards – worked hours at it and it paid off lots of times."

After Simpson, he played professionally for three or four years with the Frankford, Pennsylvania, Yellow Jackets, a forerunner of today's Philadelphia Eagles, and was paid $50 per game, his daughter said. Then he began a teaching and coaching career, first at Simpson as an assistant, then at Algona High School in northwest Iowa, then at Beloit College in Wisconsin, before he was hired in 1939 at the University of Dubuque.

He is probably remembered more widely today for his long and distinguished coaching career in nearly every sport at UD, where he served until his retirement in 1969. In those 30 years, his teams won 25 Iowa Conference team titles in football, basketball, wrestling, tennis, track and cross country. He also served as athletic director for 20 years.

When he retired as football coach in 1961, his fellow coaches in the conference presented him with a plaque still displayed at the university. It reads: "Moco Mercer – A great coach, a great friend. He won many – lost a few – enjoyed them all."

Mercer and his wife Helen, a native of Kellerton whom he met at Simpson, had daughter Melinda and son Mike, who became a placekicker in professional football for the Oakland Raiders and Minnesota Vikings. In 2005, he had retired and was living in Oregon.

Moco Mercer died in 1970 at the age of 66.

Nile Kinnick, Adel/Omaha Benson, 1936

Most people in Iowa today know that Nile Kinnick won college football's Heisman Trophy in 1939 for his All-American play with the University of Iowa Hawkeyes.

They also know that, in a tragedy that numbed the whole state, Kinnick died at only 24 years old on June 2, 1943. He was piloting a U.S. Navy Grumman Wildcat fighter plane on a training flight from the deck of a carrier in the Caribbean Sea. The plane's motor developed a serious oil leak and stalled. He made an emergency landing in the water off the coast of Venezuela, but Navy rescue teams were unable to find either him or the plane. Of course, most Iowans also recognize that Kinnick Stadium at his alma mater is named in his memory.

But before his collegiate glory, Kinnick also was an outstanding high school athlete – for three years at Adel High School, located 15 miles west of Des Moines, and then in his senior year for Benson High School in Omaha, Nebraska. The family moved there when his father Nile Sr., whose farm management career in the Adel area had been ruined by the Great Depression, landed a good job as an appraiser of farm property for the Federal Land Bank in Omaha.

Kinnick had a lineage of leadership. His mother Ada Frances Clarke Kinnick was the daughter of George W. Clarke, a Republican, who was governor of Iowa from 1913-1917. The Clarke surname became the middle name of Nile Jr., who was born July 9, 1918.

He was the oldest of three brothers, with Ben a year behind him and George eight years younger. They grew up living in the town of Adel, across the street from the school.

"We all started playing football and basketball together in about the second grade," said Randall Mortimer, 87-years old in 2005 and living in Ames, but a classmate and teammate of Nile Kinnick Jr. in Adel. "They had a barn there at their house in town, and Mr. Kinnick put two baskets up in the haymow. Every morning all winter long, we'd get up there before school and play. We'd start out with our sheepskin coats on and four-buckle overshoes, just to stay warm. Then as we'd start playing and got warmed up, we'd shed the coats and heavy clothes. We'd always put one of the littlest kids up in the cupola of the barn so he could see the schoolhouse. When he'd see the other kids starting to go in, then he'd yell to us and we'd break up the game and get over to school, just in time."

Nile Kinnick Sr., who had a degree in agronomy from Iowa State

College, where he also played football, headed a large-scale grain and livestock operation that included several farms.

"The Kinnicks were farmers, but Nile Sr. wasn't one to put on bibbed overalls and get out in the field and do the work," said Paul Baender, a retired University of Iowa English professor who edited a collection of more than 300 letters that Nile Kinnick Jr. wrote. They were published in a 1991 book "A Hero Perished – The Diary and Selected Letters of Nile Kinnick."

Baender noted that the family had tenants living on and working their farms.

"The Kinnicks owned a lot of land around there in the 1920s and early '30s," said Mortimer. "And they were pretty progressive. I think they had the first combine in that whole area. And they had a lot of cattle."

Meanwhile, by his seventh and eighth grade years, Nile Jr. was starting to receive a good deal of attention as an athlete. The Des Moines Register made mention of Nile leading the Adel Junior High football team through two undefeated seasons, and predicted he would be quarterbacking the Adel High School team before long, according to a family history compiled on the Internet by William Smith, a distant Kinnick relative in Kansas.

By the start of the high school football season in the fall of 1931, young Kinnick was indeed the starting quarterback for the Adel High Tigers – at 13 years old and about 120 pounds.

"There were four of us freshmen who made the starting line-up," said Mortimer. "Three of us – including Nile and me – all weighed about 120, and the fourth one was a little more mature and weighed a little more. But you can imagine, we got knocked around quite a bit playing varsity football.

"I don't remember for sure how the team did that year, maybe about 6 and 5 or so, but it seemed like we did all right for being so young. What I remember most is that we had an open date in that season, and it happened to fall right during pheasant hunting season in Iowa. So the coach let the players take a vote whether we wanted to schedule a game on that open date, or just skip it and go hunt pheasants. Unfortunately, we voted to add an extra game, and the coach scheduled us against Shenandoah on their home field. This was at a time when Shenandoah was ruling everything in southwest

Iowa. Well, on the first play of the game, I was playing defensive end and I ran into their backfield and somehow tripped up their back, and he went down for a loss. I think that was the last time we stopped them all day. On the next play, two of them ran right over me. And we wound up getting beat something like 60-0. We should have gone pheasant hunting."

In 1932, the sophomore year for Kinnick, Mortimer and the others, the team "got a little better," Mortimer recalled, and the Tiger fans started looking forward to the next two years.

Several of the boys were also good baseball players.

In the summer of 1932, or possibly 1933, Kinnick joined a bunch of other high school athletes from around the area west of Des Moines to play on an American Legion baseball team, since no high school baseball program was offered in the summer in those early years. Kinnick was a catcher on that team, and the star pitcher who threw to him was young Bob Feller from Van Meter, located just eight miles southeast of Adel.

"I didn't know Nile that well, since he was a couple of years older than I was," said Feller, who went on to pitching stardom with the Cleveland Indians and is a member of the Major League Baseball Hall of Fame. "My memory of him is more for his high school football and basketball, than in baseball. But he was a tough little guy, and quick."

Then came the magical 1933 football season when Kinnick, as a junior, led the powerhouse Tigers to an 11-0-1 record, outscoring opponents 393-29. The only blemish on an otherwise perfect season was an 18-18 tie with Guthrie Center. Ten of the victories were shutouts.

Kinnick was selected fifth team All-State. Family historian Smith quotes one newspaper report at the end of that season: "Kinnick, who directed the Adel team from the quarterback position, liked the rough going and he played fiercely in every tilt of a hard 12-game schedule. Kinnick was versatile and carried the ball brilliantly in the open field. His passing and punting figured prominently in every Adel game."

Adel fans claimed the mythical state championship after that season, and Kinnick and the other team members all signed an autograph football that is still displayed at Adel-DeSoto-Minburn High School in Adel.

In basketball, Kinnick was a leading scorer for Adel for three years, nd he was second team All-State in 1934 as a junior.

It had been quite a three years, and with his high school ccomplishments and what he did later, Kinnick indeed left a mark on his hometown.

Today's ADM High School is located on Nile Kinnick Drive. At he north end of town is Kinnick-Feller Riverside Park. And the school maintains a good collection of Kinnick biographical information on its Internet site.

But there is little mention anywhere of what the reaction was in Adel when the Kinnick family moved to Omaha in 1934. It meant that the community was losing one of its greatest athletes ever, right before his senior year in high school.

Surely there was sorrow, perhaps even shock. And yet, in that era, with the Great Depression raging, the economic calamity was so severe that it was not unusual for families to pick up and move when jobs became available elsewhere, and that was as true in families of great athletes as it was in all other families.

"Were we shocked? No, not really," said Mortimer. "Remember, that was during hard times. The Kinnicks and a lot of other farmers were going under at that time. The Kinnicks, with all those fat cattle, got caught at a time when the market bottomed out, and they couldn't get any price at all for them. A lot of people were moving around."

The Kinnicks actually landed pretty well when Nile Sr. got the farm appraisal job with the Federal Land Bank.

It was the fall of 1934 when the Kinnick boys enrolled at Benson High School, and Nile graduated in the spring of 1936.

Dean Westergaard, an advertising executive who lives in Adel and has become the unofficial local keeper of Kinnick lore, said Kinnick completed his athletic eligibility in the 1934-35 school year. But he took some additional high school courses in the 1935-36 school year "as sort of a fifth year senior" before he graduated.

"From what some of his old teammates have told me," Westergaard said, "Nile's parents thought that if he graduated in 1935 and started college then, he'd be awfully young, since he had a July birthday would have just turned 17 years old. They all knew he was going to play college football, and they were worried about whether he'd be ready. So they talked to the people at Benson High School, and they advised the Kinnicks to let him kind of string out his course load over those two years, and then he'd have a little extra time to mature and get stronger."

Of course, Kinnick, who was a brilliant student, easily met not only every athletic challenge in Omaha but also every academic requirement.

After his senior football season in the fall of '34, he was named All-State and All-Omaha for his play at halfback, according to Smith's family history. He was also All-State in basketball in the late winter of '35, after helping the Benson Bunnies reach the Nebraska state tournament.

That means among all of Kinnick's other honors, he could claim the distinction of being one of the few athletes ever to be named All-State in two sports in two states!

Little wonder why. In a 1991 story in the Omaha World-Herald, Lloyd Grim, who had been one of Kinnick's football teammates at Benson High, told columnist Michael Kelly: "I can see him right now. Football practice is over, and it's dark, and he's standing out there punting. He'd punt 25, 30, 40 or 50 times after practice. The reason Nile was such a champion is that he worked at it."

Kinnick graduated third in a class of 199 at Benson High, according to columnist Kelly, and he was popular enough to be chosen master of ceremonies at the senior banquet.

Of course, Kinnick gained his greatest fame while at the University of Iowa, where he enrolled in the fall of 1936, and much more is known about him as a collegian than as a high school athlete.

He was 5 ft., 8 in. tall and 170 pounds at Iowa, but the way most teammates and even opponents remember him, his size didn't matter because he was all heart on the football field, the basketball court and baseball diamond. He played football all four years, basketball his first two years and baseball only as a freshman. In that era of intercollegiate athletics, freshmen could not play on varsity teams.

In his sophomore and junior seasons, the football team was a woeful 2-13-1. Kinnick, a halfback on offense and a defensive back, was all-conference as a sophomore and repeated in his junior year despite playing part of the year on a broken ankle that he taped and ignored.

But in his senior season, in 1939, with new coach Dr. Eddie Anderson on the sidelines, the Hawkeyes went 6-1-1. The team became known as the "Ironmen," because nearly all the players were on both offense and defense. Indeed, Kinnick played nearly every minute, as he was also the drop-kicker, punter and punt returner. He was the statistical leader in nearly every category and was involved in 107 of the team's 130 points. He set a record for pass interceptions during a career, and it stood for 50 years.

He was picked on 12 All-American teams, and besides winning the Heisman as college football's outstanding player that season, he was also named the top male athlete in the U.S. – amateur or professional.

For Kinnick and the team, it had been a "two-month charge to immortality," the Des Moines Register reported, and "the nation acclaimed them."

Kinnick, who majored in "commerce" and won Phi Beta Kappa honors for his academic work, turned down the opportunity to play professional football, choosing instead to go to law school at the university.

Among the most insightful resources about him in his college and young adult years is a 2003 book "Tales from the Iowa Sidelines" by retired Des Moines Register sporstwriter Ron Maly. He portrays Kinnick as a brilliant and complex young man.

Maly notes that Kinnick was raised in the Christian Science Church, a faith with pacifist leanings, although not as much as the Quakers. While Kinnick was not particularly active in the church while at Iowa, old college friends told Maly, he did follow the news closely and was concerned about the threat of war. But, then, nearly all college men were worried. They knew who would be fighting the war if indeed the U.S. was drawn into it.

Many people can quote Kinnick's speech when he accepted the Heisman trophy in New York City in late 1939 – two years before World War II began – especially his concluding thought: "...I thank God I was warring on the gridirons of the Midwest and not on the battlefields of Europe. I can speak confidently and positively that the players of this country would much more, much rather struggle and fight to win the Heisman award than the

Croix de Guerre."

His speech is generally regarded as one of the best ever given during the Heisman ceremonies. When you look back on it with an understanding of Kinnick's religious tradition, knowledge of his concern about the war and then think about his death in military service three years later, it makes the dramatic conclusion to his speech all the more powerful and poignant.

"Some people back then might have branded him an isolationist," Maly told me. "I think some of those guys who covered his speech – some of those New York guys – wrote that Kinnick may have had isolationist views." Maly said from what he learned in his research and interviews, "I don't feel Kinnick wanted to go into the military, but he felt he had to."

During the U.S. presidential campaign of 1940, Kinnick – then apparently a law student at the University of Iowa – went to Iowa Falls when Republican candidate Wendell Wilkie was making an appearance aboard a whistle-stop campaign tour on a train. Maly learned from former Des Moines Register political writer George Mills that Kinnick introduced Wilkie to the crowd that day. Wilkie had been an isolationist, but by the time the Republicans nominated him, he had started to broaden his view. And two years later, after he had been defeated by President Franklin D. Roosevelt, he was fully supporting the war effort and stood with Roosevelt in advocating continued international involvement when and if peace resumed.

It is well documented that Kinnick, in that time period, was telling friends and family that he might eventually like to run for the U.S. Senate, or some other high office. It was a popular idea. Right after he won the Heisman in 1939, the Marion Sentinel, a newspaper in the east suburb of Cedar Rapids, endorsed Kinnick for president of the U.S. – in the 1956 election! Sports Illustrated magazine, which included that delightful political vignette in a 1987 profile of Kinnick, noted that the 1956 election would have been the first one in which he would have been eligible for the presidency, with its 35-year-old minimum age requirement.

"He captured the imagination of an entire nation," Maly wrote in the introduction to his book. "In my conversations with those who knew him, played with him and played against him, I am convinced Kinnick was destined for greatness beyond the football field. He remains the most

376

dynamic player in the 113-year history of football at the university."

When it appeared in the summer of 1941 that World War II was looming, Kinnick gave up his law school dream to enlist in the Naval Air Corps Reserve. He was called to active duty on December 10, 1941, three days after Pearl Harbor was bombed by the Japanese, bringing the U.S. into the war. A 1948 book "The Big Nine" by Howard Roberts quotes Kinnick as he was leaving Iowa City to report for military training, "I would be lacking in appreciation for all America has done for me, did I not offer what little I had to her."

He was indeed as eloquent – in speeches, in interviews and even in letters to friends and family – as you might guess from his comments here.

Paul Baender, the retired University of Iowa professor who edited the collection of Kinnick letters for a 1991 book, said the star athlete was "a very prolific letter writer. But, remember, this was before the time when people would pick up a telephone and call somebody long distance just to visit."

The Kinnick letters are still available today in the Special Collections area of the university's library.

"The letters deal with his boyhood and high school years only in passing," Baender said. "The correspondence doesn't really pick up until he's in college and a young adult."

Baender told the Omaha newspaper's Michael Kelly that in Kinnick's letters to his father Nile Sr., he would often address him as "Gus," an affectionate nickname he'd given his dad. He typically signed them "SB," which referred to the nickname the father had for Nile Jr.: "Sonny Boy."

Kinnick never married, although the collection of letters indicate he had a serious romance or two.

In 1996, deep-sea divers, using the advanced technology and diving methods of the modern era, located what is believed to be his plane on the floor of the Caribbean Sea. There was some discussion about retrieving it for a memorial adjacent to the stadium in Iowa City. However, it was ultimately decided to leave it in the waters, presumably as Kinnick's tomb.

The tragedy of his early death is still regarded by older Iowans, who lived through it, as one of the biggest heartbreaks in state history.

But it wasn't the only one in the Kinnick family.

Younger brother Ben became a bomber pilot in World War II, and he was killed in the South Pacific in 1944. The youngest brother George died in the mid-1980s of heart disease. Nile Sr. outlived the rest of his family, dying at 96 in 1989.

Bob Feller, Van Meter, 1937

In the Iowa high school spring baseball season of 1936, pitcher Bob Feller of Van Meter was throwing fastballs right past boys from places like DeSoto, Adel, Dexter and Earlham.

Two months later, in the summer of 1936, he stepped up to a higher level of competition, in fact it was the highest level – Major League Baseball.

In his first professional appearance, on July 6, 1936, the 17-year-old schoolboy from Iowa took the mound for the Cleveland Indians against the visiting St. Louis Cardinals in an exhibition game. He pitched three innings. The St. Louis hitters didn't fare any better against him than the kids from the small towns back home had in the spring. Feller struck out eight of the nine Cardinals he faced that day, including all of their heaviest hitters.

In later games that summer and early fall, he struck out 15 St. Louis Browns and 17 Philadelphia Athletics. He won five games and lost three. He became a national sensation.

And when that season came to an end in late September, Feller hurried right back to Van Meter, then a country town of about 300 people, located 20 miles west of Des Moines.

After all, he was getting a late start – for his senior year of high school! And the 17 students in his class had elected him its president.

"But Florence Wishmier did all the work," the 85-year-old Feller recalled in 2004, while talking at the Bob Feller Museum in Van Meter. "She should have been the president."

When Feller, Wishmier and the other students in the Van Meter High School class of 1937 graduated the next spring, NBC Radio did a live, nationwide broadcast of the ceremonies.

Nearly everyone knows what happened after that. Feller went on to a brilliant career pitching for the Cleveland Indians, continuing through the 1956 season.

It was a career that had a storybook start and, for a long time, became more amazing with each passing year.

Imagine this: In the 1939, '40 and '41 seasons – when he was between 21 and 23 years old – Feller's won-loss pitching records were 24-9, 27-11 and 25-13. Sportswriters were having contests to come up with colorful nicknames for him: "Rapid Robert," "Bullet Bob" and "The Heater from Van Meter."

With three such exceptional seasons in a row, what kind of success must he and Cleveland fans been looking forward to in the years just ahead?

What they got, instead, was World War II.

After Pearl Harbor was bombed, Feller enlisted, spent nearly four years in the U.S. Navy and completely missed the major league seasons from 1942 until 1944. He served as chief on an anti-aircraft gun crew on the U.S.S. Alabama during heavy fighting in the Pacific. He never whined about missing three baseball seasons in which he would have been in his prime physically. He never portrayed himself as a hero. On the contrary, he has said repeatedly in interviews, "The heroes are the ones who didn't come home."

He got back from service in time to go 5-3 in the 1945 season, and then in the next two, he was 26-15 and 20-11. He had good seasons the rest of the way, too. In 1962, he was inducted into baseball's Hall of Fame.

"The greatest in my era," a fellow Hall of Famer, the legendary slugger Ted Williams of the Boston Red Sox, said of Feller as a pitcher.

My goodness, what must the kids who were playing with and against him at Van Meter High in the early to mid-1930s have thought of him?

"Well, playing outfield, you didn't ever have much to do when Bob was pitching," said Harold Bailey, 87 years old in 2005 and living in Adel, a teammate in both baseball and basketball. "Of course, he had a fastball that was unbelievable for somebody his age. And his curve ball was pretty good, too. There were a lot of kids scared to bat against him. He usually had pretty good control, but when he did throw a little wild, it'd scare them even more."

Feller grew up on a farm two miles east of Van Meter, up a hill from the Raccoon River.

Baseball was so popular that there were ball diamonds popping up everywhere – even at community gathering points in the countryside. Feller's father Bill Feller built one of those rural ballparks and organized a team called "Oak View."

"I remember that ball park was up on a little hill and looked out over the farms," Bob Feller said. "It had been made with about 20 wood posts, with chicken wire strung between them. There was a pop stand and outhouses down the left and right field lines. I think Dad charged 25 cents per carload for fans. It was a 'Field of Dreams' in a way, built 50 or 60 years before they ever thought of the one in Dyersville."

Feller started playing for that "farm team" as a boy, and eventually pitched for it. He may have inherited some of his pitching ability, and probably received some coaching and encouragement, from his maternal grandfather, who had been a pitcher. He remembers "starting to throw curve balls when I was eight years old," which probably was not the best thing for the development of his arm.

That farm was a great place for Bob and his younger sister Marguerite to grow up, he said. His father was an active farmer, and his mother, Lena, was a school teacher and nurse at different times in her life. Economic times were tough, of course, but they were tough on everybody, not just the Feller family.

In the summers of 1931, '32, '33 and '34, Feller played American Legion baseball. The first two of those years, when he was 12 and 13 years old, he played for the Legion team from Adel. It was while he was playing there that Nile Kinnick, an Adel athlete who would go on to win college football's Heisman trophy at the University of Iowa, was one of his catchers. In 1933, Feller joined a team in Highland Park on the north side of Des Moines, and in 1934 he played for the Legion team in Valley Junction, which is now West Des Moines.

In the summer of 1935, he pitched for a team sponsored by the Iowa Farmers Union Insurance Company from Des Moines, and they played all over the state against men's teams. Stories in the Des Moines Register archives say during that summer, Feller averaged 19 strikeouts per game!

Word spread fast.

On July 22, 1935, Cyril Slapnicka, a native of Cedar Rapids who was a scout with the Cleveland Indians, "strode out through the wheat on the

Feller farm, where Bob was driving the tractor," according to the Register. He signed the 16-year-old to a professional baseball contract, "for $1 and an autographed baseball," according to a history compiled for ESPN.com by writer Nick Acocella.

Feller was to wait until the following summer, 1936, and then report to the Fargo-Moorhead team in the Class D Northern League.

But we're getting ahead of our story here about Bob Feller, the high school athlete in Van Meter.

His high school sports career started in the 1933-34 school year. The only sports offered were baseball in the spring and fall, and basketball during the winter. The coach for both sports was Leland McCosh, who was hoping to lead a rebuilding effort, as the earlier Bulldog teams had been struggling.

A decade previously, Van Meter had a good run in basketball, playing in a makeshift gym on the second story of the Chevrolet garage in a building owned by Feller's father.

"That was quite a gym," Bob recalled. "The ceiling was only 13 feet high, and it had support poles right out in the middle of the floor. The Van Meter guys learned how to be running down the floor, grab one of those poles, do a 180- or 360-degree spin, catch a pass and go for the basket. We played up there, too, when we were little guys, and I always had a basket in the barn at home and a couple of them outdoors in the barnyard."

By the time Feller was in high school, Van Meter was playing in a new gym at the school.

He was "a benchwarmer" in his freshman year, but he "grew real fast when I was 14 and 15" and was a starter as a sophomore and junior. He reached 5 ft., 11 in. and was well-built, and he became the starting center. By that time, Van Meter seldom lost.

He said he "was never much of a shot in basketball, although I was okay at free-throws. I think the most points I ever made in a game were 13, but it was usually down around eight or nine. I could rebound pretty fair, and I could always throw the ball well, getting it to my teammates."

At tournament time in 1936, Van Meter had lost only a game or two. "I think we beat Perry twice in regular season games, but they beat us in the finals of the county tournament, if I remember correctly," Feller said.

Feller was at center, Harold Bailey and Carroll Padley were the guards, and alternating at the two forward positions were Kelly Gutshall, Don Fisher and Max England.

The team went on a run through the sectional, district and substate tournaments and in a game at Marshalltown, they beat Lamoille to qualify for Van Meter's first-ever appearance in the state tournament, which was played at Drake University in Des Moines.

"What I remember most about that game at Drake is that I was sick," said Feller. "I was running a 102 degree temperature, so I doubt if I played very well."

Logan beat Van Meter in the first round.

Meanwhile, the folks in Lamoille were upset about Feller being in the Van Meter line-up.

"They'd found out I had signed a professional baseball contract, so they complained to the Iowa High School Athletic Association," Feller said. "They didn't think I should be eligible to play."

He remembers "a real serious meeting" at IHSAA headquarters in Des Moines. "Our Van Meter superintendent, O.E. Lester, Coach McCosh, Dad and I had to go in there, and I think we had to answer questions from the board members. They'd told us ahead of time how upset they were, so we took all the trophies with us, just in case we had to give them back."

The IHSAA executive secretary then was George A. Brown, and he and board member O.C. "Pop" Varner, the superintendent and well-known coach from Diagonal, led the interrogation.

"What they decided," Feller said, "was that it was okay for me to be playing as long as I had not yet played a professional game, and that wasn't going to happen until that summer of 1936."

So the Van Meter delegation took the trophies back home and Feller prepared for his last season of high school sports – spring baseball.

"From my first year of high school baseball, I pitched most of the time and played a little at shortstop," Feller recalled. "You know, I really don't remember what our record was, but I think we won most of the time."

His catcher, for most of those high school games, was Kelly Gutshall.

Late in that spring season of his junior year, the team entered the tournament series and "I pitched five games in eight days," he said. When they were finally eliminated in the district tournament by Des Moines North, Feller's arm was more than tired, it was sore – and he was supposed to be reporting soon for the start of his professional pitching career.

Cyril Slapnicka, the scout who had signed him, by then had become general manager of the Cleveland Indians. He manipulated the contract that had called for Feller to report to Fargo-Moorhead and took him instead directly to Cleveland. They wound up in a fight with the Fargo-Moorhead management, which took their case to the commissioner of baseball, Judge Kenesaw Mountain Landis. The commissioner, after talking to Feller's father, ruled the boy could indeed report to Cleveland.

"The plan was to get me there so the Indians' trainers could work on me, and then I was going to play some semi-pro ball around Cleveland," Feller said.

But then came his initial appearance in the exhibition game against the St. Louis Cardinals, and the rest is history.

So, what was it like when Feller went back to Van Meter High School late that fall, to start his senior year? It was no problem academically for him. He'd been able to keep pace with assignments during the month of classes he had missed, because the Indians hired a tutor who worked with him. They did the same thing when he left early at the end of the school year to go to 1937 spring training.

He and his sister Marguerite generally still rode the school bus back and forth to town, the Des Moines Register reported, and he often wore his Cleveland ball cap with his blue jeans.

But it did get a little crazy during that fall and winter when reporters from newspapers and magazines across the country began visiting Van Meter. They chronicled the meetings of the senior class officers. They reported how Bob had been in the Glee Club "even though I couldn't carry a tune in a bucket," he recalled many years later.

"It never got too bad with the media that year, though," Feller said. "Our superintendent Mr. Lester pretty well kept them under control."

The presence of reporters and photographers from such respected publications as the Saturday Evening Post, and the radio personalities and technicians who came from NBC Radio to broadcast his graduation, helped the townsfolk of Van Meter finally realize just how big the Bob Feller story had become.

"When Bob first left for Cleveland that summer of 1936, I don't think people here really understood what a feat he was doing," said Harold Bailey, the old teammate. "They knew he was good, and they knew major league scouts had been in to see him play in high school and Legion ball. But when he first left, people here didn't think he was going to be playing with the Indians right away."

Rather, they thought he was going to play semi-professional ball, then probably spend a few years in the minors.

"When he started having that success so quickly, then people began to see what was happening," said Bailey.

Feller was not allowed to play high school sports during his senior year, but he worked out regularly. He remembers "doing a lot of pheasant and duck hunting with Sec Taylor," who was the sports editor of the Des Moines Register and obviously recognized what a good story young Feller was becoming. Taylor, whose column was called "Sittin' in with the Athletes,' wrote frequently about Feller for the next three decades.

By the late 1930s, the town of Van Meter began saluting its most famous native son at the end of the baseball seasons with "Bob Feller Homecoming Days." It was typical for Iowa's governor and one or more congressmen to attend, as well as other major league players with Iowa ties.

As he became more affluent, Feller built his parents a beautiful new home on the farm. And he would turn heads when he'd drive into town in a big new convertible, dressed a whole lot snappier than he ever had when he was growing up in Van Meter.

His occasional brusque manner and blunt speech have caused him some trouble through the years, including in a 2003 fuss with Bernie Saggau, the executive director of the Iowa High School Athletic Association. It was a disagreement over the way Feller handled requests from IHSAA staff members to interview him on video for the new Iowa Hall of Pride. After sharp remarks between the two of them were reported in the Des Moines Register and other media, the newspaper asked in a headline whether Feller was a "prince or patoot." Both men apologized and laughed about it later, and Feller indeed sat for an extended interview. He was happy to do what he could to support high school sports, he said.

And how does he look back on his own experience at Van Meter High School?

"You know, we had a lot of fun, a whole lot of camaraderie," he said. "And I feel like we always had pretty good coaching.

"When I think about growing up back in that era, the main sports when we were little were horseracing, horseshoe pitching, boxing and baseball. There weren't all the organized teams and program for younger kids like there are today. So it was really big for us when we got to high school and could play basketball and baseball against other schools. I think that's one reason we enjoyed it so much."

Feller and his first wife Virginia raised three sons in Cleveland, Ohio. One of them, Steve, became an architect and designed the Feller Museum in Van Meter.

Bob and his second wife, Anne, now live in a suburb outside Cleveland, where in mid-2004 life was good.

"Anne and I are collaborating on a book," he said.

No, he explained, it would not be about his baseball career, which has been covered in five earlier books by various authors.

"This one will be a children's book," Feller said. "We're calling it, 'How to be a Cat' by Felix Feller, as told to Bob and Anne Feller."

He has continued his association with the Cleveland Indians since his playing career ended. He has done some coaching during spring training and clinics, and continues to make public appearances around the country and handles public relations assignments from the team. "I really don't do anything for the Indians now," he said with a wry smile, "but I still get a check every two weeks, year 'round."

He returns to Van Meter several times a year to hang out at his excellent museum. He often brings other old baseball greats with him. The last four years, he has given the "Bob Feller Pitching Award" to the top pitcher in each of Iowa high school baseball's four classes, in a nice ceremony held at the museum after the state tournament is completed.

And he enjoys knowing that since 1990, Van Meter teams have been playing their home games at the "Bob Feller Athletic Complex."

It's indeed a big story that happened in the little town.

It was in the late 1970s when Bill Clark, then a veteran scout for the Cincinnati Reds, reminded me that the Feller story is still very much alive in the hearts and minds of baseball people.

"For somebody in my business, when you're driving down Interstate 80 and see that 'Van Meter' sign, it always gets your attention," Clark said. "There've been several times I've driven in there, looked around and thought to myself, 'Hmmm – I wonder if there's another fastball coming up here.'"

Jack Dittmer, Elkader, 1946

He was 10 years old when they stuck him in rightfield for an American Legion baseball game, in which nearly all of his teammates were high school boys.

They already knew by then around the northeast Iowa town of Elkader, pop. 1,500 then and now, that Jack Dittmer was going to be an exceptional athlete.

And indeed he became one. He was a four-year starter in three sports in his high school years in the mid-1940s.

He was a feared running back and receiver in football, and he also drop-kicked the extra points and field goals on a team that won all 19 of its games his last two and one-half seasons. He scored more than 1,000 points in his basketball career at a time when the team averaged only 30 to 40 per game, plus they lost only two games his last two seasons. In baseball, he pitched or played shortstop and led his teammates to the spring state tournament in his junior year.

He turned down offers from major league baseball scouts in his senior year, choosing instead to accept a football scholarship at the University of Iowa. As a Hawkeye, he won nine letters – four in football, four in baseball and one in basketball after he decided to go out for that sport when he was a senior.

Then he played 10 years of professional baseball, including five years in the majors with the Boston Braves, Milwaukee Braves and finally the

386

Detroit Tigers.

Around Elkader at the beginning of the new century, most people are either unaware of his exceptional career in athletics, or they know it so well that it's seldom a point of conversation. In 2005, most simply thought of the 76-year-old Dittmer as one of the community's most loyal fans of high school sports, and maybe that's why Jack Dittmer Field at Central of Elkader High School is named after him. Others know he's a big fan of the Iowa Hawkeyes, since he is generally wearing a Hawkeye jacket and ball cap, the latter covering his trademark flat-top haircut. And many just think of him as "the car dealer," which he has been in the community since the 1950s.

It was while he was playing professional baseball that he went to work in the off-seasons for his father's Dittmer Motor Co., a Studebaker dealership. Not many major league baseball players today would do that, but they're all making a good deal more money than the $13,000 per year that was Dittmer's highest salary as a player. He retired from baseball after the 1959 season. When his father died of a stroke in 1962, Jack took over the car business and turned it into a Chrysler dealership. In 1985, he sold the company to Dave Brown, who renamed it Brown Sales & Leasing. Dittmer has worked for Brown ever since, now selling General Motors, Ford, Chrysler and Dodge vehicles at what is the only dealership in the community.

"Jack is a pretty modest, low-key guy," said Larry Stone, a writer who lives in the Elkader area. "He doesn't flaunt his athletic accomplishments. He likes kids – especially the athletes – and he's one of the regulars at all the high school games. He likes to chat with the athletes, especially after they've graduated and then come back to town to visit. They all like stopping in to see him. But my hunch would be that a lot of the newcomers around Elkader might not have a clue about Jack the baseball-football-basketball star."

Dittmer looks back on his high school sports career with genuine fondness.

"I had a good time wherever I played in sports, but those high school years were probably as good or better than what I experienced in college or in pro ball," he said. "We didn't have a lot of players in Elkader, so we really had to learn to play together. I think what helped us more than anything else was the fact that we had a couple of coaches early on who taught us the fundamentals of the sports, and that was a real break for us."

He recalled two personal highlights.

"In football, when I was a sophomore, we won our last three games of the season, and that started a streak of wins that was up to 19 when I graduated and went on up to 44 or 45," Dittmer said. "The game that started the streak was against Postville, which was always our biggest rival. We were behind 7-6 real late in the game and we had the ball deep in their territory, but they dug in and were holding us. On fourth down and 15 to go, we decided I'd try to drop kick a field goal. So I grabbed the ball, aimed at the right goal post, dropped and kicked it – and it ticked the left goal post as it went through. We won 9-7, and that's how the streak started!"

Those next two seasons, his junior and senior years, Elkader's football team "dominated everybody," he said.

They were nearly as dominating in basketball, too, even though small schools like Elkader (there were 21 students in Dittmer's graduating class) were thrown right in with the large schools in the one-class basketball tournament. Their only losses in those two years were to Dubuque Senior in the finals of the district tournament in his junior year and to Marshalltown in the substate tournament in his senior year.

Dittmer was 6 ft., 1 in. and 130 pounds when he was playing center, and he picked up the nickname "Skinny" that followed him on into college. He said his best game was probably in his senior year in a 33-31 victory over Loras Academy in a district tournament game – he scored 21 points.

He added some bulk by the time he became a starting pass receiver on the University of Iowa football team, playing at 165 pounds through most of his four years with the Hawkeyes. He was known for his great hands and good speed after he caught the ball.

"Despite his light weight, Dittmer never backed away from a collision on the football field," wrote Ron Maly in a story in 1988 when Dittmer was inducted into the Des Moines Register's Iowa Sports Hall of Fame. "Following a rare Iowa victory over Ohio State in 1948, Dittmer was asked about a run-in with the Buckeyes' 220-pound Joe Whisler. Although Whisler had steamrolled him, Dittmer said: 'Did you see me take him on? I wonder if he's out of the hospital yet.' "

He was also known for his competitive spirit in his four years with the Hawkeye baseball team.

Ditto for when he decided to go out for the basketball team for the first time when he was a senior. "You know, basketball was really my favorite sport, and I had missed playing it," Dittmer said. "In that senior year, I had the time, and I wanted to see how far I could go."

He and his wife Darlene have two daughters and a son, and now six grandchildren.

John Estes Jr., Des Moines North, 1946

He was "probably the best athlete the city had produced," the Des Moines Register said in a 1995 story about the high school sports career that "Johnny" Estes had at Des Moines North High School 50 years earlier.

Estes "played four sports better than anyone – ever – at North High," the late Bill Reichardt told me. "He was going to be the star for Dr. Eddie Anderson, the football coach at Iowa. He had planned for John to be the first black quarterback in all of the history of college football."

But tragedy struck.

In the summer of 1948, between his sophomore and junior years at the university, Estes was working as a lifeguard at the Good Park swimming pool in Des Moines. During a break from work, he and several of his fellow lifeguards were playing a pick-up basketball game on some adjacent courts. Estes went up for a shot, was undercut and came down hard on his left shoulder and the left side of his head.

"Right at first, I just thought I broke my left arm," he said.

But he quickly realized that he couldn't move below the waist, and "come to find out, I was paralyzed." Twelve days later, the paralysis had moved up nearly to his neck. He was totally immobile for seven months, before the paralysis retreated to his waist and settled in permanently there. Ultimately, it was determined that the sixth and seventh cervical vertebrae in his back had been crushed in the fall.

"I went through all the psychological trauma that anybody would go through," Estes said. "I realized that I'd never play any more sports. The only thing I really wanted to do was to be able to take care of myself, and not have to have someone helping me do everything."

Johnny Estes still had the heart, courage and tenacity of a great athlete. He took on the biggest challenge of his life like it was an athletic opponent. And he won.

After two years of hospitalization and therapy, which Coach Anderson arranged at University Hospitals in Iowa City, Estes came home. He was up and walking, albeit with the help of crutches. A year later, he needed only one crutch. The paralysis remained below the waist from the spine injury – he wore corrective shoes to keep his ankles from turning – but he was up and on his way. He'd use his phenomenal upper body strength to carry, swing and drag the lower half of his body.

He resumed his college education, taking courses at Drake University in Des Moines, and then decided he would follow his father and grandfather into the funeral business. He enrolled at the Kansas City College of Mortuary Science, graduated in 1952, then took advanced courses for funeral directors in facial reconstruction. When he returned to Des Moines, John Sr. renamed the business – Estes & Son Funeral Home.

John Estes Jr. went on to become one of the most influential citizens in Des Moines. He was actively involved in the National Association for the Advancement of Colored People, the National Council of Christians and Jews, the Des Moines Chamber of Commerce, Republican politics (although he has also supported many Democrats) and served as a trustee of Simpson College. When the capital city was in racial turmoil in the late 1960s, Estes walked the streets of the inner city with Des Moines Mayor Tom Urban, reassuring people that they'd be safe and their grievances would be heard.

He helped his friend Bill Reichardt in the formation and operation of the Little All-American Football League, an answer to the lack of junior high sports programs in Des Moines. Estes was also involved in the management of the Des Moines Warriors, a semi-professional football team in the mid-1960s.

Meanwhile, he and his wife Elaine Graham Estes, who served as director of the Des Moines Public Library in her 39-year career, became social and cultural leaders in Des Moines, too, with friends stretching across nearly every sociological line you could draw. People often assume they are related to opera singer and native Iowan Simon Estes, and while they are not, they've often been involved in the same community and state projects. John and Elaine Estes have lived the past 40 years in a large, stately brick home, built in 1869, that is just up a hill north from downtown, with a gorgeous view of the city.

None of John Estes' prominence during his career came as any surprise to those who knew him at Des Moines North from 1943-46, where besides all his sports glory, he served as vice-president of the student council. The yearbook in his senior year described him as "an athlete, a scholar and a gentleman."

His family had moved from Joplin, Missouri, in 1937, after his father bought the Wilson Funeral Home in Des Moines. He grew up playing "all the common sports" in his neighborhood, and by the time he was in ninth grade, word had spread about him to the coaches at North, which in that era was in a perpetual battle with East High for athletic supremacy in the city. At that time, even though ninth graders were in junior high in Des Moines, they were still eligible for high school sports competition, and Estes got some playing time that year at North in both basketball and baseball. From his sophomore year on, he was generally a starter in all four sports – football, basketball, baseball and track, even though the latter two sports were both conducted in the spring. In the summer he played more baseball, tennis and golf.

He grew to 5 ft., 10 in. and 165 pounds, and he was an All-City and All-State selection in football and basketball his last two years.

"I guess the honors came quickest for me in football," Estes said. "I started out as a quarterback in high school, but then they moved me to running back. I enjoyed basketball, even though I never scored more than about eight points a game – I was more of an assist guy and defensive player. But my favorite sport was always baseball. I probably got that from my dad, because he'd been a professional player early in his career – at the AAA level in the old Negro League. The next step up for him would have been the Kansas City Monarchs at the big league level."

Johnny Estes had great coaches at North High. Francis X. Cretzmeyer, who would later coach track for years at the University of Iowa, was coaching North's track, basketball and baseball teams, and assisting with football. The head football coach was Arden McClain, who'd "been there for years and years," said Estes. "He was a regimentator. It was always 'Be on time! Do what you're supposed to do!' He cracked the whip on us."

Those coaches got results, too. In the Estes era, the North High Polar Bears – in their distinctive pink and green uniforms – dominated the other schools in the Des Moines area. Alas, they never did very well in tournament competition. "It seemed like we could never get out of the substate," Estes said.

In the rivalry between North and East, he was a marked man by his senior year.

"I remember East had this big pep rally, and they had a big casket they carried into it, and they had my name all over it," Estes said. "Mike Augustine, the coach over there at East, made them get rid of it."

When North and East would play football, "the game would always be at Drake Stadium, and there wouldn't be a seat left," he said.

There were also some huge battles with Dowling High School, which was then a Catholic school for boys only, located one block west of North High in the inner city. "Dowling had Jerry Groom back in that time, and we always had trouble handling him," Estes said. Groom went on to become a consensus All-American center for Notre Dame.

Besides playing the other Des Moines schools, North High would travel for games in Fort Dodge, Mason City and Waterloo.

"Sometimes when we were traveling, especially if we were trying to get something to eat in a smaller town, we'd run into places where they said they wouldn't let us black players eat," Estes said. "I can still remember Coach Cretzmeyer telling restaurant owners, 'Yeah? Well, we'll all be leaving if we can't all sit down and eat together.' And a few times we didn't eat."

There was probably also some racial discrimination in the fact that Estes was not recruited by major colleges.

"I think the only schools that recruited me really were the black universities," he said. "I remember being contacted by Howard University in Washington, D.C. But there was a group of three professional men in the black community in Des Moines, and they always did a lot to support black athletes at both Drake and Iowa. They were Archie Alexander, who was an engineer; James Morris, who was a lawyer and published the Iowa Bystander newspaper, and Dr. William Ritchey, a dentist. They were insisting I should go to Iowa and walk-on, and in fact, Archie and my dad took me over there an enrolled me. So that freshman year, I was technically a walk-on, although I always told people I was more of a 'demanded walk-on.' "

As a freshman in the fall of 1946, Estes was on the Hawkeyes' scout team. But as a sophomore, Eddie Anderson started him at defensive safety and he was the third team quarterback.

Would he indeed have become the starter at quarterback, had the spinal injury not occurred in the pick-up basketball game?

"Well, maybe," Estes said. "Eddie was going from the T formation to the single wing, and I think he had me in mind to be the tailback. In that single wing, your tailback is like a quarterback – doing all the passing, the handoffs and all of that. But I never spent a lot of time worrying about whether I was going to be the first black in that position. I just wanted to play somewhere. I think there was a black fellow who was a second string quarterback at Indiana about that same time. I don't know whatever became of him." After the injury, his competitive spirit undoubtedly saved his life.

He was honored for that spirit in 1979 when the City of Des Moines named the Good Park basketball courts after him.

But Estes, 76 years old in 2005, said there's something he values even more than his tenacity. "The most important thing to me was being able to meet so many different people," he said, "and a lot of those I met became everlasting friends."

Bernie Bennett, Mason City, 1949

In a city where high school sports have a very rich heritage – and have been especially strong in the last two decades – one of the community's best athletes ever is not at all well-known by most current fans.

He is Bernie Bennett, 72 years old in 2005 and retired in Shawnee Mission, Kansas, after a career as a high school and elementary teacher, coach and referee in the Kansas City area.

But he was the talk of Mason City in the late 1940s, when he was a two-time All-State player in both football and basketball for the Mason City

High School Mohawks. And, actually, baseball may have been his best sport.

In January of 2000, when the Mason City Globe-Gazette picked the "North Iowa Athlete of the Century," Bennett was one of the three finalists, all Mason City High alumni. The newspaper named 1980s wrestler Tim Krieger, a three-time state champion, as the top athlete, and 1950s track man Bill Woodhouse as the other finalist. But Bennett was clearly more of an all-around athlete than the other two.

Another great athlete for the Mohawks, Dean Oliver, who graduated in 1997, received strong consideration but his focus in high school was more on one sport, basketball. And if athletes playing into the new century had been considered, certainly Jeff Horner, a 2002 graduate, who had an exceptional four-sport career, would have been high on the newspaper's list, as he is on the Centennial Honor Roll here.

Bernie Bennett?

"I would say that he was probably the best athlete I have ever seen," Eddie Kline, a three-time state wrestler champion himself, said of Bennett to the Globe-Gazette. "He could throw that ball from his knees down to second base – just a shot. Absolutely a wonderful person, as well as a great athlete." Duane Jewell, another outstanding Mason City athlete in the 1940s, said that Bennett stood out as the Mohawks' tailback in football. "He could throw like a bullet," Jewell said.

It was a great time to be a high school athlete, Bennett said.

"This was before television, and high school sports had a big following," he said. "My memory is that we'd get huge crowds at our games – 4,000 to 5,000 people was not unusual for a football game and sometimes for our Junior Legion baseball games in the summers."

Being involved "saved me," he says now. "Sports was really all I wanted to do. Every moment in my life it was sports, sports, sports. Schoolwork was almost secondary, but we knew we had to do our book work, too, just so we could play sports."

Bennett, who is African American, grew up in a time when Mason City's population became very diverse, with newcomers and immigrants arriving from all over the nation and overseas to fill the jobs in the area's rapidly expanding industries.

"My parents moved from Texas to Mason City in the 1930s," he said. "They came up for work. My father was a common laborer who got a job at Mason City Brick & Tile. I probably got my athletic ability from him. He loved baseball, but I don't think he ever did get to play it just because times were so tough then. All he did all his life was work."

Besides Bernie, Charlie Lloyd Bennett and his wife Ruby had two other sons, Kenneth, now deceased, and Charles, who lived in Des Moines in 2005, and a daughter Doris Bennett Wade, also from Des Moines.

They lived in a south-side Mason City neighborhood filled with immigrant families. They called the area "Powder Street," a name which local historian Arthur Fischbeck said came from a gun shop owner who kept his "powder" in a stone shed on the back of his lot.

"It was kind of a rough place with a lot of beer joints, but I wasn't part of that," said Bennett, "other than I worked a little peeling potatoes at one of the taverns. That neighborhood was just everybody – all mixed together – and we all loved each other. Greeks, Poles, Germans, Mexicans, African Americans. You know, we were really poor – we didn't even have a bathtub of our own to bathe in, no shower, either – but we all looked out for each other. It was one of those situations in which we didn't realize we were poor. When I look back on it now, it was a happy childhood. It really was. I was entirely happy."

He began developing his athletic ability in summer recreation programs played in the parks and on school grounds.

"We also spent a lot of time at the YMCA," Bennett said. "There was a guy who worked there, Gordon Blanchard, who saved a lot of us by getting us involved at the Y. He made memberships basically free to poor kids."

Bennett's first taste of real competition came at Roosevelt Junior High School in the seventh, eighth and ninth grades. In his first year of high school, he played sophomore football but then got some playing time on the varsity basketball team.

"I was always one of the young ones in my class, and in a way that hurt me," Bennett said. "When I was playing my first varsity basketball, I was only 14 years old, and I played my whole senior season of football when I was 16."

By his senior year, he was 5 ft., 10 in. tall and weighed about 170. He said he "was quick, but I wouldn't think about going out for track, because when I was in seventh grade, our phys ed teacher made us run a quarter-mile. My side was hurting so bad, I told myself that's it – no more track."

In football, his coach Harry Helgeson played him at tailback in a single-wing offense, meaning that Bennett was doing the passing in addition to a lot of the running. He thinks he "was probably close to 1,000 yards rushing" his last two years. He also played cornerback on defense and returned punts.

"We had a really good team my senior year, but we lost the conference title to Fort Dodge when a guy named Bennett fumbled a punt in the rain," he said with a chuckle.

In baseball and basketball, Bennett played for a legendary Mason City coach, Elmer Starr, who was at the school for 26 years.

"He was a real important man in my life," Bennett said. "He loved sports, and especially baseball. I don't really think back on him as being a particularly tough coach. He had a big heart, and he'd do anything for you. I can remember a lot of times when we'd practice late, and then I'd catch a ride home with him. Then in college, I worked some with him both in Junior Legion baseball and also in the summer recreation program. We stayed pretty close through later years. Whenever I'd get back to Mason City, I'd always stop to see the Starrs."

Bennett was certainly one of Starr's top performers. He was a four-year starter at catcher in baseball, and hit in the high .400s his last couple of seasons. He helped the Mason City Legion team, also coached by Starr, win the 1948 state championship.

In basketball, "I played a little my sophomore year on a team that made it to the state tournament, and then I started at guard the next two years," Bennett said. "I could shoot it pretty decent, and played good defense. Our teams were pretty average, but I just loved playing."

As brilliant as Bennett's high school career was, some thought he didn't receive the honors and especially the recruiting attention that his abilities might have warranted. Duane Jewell, a teammate two years older who went on to a career as a detective for the Mason City police force, said there was "probably some racial discrimination involved in that. There was a lot of that around back in that time." Jewell is white.

But Bennett did receive a full scholarship to play football for the Iowa Hawkeyes, his first two years under coach Leonard Raffensperger and his last two under new coach Forest Evashevski. He lettered three years playing halfback or fullback and sometimes returning punts.

"I did all right at Iowa, but I always felt I wasn't as good as I should have been because we really had poor teams," Bennett said. "I had my moments, though."

One of those was returning a punt 44 yards for the only touchdown in an 8-0 Hawkeye upset of Ohio State in the homecoming game in Iowa City in his senior season of 1952.

He had hoped to play baseball at Iowa, too, but was ordered to take part in spring football practice instead. He did play baseball his senior year at Iowa, and in the summers, he played semi-professional ball with the Mason City team.

After earning his degree in physical education, Bennett stayed on at Iowa to get a master's and during those two years, he was a graduate assistant coach on the football team. He also played with a renowned "Airliner" basketball team, which was sponsored by a popular bar and restaurant, that won the Iowa AAU basketball title.

He then spent two years in the U.S. Army before beginning his teaching career in the Kansas City area. He coached early in his career "but then I became more interested in officiating," and for more than 20 years, he did high school and small college football and basketball all over the metro area, as well as in the west half of Missouri and the east half of Kansas.

He and his wife Alice, who was also a teacher, have a son Bradley, who is an outstanding soccer and hockey player.

Bennett said that despite growing up in poverty and facing occasional racial discrimination, his memories of a childhoon in Mason City boyhood are very warm.

"Good people, good schools – and bad weather," he told the Globe-Gazette newspaper. "When I was young, I didn't even notice it, to tell you the truth. But I do now."

Gary Thompson, Roland, 1953

It's a story that reads like a novel, or a movie script, but the best part is that it's not fiction. It happened. And when it did, the boys on the Roland Rockets basketball team – from a town of only 750 people in the heart of Iowa – became genuine and enduring sports legends in this state.

They were a great team, one that through four basketball seasons beginning in 1949 and ending in 1953 went 29-2, 35-1, 32-3 and 32-2. Five of those eight losses happened in the one-class state tournaments, where they took-on and beat several teams from Iowa's largest high schools, including Waterloo West and Des Moines East.

Nearly all the Roland basketball players also played baseball – the only other boys' sport the school offered – and they made it to that sport's state tournaments three consecutive years, too.

Always in the thick of the action was one player so special that for the rest of his life, the public has turned him into the personification of that whole Roland team, that community and its run of glory.

So much so that he is known statewide as "the Roland Rocket" – Gary Thompson.

He was All-State in basketball and would have been in baseball, too, but honor teams were not picked in that sport until the 1968 season. He went on to become an All-American in both basketball and baseball at Iowa State College, as the university in Ames was known then. He is one of those athletes who never found a sport in which he wasn't good.

For crying out loud, he even won two state championships in horseshoe pitching at the Iowa State Fair after his sophomore and junior years of high school. "Junior division," he quickly points out.

Still today, more than a half-century after his high school career ended, Thompson's name is one of the first mentioned when veteran sports fans in Iowa start talking about the state's greatest athletes.

Part of that, he says, is because of all the press coverage he and his teammates received in their Roland Rocket years.

"When I look back, the coverage was so intense," Thompson said. "You know, especially for small guys like I was, and for small schools, if you do something outstanding, it's always blown up."

398

He had been raised to keep things in perspective. Well, actually, his mother Abbie Thompson made it even more plain than that.

"I think the first mention in an out-of-town newspaper I ever got for anything in sports was when I was a freshman in high school and we played a second-team game over at Nevada," Gary said. "A few days later, the Nevada Evening Journal had a sports item that called me 'a little kid you want to watch in the future.' I was kind of excited about that, but when mother saw it, first thing she said was, 'Don't you even think about getting a big head!' "

So he didn't.

But a couple of years later, many more people were watching him.

He recalls that after his team's first state tournament appearance in his sophomore year of 1951, when they carried a 35-0 record into the championship game against mighty Davenport High School, "I started getting 20 to 25 letters a day from kids and fans all over Iowa. That was the most unbelievable experience of my life up 'til then. I'd been so focused on the games, I just didn't realize how much attention people were paying to what our team was doing."

The Rockets had knocked off Hull, another Class B school, in the first round of the state tourney, which was played then at the University of Iowa Fieldhouse in Iowa City. Teams qualified for the state tournament by playing in three classes – AA, A and B – up through the sub-state. But then they were all mixed together in the "Sweet Sixteen" at state, regardless of size. After the victory over Hull, the Rockets rang up stunning upsets of Waterloo West and then Des Moines East in the next two rounds, igniting wide public interest.

Everyone wanted to know more about the Roland Rockets and especially about Gary Thompson, their skinny, short, flat-topped, sophomore guard who was such a dead-eye of a shooter. The reporters started calling and stopping by. Brad Wilson, who was the chief prep sportswriter then for the Des Moines Register, later recalled his first "interview" with Thompson.

"Gary Thompson showed up in the state basketball tournament at Iowa City in 1951 as a 5 ft., 6 in. sophomore, but with a total of more than 400 points," Wilson wrote. "No one ever heard of him outside Roland until that spring. Fans were talking about Davenport's great Carl Widseth and

Keokuk's Bill Logan. Most of us were aware, however, of Roland's record and there was a rush to interview Roland players – the tall ones.

"We mistakenly took for granted that the little guy we chatted with was Roland's water boy and equipment manager. 'Do the Roland players think they have a chance to win?' we asked the diminutive lad seated alongside the Iowa playing court, during the pre-tournament warm-up drills. 'Sure,' answered Gary, 'why not?'

"Later, as we talked to Coach O.M. 'Buck' Cheadle, we queried: 'Who's the 400-point sophomore kid you have?'

"With a twinkle in his eye, Cheadle answered, 'You were just talking with him.' " 'Pretty small,' we ventured. " 'He's just big enough to be an All-Stater,' rejoined Buck. 'Keep an eye upon that boy, he'll be the greatest.' " By that point in 1951, Roland was a town already gone wild over sports.

"Roland was already doing great before I came along," Thompson said in 2005. "They'd had years of success in baseball and girls' basketball, and then right before I started high school, we had some big boys' basketball teams – averaged 6 ft., 2 in. or better."

Indeed the varsity boys' teams the two years Gary was in junior high went 28-2 and 29-2 and got beat in the sub-state tournaments.

His own introduction to sports started even earlier.

His father Maurice Thompson, who'd grown up one of 10 children in a family in nearby McCallsburg, and his brothers had high school state tournament experience in basketball. Maurice became a carpenter, and he and Abbie Hemnes, a native of Roland, settled in her hometown after they married.

Maurice was a player-manager for the Roland town baseball team for years, staying in the line-up until he was 40 years old. His young son Gary became the batboy.

"I grew up carrying around a gunny sack of balls and bats for Dad," Gary said. "I'd help tack up the broken bats and wrap them with tape."

He had another duty with the team, too.

"We had an old 1937 Chevy that Dad would use to drag the infield on the ball diamond," Gary said. "The 'drag' was two or three big wood planks that Dad had wired together, and he'd pull them behind the car. I'd ride back there, sitting on the drag, to help hold it down. I'd wind up covered with dirt, but I loved it."

The town team would frequently play Sunday afternoon games. "Mom's credo was always if you can play ball on Sundays, then you can go to church first," Gary said. "And we always did."

The Thompsons lived in town for most of Gary's youth.

"Yeah, I was a town kid – a city slicker from Roland," Gary says with a laugh.

However, they did live two years on a farm, when Maurice was building hog houses on several farms owned by a banker in New York. Part of the agreement for free rent for the family was Gary, then an eighth and ninth grader, doing the chores. Earlier, Maurice and Abbie operated a Phillips 66 service station for a year, and Gary got his first taste of the gas and oil business, which would eventually become his career.

The Thompsons were a musical family – except for Gary.

"My parents were both real musicians," he said. "Dad could play anything with strings, Mom could sing and when my brother DeLon came along, he could sing, too. Really, our big entertainment as a family was always to go visit our cousins, maybe have dinner or supper together, and then we'd all sit around and sing. I especially remember everybody singing 'Old Red River Valley.' It was fun, but you know, I couldn't carry a tune in a bucket."

So Gary got to know organized sports up close and personal, first as a batboy, and then by sitting on the scoreboard during Roland High School baseball games and posting the score by innings. But his real introduction to competition came in pick-up games on the yards and driveways of his friends' homes around the town.

"My memory is that there was a basket and bang board in every driveway in Roland," he said. "I think one of the reasons we started having good teams was that, growing up in a small town like that, there were never enough kids so that you could just play with your own age group. You had to play with the older kids, too."

He went through being a tag-a-long in those games, as did brother DeLon, who was seven years younger than Gary. They'd often "call up our cousins over at McCallsburg and get them to ride their bicycles six miles over to Roland and play with us, too," Gary said.

The first time his talent was noticed by a coach was when Gary was in sixth grade.

"We had a new high school coach then, Kenneth Lepley, and somehow he picked me out and brought me up to play with the seventh and eighth graders on the junior high team," Gary said. "I remember him telling me, 'Gary, during the noon hours at school, I want you to go out on the basketball floor and dribble up and down that floor, and never look at the basketball. You look at the wall.' So I did that, and eventually, he'd put cones out on the floor, and I'd have to dribble around them, without looking down. He got me started working on those fundamentals.

"But here I was, a sixth grader, and really, I'm 4 ft. nothin' tall and scared to death of going up and playing with those junior high kids," he continued. "I was supposed to get out of class early to go to my first game, but it got to be 3:30 in the afternoon, and I was just too scared to ask the teacher. So I sat there, and I wound up being late getting to the game.

"Our uniforms for junior high back then were the old high school jerseys and pants, and I was so little that the arm holes on the jersey drooped clear down into my shorts. The shorts were so big, I knew I was going to have to get somebody to help me. So I was peaking around the corner of the gym, trying to get someone's attention to come and help, because the team was already on the floor. Finally someone came and got safety pins to hold up my pants – for my first organized game."

Meanwhile, Lepley's varsity teams were rapidly improving, and basketball frenzy was gripping Roland.

"When I was in my junior high years, those high school home games became real events," Thompson said. "I remember standing two hours in line outside the gym doors, waiting for them to open. The line would be three or four abreast, a block long or better."

Roland's gym had been built as a WPA (Works Progress Administration) project during the Great Depression. It had a beautiful maple playing floor – you didn't dare walk on it unless you were in sneakers or stocking feet – and was one of the biggest floors in the area, too. As many as 1,000 people would pack it for big games.

Coach Lepley moved on after the 1948-49 school year, and was succeeded by Overton M. "Buck" Cheadle, who Gary Thompson now says "was just the greatest thing ever for me."

Cheadle, born in the Chickasaw Nation in Oklahoma to an Indian father and German mother, was a real head-turner when he arrived in Roland as the 30-year-old new coach. He was tall, trim, handsome and a very sharp dresser, often wearing bow ties with his suit or sports jacket during games.

Cheadle had been a good athlete in baseball and basketball at the Chilocco Indian School, then Murray Junior College in Tishomingo, Oklahoma, and then for two years at Oklahoma City University. When OCU dropped sports as World War II was looming, Cheadle and two of his teammates decided to transfer to Central State College in Edmond, Oklahoma, where he played one more year of baseball and basketball and earned his degree in history, English and physical education.

The day after Pearl Harbor was bombed on December 7, 1941, bringing the U.S. into World War II, Cheadle and his two roommates went to a U.S. Navy recruiting center and enlisted. He was assigned as a "specialist in athletics," helping do physical training of sailors, and he spent the next five years in the Navy. The last 20 months of his service, he was assigned to a convalescent hospital in Santa Cruz, California, where he met a Navy WAVE Ruth Howard, a native of Des Moines. They eventually married, moved to Oklahoma after they were both discharged from the Navy "but she didn't like all the storms we had in Oklahoma and she brought me to Iowa," Cheadle said. He landed a high school teaching and coaching job for two years at Norwalk, just southwest of Des Moines.

"I taught four different courses, coached both boys' and girls' basketball, baseball and some junior high sports," Cheadle said. "I was young and full of energy, and they just piled it on me. In that second year, I was starting to wear out, and I thought I better start looking for another job.

"About that same time, it seemed like I kept reading in the Des Moines Register about this town, Roland, and how they not only had good sports there, but a strong music program and good academics, too. For some reason I got this idea in my head that it sounded like an ideal place, and I told myself if I ever saw a teaching and coaching job open up there, I'd go after it. In the spring of '49, I saw an ad in the Register for an opening in Roland, and I applied right away."

Cheadle had an appointment for an interview with the Roland superintendent and school board on the Thursday night before Easter.

"That was a church night for all those Norwegian Lutherans, and so I was supposed to be up there for the interview and be done in time for them to get to church," Cheadle said. "But we got hit with a blizzard that day, and the roads were terrible. I was an hour or more late when I drove into Roland. I hated that because I always made sure I was on time or early getting to appointments. I thought they might all be gone when I got to the school, but the superintendent and school board president had waited to see if I'd get there. We talked for a while, then when church was over, they were able to round up a quorum of the school board members. They came down, talked a little more and they hired me."

That was also the night he first became "Buck" Cheadle.

"One of the school board members said to me, 'Mr. Cheadle, your first name is Overton, and that just doesn't sound like a coach's name to me. Don't you have some kind of nickname you could use?'" Cheadle recalled. "The truth is, back home in Oklahoma, they'd all called me 'Cheadle Bug' because I was so little when I started playing basketball in high school. Then in college, some of my teammates started calling me 'Pro' because I had turned down a professional baseball contract. I didn't want to use either one of those nicknames, though. As a young Indian guy, I was always real proud of my heritage, so I said, 'Yes, sir, I do have a nickname – it's Buck.' I just made it up right there on the spot. A day or two later, the Des Moines Register had a little story headlined, 'Roland hires Buck Cheadle.' That's what everybody has called me ever since!"

Cheadle thinks the first time he ever saw Gary Thompson was after he'd moved to Roland and summoned the boys for the start of fall baseball practice in 1949.

"I didn't tell Gary this until years later, but when I first noticed him standing there – he might have been 5 ft., 2 in. then – my thought was, 'Well, I've got a student manager already,'" Cheadle recalled. "Little did I know that what I was looking at was an All-American in the making."

404

After the first couple of practices, Cheadle realized Thompson's potential, and he sent one of the varsity's old flannel uniforms home with him to have his mother "take it up a little and see if she can make it look a little better on you," he told the boy. "We had to do that with his varsity basketball uniform that first year, too."

Thompson says Cheadle was "a real competitor and motivator. And wow, was he ever schooled in the fundamentals of both baseball and basketball! We had all kinds of drills that we'd run through at every practice – rebounding drills, pivot drills, 3-on-2, 2-on-1, doing crisp chest passes, handling the ball on the fast break without the ball ever hitting the floor. The other thing he did that I don't think our coaches had done before was scout other teams."

Cheadle also took his team far and wide for games with schools that had powerhouse basketball programs – including Diagonal and Storm Lake. They frequently scrimmaged larger schools like Marshalltown, Boone and Ames, and he arranged for them to have practices in the Armory at Iowa State so they could get the feel of playing in an arena atmosphere.

In his freshman year, Thompson got plenty of playing time in baseball and was a reserve on the varsity basketball team, scoring 42 points for the season. From then on, he became the team leader, as a pitcher and shortstop in baseball, and as the playmaking guard and leading scorer in basketball.

Over his four years of high school baseball, he had a batting average of .450 and in his last two years he lost only three games as a pitcher – all in the state tournament.

In basketball, he averaged 20 points per game as a junior, 25 as a senior and set the state's career scoring record with 2,042 points, becoming the first Iowa player ever to top 2,000. His one-game high was 41 points against Zearing in 1953, and "Gary was over the 30-point mark many, many times his last two years," the Roland Record newspaper reported.

He was as well-known for his slick one-handed "set shot" in high school as he became for his smooth jump shot which he developed in his years as a Cyclone at Iowa State University.

Thompson said basketball fans today "often say they can remember when Roland won the state championship back in the 1950s, but we never did win one. We were second to Davenport my sophomore year in 1951, and that's when we learned there's such a difference between being 35-1 and being 36-0. But you know, that was such an achievement for our little school the way it was. If we'd have won that one, I guess we'd have been the 'Hoosiers' before the 'Hoosiers' movie came out."

That Roland team had three seniors in the line-up – Ralph Thompson, Jake Hill and Frank Egland. The other two starters were Don Holland, a junior, and Thompson. The sixth man who played extensively was Dave Peterson.

Waterloo West was favored to win the state championship, and when Roland beat the Wahawks 43-40 in the quarterfinals, the whole state was shocked. Roland had built a 31-24 lead at halftime, then slowed the scoring pace in the third quarter. Thompson fouled out with just more than six minutes left in the fourth quarter, and left the game nearly in tears.

"That's when we decided to put the ball in the deep freeze," Cheadle said. "We got Don Holland loose for a couple of baskets inside, but West kept chipping away at us. We were up 41-40 with three minutes left, and then we stalled for two minutes straight.

We finally won it when Ralph Johnson got the ball and drove for a lay-up that put us up 43-40 in the last seconds. They had the whole court lined with University of Iowa lettermen, who were the ushers, but they couldn't begin to keep the fans off the floor. They mobbed us!"

In the semifinals, the Rockets had a much easier time of it beating Des Moines East 46-37, and then they faced the defending state champions from Davenport. There was only one public high school in Davenport in those years, and legendary coach Paul Moon had put together a basketball juggernaut that won three consecutive titles.

The Roland vs. Davenport game was one in which there were no neutral fans. Several hundred were cheering for the Blue Devils, and 14,000 were cheering for the Rockets.

"I can still remember the fans chanting, 'Beat Davenport! Beat Davenport' " said Thompson. "And when they introduced the starting line-ups, they shut off all the lights in the fieldhouse, and each of us ran out into a spotlight when our name was called. If you don't think that gets a little sophomore from a small town pumped up!"

Brad Wilson, the Register sportswriter, later recalled an odd incident that happened in the final minutes of that game.

Roland led by 4 points going into the fourth quarter "and 14,000 fans were really jumping," Cheadle recalled. But "the dam broke in the last three minutes," Wilson wrote. "Davenport scored 10 straight points in 90 seconds and won going away, 50-40.

"It's history that Roland went all the way down to the wire with mighty Davenport before losing in the final quarter," he wrote. "There was an incident in that final period, too, that revealed a facet of Gary's character.

"A stray dog had somehow managed to get onto the playing court. The frightened pooch scurried about, much to the delight of fans who set up a chorus of whistling. Players and officials waved their arms to shoo the dog off. All but Gary. He walked over to the frightened dog, patted him on the head, then lifted him up in his arms and carried him off the court, accompanied by a burst of applause. Gary had won the hearts of Iowa basketball fans for all time. They liked the humane touch. Most great athletes have it."

Davenport coach Moon, incidentally, told the media after the game, "I'll bet I could collect enough money from Davenport rooters here tonight to buy Gary's dad a 400-acre farm in Scott County so he could play for Davenport High!"

Thompson, his teammates and all of Roland's fans went home a little disappointed, but not much. Some may have realized they'd just lived through one of the all-time best weeks in Iowa high school sports history. A half-century later, some would say that week in 1951 still stands as the best.

There were many more thrills the next two years, of course, with Roland finishing fourth in basketball in both 1952 and 1953, and going to state in baseball in the springs of 1951, '52 and '53 as well as the fall of 1952.

Gary Thompson also fell in love.

When he was a sophomore, his teammate Hollis Fosse, who had started driving the 18 miles from Roland to Ames to go roller skating at the Skateland rink there, came back "and told me there was a girl I needed to meet at the roller rink," Gary recalled.

And when he went to meet Janet Sydnes, of Huxley?

"Love at first sight," Gary said. "I went skating the next four years with her. We skated four nights a week – Wednesday, Friday, Saturday and Sunday. The Ames kids were too sophisticated to roller skate, but all of us from the small towns loved it. It was great. There was a live organist playing. They'd have 'Moonlight Skates' and 'Two-Steps.' And, you know, I was a darned good roller skater. Never could dance worth a darn, but I was good at roller skating!"

Jumping ahead, Gary and Janet Sydnes Thompson had been married for 50 years in 2005.

Buck Cheadle left Roland in the spring of 1952 to become head basketball coach at Burlington High School in southeast Iowa.

"My three years in Roland were so wonderful it was like living in heaven," he recalled. "I've often said I wished somebody had kicked me in the back side for even thinking about leaving before Gary Thompson's senior year. But you know how young coaches are, always looking for a bigger school, and I've always been one to look for a challenge."

He stayed eight years in Burlington, had the runner-up team to Marshalltown in 1956, then took a high school counseling job in Rockford, Illinois, for seven years. He returned to Iowa in 1967 and spent seven years at Pekin of Packwood, then moved back to Oklahoma in 1974 to start the Indian Education Program in the Putnam City schools. He eventually became a special counselor for Indian students at East Central University in Ada, Oklahoma, where he has lived in retirement since 1984 with his second wife, the former Helen Von Lienen a native of Williamsburg, Iowa. He has also worked in adult education for the Chickasaw Nation.

Cheadle was succeeded at Roland High in the fall of 1952 by Robert Looft, who continued the Rockets' run of athletic success.

Looft, who eventually became president of Iowa Western Community College in Council Bluffs, wrote later that Thompson's success at Iowa State was "no big surprise to us. We who have lived in Roland know the stuff of which you are made. We have seen your undeniable spirit and courage. What is most impressive is that you have remained humble through

408

all the glory. That is a sign of greatness."

Thompson's four years at Iowa State were almost as amazing as his run at Roland High School. He set the Cyclones' career, season and single game scoring records in basketball. He led the baseball team to the College World Series for the first time.

"…it was not just the playing ability that made Thompson the greatest of Iowa born and bred basketball players," wrote Harry Burrell, the sports publicity director at the college. "It was his attitude of devotion to the game, to its highest ideals, his fighting heart, his determination that he was going to try to be a better player every day than he was the day before – it was those things combined with an unbelivable modesty that won him a permanent place in Iowa State's history."

After graduation in 1957, his hometown had "Gary Thompson Day" and more than 2,000 people turned out in the city park on a July day to join in the celebration.

After Iowa State, Thompson spent 11 years with the Phillips Petroleum Co., living in Bartlesville, Oklahoma, during the five years he played with their champion AAU basketball team, the Phillips 66ers. After ending his playing career, he became a Phillips 66 district manager in Cedar Rapids for two years, then was reassigned back to Oklahoma to coach the 66ers the last four years the team played.

In 1968, he returned to Ames and formed Gary Thompson Oil Co., which now owns eight convenience stores in Ames and the Des Moines area. His oldest son Rick Thompson, 43 years old in 2005, is vice-president. His son-in-law Tom Wierson, married to the Thompsons' daughter Kim, is manager of operations. Youngest son Scott Thompson, bases his own Certified Public Accounting business from the Thompson Oil offices.

In the 1960s, Gary Thompson began a basketball broadcasting career, first on radio doing commentary for Ames High School and state tournament games. In 1971, he joined the television broadcast team doing Big Eight Conference college games, and continued doing commentary on television coverage of high school and college games – including the NCAA tournaments – through the end of the 2004-05 season.

Thompson's parents are both deceased, his father Maurice in 1968, his mother Abbie in 1989.

His brother DeLon Thompson was an exceptional baseball player, one who once struck out 23 batters in a seven-inning high school game, setting a national record. He went on to Iowa State where he played both baseball and basketball as a freshman, devoting himself to baseball and winning three varsity letters. He was one of the Cyclones' leading pitchers, once beating Oklahoma twice in the same day – in the first game as a starter and the second game in relief. He signed a bonus contract with the Minnesota Twins organization and played two years in the minor leagues.

DeLon went on to work for Sears, Roebuck and Co., but then left for several years of Christian missionary work that eventually took him to Nashville, Tennessee. There, besides missionary work and a job in the automotive finance business, he also began performing both Christian and country music, using some of the musical talent that had helped him become a top singer and trumpet player in high school. He later became finance manager of a large car dealership in Tucson, Arizona, and now uses that city as his base while spending full-time writing and performing country music around the country. His CDs have also developed a big following in the European markets.

Gary Thompson is a very active booster of Iowa State University athletics. He has been a key member of several recruitment efforts for Cyclone coaches, and he is generally the master of ceremonies at Cyclone Club luncheons in Ames. He is very involved in church and community activities in Ames, and still takes an interest in programs and projects in his old hometown of Roland as well as the neighboring town of Story City, where Roland-Story High School is now located.

He has become a competitive golfer in senior tournaments across Iowa and beyond. He won the state senior tournament championship in 1999 and plays 90 to 100 rounds of golf per year.

"I love the game, but what I love most about it is the competition," he said. "I always say I'm not really a golfer. I'm an athlete playing golf."

Gary Thompson is an athlete, all right. One of Iowa's very best. And the Roland Rockets? Just thinking about their time and place in Iowa sports history warms the heart of any real sports fan in this state.

Randy Duncan, Des Moines Roosevelt, 1955

He was a first team All-American on an Iowa Hawkeye football team that won the 1959 Rose Bowl, a runner-up for the Heisman Trophy and a No. 1 draft choice by the National Football League. He went on to become a star in professional football, albeit in the Canadian league that at the time paid higher salaries than the NFL.

But 68-year-old Randy Duncan looks back on it all in 2005 and says flatly that his participation in high school sports at Des Moines Roosevelt "was a hell of a lot better than later, a hell of a lot more fun.

"It was a better experience for me than playing in college or in professional football," he continued. "In college and in pro ball, there was a lot of pressure. In high school, it was all fun. It's a great program."

Ask him for the highlight of his athletic career, and his answer is immediate.

"Beating East High 14-7 in football in front of 15,000 at Drake Stadium in my senior year at Roosevelt in 1954," Duncan said. "We came into the game undefeated and untied and ranked No. 1 in the state, and East was No. 3. That's a great memory. The year before against East, we were behind 13-7 and had the ball on the one-yard line, but we couldn't get it in. So that made the 1954 win even bigger for me and my teammates."

He is formally Hearst Randolph Duncan, Jr., the son of a former high school coach. Hearst Sr. coached at Elkhart and Luther, both located in central Iowa, before deciding to go to law school. The family lived in Osage until Randy was four, then moved to Mason City for five years before settling in Des Moines.

"I played sandlot baseball, but there really weren't organized sports for young kids in Des Moines back then," Duncan said. "I never put on a pair of football pads until I was in ninth grade."

That ninth grade team he played on, incidentally, went undefeated, as did his Roosevelt sophomore team.

His last two years, varsity coach Archie Johnson made Duncan, who was 6 ft. and 180 pounds, the starting quarterback and defensive safety. The Roughriders, who were driven by his passing, lost only two games in the 1953 season before their magical undefeated season of 1954.

Thus, he was involved in only two losses in football games during high school. And the University of Iowa Hawkeye teams he played on lost only three.

He was also an exceptional basketball player on the Roosevelt teams coached by the legendary Al Comito. They made the state tournament in both 1953 and '54, finishing runner-up to Muscatine in the latter year. Duncan, averaging 22 points per game, got a big salute from sportswriter Brad Wilson in the Des Moines Register.

"Roosevelt's one-two punch, Jim McConnell and Randy Duncan, brought the Roughriders back to the state championship final for the first time in 21 years," Wilson wrote. "Surprisingly enough, Duncan, a fine ball-handling quarterback and deadly out-shooter, has surpassed McConnell's scoring in the tourney stretch. Duncan probably ranks as one of the best guards ever to wear the white and blue, and among the top performers in the state."

He was recruited for both football and basketball, and his first thought was to follow his older sister and some other friends from Des Moines to the University of Colorado.

"I basically stayed in Iowa because a lot of people were pressuring me to do so," Duncan said.

He was a mid-year graduate at Roosevelt High School in January, 1955, so he enrolled then at the University of Iowa. Since freshmen were not eligible for varsity football competition, that meant he went through two springs and one fall of practice before he ever got any playing time. He also played freshman basketball, "and might have stayed out in later years, except that in my sophomore year, we went to the Rose Bowl in football, and that knocked me out of all the early practices and games," he said.

On that 1957 Rose Bowl team, Duncan was the back-up quarterback to Kenny Ploen, then he started as a junior and senior.

After all his success at Iowa, Duncan signed with the British Columbia Lions in the Canadian league and played two years. He also began his law school studies in the off-season. He played a final year of professional football in 1962 with the Dallas Texans of the old American Football League.

He graduated from the Drake Law School in 1963 and joined the same firm his father headed in Des Moines. In 2005, Randy is the senior partner in that firm of Duncan Green Brown Langeness & Eckley. He and his wife Paula have three sons, all of whom were good football players at Roosevelt. Jed is now an investment banker in New York, Matt is a lawyer in the same practice with his dad and Scott is a teacher in St. Louis.

"High school athletics have vastly improved in Iowa through the years," Randy Duncan said. "The coaching is much better. There's more emphasis on the fundamentals than there used to be. And the caliber of athletes in Iowa is a lot better than used to be the case. But the program was already pretty good when I was playing, and it gave me a lot of my favorite sports memories."

Eddie Bedell, Burlington, 1956

His tragic death in a car accident in 1965 – just two years after he had established a dental practice in his hometown of Burlington – has meant that Eddie Bedell is not as well remembered for his athletic accomplishments at Burlington High as he probably should be.

He was an All-State football quarterback who started three years for the Grayhounds and led them to conference championships as a junior and senior.

·He was an All-State basketball player, also starting three years, the first two as a guard and then as a center just 6 ft. tall in his senior year, when Burlington lacked a taller player for inside play. But that team, playing only .500 ball in early January of 1956, went on a 13-game winning streak that saw them finishing runner-up in the state tournament to powerful Marshalltown.

What Bedell lacked in height, he made up for in quickness and mobility, and he was known "for pivoting around the defensive player, going toward the basket and shooting an underhanded scoop shot," as Dick Wagner, a former Burlington baseball coach and athletic director recalled. "Eddie would either get the basket, or they'd foul him and he'd hit the free throws. It seems to me that during those two years he played guard, he only averaged about four points a game, but when he played center that third year, he was averaging about 20 points."

Bedell captained the track team that won the conference

championship in the spring of 1956, he set the conference record in the pole vault and then he won the state championship in that same event.

He was a starter on the Grayhound baseball team, and a good hitter – although his awkward, left-handed throwing style kept him from being a star in that sport.

And he won a state junior golf championship along the way.

Put all of the above together, and Eddie Bedell was one fine all-around athlete.

"Eddie was an all-around good guy, too," said Leroy Pease, who started teaching and coaching at Burlington High in 1937, then served as principal the last 16 years before he retired in 1980. "His best attribute in sports was his head – he was a really smart athlete – and he was a real competitor. He was the star athlete of that 1956 graduating class."

Wagner, who was in high school in nearby Cantril in the same era that Bedell was starring in Burlington, agrees with Pease's assessment. "Eddie was not really a natural athlete," Wagner said. "What he accomplished came because of his competitiveness and his intellectual ability."

Bedell, an honor roll student who ranked twenty-first in his graduating class of 319, won a Nile Kinnick Scholarship to the University of Iowa, an honor that was given only to the top student athletes in the state. Pease remembers Bedell playing football at the university, but never reaching the stardom that he had in high school. In fact, he gave up football in his junior year and turned into a two-year letter winner in golf for the Hawkeyes.

He went on to dental school at the University of Iowa, graduated and came home to Burlington to open his own office. Late at night on November 24, 1965, Bedell died in a car accident south of Wapello, Iowa, on U.S. Highway 61 when he apparently lost control of the vehicle he was driving. It went into a ditch and rolled.

"It was a shock for the community. Just stunning," said Pease. "He had been a young man with such great potential."

Bedell had never married.

His basketball coach at Burlington High had been Buck Cheadle, the same man who had coached Gary Thompson for three years at Roland.

"Eddie was a really fine athlete," recalled Cheadle, who now is retired

414

in Oklahoma, as mentioned earlier. "He played with a lot of heart. He was one of those who would figure out a way to win."

Jim Wagner, Cedar Rapids Regis, 1962

Talk about a testimonial!

Dick Breitbach, the veteran coach at Cedar Rapids Regis and its successor school Cedar Rapids Xavier, has an interesting way of describing just how good a football player Jim Wagner was for Regis in the early 1960s.

"He was an All-American running back, which should tell you a lot, " said Breitbach, as he began. "But if you want to know what Jim Wagner was really like as a player, take Tim Dwight, add five inches of height, add 15 to 20 pounds of weight, and yet keep the same speed. That was Wagner. The speed is what most people remember. He was very, very fast."

Dwight, of course, was the sensational football player and trackman at City High of Iowa City in the early 1990s, before going on to a great career with the University of Iowa Hawkeyes and then into professional football. You'll read more about him later in this chapter.

But Breitbach has more about Wagner.

"Notre Dame was all over him, trying to recruit him," said Breitbach. "In November, 1961, the Fighting Irish were coming to play at Iowa. So Joe Kuharich, who was the Notre Dame coach, had his team stay in Cedar Rapids, they used our Regis football field to practice on, and they went to mass at our church Immaculate Conception – all because of Wagner."

Jim Wagner was among a dozen good athletes who came together in 1958, when Regis opened as a new Catholic high school in Cedar Rapids, a consolidation of the former Immaculate Conception and St. Wenceslaus high schools.

"Our first year in football was quite an initiation," said Wagner, 61 in 2005 and still living in Cedar Rapids. "We were playing some really strong teams, like Loras Academy from Dubuque and Alleman from Rock Island. Loras, which was as big as most college teams, beat us something like 60-0."

He was a freshman running back, and his older brother Larry Wagner was the quarterback. "I remember we had one pass play that was called 'Wagner to Wagner,' " Jim said. Larry, who had started his athletic career at

Immaculate Conception, was an All-Stater in both football and basketball, and went on to play basketball at Creighton University in Omaha.

Those early Regis teams took some lumps, but "I think we all had a high threshold of pain from the way we'd played around home," Jim said.

"We grew up southeast of downtown, and we probably had 25 kids around the neighborhood. It always seemed like most of them were older than I was, and I'd get beat up pretty good. There were eight or more of them who went on to play college football or basketball. There was a game going on in somebody's yard all the time – tackle football, or pretty rough basketball, baseball, always something. We had the Mitchell brothers next door, the Paxtons behind us, Jim Maher down the street, the Gatto brothers. They were all tough."

Of course, so were the Wagner brothers – Larry and Jim, as well as younger brothers Rick and John, who graduated in 1965 and 1967 from Regis.

Regis football came of age in 1960, Jim's junior year, when Tom Good took over as head coach. He became one of Iowa's best football coaches, a Hall of Famer.

In the 1960 season Regis went 8-2, and they were 9-1 in the fall of 1961 when Wagner was a senior. By then he was 6 ft., 2 in., weighed 190 and had sprinter's speed. All of that helped Jim pile up more than 1,300 yards rushing that season, an average of 11.3 yards per carry. He was also a leading tackler on the team.

"I loved football," said Jim Wagner. "Since most of us on those Regis teams had grown up playing together, we were all friends and nobody on the squad had an attitude."

But he had almost as much success in basketball. That started in his seventh and eighth grade years at Immaculate Conception, when a University of Iowa student named Bob "Red" Jennings filled in as the boys' basketball coach at the parochial school. In 1958, the same year Jim Wagner started high school at Regis, Jennings became the varsity basketball coach "so he coached me all the way through school in basketball," Wagner said.

Jim was elevated to the varsity squad as a sophomore, and started in both his junior and senior years. The team those two years was loaded – with

416

Saluting 25 of our greatest

Gary Thompson, Roland, 1953. Iowa State Cyclones, Phillips 66ers. *Below:* Thompson and John Walters were the play-by-play team for the telecast of the 2004 boys' state basketball tournament.

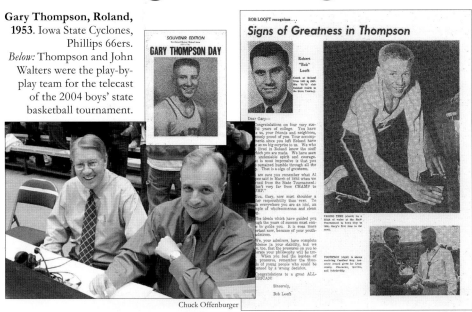

Chuck Offenburger

Personal Collection

Chuck Offenburger

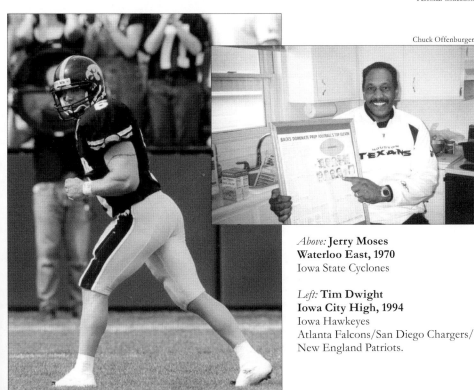

Above: **Jerry Moses**
Waterloo East, 1970
Iowa State Cyclones

Left: **Tim Dwight**
Iowa City High, 1994
Iowa Hawkeyes
Atlanta Falcons/San Diego Chargers/
New England Patriots.

Sports Information, University of Iowa

Casey Blake
Indianola, 1992
Wichita State Shock-
ers, Toronto Blue
Jays, Minnesota
Twins, Baltimore
Orioles, Cleveland
Indians

Curtis Craig
Davenport
Central, 1974
Nebraska
Cornhuskers

Cleveland Indians

Quad City Times

Burlington High School

Above: **Eddie Bedell**
Burlington, 1956
Iowa Hawkeyes

Right: **Darin Naatjes**
West Lyon, 1999
Stanford Cardinal
Philadelphia Phillies
organization

Sports Information, University of Iowa

A-D-M High School

**Nile Kinnick
Adel/Omaha
Benson, 1936**
Iowa Hawkeyes
Heisman
Trophy

Sports Information, University of Iowa

Iowa City West High School

**Nate Kaeding
Iowa City West,
2000**
Iowa Hawkeyes
San Diego Chargers

**Ed Podolak
Atlantic, 1965**
Iowa Hawkeyes
Kansas City Chiefs

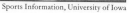

Sports Information, University of Iowa

Atlantic High School

Dan Gable
Waterloo West, 1966
Iowa State Cyclones,
Olympic Gold Medalist,
Coach, Iowa Hawkeyes

Adam Haluska
Carroll, 2002
Iowa State Cyclones/
Iowa Hawkeyes

Ron Kennedy
Storm Lake, 1970
Arizona State Sun Devils
Scavollini Cuccini, Pesaro,
Italian Professional Basketball
League

Personal Collection

Denise Sheehan

Ted Burgmeier, Dubuque Wahlert, 1974.
Notre Dame Fighting Irish
Kansas City Chiefs

Personal Collection

Right: **Jack Dittmer
Elkader, 1946**
Iowa Hawkeyes
Milwaukee Braves/Detroit
Tigers

Below: **Zeron Flemister
Sioux City West, 1995**
Iowa Hawkeyes
Washington Redskins/
New England Patriots

Sports Information, University of Iowa

Monroe County Historical Museum

Above: **Kenneth "Moco" Mercer
Albia, 1922.** Simpson Redmen
Frankford, PA. Yellow Jackets
Coach, University of Dubuque
Spartans

Right: **John Estes Jr.
Des Moines North, 1946**
Iowa Hawkeyes

Personal Collection

Bob Feller
Van Meter, 1937
Cleveland Indians
Pictured here on the left,
Feller in his heyday and below
as a high school boy playing
on his father's "Oak View"
adult team (Feller is fourth
from left in the front row).

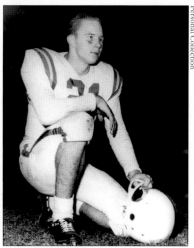

Above: **Jim Wagner**
Cedar Rapids Regis, 1962
Iowa Hawkeyes

Left: **Randy Duncan**
Des Moines Roosevelt, 1955
Iowa Hawkeyes

Right: **Bernie Bennett**
Mason City, 1949
Iowa Hawkeyes

Below: **Fred Hoiberg**
Ames, 1991
Iowa State Cyclones
Indiana Pacers/Chicago Bulls/Minnesota
Timberwolves

Below Right: **Jim Abrahamson**
Marshalltown, 1966
Iowa State Cyclones
With his family after Marshalltown won
the 1966 state basketball championship.

Personal Collection

Personal Collection

Right: **Joel Osborn**
Harlan, 2004.
Northwest Missouri State
Bobcats. With his father Coach
Mitch Osborn, left, and broad-
caster Tim Seaman after leading
Harlan to the state basketball
championship in 2004.

Chuck Offenburger

All-American Jim Cummins, Denny Phillips, Joe Schmitz, Dave Fish, John Carrigg and Wagner. The leading scorers were Cummins, who went on to play for Northwestern University, and Phillips at 20 and 15 points per game respectively. Wagner "averaged about 11 points, I think, but I really liked the rebounding more," he said.

As juniors they were 18-3. Then as seniors in 1962, they went 21-5 and won the all-one-class state championship by beating a fantastic Laurens team – led by the Ziegler brothers.

Wagner tried baseball his freshman and sophomore years but found it "too boring." Regis did not have a track team in that era.

When it came time for college, Wagner said he "was leaning toward Notre Dame or Missouri, but I really was getting a lot of pressure to go to Iowa." Notre Dame put its whole squad on display for him during that practice on the Regis field. Dan Devine had Wagner visit the Missouri campus six times, "and I loved it," he said. "Missouri was actually my first choice, but there were a lot of people around Cedar Rapids telling me I had to go to Iowa."

So he did. Even though he was not eligible to play as a freshman, Wagner earned a lot of respect for his play in practice that fall of 1962. As a sophomore, he joined the varsity and a week before the Hawkeyes' first game, he was elevated to starting running back. While scrimmaging, Wagner took a handoff, headed for the end zone and "got hit as I planted my left foot. I tore all the ligaments in my knee and ankle and had a compound fracture of ankle."

After six weeks in the hospital, he tried to resume life as a student on crutches on the sprawling campus. "It was so hard," he recalled, that he took the spring semester off, went to live with an aunt in Texas to be in warm weather and began his stretching exercises there, hoping to recover in time for the 1964 football season. He indeed rejoined the team, "could run okay, but I just couldn't cut very well." He knew his football career was over.

He threw himself into his studies in accounting, got married in his senior year and then decided to go into business before he got his degree. He went to work for Eby's Sporting Goods in Cedar Rapids, two years later bought the company, then five years later sold it.

In 1971, he started a small business in his basement, producing silk-screened and embroidered logos and apparel. He still heads that company, now called Jym Bag Co., which has 35 employees making the same products for major stores and businesses across the U.S.

Jim, who stays active athletically in golf and tennis, and his wife Nancy have five grown children, who were athletes at Linn-Mar and Cedar Rapids Washington high schools.

Life has been good for him, and he treasures the memories from his years at Regis High School, which in 1998 consolidated with LaSalle High School to form Cedar Rapids Xavier. He sometimes thinks how different it might have been had his father, the late John Wagner, not made a big sacrifice for the family in 1960.

"Dad was director of purchasing at Collins Radio in Cedar Rapids, and in my sophomore year, he and my mother Marjorie called my brother Larry home from Creighton and got the rest of us all together," Jim said. "Dad told us he'd been offered a job at the presidential level of the company, with a big salary, but we would have to move to Texas. But he said we were going to take a family vote on it, and the majority would rule. We all voted to stay, and Dad turned down the offer. He wound up being purchasing director in Cedar Rapids for 45 years. He had a great career with the company, but he must've often wondered about that decision. I think back on it, and holy cow! That was quite a choice we made for him."

Ed Podolak, Atlantic, 1965

His name is one of the most familiar and enduring in Iowa sports history.

Ed Podolak went from being a four-sport super star at Atlantic High School to being a workhorse of a quarterback and running back for the Iowa Hawkeyes. He then went on to be an outstanding running back for the Kansas City Chiefs for nine years, and in 2005 he was starting his twenty-third year as the very popular commentator on radio broadcasts of Hawkeye football. He has his own successful real estate and investment company with developments in Colorado and a beautiful seaside resort in Costa Rica.

"God's been good to me," said Podolak, 57 in 2005, who lives on a small farm outside Basalt, Colorado, with his wife Vicki, who was his high school sweetheart. Their daughter Emily, received a graduate degree in landscaping from the University of Washington, and Laura, who played basketball for the University of Iowa, was working in radio news and sports in 2005.

Ed's athletic career had what he acknowledges is "a storybook" start in the southwest Iowa town of Atlantic. Joe and Dorothy Podolak raised Ed, his younger brother Charlie and their younger sister Betty on an 80-acre farm seven miles south of Atlantic.

"As we were coming up, the head football coach in Atlantic was John Hunter, and he was wise enough that he'd come to the two grade schools in town, and he'd coach us in flag football," Ed said. "We'd have an annual game with the other grade school. And we all thought that was a big deal, of course. The same thing happened in basketball."

What the Atlantic coaches saw coming in the Class of 1965 was a wave of exceptional athletes, led by Podolak, Jim Vollmuth, Dan Gipple, Dan Duskin and Bill O'Connor. They were the heart and soul of Trojan teams in the four major sports, and golf, too.

The football team was undefeated – with only one tie – in the 1963 and '64 seasons. The basketball team made the state tournament in both 1964 and 1965, losing to eventual champion Newton the first year and a much bigger Keokuk team the next.

Always leading the way was Podolak, who grew to 6 ft., 1 in. and 183 pounds and won 13 letters in high school. He was a starter from his freshman year in baseball, playing third base and hitting about .400 in his last two varsity seasons. As a sophomore he moved into the starting line-up in basketball, and averaged scoring "in the high teens" the rest of his career. He was the starting quarterback in football both his junior and senior years. In track he ran on the sprint relay teams and was a pole vaulter.

"Ed Podolak had the heart of a champion," said Arnie Gaarde, who was his basketball coach.

Podolak, who said that when he was not busy in a sport he "was usually farming," did make time in his senior year to be editor of the Atlantic High yearbook. His successor as editor was Carl Voss, a mediocre athlete who was a year younger and who has gone on to a successful career as a photographer and editor in Des Moines. Ever since high school, Voss has enjoyed telling people that "as Ed Podolak was about to graduate at Atlantic, I tried out for his position and won it," pausing before he adds, "Okay, I shared the position with a girl – as yearbook editor."

Podolak was the subject of an intense recruiting battle in his senior year among the football coaches and fans from Wyoming, Nebraska, Iowa State and Iowa.

"Bob Devaney was new at Nebraska then, and it was pretty exciting thinking about being a part of that," Podolak said. "He'd come from Wyoming, which had a lot of talent then, and they came after me early. In fact, I signed a letter of intent to go to Wyoming, but it was binding only in their conference.

"Clay Stapleton was the coach at Iowa State, and at the semester break of my senior year, they hired my high school football coach Howard Justice, who'd been like a second father to me, to be an assistant coach on their staff. Howard had good enough credentials as a coach to get that job anyway, but they were probably hoping that would get me to Iowa State, too, and I did sign a Big Eight letter of intent for Iowa State. But Jerry Burns was the head coach at Iowa, and I was talking to him a lot, too. It was a lot of pressure for a 17-year-old, I'll tell you that."

But it was Bill Reichardt, the former Iowa Hawkeye star who was then a well-known clothier in Des Moines, who "had the most influence on me going to Iowa," Podolak said. "He spoke at our football banquet in Atlantic, and then he stayed in touch with me the rest of the year."

On the morning of "national letter intent day," Podolak was greeted "at my mother's breakfast table" by Howard Justice from Iowa State, assistant coach Whitey Piro from Iowa and another coach from Wyoming – all holding letters of intent they hoped he'd sign, committing himself to their school.

He ate his breakfast, listening to their pitches, got up and told them he "can't sign right now. Everybody leave your letters, and I'll think about them." His mother put the letters in a drawer and Ed went to school.

The pressure continued, of course. That same evening, Podolak was working at a local clothing store when Iowa coach Burns called him for a long talk.

"I hung on for a month longer," he said. "It finally came down to Iowa State and Iowa, and by the time of the state track meet at Drake Stadium in Des Moines, I had decided on Iowa. So there was my old high school coach Howard Justice, who came down from Iowa State to see us compete. I ran over to him and said, 'Coach, I've got to go to Iowa.' Telling him that was one of the hardest things I've ever had to do. He was disappointed, but he wished me the best, shook my hand and we've stayed friends the rest of our lives. In fact, when the Kansas City Chiefs inducted me into their Hall of Fame, he was the one coach I invited to be there with me. I learned more about football from Howard Justice than from any other coach I had along the way."

Ironically, Podolak never played for Burns at Iowa. He was not eligible as a freshman in 1965 and the Hawkeyes went from being the pre-season pick as the No. 1 team in the nation to finishing with one victory and nine losses. Burns was fired. Ray Nagel was hired to succeed him, and Podolak became the quarterback. He passed for more than 1,000 yards in both his sophomore and junior seasons. Then midway in his senior year, he shifted to running back to try to shore-up an injury-depleted team. He led the team in rushing that season with 937 yards. While he had strong statistics as an individual player, the team struggled those three seasons to records of 2-8, 1-8-1 and 5-5.

Podolak was thrilled to go back into a winning situation with the Kansas City Chiefs, playing on the special teams in Kansas City's 1970 Super Bowl victory and then becoming one of the top running backs in the National Football League through his last season in 1977.

During his professional years, he had settled in the Aspen area of Colorado, which he first saw on skiing vacations when he was in college – and quickly came to love. "There's nothing like the weather here," Podolak said. "Once you live here, it'd be hard to think of living somewhere else – except for some trips to warm weather places like Costa Rica."

He's been the color commentator on the WHO radio broadcasts of Iowa Hawkeye football since 1983, flying in and out of the Aspen airport to get to the games. Early on, he also did commentary on NFL games on NBC-TV but gave that up when he realized "college football is much more colorful than pro games," as he once told the Des Moines Register.

But he always keeps an eye on the high school scores in Iowa, especially the scores of the Atlantic Trojans.

"The people of Atlantic have always been very sports and education oriented," Podolak said. "There couldn't have been a better place for a high school kid to grow up than Atlantic, Iowa."

Jim Abrahamson, Marshalltown, 1966

He was the quintessential four-sport athlete in a golden era of high school sports in Marshalltown.

Jim Abrahamson quarterbacked the undefeated Bobcat football team in his senior season of 1965. In basketball, he was described as the "prototype point guard" who guided Marshalltown to a 26-1 record and the 1966 state championship title. He was a three-year regular on a golf team that qualified for state twice. And he was a crackerjack infielder, "junk ball" pitcher and .400 hitter on a baseball team that made it to the substate finals.

The 6 ft., 1 in. Abrahamson was recognized as such a "gamer" that he won a basketball scholarship at Iowa State University, where he was a three-year starter at guard, feeding the ball to the Cyclones' top scorers Don Smith and Bill Cain.

He had come from a very athletic family. His brothers Lee and Jerry were on a 1956 Marshalltown High basketball team that went undefeated and won a state championship. Lee went on to play at Coe College and Jerry at the University of Northern Iowa and Drake. Another older brother Dick was a football star, and played at UNI. Their only sister Sue grew up before girls' sports were offered in Marshalltown, but she was a cheerleader in both high school and at Coe. Their niece Katie Abrahamson-Henderson was a superstar at Cedar Rapids Washington High School, the University of Georgia and then the University of Iowa. In 2005, she was the head's women basketball coach at Southwest Missouri State University.

Jim Abrahamson, 57 years old in 2005, and living in Bentonville, Arkansas, recited that athletic lineage and said "you can tell that as a family, we were really into sports."

He said when he looks back at his own prep career, "the first thing that comes to mind is how fortunate we were in Marshalltown because of the way sports was emphasized. It wasn't that we had anything magic happen. Our magic was the fact that our parents and coaches started us early and encouraged to stay with sports as we went on through high school.

"We had five or six grade schools in a town of 23,000," he continued. "We starting competing against each other in grade school, then we went on up to one of the two junior highs in town – Anson and Central. We had a huge rivalry between those two junior highs in football and basketball. Then when we all joined together at Marshalltown High, we had a core group of 20 or more who were all the same age, and we really meshed.

"I'll tell you what – our class of 1966 was just extraordinary. We were good in every sport Marshalltown offered. There was real team pride then in all the sports. And that's what really stands out in my mind about my own personal experience. When I did well, it was in a team situation. I didn't have any extremely impressive stats, but I got to be a captain on three team sports. The opportunity to lead, and sometimes to excel, in a team situation taught me a lot of valuable lessons."

Abrahamson chuckles now, telling how in high school, he "was so totally dedicated to school and sports that I never had a date 'til the senior prom. I was so focused!"

Actually, he was in the band, too. He liked playing trumpet but hated to march.

"You know, football was really my least favorite sport, but I kept telling myself that if played football, I wouldn't have to march," he said.

But he had real success in football, quarterbacking the Bobcats his last two seasons, including the undefeated senior season when new coach Jack Blazek put in a pass-driven offensive scheme that had Abrahamson scrambling and throwing all over the field. "One of my ends was Steve Cooper, a first team All-Stater," Abrahamson said, "and it was nice having somebody that good to throw to."

Coach George Funk's basketball team was a powerhouse. Midway in the 1964-65 season, Funk settled on a line-up that had three 6 ft., 3 in.

players on the inside – Cooper, Frank Buchan and John Moore – with Abrahamson and 5 ft., 10 in. Ron Peterson at the guards. "We started really putting it together, and I think we wound up 18-3 or 18-4 that year and got beat by Grinnell before we got to state," Abrahamson recalled.

They all came back as seniors for the 1965-66 season, during which they became the first Marshalltown team to play in the just-completed, domed "Roundhouse" gymnasium, which 40 years later, in 2005, was still regarded as one of the best high school basketball facilities in the state.

"We were packing 4,000 to 5,000 people in the Roundhouse for home games," said Abrahamson, who is still proud of the fact that he made the first basket in a game there.

All five Marshalltown starters averaged scoring in double figures that season, with Moore leading the way with 20 points per game. Abrahamson averaged "about 12 or 13."

The team "pretty much blew away everybody we played that year, except for two games," he said. "In the first game of the season, we only beat Waverly-Shell Rock by a point or two – I think we still had our football muscles on. Then a little later, Des Moines Roosevelt came to Marshalltown to play us, and they were really good. In fact, I think that was the first regular season high school basketball game to be televised live in Iowa. My memory is that WHO-TV from Des Moines came up and did it. Roosevelt beat us that night, but then we were able to beat them in the sub-state finals."

All five of the players in the Marshalltown starting line-up went on to play college basketball.

Abrahamson got his degree at Iowa State University in land planning and landscape architecture. He spent five years doing regional planning for governmental agencies in Davenport and Fort Dodge, then in 1975 moved to Arkansas, where he is manager of land acquisition for Cooper Communities, Inc., a company that develops large retirement communities across the southeastern United States, and as far north as Kansas City.

Single now, he has a grown son and two stepdaughters.

After his Iowa State years, Abrahamson played a half-season with a Continental Basketball Association team in Aurora, Illinois, "but it just wasn't right for me." He continued playing Amateur Athletic Association basketball for five years with teams in Iowa and then Arkansas.

He said that "surprisingly, after college, I picked up a whole new sport for me – tennis – and I played that somewhat competitively for several years in the late 1970s. But now my sports playing is pretty well limited to golf, which I really enjoy."

Dan Gable, Waterloo West, 1966

In the Iowa high school state wrestling tournament of 1966, Dan Gable had just wrestled his last match for Waterloo West High School, won his third state championship and finished his prep career 64-0. His coach Bob Siddens remembers "tapping him on the shoulder."

Gable wheeled around into the arms of Siddens, who told him, "Daniel, you're the best I've ever had – or ever will have, I'm sure."

Thirty-one years later, the 1997 University of Iowa Hawkeye wrestling team won their fifteenth NCAA national championship under Dan Gable in his last year as head coach. The tournament that year was held in Cedar Falls, next door to Gable's old hometown. Siddens, by then long-since retired from Waterloo West, was asked by NCAA officials if he would present the championship trophy to Gable and the Hawkeyes. Siddens said he was "thrilled to be able to make the presentation," and after he did, he pulled Gable close and said above all the noise, "You know, Daniel, you were a pretty fair country wrestler. But I do think you're a better coach."

Gable, 56 years old in 2005 and an assistant to the director of athletics at the University of Iowa, has had a lifetime of big moments.

He won two individual national championships as a wrestler at Iowa State University, where he had a career record of 118-1, losing only his last match in 1970. He won the gold medal in the 1972 Olympics in Munich. He came to be regarded as the greatest wrestler ever. Sports Illustrated magazine recognized him as Iowa's greatest athlete of the twentieth century. He had the fabulously successful coaching career with the Hawkeyes.

And, yet, those two relatively private salutes from his old high school coach still rank very highly with him. Coach Siddens, better than anybody, can tell you that all of his star wrestler's achievements, honors and accolades did not come easily. Gable earned them.

"Of course, I've always been very proud of him," said Siddens. "I suppose I don't think of him as much as the Olympic champion or the coach of all those national championship teams at Iowa, like most people do. I just think of him as the cute little red-haired, crew-cut wrestler in my wrestling room, with a great work ethic.

"His intensity and focus strengthened the longer I was with him," Siddens continued. "I've had other wrestlers I've thought were more God-gifted than Daniel, but no one ever had the kind of intensity he did."

Notice how his old coach calls him "Daniel"?

"He's the only person who calls me that," Gable said. "A media guy came up to me not long ago and said he noticed Coach Siddens calls me that. He said he liked it, and he asked if he could call me that, too. I told him you have to get permission from Siddens first."

So what was Dan Gable like on his way up?

He was a swimmer before he was a wrestler, starting in the YMCA program in Waterloo when he was four years old, and he was the Y's state backstroke champion when he was 12. When he was eight, he was working for 35 cents an hour at the Y handing out towels and cleaning lockers.

His interest in wrestling was stirred by his father Mack Gable, who had wrestled in the early 1940s at Valley High School in West Des Moines. After moving to Waterloo for a job as a trucker, Mack met and married Katie Cantwell Gable, whose brother Keith had been a good wrestler at Waterloo East High School.

"Dad made some money trucking, and he decided he wanted to get into farming," Dan said. "So when I was about two years old, we moved to a farm along the Wapisipinicon River near Readlyn. Within six months, there was a flood, we lost all the crops and didn't have insurance for them, and all the animals got some disease from the flood waters and died. We lost everything my folks had invested. So we moved back to Waterloo and Dad started a real estate and construction business that he ran for the rest of his career."

Back in Waterloo, one of Mack and Katie's good friends was Don Buzzard, whose sons Bob and Don Jr. both wrestled at East High, so Dan Gable followed their careers closely as he went through grade school and junior high. Both Buzzards became All-American wrestlers at Iowa State University, and that helped start Dan's interest in also becoming a Cyclone.

Dan's first wrestling opponents included his sister Diane, who was four years older, on the 12-foot square wrestling mat that Mack Gable put in the basement of the family home. "By the time I was in fourth grade, I could beat her and some of her friends sometimes," he said. "I loved the sport immediately."

But as he went through junior high – which was three years back then in Waterloo – Dan not only wrestled, he also was a "spinning back" in the football team's single-wing offense, an infielder in baseball and he also played in a Saturday morning basketball league.

"One thing I always remember about sports when I was that age is that my imagination was really alive," Dan said. "I was Bob Cousy when I was playing basketball, or Mickey Mantle in baseball or Jim Brown in football. Or other times I was myself and I was playing against famous athletes. And beating them, too!"

He said until he was an eighth grader, "I'd never been a very good student, and I'd really been kind of a hellion in seventh grade.

"But then my junior high coach, Martin Lundvall, who was also my algebra teacher, turned my life around academically. He pushed me on how important it was to work hard in class, to study and to succeed. He got my attention, and it made a major difference. I graduated from high school with a 3.2 grade point average, and I had a 2.83 in college. A lot of the things he (Luvall) taught me about studying are the things I've used over the years working with college athletes."

Gable also moved up the job ladder, from towel boy at the YMCA to doing yard maintenance and painting for his dad's company for $1.25 per hour. In high school, he shifted over to working for Martinson Construction in Waterloo, and during his college summers he loaded, hauled and unloaded lumber for the Wheeler-Braun lumberyard in Waterloo.

"I remember when I got the job at Martinson's, Dad went to them and said he'd be glad to pay my wages if they wanted him to – he just wanted me to work in tough jobs like stirring cement and digging ditches," Dan said. "He told me I had to be gung-ho about it, too, or otherwise I'd get fired. So I really got after that job, and stayed with them all through high school. It was hard work, but it helped prepare me for competition."

When Gable started his sophomore year at West High, he was the youngest member of his class – and one of the smallest, too.

"I went to the first team meeting for football, thinking I was going to play, but I was dwarfed by everybody," he said. "Later that year I wrestled as a 95-pounder, so you can imagine how little I was. I looked at those big football players, and I thought, 'Well, maybe it's time for me to start being a single-sport athlete.' The coaches let me still report to football every day, go through their warm-ups with them and then they'd let me go to the gym and work on wrestling."

Siddens got Gable's attention early.

"One high school memory I'll always have," Gable said, "is the time Coach Siddens grabbed me by the collar, picked me up off the floor so my legs were dangling and yelled right in my face, 'Quit feeling sorry for yourself or you're never going to go anywhere!' It was a situation where I hadn't been disciplined enough in my weight control."

In his first varsity season, Gable began ringing up victory after victory, and as he did, he pushed himself harder and harder. He began a routine that he followed throughout high school.

"Our house was right by West High – not 100 yards from the school grounds – and I had a key to the school and to the locker room," he said.

From 6:30 to 7:30 a.m., four days per week, he'd be at the school running around the gym for 18 to 20 minutes, then working on sprints and then on his wrestling moves.

"At first it was me alone doing that," he said. "Then eventually when I was old enough to drive, I'd go pick up my teammate Doug Moses, come back to school and we'd work out together. Then some other guys on the team started coming in before school, too, and by late in the season, we had the whole team doing that."

Gable said when he had study hall in the late morning, "usually a couple days a week, I'd get a pass slip and go down to the gym and do some isometrics, run a little or do some weight lifting."

After school, he'd go through the regular wrestling practice from 3:30

to 5:30 p.m., "but I'd usually be there until 6," he said. "I'd get home by 6:30, eat and then study. About 8:30, I'd head downstairs – or in nicer weather go out outdoors – and run some more."

He said once the season ended, he typically "let my hair down a little bit in April, and then I'd get back to business. But every year, I increased my workout schedule even more, so that by the time I graduated, there was no more off-season. I was practicing the full year 'round."

All of that was far more than Siddens ever asked or demanded of his wrestlers.

"He had a way of making us want to do whatever it would take to get to the next level," Gable said. "He not only did that with me, he got everything out of everybody on the team. That's why West High School has all those state team championships – still more than any other school in the state." The number is 17.

After Gable won the individual state championship in his sophomore year at the 95-pound weight, he won the 103-pound title in his junior year and the 112-pound title in his senior year. Of his 64 high school victories, 39 were pins.

The young Gable was indeed "a driven person," he said. "I learned it back then, and I'm still that way today, no matter what I'm doing."

His intensity undoubtedly helped Gable get through a horrendous family tragedy late in his sophomore year of high school.

On Memorial Day weekend of 1964, his sister Diane, then 19, was raped and murdered in the Gable home by a 16-year-old neighbor boy, while Dan and his parents were away on a fishing trip. The boy Tom Kyle, who had dropped out of school not long before the incident, confessed and is serving life in prison.

After hundreds of interviews in which he has been asked about the murder – and how it has affected him on through his career and life – he no longer flinches at the questions.

"We all have some pretty heavy markers in our lives, some heavier than others," he told me.

After his parents and he got over the initial numbing shock of what happened, Gable said "the thing I was most afraid of was that it was going to break up our family. My folks weren't going to move back into our house. It was like a morgue to them, like it was haunted. But I convinced them to. I moved right into Diane's room myself. They couldn't believe I did it, but it was just something I knew I had to do."

He said Mack and Katie Gable, both of whom lived into the late 1990s, actually became much closer to each other.

Siddens, who was a guidance counselor at West High as well as being Dan's wrestling coach, spent lots of extra time with him, not only right after the murder but in the succeeding years.

"Some of the media have played it up that Diane's death is what made Daniel so intense and successful as a wrestler, but you know, I don't really think so," Siddens said.

Gable said the impact went far beyond wrestling into every aspect of his life.

"The one thing I know that I learned from my sister's death is that you've got to take adversity when it comes and face it head-on," he said. "All my life, that's how I've lived. Somehow, you eventually get over those things."

During the rest of his high school career, and on through his college, Olympic and coaching experiences, his parents became even more zealous Dan Gable fans.

"My mother was something else," Dan said. "Anytime anybody would say or write anything critical about me, she'd send them a 'Get Well' card."

Gable was a class officer during his West High years, and he was also a member of several school clubs but says that while he "had a great time, I probably did miss out on a lot of things other kids did, just because I was so focused on wrestling. I didn't do much dating. I always had crushes on girls, but they never knew about it."

When he was being recruited for college wrestling programs, "I didn't get into that stuff at all," he said. "I'm always into whatever I'm doing right at the time, so I was focusing on my high school wrestling then. I relied on my support system to decide about college. I've always had a good one (support system) around me, for big decisions like that, and I've always relied on them. Back then, it was my parents.

"Lots of wrestling coaches were calling. I did consider Michigan

State because they had a two-time champion from Waterloo. But I was a pretty loyal Iowan, then and now. When Harold Nichols had me come over and visit Iowa State, he put me in his car, drove me around Ames and we ate at McDonald's. Then he showed me Iowa State's horse barn and told me I could ride horses if I came there. I went home and said to my folks, 'Hey, what do you think, Mom and Dad?' They said, 'Well, you're kind of a homebody, maybe you'd like being somewhere close like Iowa State, and you might win a national championship there.' I said, 'Okay., no problem,' and that was it."

Gable and the Cyclones indeed won national championships.

Did he ever ride any of the horses? "No," Gable said, "but I rode a lot of wrestlers."`

In 1974, he married Kathy Carpenter, also a West High graduate, although she's six years younger than Dan so they weren't in school together. They have daughters Jenni, Annie, Molly and Mackenzie. Jenni, married to former Hawkeye and professional baseball player Brian Mitchell, and her husband are the parents of young Gable Robert Mitchell. Being a grandfather? "It's just the greatest," Dan said.

His wife and daughters have become an even stronger support system for him than his parents had been.

"When you're wrestling and then coaching, there's always some controversy, and you really need that support around you," Gable said. "For a lot of years, I was so focused on practices and meets and recruiting that I was gone a lot. But now, I'm turning more of my life over to them."

He had a brief flirtation with the idea of running for governor in the 2002 election, after top Republican Party leaders in the state asked him to consider it. He talked to his family and other advisors, grimaced at the criticism and cheap shots that started appearing almost instantly in some political pundits' columns – and decided against making the run.

"That'd be tough," he said of politics. "Politics is a full-contact sport with no rules and regulations."

Instead, he has gotten deeply into fishing – "big-time now," he said – and recently appeared as a celebrity guest on one of network television's fishing shows.

From his base in the athletic department at the University of Iowa, Gable now works with Hawkeye athletes in many sports on "performance enhancement," stays close to the wrestling program and serves as an ambassador for the university.

He is also perhaps the leading advocate internationally for the sport of wrestling. He is known globally, not only for his own wrestling career, but also as the head coach the U.S. Olympic teams in 1980, 1984 and 2000.

"When I look back, I feel like I was preparing to be a coach all my life," he said. "When I was swimming at the Y, I started learning how to deal with people and about sportsmanship. In junior high, Martin Lundvall got my attention about academics. At West High, I learned a lot from Bob Siddens about counseling. And with all the wrestling I learned from them, and from Harold Nichols at Iowa State, I think it was pretty well determined that I'd be a coach."

So, is Gable happy?

People as intense as he is always struggle with that question, and he rolled his eyes before he answered.

"I'm happy at least some of the time every day," he said, "but that doesn't mean I'm happy every minute. That's how it is when you're driven like I am. There are always things to work on. I'm a determined guy – a perfectionist – although I'm starting to learn to slow that down a little now."

Ron Kennedy, Storm Lake, 1970

Many Iowa high school basketball fans remember him as the first "big man" to play in the state.

Ron Kennedy, who was already 6 ft., 10 in. and 220 pounds as a sophomore during the 1967-68 season, led Storm Lake High to the state championship that year, a return trip to the state tournament in 1969 and a runner-up finish in 1970.

Over those three seasons, the Tornadoes posted a record of 69-4. They were playing in the large-school division of the two-class tournaments, meaning they were beating such schools as Des Moines Roosevelt and Waterloo East.

Kennedy, who is right-handed but could shoot almost as well with his left hand as his right, averaged 25.5 points and 14 rebounds per game in his senior year. He set a school single-game scoring record of 55 points against Sibley, and in 2005, he still owned the school's records for career scoring (1,431) and rebounding (981).

In track, he set a Drake Relays high school record in the discus in 1970 with a throw of 175 ft., 10 in., and he had a personal best in the shot put of 58 ft., 6 in.

In baseball, he pitched – can you imagine batting against a 6 ft., 10 in. fastball pitcher? – and occasionally played first base. Kennedy personally won a game against cross-town rival Storm Lake St. Mary's in 1968 by hitting a home run that Storm Lake Times editor Art Cullen remembers "coming down somewhere near Sulphur Springs," a tiny town four miles east of the Storm Lake ball park. Cullen, who was a young boy then, remembers the Kennedy homer especially well for two reasons – his older brother Bill Cullen was the St. Mary's pitcher who had thrown the gopher ball, and besides, Kennedy was Catholic.

"Oh, yeah, people at St. Mary's High were never real happy with our family," Ron recalled with a laugh. "We were Catholic, but our folks sent us through the public school system. When my brother Randy and I were playing for Storm Lake High, our priest was always commenting to our mother, 'Elaine, you really ought to have those kids here in our Catholic school.' But Storm Lake High was a really good place for us."

Joe and Elaine Kennedy indeed had a stable of good athletes.

Their oldest son Randy, a year older than Ron, played as the sixth man on the 1968 championship basketball team. He was 6 ft., 8 in. and 205 pounds then, and when both he and Ron were in the game, they generally gave Storm Lake control of the inside action. Another brother Steve Kennedy, a year younger than Ron, wasn't as athletically inclined in high school although he had a good run in youth baseball, in which all three Kennedy boys played for teams coached by their father. The Kennedy sisters Deb and Kim, who graduated in 1973 and '74 were both over six feet tall and played basketball, too.

But it wasn't just his size advantage that made Ron Kennedy such a star athlete.

"He was really talented, including as a student," said Barry Holtgrewe, the coach who first spotted Kennedy when he was already 6 ft. tall in sixth grade. Holtgrewe helped bring him along as a young athlete and coached him during his sophomore and junior years of high school basketball and track.

"He could've played any sport for any school in the state," Holtgrewe said. "Besides the basketball, track and baseball that people know about, I'm betting Ron Kennedy was bowling 180 in high school, and I'm sure he was one of Storm Lake's best players in tennis – and even ping pong. There didn't seem to be anything that kid couldn't do. He was unreal!"

And besides all that talent, Holtgrewe said, "Ron was such a nice kid. You couldn't find five pounds of meanness in him."

Storm Lake's junior high school in that era included seventh, eighth and ninth grades, and Kennedy played football as a ninth grader before deciding "my knees were too big a target, and I just didn't care for the game." In that one year of football, he played quarterback, occasionally tight end and also defensive tackle. Holtgrewe remembers him being "a great passer because he was so tall, he could always see all his receivers and almost threw down to them. He also had great hands when they'd throw to him, and I swear, he could punt the ball 40 yards with either foot."

Holtgrewe went on to coach men's basketball at Iowa Wesleyan College in Mount Pleasant for five years before leaving coaching to go into the insurance business at the Iowa Great Lakes and live in Spirit Lake.

He said Storm Lake's 1968 championship team that went 25-0 was a phenomenal one.

"We had so many good athletes around that town in the 1960s, it was amazing," he said. "On the 1968 team, our starting five players were really good, and our second five were almost as good. I always thought our second five could have made it to state, too. I really think that team was probably the best ever to play in the Lakes Conference."

Besides Ron Kennedy in the pivot, the Tornadoes had Jim Jorgensen and Nick Bertram at forwards, and Virg Robinson and Dewey Christensen at guards. They beat Des Moines Roosevelt by 10 points for the state championship.

When Holtgrewe left, he was replaced as coach for the 1969-70 season by Doug Schakel. He took Storm Lake all the way to the state title game, in which the Tornadoes were beaten by Davenport Central.

College coaches had started recruiting Kennedy when he was a sophomore.

"Arizona State was the first school to contact me, and they really stayed after me until I signed in my senior year," he said. "I remember that sophomore year, Barry Holtgrewe was our physical education teacher, and he took our class to the Storm Lake bowling alley. And while we were bowling there for PE, an assistant basketball coach from ASU came in to meet me. I couldn't believe it! He stayed around and watched our basketball game that night, and that's how it all started."

That summer, Joe and Elaine Kennedy parents took Ron and their two daughters on a long driving trip so Ron could visit ASU, Southern Methodist University, the University of Southern California and the University of Denver.

"I knew immediately I wasn't going any place where they had snow," Ron said. "I'd had enough of that already, growing up in Storm Lake."

At ASU, he was a three-year starter, helped the Sun Devils win a conference championship in his sophomore year and averaged about 12 points and nine rebounds per game for his career. "Actually, my focus in college became more defense and rebounding than it had been in high school," he said.

Another highlight of his college career was playing UCLA great Bill Walton to a standoff in the 1973 NCAA western regional finals tournament game, although UCLA prevailed and went on to win another of its national championships in a 30-0 season. "That was an experience," said Kennedy. "They were a great team with Walton, and I remember Keith Wilkes, Larry Farmer and Larry Hollifield. Because of my size in comparison to others that Walton played against, I was able to muscle him from his 'comfortable' position on the low post box. I remember him complaining about my 'beating me up.' "

After college, Kennedy was drafted by the old Kansas City Kings of the National Basketball Association, and was the last player cut before the season started. So he returned to Arizona for a year but stayed in shape with regular workouts. The following year, he played a year in the Italian Professional Basketball League.

In 2005, Kennedy still lives in the Phoenix area, where he has had a very successful career in international sales, ranging from precious metals to asphalt paving machines to jet engine components. Recently, however, he's moved into real estate sales. He has never married, although he and Claudia Jensen have an 18-year relationship.

"I've always felt sports provided a whole lot of socialization skills for me, as well as the lessons you learn becoming part of a team and working together for a common goal," Kennedy said. "When you're fortunate enough to win a state championship doing that, it gives you a lot of special memories."

He said he kept playing pick-up basketball games, and occasional "Old Timers Games" at ASU, "until seven or eight years ago," he said. "I finally gave it up because I felt like it was getting a little risky for a 6 ft., 10.5 in., 320-pound guy to be trying to get up and down that basketball floor."

Jerry Moses, Waterloo East, 1970

He likely was the most heavily-recruited high school athlete ever in Iowa.

They all wanted Jerry Moses of Waterloo East High School to come play football for them – Southern Cal, Notre Dame, Alabama, Ohio State, Nebraska, Colorado, Missouri, Illinois, Iowa, Iowa State, the University of Northern Iowa. (And UNI came closer to getting him than you might have realized.)

"It got to be real cloak and dagger," Johnny Majors, then the coach at Iowa State, told the Waterloo Courier. "It seemed like there were recruiters behind the trees at his house."

Majors and Iowa State won the recruiting battle. But it all came to a "frustrating" conclusion, said Moses, who turned 52 in 2005, because in three consecutive varsity seasons at Iowa State, he suffered a broken foot, a wrenched knee and a broken hand. That kept him from ever reaching his potential for the Cyclones.

"When you play the positions I played – flanker, wide receiver

– you've got to have your wheels and you've got to have your hands," Moses said. "And that's where those injuries were. It was a real emotional letdown for me. It took the fun out of football then. Now I look back on it and I can realize it was a fun time and a great experience for me at Iowa State. But I'll always wish I could've stayed healthy and had the chance to really see what I could do."

The disappointment also now makes his experience at Waterloo East High all the more precious in his mind – and in the minds of a whole lot of Iowa prep sports fans. Those who saw Jerry Moses in action know he didn't leave much, if anything, undone in his years as a Trojan.

In football, he was a first team All-American on the Sunkist-sponsored honor teams picked by Coach & Athlete Magazine. Waterloo East didn't lose a game during his three years on the varsity – in fact, they didn't lose for six consecutive seasons from 1966 through 1971. As a junior, he rushed for more than 1,200 yards and had 19 touchdowns. As a senior, when he had grown to 6 ft., 2 in. and 190 pounds, he rushed for 1,537 yards and 37 touchdowns – averaging 11.6 yards every time he touched the ball.

He had sprinter's speed, recording times of 14.5 seconds in the 120-yard high hurdles and 19.9 seconds in the 180-yard low hurdles. He high jumped 6 ft., 6.5 in. In his junior year, he won all three of those events at the state indoor track meet, and he was usually a top placer in the state outdoor meets, too.

In basketball, he was a three-year starter at guard, helping East High reach the state tournament in both his sophomore and senior years. "That sophomore year, we really thought we had the best team at the tournament, but we got beat by Storm Lake, and they beat us again in my senior year," Moses said. "We couldn't handle the Kennedy boys," whom you've just read about in this chapter. Moses averaged 14 points per game as a junior and 19 as a senior.

Meanwhile, he was a solid "B" student, served as president of his senior class and was one of the most popular kids at East High. In 2005, 35 years later, he'd probably make anybody's list of most popular citizens of the whole Waterloo/Cedar Falls metro area.

Jerry is the second oldest of the five children of James and Doris

Moses, who are in their 70s and live just a few blocks away from him in the neighborhood just north of East High School. They were teenagers when they came with their families from their native state of Mississippi, part of a wave of African Americans who began moving north in the 1930s and '40s for industrial jobs.

High school educations were frivolous to many blacks then, and neither James nor Doris ever graduated. James did prove himself an excellent athlete, playing semi-professional baseball around northeast Iowa and turning down a chance to sign a professional contract with the Chicago Cubs organization. By then, he already had a job at the Rath Packing Co., the meat processor where he spent his career. And he and Doris were already planning their family. She spent her career as a homemaker, while also cleaning houses around the two cities.

They raised daughter Marketa, their oldest child, and sons Jerry, Neal, Ricky and Timmy. All four boys were good athletes, with Neal and Timmy following Jerry as college football players.

James and Doris Moses were loving, strict parents who involved all the kids in worship and activities at the Antioch Baptist Church. Jerry, his family and many of the other second and third generation Moseses are still active at the church.

Jerry Moses had a good three years playing the full sports program at Logan Junior High School, and when he arrived at East High as a sophomore, the Trojans' athletic program could not have been any stronger. Howard Vernon was the football coach, Murray Wier was the basketball coach and Jim Miller joined the staff to coach track. All became Hall-of-Fame coaches in their respective sports.

What was Vernon like? "Coach demanded excellence," Moses said. "If you didn't know your assignment, you didn't play." He was the coach at East High through Moses' junior year, and then joined the football staff at the University of Iowa. He was succeeded at East by Bruce Wiegmann.

And what did Moses think of playing basketball for the legendary Weir? "He was really intense," Moses said. "He believed in playing five guys, maybe six, so you had to be in great physical condition. He was very demanding, very competitive and he preached winning. But he was a fun guy,

438

too – well, he was fun if we were winning. If we were losing, he was not as much fun."

Moses made the East High varsity football team as a sophomore, and three or four games later, he became a starter when another running back was injured.

"That was a real attention-getter, going up to the varsity – a big transition from junior high," he said. "I'd been used to playing with linemen who were 150 pounds, maybe up to 200 pounds. On the varsity, our offensive line averaged 250 or better, and they could move, they were very athletic. And I was shocked at how tough they were. I remember Mike Allen was this big strong lineman, a couple of years older than I was. He grabbed me and said, 'Moses, when you get the ball, you get behind me and I'll clear the way for you. I'll probably get knocked down, and when I do, you just step right on me and keep moving. You can step anywhere you want, except on my eyes. Don't step on my eyes because I've still got to be able to see.' When he told me that, I thought, 'Wow, what kind of guys are these!' "

Of course, Moses became an explosive running back, the top weapon in the Trojans' powerful offense. The team's games at Sloan-Wallace Stadium were all "standing room only," and that was after many additional sets of bleachers had been added. Games against Waterloo West would draw up to 15,000 people.

In fact, it was the victory over West in his senior year that Moses ranks as the highlight of his high school football career.

"We were unbeaten and ranked No. 1, and West was unbeaten and ranked No. 2," he said. "It was for all the marbles, and I did not want to be part of East's winning streak being broken – especially by West."

But the rivalries with West, Cedar Falls and other schools "were always good ones," he said. "I really felt like a lot of the guys on the other teams were my friends, and a lot of them still are. We'd really go after each other during the games, but afterward, it was 'Hey, good game, we'll get you next time,' or 'We'll get you in basketball' and that kind of stuff."

The effort by colleges to try to recruit Moses was like nothing the people of Waterloo and Iowa had ever seen. It began in his junior year, and by his senior year, most sports publications were identifying him as the

No. 1 recruit in the nation. More than 100 colleges contacted him. More than 40 sent coaches to visit him. He made trips to several schools, including Iowa, Iowa State and Notre Dame.

"It was really hard to turn down Notre Dame because of all their tradition, and they were so nice to me," Moses said. "But when Coach Majors came on the scene from Iowa State, that was when I started leaning that way. Deep down, I wanted to stay in the state. The coach at Iowa then, Ray Nagel, came to visit me on a Friday, and on Saturday he was fired, so that situation was too unstable. I really did think about UNI, too, because I liked their coach Stan Sheriff so much. He was talking about the new UNI-Dome and all the big things they were trying to do."

In a page one story in late April of 1970, the Des Moines Register told the story of the recruiting contest going on in Waterloo. "It's a pressure-packed decision for a high school student who a few months ago found himself thrust into the world beyond Waterloo," the Register reported. "It's a world that includes extended telephone conversations with men like University of Alabama football coach Paul (Bear) Bryant and dinners with established football stars like J.C. Caroline, formerly of the Chicago Bears and now on the University of Illinois football coaching staff."

Years later, Moses looks back and says it "was always fun, but there was a lot of pressure."

When the day approached for recruits to sign national letters of intent, it was so hectic that Moses spent the preceding night at his older sister Marketa's home. "I drove by my own house on the way to school the next morning, and there must have been 20 coaches there from different schools, visiting with my mother," he said. "A lot of those guys were still there late that night."

He finally announced he needed more time to make his decision, then in mid-May he announced he would go to Iowa State.

"Coach Majors became more than a coach to me," Moses said. "As the years have gone by, he's become more like a friend. We still talk on the phone quite a bit."

When the injuries cut his Iowa State career short, Moses "was way down in the dumps" and dropped out of school. He returned to Waterloo in 1974, healed up and played a year with the semi-professional Nite Hawks football team in Newton, Iowa. He kept working out, and had unsuccessful tryouts with the Saskatchewan team in the Canadian Football League and with the old Houston Oilers of the National Football League. He also began work as a sales representative for a beverage distributor, then a beverage manager for Hy-Vee Food Stores.

The best thing that happened to him during that time was that he met and married Shirley. She has worked more than 30 years in Deere & Company's sprawling operation in Waterloo, as a tour guide, clerk, secretary and assembly line worker.

Their son J.J. Moses, 25 years old in 2005, had an outstanding football career at Waterloo East High and Iowa State University, and in 2005, he had already played for the Houston Texans for two seasons. At 5 ft., 6 in. and 180 pounds, he is one of the smallest players in professional football, but has made his way as a wide receiver and kick return specialist. "He reflects Shirley's size, because she's only about 4 ft., 10 in., if that," Jerry said. "For him to make it in the NFL is pretty amazing."

Younger son Milan, is more his father's size at 6 ft., 1 in. and 190 pounds. Milan also had a good career at East High and in 2005 he was midway through his football years at Iowa State, where he was a dependable wide receiver.

"I've had as much fun – maybe even more fun – following our sons in sports than I did when I was playing myself," Jerry said. "They're both good kids. They try to do the right things, they listen to what we tell them and they work hard. We've always told them about believing in themselves, doing the best they can and not leaving anything on the table in sports. If you give it all you've got, and then you don't happen to achieve quite what you wanted, well, you won't feel bad about it."

As Jerry's own career advanced – he served as a jobs counselor in a program at UNI and worked as a machine operator at Deere – he always felt there was one thing he left on the table: Getting his college degree.

"I was the first person in my family ever to go to college, and I promised my parents and myself that I'd get a degree," he said. "So while we were working and starting our family, I kept working on classes through Iowa

State. I worked it out so I could pick up the 20 credits I needed by attending classes at UNI, and in 1984 I finished up my work in child psychology. I went back to Iowa State for graduation, too. That meant a lot to me."

Moses played in basketball leagues and "a little golf" through the years, but now a sometimes-painful physical condition means, "I spend more time talking about sports than doing any myself."

In 2000, he had back surgery to remove a spinal calcium deposit that had severed the sciatic nerve. Surgery was successful in removing the growth, but his legs and feet "have been tingly" ever since. That's put Moses on disability.

"I get some pain from it now and then, but I just force myself to bear with it," he said. "I remind myself all the time to be thankful that I'm still up and around and not in a wheelchair. That could have happened."

Moses said he remains a loyal and active fan of East High sports, but he has one concern about high school athletes today.

"You know, I think a lot of kids cheat themselves by not experiencing all the things they could when they're going through high school," he said. "They seem to want to specialize and limit themselves to one sport, and at East now that's mainly basketball. Nobody wants to play football or run track. When I talk to the kids, I tell them they're probably leaving a lot of full-scholarships to colleges unclaimed in the other sports. I think high school is when you want to explore other sports, and other activities beyond sports, and see what they can do for you. It did a lot for me, I know that."

Ted Burgmeier, Dubuque Wahlert, 1974

He was a left-handed All-State quarterback who led the state in total offense in his senior year, as well as leading his team to consecutive seasons with 7-2 records – which were the best in school history. In basketball, he was a guard and one of the leading defensive players on a team that finished second in the state tournament in both his junior and senior years. He was the pole vault champion in the state track meet in his senior year. In baseball, he pitched a two-hitter against a Davenport West team that went on to win the state championship.

Those credentials pretty well establish Ted Burgmeier of Dubuque

Wahlert as one of Iowa's 25 best high school boy athletes.

But there's one thing he knows he'll take a lot of kidding about, like he did almost anytime he and the Golden Eagles of Dubuque Wahlert played their way into the consciousness of the state's sports fans.

He was from Illinois. He's still from Illinois.

He lives in his boyhood hometown of East Dubuque.

Of course, life is really almost seamless between East Dubuque and Dubuque, and for that matter, several towns just to the north in the corner of Wisconsin. They are separated only by the Mississippi River and the state borders, and everybody calls the region "the Tri-State." And if you want to go to a Catholic high school, as Burgmeier did, the only one in the immediate area was and is Wahlert, which takes its name from the Dubuque family that has been a major benefactor. Burgmeier and his seven siblings all went to Wahlert. The three oldest of his four kids have all gone to Wahlert, and little John probably will when he reaches his high school years.

"Back in the 1970s, when we were playing teams during the regular season, it was never even talked about whether some of us were from out of state," said Burgmeier, who turned 49 in 2005. "It was just part of life around here. But I remember when we went to the 1974 state basketball tournament, four of our top six players were from across the border – three from towns just across the river in Wisconsin and I was from Illinois. I remember the Des Moines Register doing a big splash about that."

There is another thing a bit unusual about Burgmeier's athletic career.

"It was always my dream to go to Notre Dame," he said. "And I pretty much had to recruit myself."

A Dubuque area attorney Louie Fautsch was a Notre Dame graduate and a personal friend of the legendary Moose Krause, who was then the athletic director for the Fighting Irish.

"Any time I appeared in a newspaper article, I'd highlight it and send it off to Louie. "My dad helped me do the clippings and that went on for a long time. So one day in February of my senior year, one of my teachers at Wahlert mentioned during class that a 'Coach Kelly' was in town to watch me play basketball. When I went home after school, before that game with Dyersville Beckman, I looked in a Notre Dame football program and found

443

a George Kelly, an assistant coach, and I put two and two together. At the game, I saw this guy wearing a blue blazer and gold necktie talking to Bob Varley, our head coach in football and track. Then the next day, I met him in the school office, and he invited me to visit the Notre Dame campus."

When Burgmeier made that visit, he was taken into the football offices to meet head coach Ara Parseghian. "On top of his desk was a file two inches thick with all those clippings that we'd been sending to Louie Fautsch back in Dubuque," he said. "As a result of our effort, I wound up at Notre Dame."

The Irish got quite a deal with Burgmeier, who was named an All-American defensive back in his senior year.

He was initially a quarterback, but to take immediate advantage of his speed and sure hands, Notre Dame had him return punts in his freshman year. He was eventually switched to defense and was a starting cornerback his junior and senior years. He played in three bowl games and in his senior year, was on the national championship team. That powerhouse team had Joe Montana at quarterback, and among the defensive stars with Burgmeier were Luther Bradley, Ross Browner and Willie Fry. Ever the team player, Burgmeier was also used as a "holder" for the kickers on points after touchdowns.

"The athletic experience was unbelievable at Notre Dame, but even more important were the academic and spiritual experiences I had there," he said. He majored in finance and business economics.

Parseghian, incidentally, stepped aside as head coach after Burgmeier's freshman year, and for his last three years, the head coach was Dan Devine, who came to Notre Dame from Missouri.

Burgmeier was drafted by the Miami Dolphins, was released and then played the 1978 season as a defensive safety and returning punts for the Kansas City Chiefs. He was released after that season, tried out with several other teams and decided it was time to start his business career.

In 2005, he has been a territory manager for the Dubuque-based company A. Y. McDonald Manufacturing for 16 years, which among other things makes brass fittings for the gas and water industries. He covers northern Illinois, southeast Wisconsin and the northwest corner of Indiana.

Burgmeier looks back on his years at Wahlert High School with real fondness.

His first mentor in football was his father Jack Burgmeier, who had played in high school and at Loras College in Dubuque. His uncle Bob Burgmeier was a standout at the University of Detroit and then played professionally in the Canadian Football League.

"I was pretty much weaned on football," Ted said.

So were his seven brothers, all of whom played in high school, and their sister, who was a cheerleader at Wahlert.

"My dad actually single-handedly started the youth football program in East Dubuque – raised the money, coached the team and chalked the fields – so his boys had an opportunity to play," Ted said.

When he reached Wahlert, assistant football coach Dick Weitz, who served as the team's offensive coordinator, "was a big influence on me," Burgmeier said.

"Dick really pushed me. He'd also take me one-on-one and we'd watch game films together, and he worked with me on my mechanics as a quarterback. He really had a great offensive mind, and he taught me the strategies of the option offense we were using. I did quite a bit of running with the ball, and I'd also throw off the rollout. In my senior year, he felt like I'd learned enough that he let me call my own plays instead of sending them in from the sidelines."

Wahlert has always been known as more of a basketball school, and the 5 ft., 11 in. 185-pound Burgmeier was one of the guards for Hall of Fame coach Eddie Colbert, whose fast-breaking teams ruled eastern Iowa from the mid 1960s until 1980, when they won the state championship. Wahlert has stayed tough ever since under Colbert's successors.

In track, Burgmeier ran the low hurdles and on sprint relay teams, in addition to pole vaulting.

"Believe me, I know the risks of pole vaulting," he says now. "I lived them. I missed the landing pads many a time. I hit my tailbone on the pole box. Our pits were small enough back then that if you went a little left or right on your way down, you'd probably hit bare ground."

In his senior season, he won the state championship with a then-record vault of 15 ft. It was memorable not just for the title and record.

"The meet ran so long that it got too dark that Saturday for us to finish the pole vault competition," Burgmeier recalled. "So there were four or five of us who were told we'd have to come back on Monday to finish. We drove home that Saturday night – I really can't remember whether I practiced any on that Sunday – and then we drove back to Des Moines Monday morning."

His closest competitor missed at 14 ft., 6 in., Burgmeier cleared 15 ft. and he finally went out trying to clear 15 ft., 4 in., which would have been a national interscholastic record.

In baseball, he played only his junior season for Wahlert, compiling a 5-2 pitching record with an earned run average below 1.00. The other years, he played in the "Holy Name League," which had all the Catholic parishes in the area organizing their own teams of high school-aged players. "That was really fun, playing ball with the kids from your own parish, and I want to tell you, there were some great athletes playing in that league," he said.

Burgmeier married his high school sweetheart Julie Breitbach, who also came from a family of outstanding athletes. After taking nursing training in Minneapolis, she is now director of health services at Clarke College in Dubuque. Their oldest son Christopher played football at Morningside College in Sioux City, daughter Sarah was a softball player at Winona State University in Minnesota, daughter Stephanie was a good soccer player at Loras College, and John has started sports in elementary school.

"We've really encouraged our kids in sports, and I've been lucky enough to coach them all as they've grown up," Ted said. "I really think athletics teaches you so much, about working hard and achieving your goals. It stays with you, too. Whether you are running extra sprints, or working extra hard in getting ready for an important sales call, you know how to prepare. You learn how to maintain good health through conditioning, you learn how to be a team player, you learn how to accept defeat. There are a lot of those intangibles that are so important in life."

Curtis Craig, Davenport Central, 1974

I'll take the Craig brothers of Davenport Central, you take any other pair of brothers that ever played for an Iowa high school – and we'll beat you three-on-three in any sport.

Curtis Craig, the oldest of three sons of Elijah and Earnestine Craig, was a three-year starter on both offense and defense in football, and as a senior scored five touchdowns in the Blue Devils' 37-32 victory over Des Moines Dowling in the 1973 championship game. He placed in the state wrestling tournament in all three of his high school years, finishing runner-up in his junior year. In track, he was a sprinter, ran on state champion relay teams and competed in both the high jump and long jump, helping Central's team finish second in the state in his sophomore year and winning the state championships the next two years. In baseball – "my first love in sports, actually" – he never played high school ball because it was a spring season then, and he was committed to the track team. But he played American Legion ball in the summers, "and there wasn't a position I didn't play – pitcher, catcher, all of them."

He went on to the University of Nebraska, where he played wingback on coach Tom Osborne's early Cornhusker teams, lettering three years and playing on teams that went 37-11-1, won four bowl games and played in two others. He had tryouts with the professional Chicago Bears and Buffalo Bills, and was one of the last players cut, before starting into his career of working with juvenile delinquents and students with discipline problems, now at Southeast High School in Lincoln, Nebraska.

Coming along five years after Curtis was his brother Roger Craig, whose high school career might have eclipsed all that Curtis had accomplished, except that Roger missed nearly his entire junior year of football after breaking his leg in the season opener. But Roger went on to even greater glory in football at Nebraska, where Osborne called him "without a doubt one of the best backs we ever had," and then he helped the San Francisco 49ers win three Super Bowls in an outstanding nine-year professional career. He still lives in the San Francisco Bay area, working for a software company and doing motivational speaking.

"Our younger brother Artez Craig was also a good football player at Central," Curtis said, "and he played a couple of years of college ball at St. Ambrose in Davenport, but he just didn't have the same breaks and opportunities that Roger and I did."

The Craig brothers' four sisters "have all been athletes in their own right, although none of them ever were in competitive sports," Curtis said. "They played in the kickball, dodge ball and baseball games with us around home when we were little kids, and our oldest sister has run the Bix road race in Davenport in later years."

The Craig family moved to Davenport from the town of Preston in east-central Mississippi in the early 1960s when Curtis was six years old, joining a stream of African Americans relocating from the South for jobs in the more industrially developed Midwest and North.

The children's athletic abilities may have been inherited from their mother, who was a high school basketball player in Mississippi. Their father "was never an athlete, but he was a good musician," Curtis said. "He was an electric guitar player, and he was a really good blues player. I think he probably could've been a professional musician, but he gave it up for this family, working regular jobs so he could be at home with us."

He credits "a couple of innovative physical education teachers" at Jefferson Elementary School "for getting a lot of us involved in sports in our older years of grade school. They'd organize us in teams for everything – football, basketball, wrestling, volleyball. We tried everything. I look back and realize that it all seemed to come pretty naturally to me. I remember winning some, and losing some. But the key to all of it was that we were involved, we were competing and we were learning how much fun it was. I've always thought it was neat that those PE teachers took the initiative to do that."

By his junior high years, which included ninth grade, at J.B. Young School, Craig was starting to excel in football, wrestling and track.

He was an immediate varsity starter in those three sports when he began high school in the tenth grade at Davenport Central. There he played for two Hall of Fame coaches – Jim Fox in football and Ira Dunsworth in track – and his wrestling coach was Tom Murphy.

The Central sports program was very competitive, and highly successful in that era. "You were expected to play hard, with a big heart," Craig said.

His three years of Blue Devil football were amazing. His sophomore and junior years, he played nearly every play of every game. He was starting on both offense and defense, did both the punting and placekicking, and returned punts and kickoffs, too!

"People didn't believe how much I was doing in the games," Craig said. "It didn't bother me. In fact it really made it more fun for me. But going into my senior year, Coach Fox decided it was probably too much, so then I focused on offense and defense.

"I never did get caught up much in keeping track of statistics," he continued. "All we wanted to do back then was just play. My sophomore year, I was mainly used as a blocking back, then I became a running back the last two years. I guess I must've averaged five, six or seven yards a carry, but I'm not even sure."

In wrestling, he finished fifth in the state at 155 pounds as a sophomore, second at the same weight as a junior and then as a senior had a lower finish but still placed while wrestling at 167 pounds. "I might have done better if I'd wrestled lighter that last year," he said, "but since I was looking ahead to college football, I didn't want to cut too much weight."

He'd grown to 5 ft., 10 in. and a normal weight of about 175 pounds then, and with his sprinter's speed, he attracted a lot of attention from college football recruiters.

"That didn't really start until after the state championship game in my senior year," Craig said. "Nebraska was the first team to contact me, and I gauged everybody else against their program and Coach Osborne."

Craig majored in criminal justice, and after graduating, worked eight years with young adults in Nebraska correctional facilities, helping arrange work experiences for them. From 1987 to 1997, he lived in California and worked with delinquents there. He returned to Iowa City for three years of work with middle school students having discipline problems, and then moved back to Nebraska to become a campus supervisor for discipline at the 1,700-student Lincoln Southeast High School.

He and his wife Terri, whom he met while a student at the University of Nebraska, have a 14-year-old son Elijah Curtis II and younger daughters Briana and Erica.

As he turned 50 years old in 2005, Curtis looked back on his athletic career and said, "You know, high school sports was really the foundation for all I have today and all I've done in my life. And I'd say that my high school thrills were much greater than the thrills at Nebraska.

"I think the difference is that in high school, you're with people who've known you all your life. They've watched you grow up. They've coached you. They've been your teammates as little kids. And then there you are as juniors and seniors, playing together on varsity teams, and it's so much fun. I mean, I loved it! I have some great memories from playing for Nebraska, of course, but I have a lot more from playing in high school.

"In fact, I get goose bumps thinking about that, even after all these years. It's a matter of realizing how blessed I was with all those opportunities. And the best part, I just loved doing it."

Fred Hoiberg, Ames, 1991

It's hard to imagine any athlete having more of a lock on his hometown's heart than "The Mayor" does Ames.

Fred Hoiberg was Iowa's player of the year in both football and basketball in his senior year, when he helped the Ames High Little Cyclones to the basketball state championship. He was on a champion medley relay team in the state track meet and finished second in the high jump. He was an outstanding pitcher and outfielder in baseball.

He settled an intense recruiting battle by choosing to stay in his hometown and play basketball for coach Johnny Orr at Iowa State University, where his career was nearly as luminous as his prep years had been. He averaged 15.8 points per game for his ISU career, but more importantly, he had a 3.23 grade point average and became a first team academic All-American. Orr knew early-on that he was getting far more than just a good basketball when he signed Hoiberg, telling reporters that his prized recruit "exemplifies what a student-athlete is all about."

Hoiberg was so popular by his sophomore year at ISU that he received three votes for mayor in the 1993 Ames city election. About that same time, an ISU assistant coach is said to have quipped that, as well as Hoiberg could shoot the ball, he "must have been the mayor of Ames" when he was in high school.

It was a nickname that stuck, in a big way, and still does in 2005 when Hoiberg is 10 years into a nice career in professional basketball, playing for the Minnesota Timberwolves after earlier stops in Indianapolis and Chicago.

In Ames, Vic Roach, an employee at the Dutch Oven bakery, which is a morning coffee spot for local sports fans, told a reporter from the Minneapolis Star Tribune in 2004, "Even the mayor calls him 'The Mayor.' "

That's a fact. Mayor Ted Tedesco, who in 2005 began his eighth year in office, said he's "always said that when Fred's in town, as far as I'm concerned, he can be the mayor and do whatever he wants." He said sharing the title "The Mayor" with Hoiberg "has sure gotten a lot of publicity for me, I'll tell you that, and for my predecessor Larry Curtis, too."

Tedesco, a retired insurance agent, knows Hoiberg especially well because for more than 20 years, he was on the press bench courtside for Iowa State basketball games, keeping statistics for the television broadcasters.

"Fred was the prototypical All-American boy," he said, "good looking blond kid, outstanding student, good citizen and just an exceptional athlete. In high school, he was the talk not only of Ames but of the whole state, and he made it fun for our whole community."

Fred is the middle son of Eric and Karen Hoiberg, who have recently retired from careers in education. Eric was an associate dean of agriculture at Iowa State, and Karen was a fifth grade teacher. Their older son Steve and younger son Andrew were also good athletes at Ames High.

It is a family with deep roots in basketball, as Karen Hoiberg's father Jerry Bush played professional basketball and later coached the University of Nebraska men's team.

Fred Hoiberg, 32 years old in 2005, lives in the Twin Cities with his wife Carol, whom he met in high school, and their four children – daughter Paige, 8, and younger brothers Jack and twins Sam and Charlie.

Fred is as active with his kids as his parents were with him and his brothers.

"Let's see, I've already coached baseball, softball and soccer," he said. "My 5-year-old Jack played in a coach-pitch league in baseball, meaning a coach does the pitching. So I'm out there lobbing these balls, and it hurts your ego a little to have those little guys knocking it around the park on you!"

Fred never got knocked around much in high school sports, that's for sure.

In football, he was a three-year starter at quarterback for coach Kirk Daddow's teams.

"My sophomore year, we were 8-1 in the regular season, and then in the playoffs we got beat by Sioux City Heelan one game shy of the Dome," he recalled, referring to the UNI-Dome in Cedar Falls where the championship games are played. "Our next two seasons weren't quite as successful, but I did all right. I really loved football, and I looked at both Stanford and Nebraska when I was thinking of playing in college. I was born in Nebraska and grew up as a Big Red fan. If I'd have decided to play football, I probably wouldn't have gone to Iowa State."

In fact, when he was at Iowa State and the football Cyclones were wobbling, some fans were urging him to play both sports.

His high school basketball career was just golden.

He was a starter for three years for the Little Cyclone teams coached by Wayne Clinton. His sophomore year, when he played in the post position, the team was ranked No. 1 in the state before being upset by No. 2 Waverly-Shell Rock in a sub-state finals game. The next two seasons, Hoiberg, who had grown to 6 ft., 5 in., moved outside to play the perimeter to take advantage of his shooting ability.

In a magical senior season, Hoiberg and his teammates ran up a 21-3 record and won the championship without ever really being pushed in the state tournament games. "In that regular season, we were pretty dominant except for losing at Des Moines North and at Dowling and Valley in West Des Moines," said Hoiberg, who then laughed and added, "but it's hard to win in those places. They always cheat, you know."

The other key players on that 1991 team were Mike Bergan, Seth Anderson, Nathan Koch, Tim Legg and Rob Kain, and "we're all still very close friends," Hoiberg said.

"When I think about it, I had a great four years at Iowa State and I've really enjoyed professional ball, too, but my best sports memories come from my high school days," he continued. "When we won that state championship in basketball our senior year, to be able to share that with your teammates, the people you've grown up playing with, well, that's really special."

Hoiberg has stayed much involved in both his hometown and his home state. He rounds up several coaches and friends who played with him in high school and college and puts on a basketball camp each summer in Ames, and he has donated most of the proceeds from those camps to the Boys and Girls Clubs. An active Democrat, he has come home to campaign with such Iowa candidates as U.S. Senator Tom Harkin and Governor Tom Vilsack, and he spoke for U.S. Senator John Kerry in the 2004 presidential election. He has also served as honorary co-chair of a literacy program that Iowa First Lady Christie Vilsack organized.

In the summer of 2004, Hoiberg said he hoped "to play a little longer in professional ball, anywhere from a year to four or five years, if I can stay away from injuries."

He's already been mentioned by some political observers as an attractive future candidate for leadership positions in Iowa, if he and his family decide to settle in the state when his basketball career ends.

And they're not just thinking of him as The Mayor.

Casey Blake, Indianola, 1992

He was one of the best four-sport high school athletes ever in Iowa. He went on to become an All-American baseball player at Wichita State University. And in 2005 in his tenth year in professional baseball, he has become a star player for the Cleveland Indians.

Casey Blake, 31 years old in 2005, is quick to acknowledge that he's had a lot of success. However, he's not so sure he is one of Iowa's 25 best-ever high school boy athletes. In fact, he says it's debatable whether he's even the best athlete in his own family.

His father Joe Blake and uncle Jack Blake were outstanding athletes at Indianola High School in the 1960s, then at Simpson College. Joe went on to play professional baseball in the New York Yankees organization. Joe and his wife Chris Blake stayed in Indianola, where he is an insurance agent. He stays active in baseball by serving as pitching coach for the baseball team at Simpson College there.

All three of Casey's brothers – Joe Jr., Ben and Pete – were also all multi-sport athletes, and all have played professional baseball. Pete, 26 and trying to make a comeback from shoulder problems, is still pitching for the minor league Sioux Falls Canaries in South Dakota. Their younger sisters Jamie and Chrissy were among their best fans.

Casey, who grew to 6 ft., 2 in. and 185 pounds in high school, joined the Indianola varsity line-ups in track and baseball in his freshman year.

In track, in which his coach was Steve Carter, he ran the 400-meter hurdles, the 400- and 800-meter individual races, as well as the 400-meter leg on the medley relay. In baseball, playing for coach Jim Blythe, he was a starting pitcher and shortstop.

In basketball, coach Bert Hanson began using Blake in substitute roles during his sophomore year, when the Indians finished third in the state, and then he was a starter as a junior and senior, with the team finishing runner-up to a great Clinton team in 1992. –Blake averaged 27 points per game as a junior, then 21 as a senior on a much more balanced team.

In football, Casey became the starting quarterback his junior and senior year, after Chris Street had graduated. Street was the star athlete at Indianola High who went on to become an outstanding basketball at the University of Iowa before his death in a car accident in January, 1993.

Blake helped the team into his playoffs in his senior year before the Indians were beaten by Burlington.

He was an All-Stater in everything, but he says his statistics aren't all that impressive compared to those of his brothers and a lot of other athletes in Indianola and across Iowa.

"You know, in high school baseball, I didn't have real outstanding numbers," Blake said. "I think I hit just below .500. But one of my older brothers hit way over .500. And while I tied the school's home run record, my younger brother came along with another Indianola player Ryan Gripp, and they both demolished the record – I mean, almost doubled it."

He says Joe Jr. and Pete "were both better quarterbacks than I was in football. They were better throwers than I was, for sure, although my running with the ball was an added element."

In basketball, "I was just a shooter – a three-point shooter," he said. "We played a zone defense most of the time because I couldn't guard anybody. I didn't dribble all that well, I couldn't jump very well, so I focused on trying to be a good shooter."

In track? "Do we have to talk about that?" Casey said. "My least favorite sport." Yet, he was third in the 400-meter hurdles in the Drake Relays' high school division. "That third place at Drake was probably the track highlight for me," he said. "I had the ninth fastest qualifying time, and they were only allowing eight to run in the finals. But one other kid opted out of it because he was in so many other events, so they put me in there – and I wound up getting third. I was pretty proud of that."

What Blake treasures most about his high school sports experience is the opportunity he had to play all four sports, adding he wishes "there would have been a way I could have played golf too, because I love the sport.

"Indianola seemed like an almost ideal situation to me," he continued. "It's a small town, but the school competes in the largest class in sports, so the competition is good. In the small town, if you were an athlete, you were expected to do all the sports. All my friends, we played everything, and I loved it all.

"In fact, I hated to hear it in later years when friends would get better in one particular sport, and they'd say they were thinking about quitting the other ones so they could focus more on the one. I feel like each sport helped me in different ways, and helped me in the other sports, too. For example, track, which I didn't really care for, taught me how to run, showed me how to be a little faster and probably best of all, taught me mental toughness – and that last one has been really important to me in professional baseball."

His own four-sport years ended when he joined the high-level baseball program at Wichita State University, where he was a four-year starter at third base, was a three-year All-Missouri Valley Conference selection, was conference player of the year in 1996 and the same year was named an All-American. He was also an academic All-American.

Blake, who signed his first professional baseball contract with Toronto after his collegiate career was completed, played two and a half seasons in the minor leagues before he made his major league debut with the Bluejays in August, 1999. He had brief stretches in the majors in 2000 and 2001 with the Minnesota Twins, later in 2001 with the Baltimore Orioles and then in 2002 back with the Twins.

His real break came in 2003 when he signed with the Cleveland Indians and played his way into becoming the team's regular third baseman, hitting .257 with 17 home runs and 68 RBI. In 2004, he proved himself even more valuable with the Tribe, again playing all but 10 games while hitting .271 with 18 home runs and 88 RBI. Blake was asked to move to the outfield for the 2005 season, with veteran third baseman and slugger Aaron Boone taking over the infield spot, while retaining Blake's increasingly hot bat in the daily line-up. Blake also was given a two-year contract that the baseball news Internet site MLB.com reported will pay him more than $1 million per year, compared to his 2004 salary of $352,000.

So life in the big time is good for Casey Blake. He and his wife Abbie Archibald Blake, who was an outstanding athlete herself at Indianola High and then Simpson College, now have daughters Bailey and Lauren, who are turning 4 and 2 years old in 2005.

With all he's done in baseball, both at Wichita State and in the major leagues, can the thrills Casey had as a high school athlete in Iowa compare?

"My high school sports experiences must measure up pretty well against what I've done later, because I still have dreams about big games at Indianola," he said. "Playing in high school, I guess it was the last time I played with friends as teammates – people who really cared about each other – when placement of self wasn't even a factor. All we cared about was the team. I miss that. You don't find that much in professional ball."

The stories about Casey Blake, the team player, are still being written. Some Cleveland Indian fans – and possibly even some in Cleveland's management – were surprised when Blake so willingly gave up the third base position in early 2005 and moved to the outfield, making way for the veteran Boone at third.

"I'm not in any position that I'm going to tell them, 'I'm only going to play here or I'm only going to play there,'" Blake said in an MLB.com interview. "I'm a team player." His manager Eric Wedge noted: "I tell you, if you talk about the type of ballplayer we want here, that's it – a team player. He's willing to do whatever it takes for us to be a better team. He knows we're a better team with he and Aaron Boone on it."

But of all the stories about Casey Blake's selflessness as an athlete, and his consideration of others, the best goes back to his 1991-92 senior year at Indianola High – in fact, to his last game for the Indians.

"By that school year, Casey was 'Mr. Everything' in Iowa high school sports – everybody in Iowa knew about him," said Jack Lashier.

You may know Lashier's name as the director of special projects for the Iowa High School Athletic Association, and the executive director of the IHSAA's new Iowa Hall of Pride in Des Moines. But in early 1992, three years before he joined the IHSAA, he was just another dad from Marshalltown who had shown up in Indianola to watch his son play in a seventh grade "B" team basketball game.

"Our son Jackson was born with hemiplega, something that affects the motor development on one side of his body," Lashier said. "So, he can't use his right arm, hand and leg – except for sort of assisting and balancing. It was obvious, if you watched him play, that he had some sort of problem."

Jack was "sitting there in Indianola watching Jackson play, and a guy came over and sat down sort of close, and we started visiting. Obviously, he was a dad, too, and he asked if my son was playing, and I pointed out Jackson. As we watched the game, he asked what happened to his arm, so I told him."

The fan introduced himself as Joe Blake Sr., pointed out his youngest son Pete playing on the Indianola seventh grade team, and mentioned his older son Casey was a senior at Indianola High.

"Joe asked me for our address, and the next thing we knew, Jackson received a letter from Casey Blake," Jack Lashier said. "In fact, Casey wrote him several letters the rest of that year, all encouraging Jackson to stay involved in sports."

As the school year went on, Casey Blake was appearing in the newspaper, on television and radio all the time as the Indianola High star athlete. A wide-eyed young Jackson Lashier in Marshalltown was astonished he was continuing to receive letters from Blake.

Then came the baseball season, when Blake was expected to lead the Indians into the state tournament. Their opponent in the sub-state finals, in which a victory would qualify them for state: Marshalltown.

"The game was being played on the neutral field at Southeast Polk, so our whole family decided to go – to watch our Marshalltown Bobcats but also because we knew we'd get to see Casey," Jack Lashier said. "Indianola was supposed to beat the Bobcats, and we arranged with the Blakes that after the game, Casey would meet Jackson for the first time and they could visit in person for the first time.

"Well, Indianola got beat in the last inning and, of course, Casey was devastated. I told Jackson that Casey wouldn't feel like talking to him because this was his senior year, and going to the state would be his biggest goal that summer."

But Jackson didn't want to leave, so the Lashier family waited around in the parking lot for about 30 minutes.

Suddenly, they heard the clatter of baseball spikes from someone running across the asphalt. They turned around, and here was Casey Blake, sweat-soaked, uniform dirty, shirt untucked.

Casey apologized for being late, then turned to Jackson and a long, happy conversation began.

"I just couldn't believe he would want to take time right then to talk to a little kid from Marshalltown," Jack Lashier said. "But he couldn't have been more humble or gracious."

When they were finally saying their good-byes, Jack told Casey he was surprised he'd take the time to talk after such a disappointing loss.

"Of course I'm disappointed we didn't win," Casey told him, "but you know what? In the whole scheme of things that will happen in my life, this is just a blip. Talking to a kid who looks up to me is way more important. I admire Jackson so much for overcoming his handicap and doing what he is doing. God blessed me with lots of natural talent, and it's easy for me to do well in sports. I just want to do everything I can to encourage kids that don't have as much talent but still try, and that's why I felt like it was important to come out here and talk with Jackson."

The rest of the story?

Jackson Lashier played four sports through his middle school years, then in high school cut back to the sports that "I could do with one arm," he said. "I was a role player on special teams in football, but tennis was really my most successful sport. I lettered four years in it."

After graduating from Marshalltown High in 1997, Jackson went on to Iowa State University, graduating in 2000 in English. He received a master's degree in divinity from Asbury Theological Seminary in Kentucky, in 2005. And at 27 years old, he was recently married and planned to begin work on a Ph. D. in early church history, which he would eventually like to teach at the college level.

In some future lecture, or possibly even a homily, he will be able to draw on a lot of personal experiences. And he's got a terrific one to share from that –summer day back in 1992.

"You know, when Casey took time for me when I was in seventh grade, it was right when I'd started to run into difficulty being able to keep up with the other kids, with my physical problem," Jackson said. "It probably would've been pretty easy for me to give up sports. But with his letters, and then when he came out and talked to me even after his team lost that big game, he really did inspire me.

"To this day, I don't know what caught Casey's attention about my story, but when I look back on it, it sure didn't seem forced. It meant the world to me, I'll tell you that."

Tim Dwight, City High, Iowa City, 1994

As a high school freshman, the first time he touched the football in a varsity game, he ran 80 yards for a touchdown.

In the preceding two years, word had started to spread around the state that City High of Iowa City had a real prospect coming up from junior high competition. In his freshman year, he played on City High's sophomore team, but then was brought up to the varsity for the playoffs at the end of the regular season.

His sudden long run with the football in that late fall of 1990 confirmed what the whispers had been: Tim Dwight Jr. might become one of Iowa's best high school athletes ever.

And he did just that.

"For the next three years, he was virtually unstoppable in football," said John Raffensperger, the legendary City High track coach and assistant football coach who has compiled the school's sports history. "He had 43 touchdowns in his senior year."

That football team, coached by Larry Brown, went 13-0 and won the Class 4A state championship.

Dwight was just as good in track, in which he helped Raffensperger's Little Hawks teams to a runner-up finish at state in 1991, then led them to three consecutive team championships from 1992 to 1994. That began a streak of six state titles in a row for City High.

"Tim could do everything in track," Raffensperger said. "He won or was part of 12 championships in events in the state meets. He won the 200-meter sprint all four years, he won the long jump three times, he won the low hurdles once and he ran on four winning relay teams."

No question that Dwight, who competed at 5 ft., 8 in. and about 170 pounds in high school, had a lot of natural ability. But that is not really what made him All-Everything in high school, All-American in football at the University of Iowa and then a successful professional football player who in 2005 is in his eighth professional season.

"He was probably the hardest worker I've ever had," Raffensperger said. "He made everybody else around him better, because they could see that even with all his talent, he worked so hard."

And Dwight has always had another characteristic that helped him become one of Iowa's favorite athletes ever, as well as being one of its best.

"Tim has always had such a dynamic personality," Raffensperger said. "At every level he's been on, when he walks into a room, it's just electric. When he'd come out on the track to get ready for an event, other people would just stop to watch him. He's the only guy I ever saw in high school who had kids from competing teams ask him for his autograph. And I can't remember ever seeing him in a grumpy mood."

His football coach at the University of Iowa, Hayden Fry, hit upon that same thought in his 2001 book, "Hayden Fry: A High-Porch Picnic." The veteran Fry told his co-author George Wine: "I never coached a player I enjoyed more than Tim Dwight. He was so full of energy and inspiration that he made everyone around him better and made the game a lot more fun. Just like Jerry Levias, who I coached at SMU, Dwight brought electricity to the game. Whenever he touched the ball, something good almost always happened. Both Dwight and Levias were real game breakers, the kind of players who drove opposing coaches crazy trying to figure out how to contain them."

Dwight, at 29 years old in early 2005, looks back on his sports career as "a great run and a whole lot of fun. I just hope I have another three or four years in me in pro football."

He said he draws his athletic talent from his father Tim Dwight Sr., who was a tennis player and wrestler at Burlington High School. His mother Nancy is a Burlington Notre Dame graduate. Tim's older sisters were both athletes in the late 1980s at City High, Shelly as a softball pitcher and Chris as a volleyball player. Younger brother Jason, a 1998 City High graduate, was an outstanding sprinter in track.

Tim Sr., a retired social studies teacher and assistant coach at City High, got the kids started early in sports. And he and Nancy, also a retired office worker from the University of Iowa, instilled a strong work ethic in their children.

"My parents always told us no matter what, you show up, have fun, compete and work very hard," Tim Jr. said. "And they always said, 'Be humble about what you do.' "

It was "a great support system," he said, one that "definitely fueled your desire to do the best you could."

In his later high school years, when it was clear that no one at City High was going to knock him out of his starting positions, he had no trouble staying motivated. "I'd always compete against my own statistics and times from the year before," he said. "I'd push myself to get to the next level."

As several other outstanding athletes have said in this chapter, even though many went on to great success as college and professional athletes, "you definitely have more fun as a high school athlete," Dwight said. "The big part of that many of your teammates have been your classmates since first grade. There were a bunch of us in Iowa City who, from the time we were five years old, were talking about a goal of winning state titles."

He's always been one to have fun not only with other athletes and coaches, but also with the fans and media. One particular reporter he's enjoyed an unusual relationship with is Scott Saville, now of KCRG-TV in Cedar Rapids but who was with KGAN-TV in that city when Dwight was in high school in nearby Iowa City.

When the 1994 state track meet was nearing, Saville did a profile story on Dwight as he was getting ready for his final high school sports competition. The story had old footage of Dwight's football glory, as well as track highlights from the sprints, hurdles and long jump. As Saville was looking into the camera, narrating the end of the story, viewers could see over his shoulder that somebody was racing toward him. It was Dwight, rocketing down the approach strip toward the long jump pit at City High!

"I was sort of crouching between the jump board and the pit, and the last thing you saw when I ended the story was Tim jumping right over my head," said Saville–. "It was just kind of a wild idea I had, to add some fun to the story. Tim was such a fun kid that he was game for about anything."

Dwight and Saville had another interesting connection earlier in that school year.

"During the football season in his senior year, he was getting offers from schools everywhere – South Carolina, Notre Dame, Wisconsin, lots of others – in addition to Iowa," Saville said. "I was talking to him one time and I said if he'd sign with Iowa, I'd walk down Interstate 380 in Cedar Rapids in my boxer shorts. So when he made the decision to be a Hawkeye, he called our station and held me to what I'd said. It must've been during basketball season, because I remember it was awfully cold, but I walked from one end of Cedar Rapids to the other on the Interstate, wearing my boxer shorts."

With a full report for the television sports news, of course.

Dwight's professional football career as a wide receiver and kick return specialist has included three years with the Atlanta Falcons, four years with the San Diego Chargers and in early 2005 he signed with the New England Patriots. He's had a good career, despite injuries ranging from collapsed lungs, to a hamstring injury, to breaking his foot in the 2004 season.

He said he's uncertain which way life will lead him when his football career ends.

"I was a sports management major at Iowa, so that interests me, but I also think I'd enjoy being a track coach some day, too," Dwight said. "I also definitely am thinking that when I'm done in football, I want to take about two years off. When you go straight from high school sports, to college and then right into the NFL, you never get a chance to kick back and let yourself slide a little. I look forward to being able to do that."

The young bachelor has had fun – and connected well with people – wherever he has played.

In his San Diego years, he split his residences between San Diego during the football season, Lake Tahoe much of the rest of the year, with some time in Iowa City each summer. In San Diego, he became a familiar figure pedaling his bicycle through his neighborhood toward the Pacific Ocean, while towing a surfboard, on his way for some surfing or wake boarding. He has also become a yoga practitioner, and in 2002 opened The Studio in Iowa City for instruction in yoga and the Pilates exercise program.

As Dwight has become more affluent from professional football, he has invested in real estate and said he enjoys working on building projects. "I find I really like working with my hands," he said. "There's a feeling of creating something. It's neat at the end of the day to have something you can see that you've done."

He has also hosted football camps in Iowa City the last few summers. Proceeds were split between the Holden Comprehensive Cancer Center at the Children's Hospital of Iowa, which helped his sister Chris become a cancer survivor, and the Tim Dwight Scholarship Fund that helps young Iowans with college expenses.

He has been especially generous to the athletic programs at City High, where he's donated tens of thousands of dollars for a new scoreboard, an electrical timing system for track, new sets of starting blocks, new hurdles, new equipment in the weight room and other improvements. Each fall, he has sponsored a bus trip for players from City High, Iowa City West High and two junior high schools to attend a professional football game in either Kansas City or St. Louis. "He has a strict rule for that trip," said Raffensperger, "You can't go if you have any detentions or have been in other trouble."

Dwight said he hopes he can do more for his old high school and for young people in general in years to come.

"I was given such a great opportunity at City High," he said. "Our coaches and teachers and facilities were always so good. I've become a big believer in that you never forget about where you came from, because those people and programs molded you into whatever you've become. And if you're able, you need to give something back."

Zeron Flemister, Sioux City West, 1995

He was a running back the likes of which football fans in Sioux City and other western Iowa cities had never really seen before.

Zeron (pron. "Ze-RON") Flemister, of Sioux City West, was a 6 ft., 4 in., 210-pound powerhouse – so strong he won a city shot put championship, so agile he was first team All-State in both football and basketball, so fast he was on a state champion sprint relay team.

How the heck did opposing defenses stop him back in those three seasons from 1992 to 1994?

Not many could stop "Z," or "The Z-Man," as he was known by friends and foes alike.

"I've been covering prep sports for 25 years, and Zeron Flemister had the single best high school athletic performance I've ever witnessed," said Barry Poe of the Sioux City Journal. "It was the last game of his senior year against Council Bluffs Thomas Jefferson. He had something like 300 yards and six touchdowns – in one half! They didn't play him the whole rest of the game. Just thinking about that game brings back some great memories."

In fact, the total was 326 yards in that half on 17 carries, launching the Wolverines to a lopsided victory that night.

Flemister says he enjoys such memories now, but mostly he's grateful for all the opportunities because he grew up in Sioux City and attended West High. His experiences helped him win a football scholarship at the University of Iowa, and that launched him into professional football, in which he played four years as a tight end with the Washington Redskins. He was picked up by the New England Patriots before the 2004 season, but he ruptured an Achilles tendon in training camp, had surgery and missed the season. He went through rehabilitation, but was released by the Patriots in early 2005 and his agent began looking for another interested National Football League team.

"Sports is probably the most important thing that happened to me in life," said Flemister, who turned 28 in 2005 and lived in Denver, Colorado. "Because of sports and because of all the help I got at West High, I was able to go to college, get my education paid for and get my degree. Without sports, I wouldn't have gotten my education – I couldn't have afforded it. I'm the first person out of my family to go to college and get a degree, and I'm real proud of that."

He majored in health, sport and leisure studies at the University of Iowa, with a minor in human relations. He plans eventually to use his education to open and operate "a speed camp or gym, with personal trainers," he said. "And I wouldn't mind coaching on the high school level, but probably more as a volunteer coach rather than as my career."

Flemister figures his grandmother Dorothy Flemister may have saved his life.

"I was born in Chicago, in a really bad part of town near Comiskey Park on the south side," he said. "My mother, who was also named Dorothy, was so young when she had me that we were staying with her parents and her brothers. We'd had a couple of relatives who were killed in that neighborhood, and my grandmother decided she did not want any of us in that environment. She had some other relatives in Sioux City, so we all moved out there when I was 3 or 4 years old."

His uncles Tony, Aaron and Adonis Flemister – all of whom became West High athletes in the 1980s – started taking little Zeron to the Boys Club on the west edge of downtown Sioux City.

"They got me started in wrestling when I was six years old," Zeron said. "I wrestled three or four years, but then when I was about 10 years old, I was getting too big for the other kids, so that's when I started playing basketball and football at the Boys Club."

He said he got early direction from a volunteer coach Archie Arvin Jr., who was well-known as the owner and operator of Archie's Diner in Sioux City. Arvin, who died in 2003, coached for more than 30 years at the Boys Club, in Youth League football, Little League baseball and other sports programs for kids.

"Archie got a lot of us started in sports and kept us interested," Flemister said.

Arvin also served as an assistant coach in several sports at West High School and at nearby Woodbury Central High.

Flemister got a whole lot bigger and stronger as he went through his later elementary and middle school years. By the time he was a freshman at West High, football coach Al Charlson had him punting for the varsity team.

The next three seasons he was a starter at running back on offense, strong safety on defense and he also returned kicks.

"I pretty much did everything in football," he said. "West had a string of 40-some losses when I started high school, so my sophomore year when we won two games, everybody thought we were heroes. Then the next year, we went 8-1 and made the state playoffs, and everybody really went crazy. Heelan beat us then, but we felt like we had things on the way."

He was a three-year starter for coach Jim Hinrich's Wolverine basketball teams. He tore a cartilage in his knee early in his sophomore season and missed the rest of it, but was back starting at center as a junior and then as a shooting forward as a senior.

"I think that senior year, I averaged about 20 points a game and might have been the scoring leader in the Sioux Interstate Conference," Flemister said. "But what I remember best is that I got a dunk in every game. We had this inbounds 'Alley-Oop' play we used. It's fun to think about that.

"We never really did all that well in basketball, but like in football, we helped get the program built back up. A year after our class left, Coach Hinrich took the team to state and won the championship, so maybe we contributed a little to that."

Interestingly, "all through high school I really thought I was going to be a college basketball player instead of a football player," Flemister said. "But that changed after I ran in the Drake Relays in my sophomore year, and the football coaches found out I had some speed to go along with my size."

He saw limited action on the varsity track team in his freshman year, then became one of coach Rick Berthelsen's real workhouses the next three years. He ran the 100, 200 and 400-meter sprints, and also ran on the sprint relay teams. His 4-by-100 relay team won the state championship in 1995. He was occasionally used in the long jump and shot put, too."

Berthelsen "became a real mentor for me," Flemister said. "My greatest high school moments were with that coach."

The coach said he became aware of Flemister as "he was coming out of junior high, and he already was a big kid. And he had real talent, too. He was running 100 meters in the low 11-second range, even below 11, so we were able to work him into our varsity track team right away. We wound up going to state that year, and that whole season gave me extra time around him, and we had a lot of fun together.

"What I sensed right away was that Zeron was a big, tall, gentle giant, actually," Berthelsen continued. "I think he got into sports because he was so big, and a lot of people had expectations of him because of his size. So I tried to build a relationship with him that whether he was finishing first or second place in the sprints didn't make any difference to me, that what I admired about him was that he was out there trying and was having fun at it."

The two of them remain close still in 2005.

The 56-year-old Berthelsen, a biology teacher and coach for 19 years at West High, has also helped with the school's weight lifting program. "When Zeron gets back to Sioux City, we still get together, go pump a little iron and re-live a lot of old times," the coach said.

He said Flemister "has called regularly ever since he went on to the University of Iowa, and he still does now. We have long conversations, and it's a pretty special relationship. You know, I've always believed that when you get into teaching, you're really there to serve kids. So I try to be one that when a kid knocks on my door and says he wants to talk, I take the time. You can't be their parent all the time, but you can try to give them a little guidance and encouragement and keep them headed in the right way. Some you wind up getting pretty close to, and Zeron was one of those for me."

At the University of Iowa, Flemister became a tight end and special teams player for Hayden Fry's teams. He red-shirted as a freshman, then lettered in 1996, sat out the 1997 season for disciplinary reasons, then had good seasons as a junior and senior.

"I should have had a better career at Iowa than I did, but I had a few setbacks that were my own fault," he said. "Once I got the trouble-making days out of the way, then I went on and had a pretty good run there. And I wound up learning a good, hard work ethic at Iowa. That's what got me through four years of pro football as a free agent. It's tough to play that way, when you've got to constantly prove yourself, but I've been able to do it."

Zeron's younger brother Julian Flemister, who also starred at West High, has now played two years as a running back and kick return specialist for Wayne State College in Nebraska, where he is a junior. Julian is following Zeron's example of using sports to get an education.

"West High gave us that opportunity," Zeron said. "You know, I go back home now and visit with friends who didn't go to college, and they're not doing much. I could've been right there with them, if it hadn't been for sports.

"And I've still got relatives in Chicago, too, in that same old neighborhood. I stop to see them now and then, and there are rats as big as cats walking around there. Man, I was scared being there in the daytime. I sure didn't want to be there much after dark."

His grandmother saved him, he's sure.

Darin Naatjes, West Lyon, 1999

He grew up in a town so small it's not even on a state highway.

But by the time 6 ft., 7 in., 245-pound Darin Naatjes was finishing his high school sports career at West Lyon High School, a whole lot of very famous college coaches knew how to get to Alvord, pop. 187, in the northwest corner of Iowa. You drive to the intersection of Lyon County Roads A34 and K30, they could tell you, "and if you can't figure out which house is theirs, ask the city clerk – she's his mom."

Naatjes was a three-year All-Stater in baseball, a two-year All-Stater in football and basketball, and a two-event state champion in track. Playing seven different positions in football, he helped West Lyon win the state championship in his senior year.

Meanwhile, he also served as president of his class as a junior and graduated as its valedictorian with a 4.0 grade point average.

He landed a full-ride scholarship at highly-respected Stanford

University in California, choosing it over Iowa, Iowa State, Nebraska and Arizona State. At Stanford, Naatjes was a top player in both football and baseball. In 2002, he signed a professional baseball contract with the Philadelphia Phillies organization and spent his first two professional seasons pitching for the Phillies' minor league team in Batavia, New York. In the off-season, he returned to Stanford to complete his degree in American studies. In 2004, he had a partial tear of a tendon in the elbow of his right arm – that's his pitching arm. But after successful "Tommy John" surgery and nearly a year of intense rehabilitation, Naatjes was able to continue his baseball career in the Phillies organization during spring training of 2005.

Not bad for a kid from Alvord, Iowa, huh?

"I've been fortunate enough to see a lot of different places around the country, but when I get back to Alvord, it still seems like home," said Naatjes, at 24 years old. "As you get to know your teammates in pro ball, eventually you get around to talking about where you're from and what your hometowns are like. When I tell them about Alvord being a small farming community with about 180 people, they can't even fathom it. But I'm thankful for having grown up there, I'll tell you that."

Do people in the community realize just how special the Darin Naatjes story is?

"Oh yeah," said Wes Koedam, the grain elevator manager who has been mayor of Alvord since 1988. "Darin was always a standout in sports, from day one as a PeeWee League baseball player, but he's always been the kind of kid who didn't gloat over his talents. You know, when you live in a town this small, everybody's kids are like your own. So everybody here has watched Darin all through these years, and we've all known his whole family. So while some people might put Darin on kind of a pedestal, here in Alvord, we still treat him as 'just Darin.' I think he probably likes it that way, too."

The fact is there have been a lot of good athletes in Alvord and also around Larchwood and Inwood – the larger towns that make up the West Lyon school district. LaVar Woods, who would go on to play football at the University of Iowa, and Kyle Vanden Bosch, who went on to a great football career at the University of Nebraska, were in their last two years at West Lyon High when Naatjes started there. Woods and Vanden Bosch have gone on to good professional football careers, both playing for the Arizona Cardinals in 2004.

But "Darin was the one who kind of rose to the top of them all," said Mayor Koedam.

Both of Darin's parents, David and Diane Naatjes, were good athletes at West Lyon High. Both were basketball players, and David was an outstanding softball player well into his 40s. By 2005, they were divorced, with David working at an industry in Sioux Falls, while Diane works as a secretary at a car dealership in Sheldon and also at a café in Alvord, in addition to having served as the city clerk for more than 25 years.

Darin's sister Dawn Meyer, who lives now in the Alvord area, was a three-sport athlete at West Lyon and brother Danny, of Sioux Falls, was a football player.

How did Darin develop into such an outstanding athlete?

"With having LaVar and Kyle and a lot of other good athletes just ahead of me, I learned a lot," he sad. "And you know, in the small school, we played all four sports, and I think that made us better all-around athletes. At the time, we took that for granted that we'd play everything, but now I look back and realize how blessed I was to get to do that. A lot of high school players around the country have to start specializing in one sport.

"Another factor for me is that we had great coaches at West Lyon, and they all had a big impact on me."

He credits Eric TeGrootenhuis as one coach "who really helped me."

TeGrootenhuis is a Farm Bureau Insurance agent who since 1987 has been a volunteer assistant football coach at West Lyon. One of his coaching specialties is weight lifting.

"Eric got me into weight training, and he worked with LaVar and Kyle and a lot of other athletes," Naatjes said. "He'd get up at 5:30 in the morning, pick us up when we were too young to drive ourselves, and we'd go lift at the high school before school started. He didn't have to do that, but he's a guy who believed in the athletic program so much he wanted to do what he could to help us get stronger."

TeGrootenhuis said, "Because these guys were all four-sport athletes, they all had practices after school, so the early morning was about the only time they had for lifting. And I want to tell you, those three were really committed to the weight training. We'd go Tuesday, Thursday and Sunday mornings, and these kids wouldn't miss. Even if Christmas fell on one of those days we lifted, we were there."

When he began working with Naatjes after his freshman basketball season, TeGrootenhuis described him as "a skinny little thing – well, maybe not so little because he was probably 6 ft., 5 in. already. As he grew up and filled out, we were able to make him a whole lot stronger."

He said he now often thinks about having had Woods, Vanden Bosch and Naatjes go through West Lyon, all in one generation of high school students, and shakes his head in amazement.

"When they're going through, you're working with them every day and you kind of take them for granted," TeGrootenhuis said. "Then when they leave, you realize how good they really were, and you wonder, 'Will we ever have anybody like those three here again?' "

Tim Snyder, who coached them in basketball and baseball, knows the feeling.

"Boy were we spoiled!" said Snyder, who in 2005 was the elementary school principal in the West Lyon schools. He noted having coached the NFL players "and almost a dozen NCAA Division I athletes," and said Naatjes is "without a doubt the best all-around athlete I've ever seen at any level."

Naatjes' football coach was Jay Rozeboom, and Gary Kruse was his track coach.

Jeff Parkinson, sports editor of the Lyon County Reporter in Rock Rapids and the West Lyon Herald in Inwood, noted in 2004 – five years after Naatjes graduated – he still owned 15 or more school records at West Lyon.

His high school baseball statistics were especially amazing, as he had a .507 career batting average with 22 home runs, 117 runs batted in, 45 stolen bases and, as a pitcher, 182 strikeouts in 125 innings.

"I've seen a lot of excellent high school baseball players," said Parkinson, "but Darin's line drives were the only ones that sliced. That's how hard he hit the ball."

At Stanford, he played tight end in football, and in baseball he spent first two seasons in the infield and outfield. Then his coach Mark Marquess asked him to make the switch back to pitching full-time. "You can't coach what he has," Marquess told the press about Naatjes. "You can't coach being 6 ft., 7 in., athletic and throwing 94 miles per hour."

It's probably testimony to his athletic ability that Naatjes was able to make the transition back to pitching – after two years as a position player – as well as he did. Coming out of the bullpen in that junior season, he made 19 appearances, ran up a 4-0 record and had two saves with the third lowest earned run average on the team. He signed with the Phillies in August of 2002.

Naatjes had a promising start to his professional career with the Class A Batavia Muckdogs in New York late in the 2002 season and the entire 2003 season. His elbow injury occurred in early April 2004. That May, he had the intricate "Tommy John" surgery to repair the tendon damage and he spent the rest of the year at the Phillies' spring training facility in Clearwater, Florida, doing rehabilitation. The surgery is named after a former major league pitcher who had the tendon repair and was able to resume his career. Naatjes hopes to do just that.

"This injury is almost as much of a mental thing as a physical thing because the rehabilitation is so long – a good 12 months," Naatjes said during spring training of 2005. "It was really disappointing because I felt like I was making some real progress after just getting back into pitching again in my junior year of college. But I feel fortunate that this surgical procedure has been developed, because it has saved a lot of guys' careers in recent years, and it helps to be able to compare thoughts with some of them while I'm going through the rehab."

His spring training regimen in 2005 included pitching simulated games in the bullpen, then pitching some batting practice, then some limited pitching appearances in exhibition games. He expected to spend the 2005 season with a Phillies' Class A team, either in Clearwater or in Lakewood, New Jersey.

But no matter what his professional career winds up being, his high school glory will be the talk of northwest Iowa in general, and of little Alvord and Lyon County in particular, for generations to come.

"It was really a golden era at West Lyon," said local sports editor Parkinson.

Nate Kaeding, Iowa City West, 2000

In football, he was the star kicker on a team that won back-to-back state championships in 1998 and 1999. In basketball, he was a starting guard and key defensive player on a team that won the state championship in 2000. In soccer, he kicked the winning goal in an overtime shootout that gave his team the 2000 state championship. Think of that – in his senior year, this athlete was on three state championship teams at the highest level of prep competition in Iowa.

And yet, what people may remember longest about Nate Kaeding of Iowa City West is that he was one of the most fiery, competitive athletes who ever played in the state.

That's partially because so many Iowans came to know him in his college years as the unflappable, always reliable and supremely confident place kicker in football for the University of Iowa Hawkeyes, with whom he became a two-time first team All-American. And he had a great first year of professional football in 2004 kicking for the San Diego Chargers.

"We knew about Nate Kaeding when he was in junior high," said Reese Morgan, the coach who built a football powerhouse at Iowa City West from 1991 to 1999, and then became an assistant football coach at the University of Iowa.

"We identified him then as an athlete who was very skilled in all the sports. The first time I worked with him directly was his sophomore year at West High. We brought him up to the varsity as a kicker. He was a tad bit more confident than you'd like to see a sophomore. I won't use the word 'cocky.' He was just very, very competitive, and he would be extremely upset if he wasn't successful or didn't win."

Kaeding learned to control some of that with maturity and experience, and now his old high school coach says what he remembers most about his star kicker and punter is "his tremendous work ethic.

"Nate would lift weights with the team, and then he'd go out and run through his own kicking workout every day," Morgan said. "He'd stay out kicking a couple of hours every day, going through a routine he developed. He'd do a certain number of kickoffs, and a certain number of punts. Then he'd work on high kicks. Then he'd get out a set of soccer cones and he'd kick to a specific target from all angles of the field. He'd log everything he did – write it down – and he worked on those skills religiously.

"He was very self-motivated. It didn't just happen that he was a good kicker. He was a real athlete, one who was gifted with a good soccer leg, but he did the work he had to do, to get as good as he is now."

Morgan noted that Kaeding's teammates respected him so much that in his senior year at West and for two years at Iowa, he was selected as a team captain – a rare honor for a kicker.

"When I was at West, I had a couple coaches from other high schools tell me they couldn't believe the role Nate played on our team," Morgan said. "They'd see our team get gathered together before the game, and one player would be out front doing the yelling, getting everybody ready to play. It wasn't our quarterback, or some big lineman. It was our kicker!"

Kaeding showed the same kind of leadership on coach Steve Bergman's basketball teams and coach Matt Wilkerson's soccer teams.

"He's a winner," said Morgan. "He likes the pressure situations, when it's all on him. That's good in a kicker. I remember how at Iowa, when we were playing Wisconsin in his senior year, he was going to kick a field goal that would win the game for us. Wisconsin called two consecutive timeouts, trying to ice him. That might bother some kickers, but Nate was over there yapping at their sidelines, telling them to call another one. He's got a real competitive spirit."

The 6 ft. tall, 187-pound Kaeding comes from an athletic bloodline. His grandfather, the late Jim Kaeding, was the basketball coach at Muscatine High School. His father Larry Kaeding played basketball for his father and ran track at Muscatine High. Larry, a chemist for the Cedar Rapids water department, and his wife Terry Kaeding, a finance officer for the City of Coralville, have two other children. Nick, two years older than Nate, was a baseball player at West High. Their sister Jackie, a senior in 2005, has been a basketball and soccer star at West, and the University of Iowa awarded her a soccer scholarship.

474

"I've always been ultra-competitive, even as a little kid," Nate said. "It couldn't be just for fun – I had to win."

His earliest actual competition on teams came in baseball and soccer.

"I wound up giving up baseball after junior high school because it always frustrated me that I didn't seem like I was part of the game most of the time," he said. "It seems funny to say that now as a kicker, when I may only be involved in 10 or 11 plays during a game."

In Kaeding's sophomore year of football at West, the Trojans were undefeated until the first round of the playoffs and then were beaten by cross-town rival City High. "That disappointment drove us the next two years, and we went 26-0 and won the two state championships," he said.

Kaeding made 65 points-after-touchdown in a row without ever missing, and also set school records in punting and touchbacks.

In the title game in his senior year, West won in overtime when Nate Dvorak intercepted a Cedar Falls pass to end the game. There was a big pile of players on the field, with Kaeding on the bottom of the pile. "When we were getting back to Iowa City that night, I thought, 'Wow, my shoulder really hurts,' " he said. "I wound up going to the hospital to get it checked it out, found out I had a broken collar bone and then missed the first six weeks of basketball because of it. That was a little embarrassing – going all through high school football without ever getting hurt, then breaking my collar bone in the victory celebration."

In basketball, Kaeding "only played scrap minutes" in his junior year – until the sub-state finals against Cedar Rapids Jefferson. "We were behind and not playing very well, and all of a sudden Coach Bergman called my name and threw me into the game for my first varsity minutes that really mattered," Kaeding said. "We got beat, but it at least gave me a chance to show what I could do when the game still mattered."

In his senior basketball season, he missed the early-season practices and games because of the football playoffs and then the broken collarbone, but then he came back as team captain, an off-guard and a defensive specialist usually assigned to the opposition's top perimeter player. Coach Bergman "told me my job was to play smart and be a leader on the floor." Kaeding took a starting position alongside his longtime friends Glen Worley,

Kevin Long, Jamie Lang and Seth Schroeder.

"We were supposed to have a great team, but we were really struggling," Kaeding said. "Kevin was the quarterback in football, and the two of us had just come off a 13-0 season and a state championship. But in basketball, the five of us weren't playing very well together, and that was really chewing on me with all the success we'd had in football. I think our attitudes were colliding. We lost 10 or 11 games through the season. But then we had a team meeting before the tournament games started, and we got things back on track. We started playing really tough defense, holding our opponents to 35 or 40 points per game. We did that all the way to the state title, and it turned out to be a really fun ride."

In soccer, he started playing on traveling teams when he was 12 years old, competing in tournaments around the Midwest. And it was in soccer that he saw his first varsity action at West High.

"In my freshman year, I played on both the sophomore team and the varsity," Kaeding said, "and then in my sophomore year, I got to be one of the varsity starters. We won conference titles all four years I played, but when Matt Wilkerson came back as coach going into our senior year, that's when our program really took the next step. He'd been a great player at West, and then he had some semi-pro experience. The biggest thing he did when he came back as coach was to take an athletic approach to soccer, and we all bought into it. I think of the 11 starters on that team my senior year, eight of us had been on the same team for several years. In a tournament that opened the season, we lost a game, 1-0, to Valley of West Des Moines, and then we didn't lost another one the rest of the season."

When it came down to his kick in the overtime shootout in the state championship game of 2000, the pressure was no problem.

"I was out there competing, just having fun," Kaeding said. "You know, I already had a football scholarship to Iowa, we'd won the state championships in football and basketball. So I just looked at that kick as opportunity to win one in soccer, too – and as a great culmination to my high school career.

"The pressure has never gotten to me in sports. In fact, I've always loved it. I play for those games that come down to one play, and I love being

476

part of them. Some guys get caught up in the pressure and have trouble, but I've always enjoyed it. That's as true now that I'm playing on Sunday afternoons as it was when I was playing on Saturday afternoons or Friday nights. You learn in pro football that it's about the money for a lot of people, but for me, it's still a lot about my competitive spirit. It's the whole risk-reward thing."

While at Iowa, Kaeding majored in history and became "sort of a history nerd." He was certified to teach in social studies, did his student teaching at Wilton High School in American history and loved it. He said he eventually looks forward to a career in teaching and coaching. "I definitely want to be involved with young people," he said.

After so much success in three sports in high school, in college football and now at the professional level, is there one moment or accomplishment that has been Kaeding's biggest thrill?

"Really not," he said. "If I look back and think about why I've been successful, it's really because I didn't sit and bask in success when it came my way. I always immediately started looking at whatever the next challenge was going to be."

Adam Haluska, Carroll, 2002

Like many sports editors of local newspapers, Ashley Schable of the Carroll Daily Times Herald usually closes the calendar year by picking the top 10 local sports stories of the previous 12 months. When she did that in 2001, she wrote that "the title for the top area sports story" could be "All Things Adam."

And actually, the best was yet to come in the second half of Adam Haluska's senior year at Carroll High School.

He completed that basketball season with a scoring average of 30 points per game, upping his career average for his four years as a starter for the Tigers to more than 17 points per game. He was named first team All-State for the third year in a row.

His track season was even more phenomenal. In less than three hours during the finals at the state track meet in May, 2002, Haluska won the 100-meter dash, the 200-meter dash, the 400-meter dash and the long jump. He scored 28 of Carroll's total of 30 points in the meet, which gave his team second place overall. That stands as one of the most prolific individual performances in state track meet history, and it pushed his total number of individual state championships in his track career to eight. Also, for the second straight year, he was named the meet's outstanding individual athlete.

"That last state track meet was something I'll never forget," Haluska said. "Because of the way the events were scheduled, I went straight from the long jump to the 100, back to the long jump, then the 200 and then the 400 – and I was done. I was exhausted. It was a warm day and I was dehydrated. But I won them all, and I remember being so relaxed after that. It was like 1,000 pounds off my shoulders. I felt very blessed and fortunate. It was a good way to finish my high school career, that's for sure."

Earlier in his high school years – before he started narrowing his focus to basketball and track – he was an 88-miles-per-hour fastball pitcher and won All-State mention as a wide receiver in football.

The 6 ft., 5 in., 215-pound Haluska began his college basketball career at Iowa State University. He immediately joined the starting line-up and was on the Big 12 Conference's all-freshman honor team. Then when the bottom fell out of the Cyclones' program and coach Larry Eustachy was fired for off-court improprieties, a weary and ailing Haluska decided to transfer to the University of Iowa.

"There wasn't an event that happened – no one thing – that made me decide to transfer," he said. "I just wasn't happy at Iowa State. I'd come to play for Larry and the rest of his staff, and they were all leaving. Then I got sick – sinus infection, ear infection, respiratory infection – for about a month in the middle of the Big 12 season. I dropped from 215 pounds to 190. I was so weak I remember barely being able to dunk at the end of the season, and I've been a guy who could get my elbow above the rim."

Haluska already knew most of the players at the University of Iowa, from AAU basketball and other competition, and Hawkeye coach Steve Alford had tried to recruit him in his late high school years. So he made the move in June, 2003, then sat out a season to comply with NCAA rules, and then quickly became a star in the Hawkeyes' 2004-05 season. For the year, he averaged 14 points and four rebounds per game while generally playing on the perimeter. But in the second half of the season, after leading scorer Pierre Pierce was dismissed from the team, Haluska stepped up to become Iowa's chief offensive weapon and averaged 18 points per game down the stretch.

In 2005, he was 22 years old, and happy again in basketball, doing well academically as a finance major and looking forward to two more seasons of eligibility with the Hawkeyes.

You'd have to say Adam Haluska was genetically destined to be an exceptional athlete.

He proudly tells the story of how his grandmother Helen Corrick Baker, who played girls' basketball in the late 1940s for little Keswick High School in southeast Iowa, once scored 101 points in a game. Indeed, she set the single-season and career scoring records for Iowa girls, although those were later broken. "She played for the Keswick Kittens," Adam said. "She still loves basketball, too. Sometimes she'll come out and shoot with us on the driveway."

Both his dad, Steve Haluska, and his mother, Kim, were good athletes at Albia High School in southern Iowa. Kim was a guard on the basketball team, and Steve was good enough that he won a basketball scholarship to Lamar University in Texas. He wound up returning to Iowa to play at Southeastern Community College in Burlington, then completed his degree and basketball career at William Penn College in Oskaloosa.

Their careers took Steve and Kim Haluska to Adair-Casey in west central Iowa, where he taught driver's education, health and physical education, and served as head track and basketball coach, and she was school secretary. And that's where Adam, the oldest of their three sons, started showing great promise as an athlete.

"Because my dad was the track coach, I started running with his varsity track team when I was a real little kid – even as a kindergartner, I think," Adam said. "I'd watch what they were doing, and try to do it too. Track was my first love for a long time. But I liked basketball, too, and I started playing in first and second grade."

In the third grade, Adam entered the Elks' free-throw shooting competition, won the regional and state contests and finished sixth in the nation in his age group. "That was a lot of nerves," Haluska said with a laugh. "The nationals were at Market Square Arena in Indianapolis, and I was used to shooting in the little gym in Adair!"

The family moved to Carroll when Adam was in the fifth grade, and he was immediately involved in the local youth sports programs in baseball, basketball and track. In middle school, he could already dunk a basketball. He also continued to follow his dad, who was the Carroll High track coach, to the varsity practices and run with the high school athletes.

Steve became the Carroll High principal when Adam was a freshman and is still in that position. Kim is now an administrative assistant at Farner-Bocken Company, a food products wholesaler in Carroll.

"My parents have been very influential in the success I've had in sports," Adam said. "It helps having someone like my dad who has access to a gym all the time. And they were real involved in getting us to the Iowa Games, AAU track meets and other competitions like that."

He said he also realizes now what a benefit it was growing up in Carroll, which "is just a great sports town, with excellent facilities and coaches and community support." He said his basketball coach Keith Stribe "is one of the most caring coaches a guy could play for. He's put together a very successful program at Carroll High. It was an honor to play for him."

Stribe, incidentally, has now benefited from having another Haluska in his program. Sean, who finished his varsity career in 2005, moved into the starting line-up when Adam graduated. The 6 ft., 2 in. Sean went on to become an All-Stater, averaging 25 points per game as a senior and being named Class 3A player of the year. He then signed to play in the strong basketball program at Indian Hills Community College in Ottumwa.

"It's hard to live in someone's shadow, but I'm really proud of the way Sean has handled it," Adam said. "You know, he's better than I am in a lot of things in basketball. He's got better court vision. He's a better guard than I am, and he has a way better left hand than I do."

Plus, Sean led the Tigers into the Class 3A state tournament in 2005, something his older brother did "even though it was one of my real goals," Adam said. "We got beat in the sub-state finals both my sophomore and junior years. It's a lot tougher to get to state than most people think."

480

Meanwhile, their younger brother Blake is completing seventh grade in 2005 and is a promising player.

Coach Stribe recorded his 300th career coaching victory during the 2004-05 season. How many of those victories could he attribute to the two Haluskas? "Quite a few," he said. "It takes good players if you're going to win a lot, and they were both good players."

He said it was evident by the time Adam Haluska was in junior high that he was going to be a great player.

"By the time he was into his high school years, Adam was so fast and could jump so well, that he could jump over most defenders," Stribe said. "That meant there were really no bad shots for him, unless he was off-balance, because otherwise, the defensive players couldn't block it."

His work ethic "was tremendous," Stribe said. "He spent hours and hours in the gym. And you know, one nice thing about that, Sean was the younger brother coming along, and he wanted to make a name for himself, too. He saw what kind of time and effort it took for Adam to become as good as he was, and Sean picked up those same work habits."

Adam Haluska said when he stops to think about it, "I really did have a great high school career, and I'm so grateful for all the opportunities I had. I tried to make the most of it. I did all I could with the time I had available. But if I had it to do all over again, I might have explored more than I did – other courses, activities even other sports. There just never seemed to be enough time to do all the things I wanted to do."

As an Iowa Hawkeye, he said, he is "focused on what we can accomplish in basketball the next few years, and hope we can get in the Elite Eight or Final Four. I'll see where sports take me. I've thought some that if basketball doesn't work out, it might be fun to get back into track and try the decathlon, although I'd have to learn a few other events that would be new to me. Eventually, though, I'll get into a career. I definitely want that to be in Iowa. It's sure been a great place to grow up, I know that."

Joel Osborn, Harlan, 2004

Of all the Iowa high school athletes I've watched in action over the years, two had an absolutely uncanny ability to help their teammates snatch victory from the jaws of defeat, and both of them played in recent times. They are Erica Junod, who starred in basketball and softball at Ankeny from 1997 to 1999, and Joel Osborn, a three-sport superstar at Harlan.

Junod went on to an excellent basketball career at Iowa State University. Osborn, after his storybook prep career, has had a promising freshman year in both football and basketball at Northwest Missouri State University in Maryville.

More so than any other athletes I've ever known, they'd find a way to beat all foes.

In the 2003 state championship football game against Mount Vernon, undefeated Harlan was trailing 35-23 with 5:50 left to play. In the next three minutes, Osborn electrified the crowd in the UNI-Dome in Cedar Falls by throwing touchdown passes to Greg Applegate that went for 80 and 67 yards. Harlan won it 38-35, clinching its ninth state football title.

In the 2004 state basketball championship game against Crestwood, undefeated Harlan was trailing Crestwood 51-38 with 6:01 left to play. With Osborn as the playmaker guard and constant three-point threat, Harlan went on a 22-3 run that gave the Cyclones a 60-54 victory, the state title and a 27-0 season. He'd averaged 20 points per game his senior season, had 17 in the championship game and was named captain of the all-tournament team.

"It was a special feeling, coaching Joel this year," his father Mitch Osborn told the media after the game. Besides being head boys' basketball coach, Mitch is also the school's athletic director. When he was asked to assess his son's athletic ability, he paused, shook his head and said, "Joel's biggest attribute? Well, he's not the quickest, and he can't jump the highest, but his mental toughness is exceptional. Of course, when he's had me coaching him since birth, he's had to develop mental toughness to put up with me, probably. The rest of our players key off that."

Joel Osborn, at 6 ft., 2 in. and 190 pounds, was a special athlete at a special time in a special athletic program.

Harlan finished second in the Class 3A state basketball tournament of 2003, then unexpectedly won the state track championship in the spring of 2003, and perhaps that's what launched an incredible run of success for the Cyclones. However, the baseball team in the summer of 2003 started off a bit wobbly. "We were 12-7 at one point, and then we won 17 in a row," Osborn said. "It was like we couldn't lose."

The last of those 17 victories was 4-3 over Waukee for the state championship, and shortstop Osborn started the double play that ended the game and clinched the title. Then they won 13 consecutive football games, then 27 consecutive basketball games.

The 57-game victory streak through three sports seasons finally ended with the opening game of the 2004 baseball season, when Carroll High prevailed 4-3, although Harlan went on to a fine 27-7 season and made it to the quarterfinals of the state tournament before bowing out.

Harlan's consecutive state championships in track, baseball, football and basketball from 2003 into 2004 is unparalleled in Iowa high school history, and Joel Osborn was a driving force in all of them but the track crown. He was All-State in football, basketball and baseball. He was the Des Moines Register's male high school athlete of the year as a senior. And he relished every minute of it.

"You look back now that it's over, it's been a blast," he told the Register's chief prep sportswriter John Naughton.

But as Osborn was quick to tell everybody, he was just one good player in a flock of them that all came through Harlan High School at the same time. Cyclone fans will be recalling them for decades to come – Applegate, Stein, Miller, Bissen, Kaufmann, McCutcheon, Arentson, Martin, Daeges and, yes, Osborn.

Joel is the oldest of three sons of Mitch and Nancy Blum Osborn, who is a nurse. In 2005, brother Kevin completed his junior year in 2005, and is an all-around athlete. Their younger brother Zach completed fifth grade in 2005 and is also showing promise.

Both parents were athletes growing up in Walnut, and Nancy averaged 36 points per game as a senior in basketball. After they married, Mitch began his teaching and coaching career at Elk Horn-Kimballton, then moved on to Pomeroy-Palmer when Joel was five years old.

"That school had a great basketball tradition," Joel recalled. "We lived in Palmer, and I remember walking into the Palmer gym, seeing all those trophies and thinking how it was like a shrine."

In his grade school years, he turned himself into a gym rat, walking over to superintendent and former coach Alden Skinner's house, "asking for the key to the gym, opening up myself, going in there alone and shooting for hours at a time.

"One thing that really helped me was that, being in a small town like that, I played all the time with kids who were older than I was," Osborn said. "I remember I was a second grader playing on a team of guys who were in fourth grade. Nick Ford was one of them, and he later helped Pomeroy-Palmer win two state championships. But back then, our little team went to some tournaments for fifth graders – and we won!"

He said he was playing in pick-up football games with older boys, too.

"I was one of the littlest kids," he said, "so I was always the quarterback because I didn't want to get creamed. Since then, I've always been able to throw. Dad would work with me, and we'd play a lot of catch."

Mitch Osborn landed the Harlan basketball coaching job when Joel was 11. "I didn't know anything about Harlan when we moved here," Joel said. "I was really upset, actually, because all my friends were at Pomeroy-Palmer."

But he soon found lots of new friends – and a whole lot more athletes – around Harlan, and they started being successful playing together in AAU competition and then middle school sports.

In football, he was still the quarterback, helping both his seventh and eighth grade teams to 4-1 records. He also quarterbacked the freshman team that went 7-2.

As a sophomore, legendary Harlan football coach Curt Bladt made young Osborn the starting quarterback for the Cyclones – and he was the first quarterback to lead the team for three years in the Bladt era. The teams went 10-2, 9-2 and then the magical 13-0 in 2003.

Throughout the track season of 2003, and even moreso that summer, Osborn was like a pest to his top three or four receivers on the football team. He insisted they do football workouts with him three times or more a week, running the team's pass patterns until he'd complete 100 or more passes.

"Joel is a special person," said Bladt. "He'd yank those receivers out of bed all through that summer and throw to them. I don't know exactly what time they'd start, but they didn't really want to be up then, I know that."

Later in the summer, the Cyclones went to a three-day team camp in South Dakota, and scrimmaged Des Moines East. Harlan, throwing passes all over the field, scored the first five times it took the ball on East's 40-yard line. "East was a little dazed," Osborn said. Added Bladt: "It was obvious how much work Joel and his receivers had done together."

It also showed during Osborn's senior season in the fall of 2003, when he set state records for touchdown passes in a season (42) and passing yards in a season (3,254).

Bladt said his game-breaking quarterback "has good size, he's not super fast but with his arm, he can throw a raspberry through a battleship He's very accurate, he's very smart, he is a student of the game and you are not going to out-work the kid. In conditioning and agility, he'll still be out there working when the cows go home."

Osborn claims "it's the tradition" that drives Harlan athletes.

"It's pretty amazing what's happened here," he said. "As a little kid, you just dream of playing for the Cyclones. And you don't want to let the tradition stop with you."

THE CENTENNIAL HONOR ROLL

Here are 125 names that were most repeated as being Iowa's best high school boy athletes of the past century, in a survey of more than 250 long-time coaches, athletic directors, school administrators, officials, sportswriters and fans.

The qualifications: 1) Multi-sport athletes had to be given extra consideration, 2) if a person was a one-sport athlete he had to be so dominating that there could be no argument about his ability, and 3) nominations should be based on what the athletes did in high school, more than what they did or didn't do later in the collegiate and professional ranks. The athletes are presented here alphabetically. They are listed under the decade of their high school graduation year.

1910s
Charles Hoyt, Greenfield
Gordon Locke, Denison
Fred "Duke" Slater, Clinton

1920s
Willis Glassgow, Shenandoah
Lynn King, Villisca
Kenneth "Moco" Mercer, Albia
Morgan Taylor, Sioux City High School

1930s
Jay Berwanger, Dubuque Senior
Ed Bock, Fort Dodge
Al Couppee, Council Bluffs Thomas
    Jefferson
Dick Crayne, Fairfield
Bob Feller, Van Meter
George "Sonny" Franck, Davenport
Nile Kinnick, Adel/Omaha Benson
Marcellus McMichael, Des Moines
    Roosevelt
Bob Saggau, Denison
Ben Trickey, Marshalltown

1940s
Bernie Bennett, Mason City
Duane Brandt, Waverly
Dean Corson, Rockwell City
Jack Dittmer, Elkader
John Estes Jr., Des Moines North
Bill Evans, Nevada
Jerry Groom, Dowling, Des Moines
486

Dick Hoerner, Dubuque Senior
Dick Ives, Diagonal
Bill Reichardt, City High, Iowa City
Jim Sangster, City High, Iowa City
Murray Wier, Muscatine

1950s
Eddie Bedell, Burlington
Bob Brandt, Denison
Chuck Dostal, Cedar Rapids Roosevelt
Randy Duncan, Des Moines Roosevelt
Tom Hertz, Creston
Bill Logan, Keokuk
Roger Nielsen, Manning
Don Perkins, Waterloo West
Kenny Ploen, Clinton
Mike Reilly, Dubuque Senior
Larry Swift, Keokuk
Gary Thompson, Roland
Sherwyn Thorson, Fort Dodge

1960s
Jim Abrahamson, Marshalltown
Tom Altemeier, Newton
Tony Baker, Burlington
Van Brownson, Shenandoah
Steve Carson, Red Oak
Vern Den Herder, Sioux Center
Clyde Duncan, Des Moines North
Jim Dunegan, Burlington
Al Feuerbach, Preston
Dan Gable, Waterloo West
Rex Harvey, Dexfield

Ron Jessen, Council Bluffs Thomas
    Jefferson/Creston
Duane Josephson, New Hampton
Merv Krakau, Guthrie Center
Doug Lane, Cedar Rapids Jefferson
Larry Lawrence, Cedar Rapids Jefferson
Randy Long, Creston
Dick McVay, Norway
Ed Podolak, Atlantic
Bob Steenlage, Britt
Jim Wagner, Cedar Rapids Regis
Rick Wanamaker, Marengo

1970s

John Arnaud, Sioux City North
Ted Burgmeier, Dubuque Wahlert
Mike Boddicker, Norway
Mike Courey, Sioux City Heelan
Curtis Craig, Davenport Central
Roger Craig, Davenport Central
Neil Fegebank, Paullina
Bobby Hansen, Dowling, Des Moines
Ron Kennedy, Storm Lake
Doug Lockin, Aurelia
Jerry Moses, Waterloo East
Lon Olejniczak, Decorah
Kevin Rhomberg, Dubuque Hempstead
Kevin Sigler, Council Bluffs Abraham
    Lincoln
Mike Stensrud, Lake Mills
Marti Wolever, Council Bluffs St. Albert

1980s

Trev Alberts, Northern University High,
    Cedar Falls
Todd Berkenpas, Maple Valley
Marv Cook, West Branch
Steve Eddie, Albert City-Truesdale
Cal Eldred, Urbana
Todd Frain, Treynor
Chad Hennings, Benton of Van Horne
Treye Jackson, Newton
Kip Janvrin, Panora-Linden

Randy Kraayenbrink, Paullina
Kevin Little, Ankeny
Nick Nurse, Carroll Kuemper
Kurt Warner, Cedar Rapids Regis

1990s

Tavian Banks, Bettendorf
Casey Blake, Indianola
Dallas Clark, Twin River Valley
Nick Collison, Iowa Falls
Tim Dwight, City High, Iowa City
Zeron Flemister, Sioux City West
Kirk Hinrich, Sioux City West
Fred Hoiberg, Ames
Raef LaFrentz, MFL/Mar-Mac of
    Monona
Brent MacLagan, Jefferson-Scranton
Kyle McCann, Creston
Jeff McGinnis, City High, Iowa City
Darin Naatjes, West Lyon
Dean Oliver, Mason City
Sage Rosenfels, Maquoketa
Sean Shafar, Bedford
Chris Street, Mormon Trail of Garden
    Grove/Indianola
Dedric Ward, Cedar Rapids Washington
Parker Wildeman, Cherokee
Joey Woody, City High, Iowa City

2000-2005

Tyler Blum, Walnut/Atlantic
Jeff Clement, Marshalltown
Calvin Davis, City High, Iowa City
Adam Haluska, Carroll
Jeff Horner, Mason City
Nate Kaeding, Iowa City West
Matt Macri, Dowling, West Des Moines
Brooks McKowen, Wapsie Valley of
    Fairbank
Nik Moser, Fort Dodge
Brad Nelson, Bishop Garrigan, Algona
Joel Osborn, Harlan
Jason Scales, Valley of West Des Moines

EPILOGUE

"Bernie," the governor said, we'll "never be able to repay you" for the "tens of thousands of young people who have been raised in this state and have been touched by you. They are now across this country and around this world, living up to the standard that you set."

Bernie Saggau's retirement as executive director of the Iowa High School Athletic Association was honored on March 20, 2005, when the Board of Control hosted a four-hour reception at the Iowa Hall of Pride in Des Moines. More than 500 people from all over Iowa attended. In a 45-minute testimonial that afternoon, Saggau was saluted by a line-up of speakers that included Governor Tom Vilsack; Judy Jeffrey, the director of the Iowa Department of Education; Robert Kanaby, of Indianapolis, the executive director of the National Federation of High School Associations; David Stead, current president of the NFHSA and an Iowa native who is executive director of the Minnesota State High School League; Mike Billings, chairperson of the IHSAA Board of Control, and Rick Wulkow, the successor to Saggau as executive director of the IHSAA. The remarks of the governor, who spoke last and used no notes, were especially profound. A transcript prepared from a video of the ceremony made by David Bingham of Keep It Memorable Sports, allows us to share them here. They seem an appropriate epilogue to this book.

Governor Tom Vilsack:

"Bernie, I'm really glad that you aren't speaking today, because that way we won't have to be compared to your oratorical skills.

"But I will tell you, you need to take a look at this audience, as I have from my seat here. There are governors in attendance, there are college presidents in attendance, there are noted authors in attendance, there are teachers and principals and administrators and coaches – all here because we owe you a debt of gratitude.

"I suppose as governor of this state, I'm supposed to talk on behalf of the people generally. But you'll permit me if I talk as a father. See, I have two sons, and when I first came to Iowa, the very first thing I learned about my state and my town is that they had an undefeated, untied and unscored-upon football team in 1963. I had a father-in-law who relived every single one of those games because his son was the captain of that team. So the expectation was pretty high.

"But, because of your work, I saw two young fellows trot on to a field and a court, and I saw them learn a lot of life's lessons. While in the stands, I had the opportunity to watch one of them go 89 yards for a touchdown in the first game he started as the varsity quarterback for the Mount Pleasant Panthers. Bernie, I'll never be able to repay you for that. That's a feeling I'll never lose. I watched that same son sink a last-second basket to win a game against Ottumwa. That memory is forever etched in my mind.

"I also saw my sons learn lessons about the difficulties of life, on those fields.

"My younger son was not the athlete than my older son was. His sport, if you will, or his talent, was in music. So, while he didn't fare very well in athletics, I had the chance to see, after I was elected governor, him perform in the All-State Chorus, and I'll never forget that memory.

"See, Bernie, that's what your life is about. It's about thousands of those memories, and every parent – every mother and every father – who watched their child perform in any activity owes you a debt of gratitude.

"So the first thing I wanted to do today is to thank you as a father, because you helped raise my two boys. They're never going to perhaps know about your contribution, because you set a structure and a system that allowed them to learn, and allowed them to grow up.

"I also want to thank you as an Iowan, because as was stated earlier, you have defined for all of us what it means to be an Iowan. You see, Bernie has dedicated his life to a sense of community – in creating a sense of community. What's most important about a community are it values.

"This association basically starts with a premise that we all have a responsibility to our young people, and Bernie taught that every day. It's a responsibility to make sure they are equipped for the challenges of the future. They learned those lessons, again, on the courts and fields that Bernie helped to construct. It's also about opportunity. It's a recognition that you don't necessarily have to be a star, if you're just given a chance to participate, because those who participate go on with that lesson, and are never afraid to try different experiences. It's also about security. It's about the notion that there is a community that cares enough about your son or your daughter, that they would set up a process in which they could learn these very difficult and tough lessons, in a loving environment, a caring environment. And that is reflected in the work of this man.

"The Hall of Pride has been mentioned as a legacy for this man, but I would suggest to you that it is not the legacy. And as great as that facility is, Bernie, and it is great, the real legacy are the tens of thousands – tens of thousands of young people – who have been raised in this state and who have been touched by you. They are now across this country and around this world, living up to the standard that you set. That's a living monument and one that will go on for a long, long time.

"Ladies and gentlemen, it has been said that the only thing that we give of freely is our time. Some use time to accumulate great wealth, and some use it to accumulate great power. But this man, this man we honor today, he used it to build stronger and better children, and societies and communities. He used it not for his own benefit, but for our benefit. And, Bernie, that's why there are so many people here today that want to simply say, 'Thank you.'

"I would be remiss if I did not also thank Lois Saggau, because as strong a guy as you are, Bernie, she's stronger. I live in one of those households, too. Lois, no man accomplishes it by himself, and Bernie would be the first to acknowledge that. You have been there during those days when perhaps things were not quite as rosy as they are today. I just want to acknowledge your sacrifice and your involvement. Each one of those living memorials to Bernie that is walking around here is also yours as well.

"So, Bernie, as a father, as an Iowan, as a governor – thank you very much for what you have done.

"You will continue to touch lives, you will continue to make a difference, and you have set a standard and an example that will be very difficult for us to follow."

INDEX

L

M

List of Reprints

1. "A Great Father's Day Gift," by Marty Gallagher – page 83
2. "Catching up years later with Jack Mustapha, Boone high school's baseball legend," by Chuck Offenburger, Des Moines Register – page 92
3. "Loss of legs no deterrent, Ackerman compiles 26-3 record with special ability," by Dan McCool, Des Moines Register – page 98
4. "The most incredible finish to a high school football game that I've ever heard of," by Chuck Offenburger, Des Moines Register – page 106
5. "State wrestling tourney remains remarkable event," Mason City Globe-Gazette – page 116
6. "PAUL MOON: Winning, winning, winning…with class," by Dearrel Bates, Quad-City Times – page 140
7. "An Open Letter to Tom Rader," by Ed Peck, The Newton Daily News – page 173
8. "Jump Shots," by Robert James Waller, printed by permission of Warner Books, Inc. - page 342